View of the Constitution of the United States

View of the Constitution of the United States

With Selected Writings

ST. GEORGE TUCKER

Foreword by Clyde N. Wilson

LIBERTY FUND

This book is published by Liberty Fund, Inc., a
foundation established to encourage study of the ideal
of a society of free and responsible individuals.

⟦⚹⟧ ⚒⟍⫸

The cuneiform inscription that serves as our logo and as
the design motif for our endpapers is the earliest-known
written appearance of the word "freedom" (*amagi*), or
"liberty." It is taken from a clay document written about
2300 B.C. in the Sumerian city-state of Lagash.

Frontispiece photography of St. George Tucker courtesy
of Swem Library, College of William and Mary

Library of Congress Cataloging-in-Publication Data

Tucker, St. George, 1752–1827.
View of the Constitution of the United States: with
   selected writings / St. George Tucker; foreword by
   Clyde N. Wilson.
      p.   cm.
Includes bibliographical references and index.
ISBN 0-86597-200-1 (hc: alk. paper).—ISBN 0-86597-201-X
(pbk.: alk. paper)
1. Constitutional law—United States.   2. Common
law—United States.   3. Slavery—Virginia.   I. Wilson,
Clyde Norman.   II. Title.
KF4550.T82   1999
342.73'02—DC21   98-11927

11   22   23   24   C   7   6   5   4   3
22   23   24   25   P   10   9   8   7   6

Liberty Fund, Inc.
11301 North Meridian Street
Carmel, Indiana 46032
libertyfund.org

❧ Contents

ᗒᗋ Foreword

ST. GEORGE TUCKER's *View of the Constitution of the United States* was the first extended, systematic commentary on the Constitution after it had been ratified by the people of the several states and amended by the Bill of Rights. Published in 1803 by a distinguished patriot and jurist, it was for much of the first half of the nineteenth century an important handbook for American law students, lawyers, judges, and statesmen. Though nearly forgotten since, Tucker's work remains an important piece of constitutional history and a key document of Jeffersonian republicanism.

Two reasons may account for the neglect of Tucker's work and of related, supportive writings. First, his view of the federal government as an agent of the sovereign people of the several states, and not as the judge of the extent of its own powers, was buried by the outcome of the Civil War, the ground for the triumphant views of Abraham Lincoln having been well prepared by Justice Joseph Story of the Supreme Court and lawyer, orator, and Senator Daniel Webster. Second, Tucker's constitutional writings were appended as essays to a multivolume densely annotated edition of Sir William Blackstone's *Commentaries on the Laws of England* that was never reprinted.

St. George Tucker was born in 1752 in the British colony of Bermuda. The Tuckers were a numerous and talented family, many of whom emigrated to the mainland colonies in North America, where several made their fortunes. For example, St. George's brother, Thomas Tudor Tucker, made his way to South Carolina, represented that state in the first two Congresses, and was treasurer of the United States from 1801 until 1828, on appointment of President Thomas Jefferson.

St. George Tucker reached Virginia in 1771. For a year he studied law at the College of William and Mary (as did Thomas Jefferson and John Marshall) under George Wythe, who shortly thereafter became a signer

of the Declaration of Independence and chief justice of Virginia. Talented, urbane, and sociable, Tucker had no trouble making his way in
the best society. In 1775, at the age of twenty-three, he was admitted to the
bar. In that same year he was present in Richmond when Patrick Henry
made his stirring appeal to "liberty or death!" Tucker then took part in
an expedition to Bermuda that gained possession for the colonists of a
large quantity of military stores that were of great use to the army of
George Washington.

St. George married well, in 1778, to a wealthy widow, Frances Bland
Randolph, and acquired large estates in Chesterfield County. He also
acquired three stepsons, one of them the five-year-old John Randolph,
later to be famous as "Randolph of Roanoke." The relationship between
Tucker and Randolph was often tense.

Tucker took an active part in the Revolutionary War. In addition to
the expedition to Bermuda, he was elected colonel of the Chesterfield
County militia and led them to Nathaniel Greene's army in North Carolina, and is said to have distinguished himself at the Battle of Guilford
Court House. During the Yorktown campaign, serving as a lieutenant
colonel of horse and an aide to Governor and General Thomas Nelson,
he was wounded.

Tucker's letters to his wife during his military service were published
in the *Magazine of American History* in July and September of 1881, and,
in addition to exhibiting marital felicity, are a valuable source of historical information on the Revolution's last Southern campaign.

After the war, Tucker's law practice flourished. He was appointed one
of the committee to revise the laws of Virginia, and he served with James
Madison and Edmund Randolph as Virginia commissioners to the
Annapolis Convention. Tucker's career as an expounder of the new constitutions of Virginia and of the United States began in 1790 when he
succeeded Wythe as professor of law at William and Mary.

Contemplating the necessities of instruction, Tucker decided to use as
a text Blackstone's famous *Commentaries on the Laws of England*. Blackstone (1723–80) had for the first time brought the great chaotic mass of
statutory and common law into a system that could be approached by

students. Published in four volumes, from 1765 to 1769, his work largely supplanted the *Institutes* of Sir Edward Coke (1552–1634) as the premier legal text of the English-speaking world.

Though Blackstone's work was indispensable, for Americans it was problematic because it was suffused with the principles of a monarchial and aristocratic state that Americans had only recently repudiated. Americans had exhibited to the world constitutions in which the people exercised their sovereign authority to create governments that rested specifically on the people's consent at an identifiable moment of history and not on a long growth of authority and precedent. Such governments were delegates rather than masters of the people and were limited to those specific powers which the people had granted them. And, through regular elections—or if necessary a drastic reassertion of sovereignty—the American people could change their government and their governors.

It was necessary, then, to republicanize Blackstone. This task Tucker accomplished by extensive notes to the body of Blackstone's work, and by writing several dozen essays, the longest of which were *View of the Constitution of the United States* and "Of the Constitution of Virginia." These essays appeared as appendices in the various volumes of Blackstone's work, and expanded Blackstone's four volumes to five. Tucker's revised, Americanized Blackstone was published in Philadelphia in 1803 and was widely used thereafter.

While the use of Tucker's work cannot be quantified, all authorities agree that it was influential. Later American editions of Blackstone followed Tucker's method, and there is evidence of the extensive use of Tucker's work in Pennsylvania, South Carolina, and Virginia. Doubtless it was taken westward by young Virginians who emigrated to every state in the nineteenth century.

In addition to *View of the Constitution of the United States*, this book includes seven other essays lifted from Tucker's edition of Blackstone. These are the most important writings in regard to Tucker's political and constitutional thought. A great deal that was more narrowly legal has not been selected.

In addition to his edition of Blackstone, Tucker published several political pamphlets and articles, sometimes under pseudonyms, as was customary at the time. These included "Reflections on the Policy and Necessity of Encouraging the Commerce of the Citizens of the United States," in *American Museum* (September 1787): 267–74; *Remarks on the Treaty of Amity... Between Lord Grenville and Mr. Jay* (Philadelphia: M. Carey, 1796); *Cautionary Hints to Congress, Respecting the Sale of Western Lands,* by "Columbus" (Philadelphia: M. Carey, 1796); *Letter to a Member of Congress, Respecting the Alien and Sedition Laws,* by "Columbus" (Richmond: 1799); *Reflections on the Cession of Louisiana to the United States,* by "Sylvester" (Washington, D.C.: printed by Samuel Harrison Smith, 1803); and possibly others. The essays on the common law and on slavery that are published here had been printed as pamphlets before they were included by Tucker in his Blackstone.

St. George Tucker was also by avocation a writer of moderately good verse, both patriotic and humorous. These have been collected, with an interesting introduction, in William S. Prince, ed., *The Poems of St. George Tucker of Williamsburg, Virginia, 1752-1827* (New York: Vantage Press, 1977).

In 1803 Tucker became a judge of the highest court in Virginia. In 1813 he was appointed by President James Madison to be the United States district judge for Virginia, an important post in which he had a distinguished career, resigning shortly before his death in 1827. As a jurist Tucker never wavered from the principles he had set forth as a professor of law.

Tucker established a virtual dynasty of legal and constitutional talent that carried on Jeffersonian principles through successive generations. A son, Henry St. George Tucker (1780–1848), served in the state legislature and the U.S. House of Representatives, was chief justice of Virginia, conducted a successful private law school at Winchester, Virginia, declined President Andrew Jackson's appointment as attorney general of the United States, became professor of law at the University of Virginia, and published books on natural law, constitutional law, and the laws of Virginia.

Another of Tucker's sons, Nathaniel Beverley Tucker (1784–1851), became professor of law at William and Mary and published three novels and a number of works on political economy and public issues. He is a major figure in the intellectual history of the Old South.

In the next generation, St. George Tucker's grandsons were equally distinguished. John Randolph Tucker (1823–97), son of Henry St. George Tucker, was attorney general of Virginia, professor of law at Washington and Lee University, counsel in numerous major cases before the United States Supreme Court, served in the U.S. House of Representatives from 1875 to 1887, and published, among other works, *The Constitution of the United States* (2 vols., 1899). Another son of Henry St. George was Nathaniel Beverley Tucker (1820–90). He edited an antebellum newspaper in Washington, D.C., was U.S. consul at Liverpool, and served the Confederate States as an economic agent abroad.

St. George Tucker's great-grandson, Henry St. George Tucker (1853–1932), son of John Randolph Tucker, represented Virginia in the U.S. House of Representatives from 1876 to 1889 and again from 1922 to 1932, carrying on the states' rights, populist, anti–big business tradition of his family and state. He was also professor of law at Washington and Lee University, and published *Limitations on the Treaty-Making Power Under the Constitution of the United States* and *Woman's Suffrage by Constitutional Amendment.*

Given the massive changes in the extent and distribution of political power since the Civil War, and the resulting adjustments in accepted understandings of the Constitution, Tucker's principles of states' rights and limited government are likely to seem strange to Americans today, unless it is remembered that these principles were the prevailing ideas not only during Tucker's time but also for several generations after.

The Constitution that Tucker explicates is the Constitution that was ratified by the people of the several states. It is to be understood as explicated by the ratifiers, including their reservations, some of which were embodied in the first ten amendments, which were a further limitation on the delegated powers of the new general government. For the assumption that the meaning and authority of the Constitution is to be found in its ratifiers, and not in the learned discussions of the Framers at Philadelphia, who were, after all, only drafting a proposal for the people's consideration, Tucker has the support of Madison himself. (See Madison's letter to Thomas Ritchie, September 15, 1821.)

Tucker, then, does not stand in awe of the *Federalist Papers*. He recognizes them as special pleadings for the Constitution before ratification and amendment. He finds some things in them admirable, particularly the defense of an independent judiciary, but he quotes them most often in support of the limited nature of the new federal government. Though Tucker is well read in political philosophy, he does not need a long historical exposition of ideas to explain the Constitution. The document is for him generally clear and specific, self-evident to those who ratified it. This is not to suggest, however, that Tucker cannot when necessary call upon Justinian, Grotius, Pufendorf, Vattel, Montesquieu, Locke, Rousseau, or other more nearly contemporaneous writers.

Tucker is the exponent of Jeffersonian republicanism, or what has been called "South Atlantic republicanism," in contrast to the commercial republicanism of New England that has since the Civil War been taken to be the only true form of American philosophy. The political background of Tucker's work is significant. The Constitution had been ratified reluctantly and with reservations by Virginia and New York (and not at all by North Carolina and Rhode Island) only on the understanding that amendments would be made. Twelve such amendments were proposed by the First Congress, and ten of them swiftly were ratified. This "Bill of Rights" was to reassert the limited nature of the new government's powers and their dependence solely on the delegation of the people of the several sovereign states.

Hardly had the federal government gotten under way, however, than the largely Northern political faction gathered under Hamilton and Adams launched an initiative to stretch those powers as far as they would go, and to make light of the limits. Much of this expansion represented a desire to use the government in mercantilist ways—for example, a national bank, a funded national debt, a commercial treaty with Great Britain. All were policies that profited the commercial classes of the

North and were burdensome to the free-trade agricultural empire of the South.

Into this domestic conflict burst the French Revolution. The great ideas of revolution and reaction that tore apart Europe could not go unnoticed in the New World, which had just experienced its own revolution and whose leaders were well aware of the power of ideas. The relation of American neutral commerce to the belligerent powers in Europe was a vexing practical issue, and the ideological heat from Europe intensified the intra-American conflict over the nature and powers of the general government.

Thus, for example, the Puritan clergy of New England during the presidential election of 1800 denounced Jefferson as a Jacobin atheist who would set up the guillotine and undermine the moral foundations of American society. Probably the conflict was really cultural, contrasting the highly ordered, communal society of New England—where most of life was regimented under leaders of proper principle—and the easygoing laissez-faire life of the South. It is a curious fact that the bourgeois leaders of the North had visions of imminent uprisings of Jacobin mobs and supported such policies to stifle dissent as the Alien and Sedition acts, whereas the aristocratic leaders of the South declared for the people and for policies of liberality. While Jefferson in Virginia rested among his two hundred slaves, John Adams was barricaded in his Philadelphia mansion against an expected attack of the revolutionary mob.

These differences of culture were also evident in political styles. Plain John Adams rode to his inauguration in a coach drawn by white horses, insisted on being addressed as "His Excellency," and demanded the strictest social protocol. By contrast, the genuinely aristocratic Jefferson walked to his inauguration with the Virginia militia, established the order of pell-mell at leisurely functions in the White House, and sent his messages unostentatiously to Congress in writing rather than appearing in person.

If the Federalists called their opponents Jacobins, the Jeffersonians could reply that the Federalists were dangerously imbued with "monarchical" tendencies. To Jeffersonians, the Federalists did not actually trust the people, gave only lip service to republicanism, and wanted a government of large, even unlimited, authority. Both Hamilton and Adams were declared admirers of the British constitution, to which they attributed most of what was valuable in American constitutions. By comparison, in *View of the Constitution of the United States,* Tucker carefully contrasts the British and American constitutions, to the credit of the latter.

Most of what Federalists admired in British principles Tucker considers to be imaginary rationalizations for quite different realities. This is his response to those who he believed over-emphasized the British inheritance. What Americans had deliberately created was superior to what had merely evolved in a system that did not honor the sovereignty of the people.

In 1798 the Federalist Congress passed and Adams signed the Alien and Sedition acts. The Alien Act allowed the president to deport any noncitizen he deemed undesirable. No judicial proceeding was involved. For Tucker and other Jeffersonians this was an assumption by the federal legislature and executive of powers not delegated and also a violation of the separation of powers since it gave the president authority that belonged properly to the judiciary.

Even worse, in Tucker's judgment, was the Sedition Act, which provided for criminal prosecution in federal courts of persons deemed to have made publications that tended to bring the officers of the federal government into disrepute. Several conspicuous prosecutions were made. Tellingly, the Congress that passed the act designed it to expire on the date they would leave office, in case their opponents gained control. For Jeffersonians such as Tucker, the Sedition Act was a violation of individual liberties, an assumption of power that never had been delegated to any part of the government (after all, the states had just ratified the Tenth Amendment), a subversion of state rights, and obviously an attempt to suppress political opposition and criticism of those in power.

The Jeffersonian response was the series of reports and resolutions that came out of the legislatures of Kentucky and Virginia from 1798 to 1800 and which were written by Jefferson and Madison. These resolutions reasserted that the federal government was of specific, limited, and delegated powers, and that the federal government was the agent of the sovereign people of the states and not the judge of its own limits. The resolutions also declared that, when the federal government egregiously overstepped its limits, the states possessed both the right and the duty to interpose their authority and render such usurpations null and void.

The conflict between federal and state power remained theoretical and potential as long as its issues were settled by normal political processes. Jefferson and his party triumphed in 1800 and remained in power for a quarter of a century (during which New England states asserted similar rights in protest of federal commercial and military policies). There was no showdown, but for Tucker and many others, for several generations, the "Principles of 1798" remained a primary text of constitutional discourse.

Tucker takes for granted the option of secession. If the Constitution draws its authority from the consent of the sovereign—which is the people of the several states—then the sovereign may withdraw that consent (not, of course, something to be done lightly). The people's consent to the Constitution is not a one-time event that forever after binds them to be obedient to the federal government. A state's right of withdrawal remains always an open option against a government overstepping its bounds, and is affirmed in the nature of the Constitution itself and in the right of revolution propounded by the Declaration of Independence.

One of Tucker's principal concerns as a legal and political thinker is to affirm the standing of the judiciary as an independent and coequal power with the legislature and executive. This is an American accomplishment, to be supported in state and federal governments both. For him the judiciary is the realm in which individuals may seek relief from the oppressions of government. The judiciary's power and independence are therefore essential.

But by no means does this principle encroach upon the even more fundamental federal principle. Tucker insists that it is the duty of the federal courts to restrain the other branches of the federal government, not to make policy and certainly not to invade the rights of the states. The jurisdiction of the federal courts is rightly limited to the delegated sphere of federal power, and carries no imprimatur of supremacy over the state courts and their jurisdictions.

But Tucker sensed the potential for just such extensions of power, something that he and other Jeffersonian jurists were committed to resist. This is reflected in his serious attention to the question of the common law and its application to federal jurisprudence. To infuse the common law into federal jurisprudence would, in his view, give the federal courts power over every question in society. This was the path taken, successfully, by Justice Joseph Story in both teaching and decree, and it is the path that led eventually to the judicial supremacy of the twentieth century. For Tucker there was a clear defense against this possibility: the common law was infused into American law because each of the colonies had adopted such parts of it as were relevant or expedient. Each state was different in this respect, and each state was the judge of its own business. The federal judiciary was created by the people with specific, limited, delegated powers. It was not among those powers to evolve or assume legal principles from some other source. The Constitution and the laws themselves were plain enough, and, unlike the common law, rested upon the consent of the people.

This conviction of states' rights is dismissed conventionally as a rationalized defense of minority interests, particularly in regard to slavery in the antebellum South. Accordingly, Tucker's writings on slavery are especially interesting. In 1796 he published a pamphlet that proposed for Virginia a plan of gradual emancipation, and he included this plan as an appendix to his edition of Blackstone. His reasoning and proposals came to naught, but they show what it was still possible to consider and to discuss in the South of Tucker's time. His time was, of course, before the rise of militant abolitionism in the North, and when the question was for Virginians alone to decide.

Tucker can be seen as prophetic in a number of ways. For instance, one of the chief defects or dangers he finds in the Constitution has to do with the president, and especially with the president's powers in foreign affairs and the military. Tucker would have preferred to have the House of Representatives as well as the president and the Senate to approve treaties. He understands that it would be potentially in the power of a president to bring on war by creating a situation in which the required declaration by Congress would be no more than an after-the-fact recognition.

Tucker remains a valuable expositor of early American republicanism, well worth the attention of any who wish to understand the origins of our system, both in regard to the Constitution and in regard to the larger conception of republican government that underlies it. Scattered through his disquisitions are many gems of quotable aphorism, as when he comments that a prosperous government and a prosperous people are not necessarily the same thing. Perhaps his thinking is most concisely distilled in this statement: "It is the due [external] restraint and not the moderation of rulers that constitutes a state of liberty; as the power to oppress, though never exercised, does a state of slavery."

CLYDE N. WILSON

SOURCES ON ST. GEORGE TUCKER

Elizabeth Kelley Bauer, *Commentaries on the Constitution, 1790-1860* (New York: Russell and Russell, 1965).

William Cabell Bruce, *John Randolph of Roanoke, 1773-1833: A Biography* (New York: G. P. Putnam, 1922).

Charles T. Cullen, "St. George Tucker," in W. Hamilton Bryson, ed., *The Virginia Law Reporters before 1880* (Charlottesville: University Press of Virginia, 1977), 96-105.

Dictionary of American Biography, vol. 19.

Jay B. Hubbell, *The South in American Literature, 1607-1900* (Durham, N.C.: Duke University Press, 1954).

Craig Evan Klafter, *Reason over Precedence: Origins of American Legal Thought* (Westport, Conn.: Greenwood Press, 1993).

❧ Note on the Text

THE TEXTS for all the writings of St. George Tucker published herein are taken from essays he appended to his edition of Blackstone: *Blackstone's Commentaries: With Notes of Reference, to the Constitution and Laws, of the Federal Government of the United States; And of the Commonwealth of Virginia*, 5 vols. (Philadelphia: Published by William Young Birch and Abraham Small. Robert Carr, Printer, 1803). The texts here preserve the original eighteenth-century spelling and punctuation and the liberal use of italics and small capitals common at the time.

It has, however, been necessary to make considerable alteration in Tucker's footnotes. These are voluminous. Many are references to obsolete compilations of laws or to now familiar specific clauses of the Constitution of the United States, which was then a new document. (Blackstone's *Commentaries* was, after all, primarily a reference work for law students.) Tucker's notes were marked by archaic printer's symbols, used generalized rather than precisely specific titles of works, and often cited page references to eighteenth-century editions of classic works that are not likely to be available to readers today.

Many footnotes that seemed no longer useful have been eliminated. In those retained, Tucker's style has been preserved as far as possible. At the end of most essays, a recapitulation of the major works referred to by Tucker has been added. In addition, some new footnotes have been placed in the present edition where it seemed useful for the contemporary reader. In every case, such new material is preceded by the tag "*Editor's note.*" All footnotes, new and old, have been renumbered in one series for each essay.

CLYDE N. WILSON

℘ Note on Tucker's Numbering of the Amendments

A WORD to the reader who otherwise is likely to be disconcerted by Tucker's manner of labeling the first ten amendments to the Constitution. The First Congress proposed twelve amendments, designed to meet objections raised by Virginia and other states. Two of these amendments, though ratified by Virginia, were never ratified by a sufficient number of states, a fact of which Tucker apparently was not aware when he prepared his edition of Blackstone for the printer. So he refers often to "the twelve articles of the amendments." Even more disconcertingly, he assigns the amendments numbers that do not correspond to later practice. For instance, when he writes "the twelfth article of the amendments," he means the Tenth Amendment. When he writes "the third article of the amendments," he means the First Amendment. Once this peculiarity is grasped the exposition becomes clear.

View of the Constitution of the United States

᎒ᐤ On the Study of Law

"On the Study of Law" was Tucker's "Editor's Preface" to his edition of *Blackstone's Commentaries*. In it he surveys the conditions for the study of law in the United States. But his chief concern is how to Americanize (or Virginianize) and republicanize a work so essential as Blackstone, yet so suffused with monarchical principles. It is this goal that justifies the numerous appendices that he has added to the work, each an essay on a particular area for which Blackstone is an inadequate guide for American students. Two of the most important essays are those on the Constitution of the United States and the Constitution of Virginia. Tucker stresses that American constitutions are *written declarations* ratified by the people of the states, and they are to be interpreted through their plain texts and through the instruments of the people's consent, and not by speculative writers on government or by office-holders, the people's delegates. Other important questions for Tucker are to what extent the common law is operative in the United States, and what are the boundaries of federal and state judicial jurisdiction. Finally, Tucker assures fledgling lawyers that, as future framers of law, they must have a knowledge of the constitutions and history of their country, as well as of law itself, if liberty is to be preserved.

WHEN A WORK of established reputation is offered to the public in a new dress, it is to be expected that the Editor should assign such reasons for so doing, as may not only exempt him from the imputation of a rash presumption, but shew that some benefit may be reasonably expected to result from his labours.

Until the COMMENTARIES *on the laws of England* by the late Justice Blackstone made their appearance, the students of law in England, and its dependencies, were almost destitute of any scientific guide to conduct their studies. "A raw and unexperienced youth," he remarks, "in the most dangerous season of life is transplanted on a sudden into the midst of allurements to pleasure without any restraint or check, but what his own prudence can suggest; with no public direction in what course to pursue his inquiries; no private assistance to remove the distresses and difficulties which always embarrass a beginner. In this situation he is expected to sequester himself from the world, and by a tedious lonely process to extract the theory of law from a mass of undigested learning." "How little, therefore, is it to be wondered at" he adds, "that we hear of so frequent miscarriages, that so many gentlemen of bright imaginations grow weary of so unpromising a search; and that so many persons of moderate capacity confuse themselves at first setting out, and continue ever dark and puzzled during the remainder of their lives!" Such is the picture which our author gives us of the difficulties which at that time attended the study of the law, even in those Inns of court whither those who sought to acquire a knowledge of the profession, generally repaired for instruction. On the appearance of the COMMENTARIES, the laws of England, from a rude chaos, instantly assumed the semblance of a regular system. The *viginti annorum lucubrationes* it was thought might thereafter be dispensed with, and the student who had read the COMMENTARIES three or four times over, was lead to believe that he was a thorough proficient in the law, without further labour, or assistance; the crude and immethodical labours of Sir Edward Coke were laid aside, and that rich mine of learning, his Commentary upon Littleton, was thought to be no longer worthy of the labour requisite for extracting its precious ore. This sudden revolution in the course of study may be considered as having produced effects almost as pernicious as the want of a regular and systematic guide, since it cannot be doubted that it has contributed to usher into the profession a great number, whose superficial knowledge of the law has been almost as soon forgotten, as acquired. And this evil we may venture to pronounce has been much greater in the Colonies dependent upon Great-Britain, than in England itself, for the laws of the Colonies not being at all interwoven with the COMMENTARIES, the colonial student was wholly without a guide in some of the most important points, of which he should have been informed; admitting that he were acquainted with the law of England upon any particular subject, it was an equal chance that he was ignorant of the changes introduced into the colonial codes; which either from inexperience, inattention, or other accidental circumstances have undergone a variety of modifications, provisions, suspensions, and repeals, in almost all the colonies dependent upon great Britain. The COMMENTARIES, therefore though universally resorted to as a guide to the colonial student, were very inadequate to the formation of a lawyer, without other assistance; that assistance from the partial editions of colonial laws (at least in Virginia) was extremely difficult to be obtained. Few gentlemen, even of the profession, in this country, have ever been able to boast of possessing a *complete* collection of its laws; the Editor confesses that his own endeavours to procure one have hitherto been ineffectual.

Not many years after the reception of the COMMENTARIES into the libraries of gentlemen of the profession, and the adoption of them as a guide to those who wished to acquire it, the revolution which separated the present United States of America from Great Britain took effect; this event produced a corresponding revolution not only in the principles of our government, but in the laws which relate to property, and in a variety of other cases, equally contradictory to the law, and irreconcileable to the principles contained in the COMMENTARIES. From this period, that celebrated work could only be safely relied on as a methodical guide, in delineating the general outlines of law in the United States, or at most, in apprizing the student of what the *law had been;* to know *what it now is,* he must resort to very different sources of information; these, although the period which has elapsed since their first introduction is scarcely more than twenty years, are now so numerous, (at least in this state) and so difficult to be procured, that not one in fifty students of law has at this day any chance of perusing them.

Notwithstanding these circumstances, the COMMENTARIES have continued to be regarded as the *student's guide,* in the UNITED STATES; and many there are, who without any other aid have been successful candidates for admission to the bar in this state, and perhaps in others: it cannot, therefore, be surprising that so many who have obtained licences to practice, discover upon their entrance into the profession a total want of information respecting the laws of *their own* country. A misfortune which their utmost diligence thereafter is required to remedy. A misfortune unavoidably attendant on that obscurity into which the laws of this state have been thrown, by *partial editions,* and by the *loose* and *slovenly* manner in which the acts of the legislature are *stitched* together, and dispersed throughout the country in *unbound,* and even *uncovered sheets,* more like ephemerons than the perpetual rules of property, and of civil conduct in a state.

These inconveniences had been sensibly felt by the Editor, whose utmost diligence had been in vain applied to their removal, when he was *unexpectedly* called to fill the chair of the professor of law in the university of WILLIAM AND MARY, IN VIRGINIA, then vacant by the resignation of a gentleman,[1] to whose advice and friendly instruction he was indebted for whatever talent he might be supposed to possess for filling the office of his successor. Great as he felt the distance between himself and his predecessor, the partiality of his friends persuaded him to accept an office which he was by no means prepared to discharge to his own satisfaction. To prepare a regular course of *original lectures* would have required some years of study, and of labour, not only in collecting, but in methodizing and arranging his materials. The exigencies of the office did not permit this: he was obliged, in the short period of two or three months, to enter upon the duties of it: he determined to be *useful* to his pupils as far as his best endeavours would enable him to be so, without regarding the form in which his instructions might be conveyed. The method, therefore, which he proposed to himself to adopt, was to recur to *Blackstone's Commentaries* as a text, and occasionally to offer remarks upon such passages as he might conceive required illustration, either because the law had been confirmed, or changed, or repealed, by some constitutional or legislative act of the *Federal Government,* or of the com-

---

1. Mr. [George] Wythe the present chancellor of Virginia.

monwealth of *Virginia.* This method he was led to adopt, partly, from the utter impracticability of preparing a regular course of lectures, for the reasons before mentioned; and, partly, from the exalted opinion he entertained of the Commentaries as a model of methodical elegance and legal perspicuity: a work in which the author has united the various talents of the philosopher, the antiquarian, the historian, the jurist, the logician and the classic: and which has undergone so many editions in England, Ireland, and America, as to have found its way into the libraries of almost every gentleman whether of the profession, or otherwise; and from general acceptance, had become the *guide* of all those who proposed to make the law their study. By these means he proposed to avail himself not only of the Commentator's incomparable method, but of his information as an historian and antiquarian, his classical purity and precision as a scholar, and his authority as a lawyer; without danger either of loss, or depreciation, by translating them into a different work; he was also encouraged to hope that by these means he might render that incomparable work a *safe,* as well as a delightful guide to those who may hereafter become students of law in this commonwealth.

It was foreseen, that the execution of this plan would not consist merely of short explanatory notes, and references to our state code: but that the prosecution of it would not unfrequently lead to inquiries, and discussions of subjects which neither form a part of, nor even bear any relation to, the laws of England. The CONSTITUTION of the UNITED STATES of America, and the particular Constitution of the state of VIRGINIA, it was supposed would afford a field of inquiry which yet remained to be fully explored; it was considered that it would be necessary to investigate the nature of that compact which the *people of the United States* have entered into, one with another; to examine the powers entrusted to those who exercise the government, and to satisfy ourselves of their just extent and limits; to consider the connection between the federal government, and the state governments; to trace with accuracy, as far as the novelty and intricacy of the subject would permit, their respective rights, dependencies, and boundaries; to survey, with attention, the whole complicated structure of our government, and consider how far the parts of a machine so immense, intricate and complex, are likely to correspond, or interfere with the operations of each other. Such a discussion would necessarily lead to an examination of the principles of our government, in the course of which a dissent from the received maxims of that which we had shaken off would be unavoidable; and in such an investigation it was conceived that it would be more proper to rely on the authority of the American Congress, or of the several State Conventions, than the opinions of any speculative writers on government whatever: inasmuch as the declarations and acts of those BODIES were the foundation of the late revolution, and form the basis of the several republics that have been established among us; and have thus become *constitutional declarations* on the part of the PEOPLE, of their natural, inherent, and unalienable rights. From this circumstance, those acts and declarations might be considered, *in our own republic at least,* as settling the controversy between speculative writers, in all cases to which they extend. *Mr. Locke,* for example, contends that all power is vested in the people: this opinion is controverted by some, and doubted by other eminent writers on government, among whom it is sufficient to mention the learned *Grotius,* and the author of these *Commentaries.* Were it required to investigate this question hypothetically, it might be necessary to recur to the arguments on both sides, and decide according as they may be found to preponderate, since no preference could be given to the bare *authority* of either of these great names. But when we find this principle asserted by CONGRESS in the *Declaration of Independence;* and by the CONVENTION of VIRGINIA in our *Bill* of *Rights;* insisted on, again, by the CONVENTION of the STATE upon the *ratification* of the *Constitution* of the *United States;* and finally acknowledged by the AMENDMENTS proposed to the *Constitution* by Congress, and since ratified by the several states, the contest, as it applies to the *principles of our government,* is at an end; and we are authorised to insist on the *affirmative,* with whatever ingenuity the opposite argument may be maintained.

The CONSTITUTION of VIRGINIA formed under circumstances which have occasioned its authority to be doubted, even by one of the most enlightened politicians that this country has produced, it was also supposed, would require a full and candid discussion. Framed at a time when America might be supposed to be in the cradle of political science, it will not be surprising if many defects have been discovered in it: to examine them impartially, and to propose a remedy for them, or at least for the most obvious and dangerous, it was presumed, could not be an unprofitable undertaking, and would naturally fall in with the plan which the editor proposed to adopt.

The authority and obligation of the COMMON LAW of *England* in the *United States,* was another subject, which it was deemed both necessary and proper to inquire into. If the arguments upon which the learned commentator founded his opinion, that "the common law of England, as such, had no allowance or authority in the British American colonies," antecedent to the revolution which separated them from each other, seem questionable, on the one hand, the opinion that it is NOW the *general law* of the land in the *United States,* in their *collective* and *national* capacity and character, appears not less questionable on the other. The Editor has therefore bestowed some considerable attention on the subject; and though he cannot flatter himself that his researches and conclusions will prove satisfactory, or convincing, to all parties, he cannot but persuade himself that those who impartially seek after truth, will incline to the same opinion with himself.

And, again; although the common law is by express legislative adoption the law of the land in VIRGINIA, under certain restrictions, yet it has from time to time undergone such a variety of amendments, both statutory, and constitutional, that no student without some guide to assist him, can possibly know what to receive, or what to reject; it was, therefore, thought indispensibly necessary to advertise him in what cases its authority and obligation have been either in part diminished or totally destroyed by such amendments. And lastly, as the common law is a collection of *general* customs, it might not be amiss to inquire whether *particular* customs have any, or what force, among us.

The frequent recurrence to the *statute law of England,* in the *Commentaries,* might lead an unwary student to presume that all its provisions were in force in this country; or if he had heard that a part of the statutes only, were received and acknowledged as binding upon us in this commonwealth, he would be left in a state of the most absolute uncertainty respecting them; neither knowing which to receive, nor which to reject, as in the case of the provisions of the common law just mentioned. If he had been informed of the positive repeal of all British statutes by a late act of the legislature of Virginia, he might be tempted to suppose that it would be merely loss of time to peruse the abstract of them in the *Commentaries,* although a short marginal note, might instruct him, perhaps, that they still are retained in our code, and form an important part of our jurisprudence. True it is, those provisions have no longer authority as acts of the British parliament: but a great number of them have been expressly adopted by our legislature; others have undergone some alteration the better to adapt them to our use; in some the very words of a statute have been retained, whilst in others the phraseology has, perhaps more from inadvertence than design, been changed; a considerable number have also been either tacitly, or expressly, rejected, or repealed. To a student pursuing a systematical course of study it must be highly important to be delivered from a labyrinth of uncertainty, by casting his eye to the bottom of the page, and there finding whether the statute he is considering still forms a part of, or has been expunged from, that code, which he wishes to understand.

Not only the regulations contained in the STATUTES, but many of the rules of the COMMON LAW have been occasionally interwoven in, or where doubtful, explained by legislative acts; thereby ascertaining their meaning, and placing their validity beyond a doubt. To point out these cases, might save the student infinite labour, time, and error.

But, the almost total change in the system of laws relative to property, both *real* and *personal,* in Virginia, appeared more particularly to demand a strict scrutiny, and investigation; in the course of which it might not only be necessary to remark the more obvious, but the imperceptible, and perhaps unintended, changes, wrought by a loose, or incautious phrase, or reference. Instances of this kind have unfortunately more than once occurred in our code, and are the unavoidable result of frequently tampering with the rules of property.

The regulations of our internal police, the organization of our courts of judicature, both in the *federal* and *state* government; their respective jurisdictions, and the mode of proceeding therein; are moreover subjects, concerning which the student can expect to receive very little information from the Commentaries, without the aid of notes to direct his attention to such as have been established here with similar powers. The courts of judicature in England have in general afforded the models of ours; but local circumstances have necessarily introduced a variety of new regulations, which by imperceptible and gradual changes, have lost all resemblance to the British original.

But independent of those alterations in the system of our jurisprudence to which local circumstances might be supposed to have given birth, there are a great number which appear to be merely the suggestions of political experiment, or a desire to conform to the newly adopted principles of republican government; among these we may reckon the ABOLITION of *entails;* of the right of *primogeniture;* of the preference heretofore given to the *male* line, in respect to real estates of inheritance; and of the *jus accrescendi,* or right of survivorship between *joint-tenants;* the *ascending* quality communicated to real estates; the *heretability* of the *half-blood;* and of *bastards;* the *legitimation* of the latter, in certain cases; and many other instances in which the rules of the COMMON LAW, or the provisions of a statute, are totally changed.

Many parts of the laws of England are also either obsolete, or have been deemed inapplicable to our local circumstances and policy; these it might be proper to recommend to the perusal of the student, rather as matter of curiosity, than of necessary information to him as an American Lawyer. To this class might be referred the learning respecting ancient feudal tenures; the whole doctrine of copy-holds, and tithes, and whatsoever relates to special or particular customs. The constitution of the crown and parliament, with their several rights, prerogatives, and privileges, would at first appear to fall into the same class: but it was conceived that it might not be uninstructive to shew how far they have been rejected in our own constitutions; or where retained, in what manner they have been distributed thereby. In some cases it would be found that they have been confided solely to the President of the United States; that in others they are participated by the Senate, as an executive council; in other instances, Congress, taken collectively, are the depositaries of the sovereign will and authority of the people; and, if the Editor's partiality does not deceive him, it will be found, upon a candid investigation of the subject, that wherever the constitution of the United States departs from the principles of the British constitution; the change will, in an eminent degree, contribute to the liberty and happiness of the people, however it may diminish the splendour of the government, or the personal influence of those who administer it. For these reasons, it was conceived, that a more particular attention might be proper to those parts of the *Commentaries*, which treat on these subjects, than at first view might appear to be necessary.

The subject of domestic slavery, which, happily for the people of England, it was unnecessary to treat of in the Commentaries, is one, which a student of Law in Virginia ought not to pass over without attention. How far the condition of that unfortunate race of men, whom the unhappy policy of our forefathers has reduced to that degraded condition, is reconcileable to the principles of a free republic, it might be hard for the advocates of such a policy to shew. It was, at least, presumed that in this enlightened age, when philanthropy is supposed to have been more generally diffused through the civilized nations of the earth than at any former period; and in this country, where the blessings of liberty have been so lately, and so dearly purchased, it could not be deemed improper to inquire whether there was a due correspondence between our avowed principles, and our daily practice; and if not, whether it were practicable, consistently with our political safety, to wipe off that stigma from our nation and government. Though the rights of nature, and the dictates of humanity, might heretofore have yielded to the suggestions of interest, the prejudices of education, or the apprehensions of timid politicians; it was still hoped to be demonstrable that reason and justice are reconcileable to our political and domestic interests.

The late revision and republication of the laws of this commonwealth, might at first view appear to supersede the necessity of particular references thereto; the subjects being generally arranged under their proper heads, in bills of considerable length, it might be supposed, would enable the student to consult the statutes, and form his own notes of their operation. But the inconvenience formerly hinted at, arising from *partial*, instead of *complete* editions of our statute law, has full operation in consequence of the omission of a multitude of acts, whose various and often contradictory provisions (so far as they could be reconciled) were consolidated into single bills; in the formation of which the date of the original law, and not only the date, but the alterations produced by amendatory acts, have unavoidably been lost sight of. Hence, the late code can only be considered as operating upon cases *subsequent* to the revisal; for a knowledge of the law *antecedent* thereto, the student must hunt through five other partial compilations, or through the scattered pages of the unbound Sessions's acts, scarcely less difficult to be collected than the leaves of the Sybils. To assist his labours, and often to supply the want of a *law* which no diligence might enable him to procure, was deemed an object of no small importance. And here we may be permitted to remark, that the settlement of this country is too recent not to render that policy very questionable, which consigns to oblivion not only temporary and occasional acts, but the laws which regulate personal property, (which have, *perhaps without intention,* been repeatedly altered and omitted) and even those, by which the titles to lands have been originally acquired, and are still held; not to mention those, by which counties have been divided, courts established, records removed, and a multitude of other arrangements made, altered, and repealed; so as to render a complete acquaintance with the laws of this country, one of the most difficult of human acquirements. A general view of such of the omitted laws as relate to the original acquisition, and subsequent disposal of lands, and other estates of persons dying intestate would well deserve the attention of the student; and although most of them are now out of print, a bare enumeration of their titles, with the periods of their enaction, suspension, or repeal, might be of singular use to those whose interests are likely to be affected by their temporary existence. In researches of this nature a stock of knowledge is acquired whose value is the more precious as it becomes more scarce. To form a complete digest of statute law appears to have been a favourite object with the legislature of Virginia from its first settlement...but unfortunately every attempt of the kind seems to have been the parent of new perplexities, by the introduction of new laws; and the re-enaction, omission, or suspension of former acts, whose operation is thus rendered *doubtful,* even in the most important cases. It has been supposed, for instance, that whenever the legislature have had a bill before them, the rejection of any particular clause therein contained is to be considered as a declaration of the legislative will, that the part rejected shall not be law; or if it be law already, that it shall thenceforth cease to be the law of the land: but will it be supposed that it was the intention of the legislature in 1792, when they struck the act of 1788, c. 23. out of the slave law, to repeal *that act,* by which the act of 1748, declaring that a *person guilty of the manslaughter of a slave should incur no punishment for it,* had been but a few years before *repealed;* under circumstances which excited a just horror that such an act should so long have disgraced our code. On the other hand, would it not probably be equally wide of the truth to presume it was the intention of the legislature to continue in force those parts of the act of 1748, which were also stricken out of the same bill, in the year 1792, and by which the *outlawing* and *shooting* of run-away slaves had been formerly authorised? Though no *general rule* can therefore be laid down upon this subject, it appeared practicable to assist the student in forming a tolerably just conclusion in particular cases. To aid his researches in the several instances before pointed out, was another object of the Editor's undertaking.

Such being the outlines of his plan, he entered upon the execution of it with a zeal, which, if it had been seconded with equal ability, would doubtless have produced a valuable system of FEDERAL and STATE JURISPRUDENCE, so far at least as relates to the COMMONWEALTH OF VIRGINIA .... to have engrafted the laws of all the states in the union, was a work too extensive in the plan, and would have been too voluminous in its execution for him to undertake, whatever might have been his aids, or his talents for such an undertaking: he therefore contented himself with the hope of being particularly useful to the students of law in his *own* state, and generally so, to those in *other* states, who were solicitous to become acquainted with the principles of the *constitution* of the *federal government*, and the *general laws* of the *union*.

Before he concludes, it may not be improper to add a few remarks on the study of the law in this country. If it be true that those nations which have been most distinguished for science, have been also most distinguished for the freedom they have enjoyed, the conclusion would immediately follow that liberty and science were inseparable companions. But here an objection immediately presents itself, that illiterate and barbarous nations are found to possess a greater portion of freedom, in their constitutions and government, than is to be met with in any civilized nation whatsoever. The ancient Gauls and their neighbours the Germans, not to mention other barbarous nations, appear to have lived under a kind of government as free as that of the Indians of this continent, and were equally strangers to literature and to science. But with these and all other barbarous nations, government hath always been a most simple machine, adapted to very few purposes, and those such as might obviously be effected by the aid of a simple contrivance. Their dress, their houses, their mode of living, and their mode of warfare, all partook of the same simplicity. An itinerant nation, or one living in common, would have few ideas respecting the rights of property; their martial temper rendered every individual the arbiter, asserter, and avenger of his own personal rights. Hence very few cases occurred where there could be room for the authority of the civil magistrate to interfere: such magistrates, therefore, appear to have been unknown among them: even their military chiefs seem to have possessed no personal authority but in war; and it is not improbable that their military institutions partook in an eminent degree of the simplicity of the civil. The principles, upon which the government, whether civil or military, was to be administered, being few and simple, were easily understood. Government in this state may be compared to a seedling oak, that has just burst the acorn and appears above the surface of the earth with its first leaves; it advances with civilization, rears its head in proportion as the other increases; and puts forth innumerable branches till it covers the earth with an extensive shade, and is finally regarded as the king of the forest: all behold it with reverence, few have any conception of its magnitude, or of the dimensions, or number of its parts; few are acquainted with the extent of its produce, or can compare the benefits derived from its shade, with the loss of soil which it appropriates to its own support. In such a state, in vain would the rude hand of the barbarian attempt to trace its figure; science, only, is equal to the task, and, even she will find it painful, laborious, and incessant; since every year is the parent of new branches, or the destroyer of old ones: nor will a superficial observation of its exterior alone, suffice; the roots may be decayed, the trunk hollow, and the monarch of the forest ready to fall with its own rottenness and weight, at the moment that its enormous bulk, extensive branches, and luxuriant foliage would seem to promise a millennial duration.

Moreover, society and civilization create a thousand relations unknown to savage life: these are extended and diversified in such a manner that the machine of government becomes necessarily more complex in its parts, in proportion as its functions are multiplied. Those who administer it acquire a mechanical acquaintance with its powers, and often, by a slight alteration in the frame, produce an entire revolution in the principles of its action; to detect the cheat requires a thorough acquaintance with the principles of its original construction, and the purposes to which it was intended to be applied. Hence the facility with which governments, free in their institution, have been overturned by the usurpations, or contrivances, of those, to whom the administration of them hath been committed. Science counteracts this mechanical monopoly of knowledge, and unfolds to its votaries those principles which ought to direct the operations of the machine; discloses the application of other powers, and demonstrates the source from which they spring, and the effect they are calculated to produce. Hence, since the introduction of letters, those nations which have been most eminent in science, have been most distinguished by freedom. Man only requires to understand his rights to estimate them properly: the ignorance of the people is the footstool of despotism.

The study of the law may seem in all countries, in some degree, to be connected with the study of the constitution of the nation. Yet in arbitrary governments questions concerning the constitution rarely occur, and are still more rarely discussed; hence in such governments the study of the law, merely as a profession, does not seem necessarily to require the study of the constitution; the former being limited to such controversies between individuals, as do not involve in them any question of the authority of the government itself: and the latter being supposed to be a theme too exalted for the comprehension of a private individual, and as such discouraged and neglected, until time or accident hath directed the attention of men of talents to a subject so important to the happiness of mankind. But in America the force and obligation of every positive law, and of every act of government, are so immediately blended with the authority of the government itself, as confided by the people to those who administer it, that no man can pretend to a knowledge of the laws of his country, who doth not extend that knowledge to the constitution itself. Yet the study of the constitution is not more necessary to the right understanding of the force and obligation of any positive law, than the study of the law, as a science, is to a full and perfect understanding of the constitution: for the rules of law must not unfrequently be consulted, to explain the principles contained in the constitution: thus, they mutually contribute to the due investigation and understanding of each other.

In a government founded on the basis of equal liberty among all its citizens, to be ignorant of the law and the constitution, is to be ignorant of the rights of the citizen. Ignorance is invariably the parent of error: where it is blended with a turbulent and unquiet temper, it infallibly produces licentiousness, the most terrible enemy to liberty, except despotism: and even more terrible than despotism itself, were it not invariably short lived, whilst the other endures for ages; on the contrary, when ignorance is united with supineness, liberty becomes lethargic, and despotism erects her standard without opposition. An enlightened people, who have once attained the blessings of a free government, can never be enslaved until they abandon virtue and relinquish science. These are the nurses of infant liberty and its fostering genii when matured. To seek their favour is to secure it; to neglect, is infallibly to lose it.

If an acquaintance with the constitution and laws of our country be requisite to preserve the blessings of freedom to the people, it necessarily follows that those who are to frame laws or administer the government should possess a thorough knowledge of these subjects. For what can be more absurd than that a person wholly ignorant of the constitution should presume to make laws pursuant thereto? or that one who neither understands the constitution nor the law, should boldly adventure to administer the government! Yet such instances occur not unfrequently in all countries, and the danger that they will frequently occur in this, is perhaps greater than in any other. The road to office, in most other countries is filled with a thousand turnpikes, which are rarely opened but to the rich and powerful. These possess at least the means of education and information. With us it is equally open to all; but men of talents and virtue are not always the foremost in the course; persons of this description are generally more backward, than those of inferior pretensions, to the confidence of the people; a confidence which, if they do not, they are infinitely more liable to abuse, than if their minds had been properly enlightened by study and application.

Not only the study of the constitution, but an acquaintance with the civil history of our country, seems necessary to constitute a thorough knowledge of its laws. The several epochs required to be well known, when the laws of England were the sole rule of jurisprudence among us; or were interwoven with the laws of our own institution; which last were nevertheless considered in a subordinate degree of authority; or when the authority of the former was wholly superseded, and the latter substituted entirely in their stead, without any check or controul; and, lastly, when by an entire change of the government a new order of things was introduced, and the authority of a part of the laws of the commonwealth were submitted to the controul of the federal constitution, and jurisprudence; otherwise the student can never be certain of the validity of a law, but must wander perpetually in the mazes of doubt and error. To assist his researches in all these respects has been particularly the object of the Editor's labours; in submitting the result of them to the public, he is not without hope that the design will be approved, however the execution may fall short of his own wishes, or the public expectation.

St. Geo. Tucker.

July 10th, 1802.

On Sovereignty and Legislature

This brief essay is Tucker's Appendix A to the first volume of *Blackstone's Commentaries*. In it he wishes to make the point that, with the Revolution, a new basis of sovereignty was established—that of the people, in contrast to the states of the Old World. This was a necessary preface to the succeeding essay "Of the Several Forms of Government."

Blackstone's Com. page 46. "Sovereignty and Legislature are indeed convertible terms; one cannot subsist without the other."

The generality of expression in this passage might lead those who have not considered with attention the new lights which the American revolution has spread over the science of politics, to conclude with the learned commentator, that, "By the sovereign power, is meant the making of laws; and where-ever that power resides, all others must conform to and be directed by it, whatever appearance the outward form and administration of justice may put on. It being at any time in the option of the legislature to alter that form and administration by a new edict or rule, and to put the execution of the laws into whatever hands it pleases: and all the other powers of the state must obey the legislative power in the execution of their several functions. . . . or else the constitution is at an end."

Before we yield our full assent to this conclusion, we must advert to a fact, probably truly stated by the learned author at the time he wrote; "That the original written compact of society had, perhaps, in no instance, been ever formally expressed, at the first institution of a state."

In governments whose original foundations cannot be traced to the certain and undeniable criterion of an original written compact. . . . whose forms as well as principles are subject to perpetual variation from the usurpations of the strong, or the concessions of the weak; where tradition supplies the place of written evidence; where every new construction is in fact a new edict; and where the fountain of power hath been immemorially transferred from the people, to the usurpers of their natural rights, our author's reasoning on this subject will not easily be controverted.... But the American revolution has formed a new epoch in the history of civil institutions, by reducing to practice, what, before, had been supposed to exist only in the visionary speculations of theoretical writers.... The world, for the first time since the annals of its inhabitants began, saw an original written compact formed by the free and deliberate voices of individuals disposed to unite in the same social bonds; thus exhibiting a political phenomenon unknown to former ages.... This memorable precedent was soon followed by the far greater number of the states in the union, and led the way to that instrument, by which the union of the confederated states has since been completed, and in which, as we shall hereafter endeavor to show, the sovereignty of the people, and the responsibility of their servants are principles fundamentally, and unequivocally, established; in which the powers of the several branches of government are defined, and the excess of them, as well in the *legislature,* as in the *other* branches, finds limits, which cannot be transgressed without offending against that greater power from whom all authority, among us, is derived; to wit, the PEOPLE.

To illustrate this by an example. By the constitution of the United States, the solemn and original compact here referred to, being the act of the people, and by them declared to be the supreme law of the land, the legislative powers thereby granted; are vested in a congress, to consist of a senate and house of representatives. As these powers, on the one hand, are extended to certain objects, as to lay and collect taxes, duties, &c. so on the other they are clearly limited and restrained; as that no tax or duty shall be laid on articles exported from any state ... nor any preference given by any regulation of commerce or revenue to the ports of one state over those of another, &c. These, and several others, are objects to which the power of the legislature does not extend; and should congress be so unwise as to pass an act contrary to these restrictions, the other powers of the state are not bound to obey the legislative power in the execution of their several functions, as our author expresses it: but the very reverse is their duty, being sworn to support the constitution, which unless they do in *opposition* to such encroachments, the constitution would indeed be at an end.

Here then we must resort to a distinction which the institution and nature of our government has introduced into the western hemisphere; which, however, can only obtain in governments where power is not usurped but delegated, and where authority is a trust and not a right... nor can it ever be truly ascertained where there is not a written constitution to resort to. A distinction, nevertheless, which certainly does exist between the indefinite and unlimited power of the people, in whom the sovereignty of these states, ultimately, substantially, and unquestionably resides, and the definite powers of the congress and state legislatures, which are severally limited to certain and determinate objects, being no more than emanations from the former, where, and where only, that legislative essence which constitutes sovereignty can be found.

❧ Of the Several Forms of Government

This was Tucker's Appendix B to volume 1 of his edition of *Blackstone's Commentaries*. Tucker considered it a necessary introduction to his lengthy treatment, in the next two appendices, of the constitutions of Virginia and of the United States. His strongest point of insistence is on the necessity for governmental power to be restrained within specifically delegated limits. Of course, it is this emphasis on the limitations, rather than the uses, of power that separated the Jeffersonian Republicans from the Federalists. "But, if the efficient force or administrative authority be, altogether, unlimited; as if it extends so far as to change the constitution, itself, the government, whatever be its form, is absolute and despotic. . . ." By Tucker's definition, the modern federal government, particularly in its judicial branch, qualifies as despotic. For Tucker, as for Calhoun, society, or the "body politic," takes precedence always over the government, or state. And for Tucker, unlike Lincoln, the people may resume their sovereignty at any time. The discussion is most of all, perhaps, an answer to those Federalists, like John Adams and Alexander Hamilton, who emphasized the evils of democracy and the need for it to be restrained. Tucker's arguments about the failings of "aristocracy" can be seen as a reply to the Federalist philosophers and also perhaps as a prophecy of later times. And Tucker's long explanation of the characteristics and virtues of "confederate governments," such as the United States, though strange to modern ears, represents a predominant American understanding of his own time and long after.

THE CONCISE MANNER in which the commentator, has treated of the several forms of government, seems to require that the subject should be somewhat further considered: this has been attempted in the following pages; in the course of which the student will meet with considerable extracts from the writings of Mr. Locke, and other authors, who have copiously treated the subject; of which an epitome, only, is here offered for the use of those who may not possess the means of better information.

PRELIMINARY REMARKS.

A nation or state is a body politic, or a society of men united together to promote their mutual safety, and advantage, by means of their union.

From the very design, that induces them to form a society that has its common interests, and ought to act in concert, it is necessary that there should be established a public authority, to order and direct what ought to be done, by each, in relation to the end of the association.

This political authority, is by some writers denominated the sovereignty;[1] but, for reasons which will be hereafter explained, I prefer calling it the government, or administrative authority of the state, to which each citizen, subjects himself by the very act of association, for the purpose of establishing a civil society.

All men being by nature equal, in respect to their rights, no man nor set of men, can have any natural, or inherent right, to rule over the rest.

This right cannot be acquired by conquest, for the few, are, in a state of nature, unable to subdue the many.

Were it ever possible that the few could triumph over the many, the power thus acquired, can not be transmissible by inheritance, since it may fall into hands incapable of maintaining it.

The right of governing can, therefore, be acquired only by, consent, originally; and this consent must be that of at least a majority of the people.[2]

1. Vattel.
2. See Rousseau's Social Compact.

Since no person possesses any inherent right to govern, or rule over the rest; and since the few cannot possess, naturally power enough to subdue the many; the majority of the people, and, much more the whole body, posses all the powers, which any society, state, or nation, possesses in relation to its own immediate concerns.

This power which every independent state or nation, (however constituted, or by whatever name distinguished, whether it be called an empire, kingdom, or republic and whether the government be in its form a monarchy, aristocracy, or democracy, or a mixture or corruption of all them,) possesses in relation to its own immediate concerns, is unlimited, and unlimitable, so long as the nation or state retains its independence; there being no power upon earth, whilst that remains, which can control, or direct the operations, or will, of the state in those respects.

This unlimitable power, is that supreme, irresistible, absolute, uncontrollable authority, which by political writers in general, is denominated the SOVEREIGNTY; and which is by most of them, supposed to be vested in the government, or administrative authority, of the state: but, which, we contend, resides only in the people; is inherent in them; and unalienable from them.[3]

Except in very small states, where the government is administered by the people themselves, in person, the exercise of the sovereign power is confined to the establishment of the constitution of the state or the amendments of its defects, or to the correction of the abuses of the government.

The constitution of a state is, properly, that instrument by which the government, or administrative authority of the state, is created: its powers defined, their extent limited; the duties of the public functionaries prescribed; and the principles, according to which the government is to be administered, delineated.[4]

The GOVERNMENT or administrative authority of the state, is that portion only of the sovereignty, which is by the constitution entrusted

3. Burgh's Political Disquisitions.
4. Paine's Rights of Man.

to the public functionaries: these are the agents and servants of the people.

Legitimate government can therefore be derived only from the voluntary grant of the people, and exercised for their benefit.

The sovereignty, though always potentially existing in the people of every independent nation, or state, is in most of them, usurped by, and confounded with, the government. Hence in England it is said to be vested in the parliament: in France, before the revolution, and still, in Spain, Russia, Turkey and other absolute monarchies, in the crown, or monarch; in Venice, until the late conquest of that state, in the doge, and senate, &c.

As the sovereign power hath no limits to its authority, so hath the government of a state no rights, but such as are purely derivative, and limited; the union of the SOVEREIGNTY of a state with the GOVERNMENT, constitutes a state of USURPATION and absolute TYRANNY, over the PEOPLE.

In the United States of America the people have retained the sovereignty in their own hands: they have in each state distributed the government, or administrative authority of the state, into two distinct branches, internal, and external; the former of these, they have confided, with some few exceptions, to the state government; the latter to the federal government.

Since the union of the sovereignty with the government, constitutes a state of absolute power, or tyranny, over the people, every attempt to effect such an union is treason against the sovereignty, in the actors; and every extension of the administrative authority beyond its just constitutional limits, is absolutely an act of usurpation in the government, of that sovereignty, which the people have reserved to themselves.

These few preliminary remarks will be somewhat enlarged upon in the sequel.

SECTION I.

Government, considered as the administrative authority of a state, or body politic, may, in general, be regarded as coeval with civil society, itself: Since the agreement or contract by which each individual may be supposed to have agreed with all the rest, that they should unite into one society or body, to be governed in all their common interests, by common consent, would probably be immediately followed by the decree, or designation, made by the whole people, of the form or plan of power, which is what we now understand by the constitution of the state; as also of the persons, to whom the administration of those powers should, in the first instance be confided. Considered in this light, government and civil society may be regarded as, generally, inseparable; the one ordinarily resulting from the other: but this is not universally the case: man in a state of nature hath no governor but himself: in savage life, which approaches nearly to that state, government is scarcely perceptible. In the epoch of a national revolution, man is, as it were, again remitted to a state of nature: in this case civil society exists, though the constitution or bond of union be dissolved, and the government or administrative authority of the state be suspended, or annihilated. But this suspension is generally of short duration: and even if an annihilation of the government takes place, it is but momentary: were it otherwise, civil society must perish also.

Even during the suspension, or annihilation of government, the laws of nature and of moral obligation, which are in their nature indissoluble, continue in force in civil society. Hence social rights and obligations, also, are respected, even when there is no government to enforce their observance. This principle, during state convulsions, supplies the absence of regular government: but it cannot long supply its place; government, therefore, either permanent or temporary, results from a state of civilized society.

As the natural end and sole purpose of all civil power is the general good of the whole body, in which the governors, or public functionaries, themselves are necessarily included as a part, so, that civil power alone can be justly assumed, or claimed by any governor, or public functionary, which is delegated to him by the constitution of the state, as necessary, or conducive to the prosperity of the whole body united; what is not so delegated is unjust upon whatever pretence it is assumed. Any contract or consent conveying useless or pernicious powers is invalid, as being founded on an error about the nature of the thing conveyed, and its tendency to the end proposed.[5]

The most natural method of constituting, or continuing civil power must, since the general use of letters, be some deed, or instrument of convention, between those who set about to establish a civil society or state, to serve as an evidence of their common intentions in forming such an association; to limit the powers which they meant to confer upon their public functionaries, and agents; and to prescribe the mode by which those agents shall be from time to time appointed, and the powers confided to them administered. And if it should happen that time and experience may demonstrate that the people have adopted, or consented to a pernicious plan; whose destructive tendency they have discovered; and now see their error; taking that plan to tend to their good, which they find has the most opposite tendency; they are free from its obligation, and may insist upon a new model of polity.

These speculative notions may be regarded as having received the most solemn sanction in the United States of America; the supreme national council of which hath, on the most important occasion, which hath ever occurred since the first settlement of these states by the present race of men, declared, "that all men are created equal; that they are endowed by their Creator with certain unalienable rights; that among these are life, liberty, and the pursuit of happiness; that to secure these rights, governments are instituted among men, deriving their just powers from the consent of the governed: that whenever any form of government becomes destructive of these ends, it is the right of the people to abolish it, and to institute a new government, laying its foundations upon such principles, and organizing its powers in such form, as to them shall seem most likely to effect their safety and happiness." Such is the language of that congress which dissolved the union between Great Britain and America. Few are the governments of the world, ancient or modern, whose foundations have been laid upon these principles. Fraud, usurpation, and conquest have been, generally, substituted in their stead.

5. Hutchinson's Moral Philosophy.

When a government is founded upon the voluntary consent, and agreement of a people uniting themselves together for their common benefit, the people, or nation, collectively taken, is free, although the administration of the government should happen to be oppressive, and to a certain degree, even tyrannical; since it is in the power of the people to alter, or abolish it, whenever they shall think proper; and to institute such new government as may seem most likely to effect their safety and happiness. But if the government be founded in fear, constraint, or force, although the administration should happen to be mild, the people, being deprived of the sovereignty, are reduced to a state of civil slavery. Should the administration, in this case, become tyrannical, they are without redress. Submission, punishment, or a successful revolt, are the only alternatives.

It is easy to perceive that a government originally founded upon consent, and compact, may by gradual usurpations on the part of the public functionaries, change its type, altogether, and become a government of force. In this case, the people are as completely enslaved as if the original foundations of the government had been laid by conquest.

Thus, the nature of a government, so far as respects the freedom of the people, may be considered as depending upon the nature of the bond of their union. If the bond of union be the voluntary consent of the people, the government may be pronounced to be free; where constraint and fear constitute that bond, the government is no longer the government of the people, and consequently they are enslaved.

And, as the nature of the government, whether free, or the reverse, depends upon the nature of the bond of union, whether it be the effect of a voluntary compact, and consent, or of constraint, and compulsion; so the form of any government, depends altogether upon the manner in which the efficient force, and administrative authority of the state is distributed, and administered. But, if the efficient force or administrative authority be, altogether, unlimited; as if it extends so far as to change the constitution, itself, the government, whatever be its form, is absolute and despotic; the people in this case are annihilated.... Their regeneration can only be effected by a revolution.

On the contrary, when the constitution is founded in voluntary compact, and consent, and imposes limits to the efficient force of the government, or administrative authority, the people are still the sovereign; the government is the mere creature of their will; and those who administer it are their agents and servants.

From hence it will appear that the nature of any government does not depend upon the checks and balances which may be provided by the constitution, since they respect the form of the government, only; but it depends upon the nature and extent of those powers which the people have reserved to themselves, as the Sovereign: or rather, upon the extent of those, which they have delegated to the government; or, which the government in the course of its administration may have usurped. An usurped government may be no less a government of checks and balances, than a government founded in voluntary consent and compact: witness the government of England, where the parliament according to the theory of their constitution (and not the people,) is the sovereign. The checks and balances of that Government have been the topic of applause among all those who are opposed alike to the government of the people, or of an absolute monarch. But no people can ever be free, whose government is founded upon the usurpation of their sovereign rights; for by the act of usurpation, the sovereignty is transferred from the people, in whom alone it can legitimately reside, to those who by that act have manifested a determination to oppress them.

SECTION II.

"How the several forms of government we now see in the world at first actually began," says the learned commentator,[6] "is matter of great uncertainty, and has occasioned infinite disputes." The celebrated author of the Rights of Man observes that the origin of all governments may be comprehended under three heads; superstition, power, and the common rights of man. The first were governments of priest-craft, through the

6. Ibid.

medium of oracles; the second being founded in power, the sword assumed the name of a sceptre; the third in compact; each individual in his own personal, and sovereign right entering into the compact, each with the other, to establish a government. A late political writer in England,[7] remarks, that all the governments that now exist in the world, except the United States of America, have been fortuitously formed. They are the produce of chance, not the work of art. They have been altered, impaired, improved, and destroyed by accidental circumstances, beyond the foresight, or control of wisdom. Their parts thrown up against present emergencies, form no systematic whole. These fortuitous governments cannot be supposed to derive their existence from the free consent of the people; they are fruits of internal violence and struggles, between parties contending for the sovereignty; or of fraudulent and gradual usurpations of power by those to whom the people have entrusted the administration of the government, or of successful ambition, aided by the operation and influence of standing armies. A democratic government, however organized, must, on the contrary, be founded in general consent and compact, the most natural and the only legitimate method of constituting or continuing civil power, as was observed elsewhere. It is the great, and, I had almost said, the peculiar happiness of the people of the United States, that their constitutions, respectively, rest upon this foundation.

SECTION III.

The fundamental regulation that determines the manner in which the public authority is to be executed, is what forms the constitution of the state. In this is seen the form by which the nation acts in quality of a body politic: how, and by whom the people ought to be governed, and what are the laws and duties of the governors.

From this definition of a constitution, given us by Vattel, we might reasonably be led to expect, that in every nation not reduced to the

---

7. Mackintosh on the French Revolution.

unconditional obedience of a despotic prince, there might be found some traces, at least, of the original compact of society entered into by the people at the first institution of the state. Yet it seems to be the opinion of the learned commentator that such an original compact had perhaps in no instance been expressed in that manner. But it is difficult not to imagine that such an original contract must have been actually entered into, and even formally expressed, in every state where government hath been established upon the principles of democracy. The various revolutions in the ancient states of Greece were often attended with the establishment of that species of government: The original constitution of Venice was a pure democracy; and the constitutions of several of the Swiss cantons partake also, in a great degree, of the same character. Can we conceive such regulations to have been established without being in some degree formally expressed? That the evidences of them have not been handed down to us is not, I apprehend, a sufficient reason for rejecting the opinion that they have had existence. If, therefore, the opinion of the learned commentator be, that there never was an instance in which government had been instituted by voluntary compact, and consent of the people of any state, it would seem that there is room to doubt the correctness of such an opinion. If, on the contrary, the opinion be referred to the primitive act of associating by individuals totally unconnected in society, before, I shall not controvert it any further.

For it is evident that the foundations of the state or body politic of any nation may have been laid for centuries before the existing constitution, or form of government of such state. In England, the foundation of the state (such as it has been from the time of the Heptarchy,) is agreed to have been laid by Alfred. And from that period till the union with Scotland, in the days of Queen Anne, the state remained unchanged: but the government during the same period was incessantly changing. Before the conquest it seems to have resembled a moderate, or limited monarchy. From that period it seems to have been, alternately, an absolute monarchy, a feudal aristocracy, an irregular oligarchy, and a government compounded, as at present, of three different estates, alternately, vieing with each other for the superiority, until it has finally settled in the crown. The foundations of the American States were laid in their respective colonial charters: with the revolution they ceased to be colonies, and became independent and sovereign republics, under a democratic form of government. When they became members of a confederacy, united for their mutual defense against a common enemy, they renounced the exercise of a part of their sovereign rights; and in adopting the present constitution of the United States, they have formed a closer, and more intimate union than before; yet still retaining the character of distinct, sovereign, independent states. In all these permutations of their constitutions or forms of government, the states or body politic of each of the members of the American confederacy, have remained the same, or nearly the same, as before the revolution.

Thus, as has been already mentioned, society may not only exist, though government be dissolved; but the state, or body politic, may remain the same, whilst the government is changeable. Whenever the form of government is fixed, the constitution of the state is said to be established; and this, as has been observed before, may be effected either by fraud, or by force; or by a temporary compromise between contending parties; or, by the general, and voluntary consent of the people. In the two first cases, the constitution is merely constructive, according to the will and pleasure of those who have usurped, and continue to exercise the supreme power. In the third case likewise, it is in general, merely constructive; each party contending for whatever power it hath not expressly yielded up to the other; or which it thinks it hath power to resume, or to secure to itself. Where the constitution is established by voluntary, and general consent, the people, and the public functionaries employed by them to administer the government, may be apprised of their several, and respective rights and duties; and the same voluntary, and general consent is equally necessary to every change in the constitution, as to its original establishment. The constitution may indeed provide a mode within itself for its amendment; but this very provision is founded in the previous consent of the people, that such a mode shall supercede the necessity of an immediate presumption of, the sovereign power, into their own hands, for the purpose of amending the constitution; but if the government has any agency in proposing, or establishing amendments, whenever that becomes corrupt, the people will probably find the necessity of a resumption of the sovereignty, in order to correct the abuses, and vices of the government.

And herein, I apprehend, consists the only distinction between limited and unlimited governments. If the constitution be founded upon the previous act of the people, the government is limited. If it have any other foundation, it is merely constructive, and the government arrogates to itself the sole right of making such a construction of it, as may suit with its own views, designs, and interests: and when this right can be successfully exercised, the government becomes absolute and despotic. In like manner, if in a limited government the public functionaries exceed the limits which the constitution prescribes to their powers, every such act is an act of usurpation in the government, and, as such, treason against the sovereignty of the people, which is thus endeavored to be subverted, and transferred to the usurpers.

Inseparably connected with this distinction between limited and unlimited governments, is the responsibility of the public functionaries, and the want of such responsibility. Every delegated authority implies a trust; responsibility follows as the shadow does its substance. But where there is no responsibility, authority is no longer a trust, but an act of usurpation. And every act of usurpation is either an act of treason, or an act of warfare.

Legitimate government, then, can be established only by the voluntary consent of the society, who by mutual compact with each other grant certain specified powers, to such agents as they may from time to time choose to administer the government thus established, and their agents are responsible to the society for the manner in which they may discharge the trust delegated to them. The instrument by which the government is thus established, and the powers, or more properly the duties, of the public functionaries and agents, are defined and limited, is the visible constitution of the state. For it has been well observed by the author of the Rights of Man, "that a constitution is not a thing in name only, but in fact. It has not an ideal, but a real existence; and whenever it cannot be produced in a visible form there is none. A constitution is a thing antecedent to a government, and a government, is only the creature of a constitution. It is not the act of the government but of the people constituting the government. It is the body of elements to which you can refer, and quote article by article; and which contains the principles on which the government shall be established, the manner in which it shall be organized; the powers it shall have; the mode of elections; the duration of the legislative body, &c." Hence every attempt in any government to change the constitution (otherwise than in that mode which the constitution may prescribe) is in fact a subversion of the foundations of its own authority.

The acquiescence of the people of a state under any usurped authority for any length of time, can never deprive them of the right of resuming the sovereign power into their own hands, whenever they think fit, or are able to do so, since that right is perfectly unalienable. Nor can it be supposed with any shadow of reason, that in a government established by the authority of the people, it could ever be their intention to deprive themselves of the means of correcting any defects which experience may point out or of applying a remedy to abuses which unfaithful agents may practice to their injury. The sovereign power therefore always resides ultimately, and in contemplation, in the people, whatever be the form of the government: yet the practical exercise of the sovereignty is almost universally usurped by those who administer the government, whatever may have been its original foundation.

It is the proper object of a written constitution not only to restrain the several branches of the government, viz. the legislative, executive, and judiciary departments, within their proper limits, respectively, but to prohibit the branches, united, from any attempt to invade that portion of the sovereign power which the people have not delegated to their public functionaries and agents, but have reserved, unalienably, to themselves.

A written constitution has moreover the peculiar advantage of serving as a beacon to apprise the people when their rights and liberties are invaded, or in danger.

It has been before remarked, that the constitutions of the several

United States of America, rest upon the ground of general consent, and compact, between the individuals of each state respectively. To this it may be added, that in every state in the union (Connecticut and Rhode Island excepted) their constitutions have been formally expressed in a visible form, or writing, and have been established by the suffrages of the people, in that form, since the revolution.

The federal government of the United States rests likewise upon a similar foundation; the free consent and suffrages of the people of the several states, separately, and independently taken, and expressed.

It is therefore a fundamental principle in all the American States, which cannot be impugned, or shaken; that their governments have been instituted by the common consent, and for the common benefit, protection, and security of the people, in whom all power is vested, and from whom it is derived: that their magistrates, are their trustees and servants, and at all times amenable to them; and that when any government shall be found inadequate, or contrary, to the purposes of its institution, a majority of the community hath an indubitable, unalienable and indefeasible right to reform, alter, or abolish it, in such manner as shall be judged most conducive to the public weal.

SECTION IV.

Political writers in general seem to be agreed that the several forms of government, which now exist, may be reduced to three; viz. first the democratic; or that in which the body of the nation keeps in its own hands the right of commanding: secondly, the aristocratic; or that in which that right is referred to, or usurped by, a certain number of citizens, independent of the concurrence or consent of the remainder; and thirdly, that in which the administration of the affairs of the state is vested in a single person, which is denominated a monarchy.... These three kinds may be variously combined, and united, and when so combined and united they obtain the general appellation of mixed governments; and sometimes of limited governments. Thus the Roman commonwealth, after the establishment of the tribunes of the people, contained a mixture of democracy, with aristocracy: the former being vested in the assemblies of the people; the latter in the senate: thus, also, the government of Great Britain, in which there is supposed to be a portion of all three of these forms, is not infrequently styled a limited monarchy.

SECTION V.

When the body of the people in a state keeps in its own hands the supreme power, or right of ordering all things relative to the public concerns of the state, this, as was before observed, is a democracy. And, in such a state, says Montesquieu, the people ought to do for themselves, whatever they conveniently can; and what they can not well do, themselves, they should commit to the management of ministers chosen by themselves.

A democracy, therefore, may be either a pure and simple government, in which every member of the state assists in the administration of the public affairs, in person; or, it may be representative, in which the people perform that by their agents, or representatives, to the performance of which in person, either insurmountable obstacles, or very great inconveniences, are continually opposed.

1. A simple democracy must necessarily be confined to a very small extent of territory: for if it be the duty of every citizen to attend the public deliberations and councils; to make laws; to administer justice; to consult and provide for the protection and security of the state against foreign enemies; or to compose domestic factions and strife; this will be impracticable if the territory of the state be extensive; and, moreover, the important business of agriculture, every species of industry, and the necessary attention to the domestic concerns of each individual must be neglected; and where this continues to be the case for any considerable length of time, the state must inevitably perish.

Where the limits of a state are so confined as that the people can assemble as often as may be requisite, for the administration of the public concerns from every part of the state, such state must have too small a population to protect itself against the hostile designs and attacks of powerful, or ambitious neighbors; or, too small a territory to support the number of its inhabitants; either of which circumstances must continually endanger its safety and independence.

A pure democracy seems, therefore, to be compatible only with the first rudiments of society, and civil government; or with the circumstances and situation of a people detached from the rest of the world; as the inhabitants of St. Marino, in Italy, are said to be, by the inaccessible cliffs of the mountain, whose, summit they inhabit. And it may be doubted (for reasons that will hereafter be mentioned), whether there ever has been such a form of civil government established among civilized nations. Perhaps nothing can be found so nearly approaching to it, as in the history of the Aborigines of this continent, as given us by the author of the history of Vermont.[8] The form and manner of the Indian government, as that historian informs us, was the most simple that can be contrived or imagined.... There was no king, nobility, lords, or house of representatives, among them. The whole tribe assembled together in their public councils: their most aged men were the depositaries of what may be gathered from experience, observation, and a knowledge of their former transactions. By them their debates and consultations were chiefly carried on. Their councils were slow, solemn and deliberate, every circumstance that could be foreseen was taken into consideration. The whole was a scene of consultation and advice. And the advice had no other force or authority, than what it derived from its supposed wisdom, fitness and propriety.

The strength, or power of the government, adds this author, is placed wholly in the public sentiment. The chief has no authority to enforce his counsels, or compel obedience to his measures. He is fed and clothed like the rest of the tribe; his house and furniture is the same as that of others; there is no appearance or mark of distinction; no ceremony, or form of induction into office; no ensigns or tokens of superiority, or power. In every external circumstance, the chiefs are upon a level with the rest of the tribe; and that only which gives weight and authority to

8. Samuel Williams.

their advice, is the public opinion of their superior wisdom and experience. Their laws stand upon the same foundation. There was no written law, record, or rule of conduct.... No public precedent, established courts, forms or modes of proceeding. The causes and occasions of contentions were few, and they did not much affect the tribe. And when the chiefs interposed in the concerns of individuals, it was not to compel but only to counsel and advise them. The public opinion pointed out what was right; and an offender who had been deeply guilty fled from the tribe, &c.

Were we not (after the example of the ancient Greeks and Romans) in the habit of considering all those nations who are not seduced by the allurements of polished life, as barbarians, and savages, should we not esteem this picture of society, as the dream of a poet, describing the golden age, rather than a just representation of the actual state of a people, whom we despise for their ignorance; and of mankind, in those situations where the poisonous effects of artificial refinement have not yet manifested themselves.

And here it may not be amiss to mention another objection that is frequently made to a democratic government; because, if such an objection exists, it can only apply to such an one as we have just described. It is this; that all power being concentrated in the people, whenever the whole people assemble to deliberate upon any matter, there lies no appeal from their decision, however hasty or ill-advised it may be, there being no law, nor constitution to limit or control their determinations. Consequently they may revoke today, what they established yesterday; and tomorrow, may adopt a new rule, different from either, which, in its turn, may be again superceded the day after. Hence, a perpetual fluctuation of councils is inseparable from a pure democracy.

Another objection, which is also frequently urged against this species of government is, that it is, more than any other, subject to be agitated by violent commotions excited by turbulent and factious men, who aim at grasping all the power of the state into their own hands and sacrifice every obstacle to the attainment of their nefarious ends.

As the first of these objections applies only to a pure, or simple democracy, such as has been above described, it may be time enough to answer it, when we find ourselves in danger of falling into such a form of government. But I am inclined to suppose, that the objection would be altogether without force, where the state of society among those about to establish a new form of government may happen to be such, as that no other inconvenience, (which might be apprehended from such a form of government) should constitute an objection to its adoption. For where there is such a separation from the rest of the world, and such a simplicity of manners, united to the existence of a very small society, as to recommend the adoption of a government perfectly, and simply, democratic, we may venture to affirm that no very great inconvenience need be apprehended from instability of counsels. And with regard to the evils to be apprehended from violent commotions, we shall hereafter see, that they mark the period when the democracy is subverted, or in imminent danger of it, rather than that in which it flourishes: and such commotions are equally incident to other governments during the period of their decline, as to democracies; and in such governments they are likewise more violent, and more fatal.

2. But all the disadvantages of a pure, or simple democracy, such as we have hitherto been speaking of, may, I apprehend, be effectually guarded against, by one that is representative: that is, in which the people administer the government by means of their agents, or representatives, chosen from time to time by themselves, and removable from the trust reposed in them whenever they cease to possess the public confidence, in their wisdom, integrity, or patriotism.[9]

---

9. It has been said, that to call a government "a representative democracy, is a contradiction in terms, and as improper as to call it a democratic aristocracy.".... Swift's Laws of Connecticut, vol. 1, 21.... With all deference to this opinion, I would ask, whom do these representatives represent? If they represent themselves, only, then I grant the government is not a representative democracy, but an elective oligarchy, or if you please, a democratic aristocracy: in which the people have indeed no power but to "chuse their rulers.".... But if these representatives represent their constituents, that is, the people; then is their authority not their own, but the authority of the people; and a government administered either directly or indirectly by the authority of the people is a democracy, as is agreed on all hands; if administered by the people themselves, then is it a simple democracy; but if the people appoint some few from among themselves to represent

It is not necessary that the limits of a representative democracy should be so confined, as to expose it to the danger of famine on the one hand, or to the incursions and attacks of powerful and ambitious nations on the other; no interruption need be given to agriculture and other necessary occupations; the constitution of the state may be permanently fixed, by the people, and the duties and functions of their representatives and agents so distributed and limited, as that the laws of the state, and not the versatile will of a giddy multitude shall always prevail.

SECTION VI.

Governments, says an American writer, may be variously modified on the democratic principle. That which possesses the most energy, and at the same time best guards its principles, is the most perfect. A democratic government ought to have the most perfect energy; because there can be no excuse for disobedience to an authority which is delegated by the community at large, and only held during pleasure. But in communicating energy without gradual and cautious experiment, there is danger of communicating with it, the power of fencing in the government, and changing its principles. This was the danger apprehended by many, at the time of adopting the present federal constitution. Nor was it a groundless apprehension, says the writer, to whom I am indebted for these remarks. The democratic principle being at that time, as it were, forlorn, destitute, and despised by the world, was in danger of being laughed out of countenance even in this country, and of being banished from it as a thing of too mean an origin to be admitted into polished societies.[10]

I repeat it says the same writer, that a democratic government ought to possess the most perfect energy; without which, true freedom, and the real and essential rights of man, are without protection. Many maxims taken from other governments are inapplicable to ours, and therefore

---

them, then I conceive such a government may, with the strictest propriety, be called a representative democracy.

10. *Editor's note:* Tucker never identifies the writer referred to here.

with respect to us, are erroneous. All monarchies, however modified, are governments of usurpation, or prescription. In the exercise of their authority, the interest and pleasure of the governing party are more considered, than the general welfare: of course, the more energetic such authority is, the greater is the oppression felt from it. In governments by compact, where, of course, the authority is legitimate, and exercised for the general good, the reverse is true. Energy in such a government, is the best support that freedom can desire; and freedom is more perfect in proportion to the degree of energy.... If the laws of a democracy prove unwholesome in their effects, it is because the members of the legislature have erred in their judgment, as the best and wisest men are liable to do; in which case, they will soon correct the error; or because they have been improperly chosen, in which case, it depends on the people to correct it, at the next election. In a democracy a legislator, as well as every other public functionary, is responsible to the community for the uprightness of this conduct. If he concurs in an unconstitutional act, he is guilty of usurpation, and contempt of the sovereign authority, which has forbidden him to pass the bounds prescribed by the constitution. He has violated his oath, and the most sacred of all duties. To omit him at the next election is not an adequate punishment for such a crime. Abuse of power is despotism, and the democracy that does not guard against it, is defective. If in any department of government, a man may abuse, or exceed his powers, without fear of punishment, the right of one man is at the mercy of another, and freedom in such a government, has no existence.

It is indispensably necessary to the very existence of this species of democracy, that there be a perfect equality of rights among the citizens, the unqualified use of the term equality has furnished the enemies of democracy with a pretext to charge it with the most destructive principles. By equality, in a democracy, is to be understood, equality of civil rights, and not of condition. Equality of rights necessarily produces inequality of possessions; because, by the laws of nature and of equality, every man has a right to use his faculties in an honest way, and the fruits of his labor, thus acquired, are his own. But some men have more strength than others; some more health; some more industry; and some more skill and ingenuity, than others; and according to these, and other circumstances the products of their labor must be various, and their property must become unequal. The rights of property must be sacred, and must be protected; otherwise there could be no exertion of either ingenuity or industry, and consequently nothing but extreme poverty, misery, and brutal ignorance.

It is further indispensably necessary to the very existence of this species of democracy, that the agents of the people be chosen by themselves; that in this choice, the most inflexible integrity, be regarded as an indispensible constituent; and where that is found, it is but reasonable to be satisfied with something beyond mediocrity, in other qualities. A sound judgment united with an unfeigned zeal for the public weal, will be more certain of promoting and procuring it, than the most brilliant talents which have not the foundation of integrity for their support, and the stimulus of an active zeal for the public good, for its advancement. Besides, if none but men of the first talents were to be employed as public agents, even where no superiority of talents may be required, such a circumstance would inevitably discourage modest merit from offering its services, or accepting an offer of the public confidence, on any occasion: and such a discouragement would soon operate to substitute the glare of superficial talents, for the solid worth of integrity, sound judgment, and love of the public weal.

In this species of democracy, it is further indispensably necessary to its preservation, that the constitution be fixed, that the duties of the public functionaries be defined, and limited, both as to their objects, and their duration; and that they should be at all times responsible to the people for their conduct. The constitution, being the act of the people, and the compact, according to which they have agreed with each other, that the government which they have established shall be administered, is a law to the government, and a sacred reverence, for it is an indispensable requisite in the character and conduct of every public agent. A profound obedience to the laws, and due submission to the magistrate entrusted with their execution, is equally indispensible on the part of every citizen of the commonwealth, in order to preserve the principles of this government from corruption. Neglect of the principles of the constitution by the public functionary is a substitution of aristocracy, for a representative democracy: such a person no longer regards himself as the trustee, and agent of the people, but as a ruler whose authority is independent of the people, to whom he holds himself in no manner accountable; and he so degenerates into an usurper and a tyrant. On the other hand, when any individual can with impunity defy the magistrate, or disregard the laws, the sinews of the government are destroyed, and the government itself is annihilated. As distant as heaven is from earth, says Montesquieu, is the true spirit of equality from that of extreme equality. The former does not consist in managing so that every body should command, or that no one should be commanded; but in obeying and commanding our equals.

The constitution of Athens, as established by Solon, was in some measure representative; there was a senate, consisting of five hundred deputies who were annually elected; so were the archons, and other magistrates of the republic. But the whole body of the people likewise assembled, both ordinarily, on stated days, and also on extraordinary occasions. By the constitution it proved that the people should ratify or reject all the decrees of the senate; but should make no decree which had not first passed the senate. This regulation in process of time was so far disregarded, as, the amendments to the decrees of the senate were at first proposed; which being acquiesced in, other decrees, afterwards, were substituted in stead of those of the senate. This innovation in the constitution changed the nature of the government entirely, and introduced all the mischiefs of faction, corruption, and anarchy; the people delivered themselves over to the influence of their vicious and corrupt orators, and intriguing demagogues; and the event finally proved that the smallest innovations are capable of subverting the constitution of a state.

Thus while a democracy may be pronounced to be the only legitimate government, and that form of government, alone which is compatible with the freedom of the nation, and the happiness of the individual, we may perceive that it is on every side surrounded by enemies, ready to sap the foundation, convulse the frame, and totally destroy the fabric. In such a government a sacred veneration for the principles of the constitution, a perfect obedience to the laws, an unremitting vigilance on the part of the people over the conduct of their agents, and the strictest attention to the morals and principles of such as they elect into every office, legislative, executive, or judiciary, seem indispensably necessary to constitute, and to preserve a sufficient barrier against its numerous foes.

The enemies of a democratic government fail not on all occasions to magnify, and to multiply, at the same time, all the disadvantages of this species of government, just as some curious opticians have contrived lenses, which represent the same object, magnified, in an hundred different places, at once. They are ready to mention on all occasions the tumults at Athens, and at Rome (which last was in no sense whatever a democracy,) and they repeat the banishment of Aristides, the imprisonment and fine of Miltiades, and the death of Socrates, with so much indignation, that one might almost suppose they were the only examples to be found in history, where virtuous men had ever been oppressed by a government; or where cruelty had ever been exercised towards the innocent. But cruelty and even violence in a republic, are very different in their effects from cruelty, or violence in a monarch. In a republic ten thousand people, or the whole state, combine to oppress one man: in the other case, one individual inflicts torture upon a whole nation, or the whole human race. Not to mention the tyrants who have deluged their territories with the blood of their own subjects, and whose names are held in detestation by the whole human race. Alexander of Macedon, the favorite of historians, both ancient and modern, crucified two thousand Tyrians round the walls of their city, because they would not submit to him as a conqueror, but offered to receive him as a friend, and ally; and the same abominable tragedy was afterwards repeated by him at Gaza.[11] In the scale of good and evil, is it better that a whole nation should be sometimes unjust, and even cruel, to a Socrates, or a Miltiades, or that one man should possess the power of tyrannizing over the whole human race?

11. Robertson's History of Greece.

But in America, such scenes of violence, tumult, and commotion, as convulsed and finally destroyed the republics of Athens and Rome, can never be apprehended, whilst we remain, as at present, an agricultural people, dispersed over an immense territory, equal to the support of more than ten times our present population. Nothing can be more inconsistent with the habits and interest of the farmer and the husband-man, than frequent and numerous assemblies of the people. In a coun-try, whose population does not amount to one able bodied militia man for each mile square, would it not be absurdity in the extreme, to pre-tend, that the same dangers are to be apprehended, as in those ancient cities; or in the modern capitals of France, or England, whose inhabi-tants, respectively, may be estimated as equal to the population of the largest state in the American confederacy? Or can we expect the same readiness in an independent yeomanry to excite, or to favor popular commotions, as in the Athenian populace, hired by their demagogues to attend the public meetings; or bribed, like the degenerate citizens of Rome, when they contented themselves with demanding from their rulers, bread, and the exhibition of public games, as all they required? Those who pretend to draw any parallel between those ancient republics, and the American states, must either be totally ignorant, or guilty of wil-ful misrepresentation. Attica was a small but an immensely populous state: the people had arrived at the summit of luxurious refinement, indolence, and corruption. The public orators were often secretly in the pay of the factious demagogues contending for preeminence within the state; or, of its enemies without. The delusions of eloquence were con-stantly, and successfully employed to beguile an enervated and infatu-ated people to their destruction. The multitude were on all occasions agitated by the breath of their orators as the waves of the sea by the wind. The Roman metropolis, on the other hand, was a military city in which every citizen was a soldier, and a sovereign, for Rome was not the head of the republic, but the mistress of the empire, and of the globe. Her citizens may be regarded as the lords of the human race, in the forum they tyr-annized over the rest of the world, and in the *campus martius,* over each other. A Martius, a Scylla, an Anthony, and an Octavius, were by turns their idols, and their scourges. Who can perceive the most distant resemblance between either of these republics; and, the states of New England, of Pennsylvania, of the Carolina's, or Virginia? Who will venture to compare those of Delaware, Georgia, Kentucky, or Tennessee, to them. But the improvements which the representative system has received in America, will I trust prove an effectual guard against those scenes of violence, which have stained the annals of the ancient republics, without weakening, or in any degree impairing the public, force, and energy, on the one hand, or endangering the liberties of the people, on the other; this leads us to a short digression concerning:

SECTION VII.

The analysis and separation of the several powers of government, which if not a discovery reserved for the eighteenth century, bids fair to be practically understood, more perfectly than in earlier times. It consists in the just distribution, of the several distinct functions, and duties, of the public agents, according to their respective natures.

The essential parts of civil power may not improperly be divided into the internal, or such as are to be exercised among the citizens of a state, within the state itself; and the external, or such as may be exercised towards foreign nations, or different and independent states: the design of civil government being, both to promote peace and happiness with an undisturbed enjoyment of all their rights, to the citizens of the state, by good order at home, and to defend the whole body, and all its members from any foreign injuries; and to procure them any advantages that may be obtained by a prudent conduct towards foreigners. These powers, which in all great empires, and monarchies, and even in smaller states, are generally united in one and the same man, or body of men, according to the system adopted by the states of the American confederacy, are, as was before observed, separated from each other; the former branch, being with some exceptions, confided to the state-governments; the latter to the federal government.

The former branch of these powers, or that which is to be exercised within the state, are, shortly, these. First, the power of directing the actions of the citizens by laws requiring whatever is requisite for this end, and prohibiting the contrary by penalties: determining and limiting more precisely the several rights of men, appointing the proper methods for securing, transferring, or conveying them, as the general interest may require, and even limiting their use of them, in certain cases, for the same general purpose. Secondly, another power of the same class is that of appointing in what manner, and what proportion each one shall contribute towards the public expenses out of his private fortune, or private gains, by paying taxes, as the state of the people will admit. These two branches of power are commonly called legislative; and in this state, and I believe in every other in the union, they are confided to two distinct bodies of men chosen at stated periods by the people themselves, one of which is called the house of delegates, or representatives, the other the senate; the first being generally vested with the initiative authority, or right of commencing all laws; the other, that of amending, ratifying, or rejecting. Both bodies being absolutely independent of each other.

The power of jurisdiction in all cases of controversy between the citizens of the state about their rights, by applying the general laws to them; and of trying, and enforcing the penalties of the laws, against all such as are guilty of crime which disturb the public peace and tranquility, constitutes the second subordinate branch of those powers which are to be exercised within the state and this power is vested, partly in persons selected for their superior knowledge of the laws of the states, whose province is to pronounce what the law is in each particular case, and who hold their office during good behavior, who are styled judges; and partly by persons indifferently chosen on the spot, to decide upon the matters of fact which are disputed in each case, who are denominated juries; being sworn well and truly to decide between the parties. And without their unanimous verdict, or consent, no person can be condemned of any crime. This is commonly called the judiciary department. And in this state no person can be at the same time a legislator, and a judge, or a member of the executive department of the government, of which it now remains to speak.

The power of appointing inferior magistrates (that of appointing the judges of the superior courts being by the constitution of this state vested in the legislature) and ministerial officers to take care of the execution both of the ordinary laws, and of the special orders of the state, given by the proper departments, and of collecting the public revenue; paying the public creditors, defraying the public charges; and commanding, and directing the public force, pursuant to the law and constitution of the state, is ordinarily called the executive department: and in this state, this subordinate branch of internal powers, is confided to the discretion of another distinct body, composed of the governor, and the executive council, or council of state; by whose advice the governor administers the executive functions according to the laws of the commonwealth.

The external powers, or such as are to be exercised towards foreign, or other independent states, are these two; the first that of making war for defense of the state, and for this purpose arming and training the citizens to military service; and appointing proper officers to conduct them; erecting necessary fortifications; and establishing a naval force: And the second, that of making treaties, whether such as fix the terms of peace after a war, or such as may procure aliens or confederates to assist in it, or such as without any view to war may procure, or confirm to a state and its citizens any other advantages by commerce, hospitality, or improvements in arts; and for this purpose the power and right of sending ambassadors, or deputies to concert such treaties with those of other nations. . . . To which we may add, thirdly, the power of deciding amicably any controversies which may possibly arise between different states, members of the same confederacy; all of which powers some authors include under one general name, viz. the federative; and all these, and some others of pretty extensive operation are vested in the federal government of the United States. The first appertain generally to the congress, composed like the state legislature, of two bodies, the one chosen by the people; the other appointed by the state legislatures. The second subordinate class belongs to the executive department, or president of the United States, assisted with the advice and consent of the senate. The third subordinate branch appertains to the federal judiciary; the judges of which, like those of the state, hold their offices during good behavior, though differently appointed, viz. by the president and senate, instead of the legislative body as in this state.

Power thus divided, subdivided, and distributed into so many separate channels, can scarcely ever produce the same violent and destructive effects, as where it rushes down in one single torrent, overwhelming and sweeping away whatever it encounters in its passage.

This analysis and separation is perfectly impracticable in a simple democracy, and is equally irreconcilable to the principles of monarchy; for in both these the sovereign power seems to be indivisible, and exerts itself every where, and on all occasions: In the former, the people being at once legislator, judge, and executive magistrate, and acted upon by the same impulse, they may at the same time make a law, and condemn the previous violation of it; and, as in the case of Socrates, in the same moment wreak their vengeance on the victim of their fury. But no such case can happen in an extensive confederacy, composed of states possessing respectively a representative form of government and in which the constitution is fixed, the limits of power are defined and ascertained, and uniform laws, and modes of proceeding are prescribed to be observed in every case; according to its nature before it occurs.

Thus the sovereignty of the people, and the responsibility of their representative democracy, however, organized, or in other words, however the several powers of government may be distributed, or by whomsoever they may be exercised, the censorial power of the people, which is in effect a branch of the sovereign power itself, may be immediately exercised upon that representative or agent who forgets his responsibility. It is this powerful control, which without resumption of the sovereign power into the hands of the people, as is sometimes necessary for the reformation of the constitution, preserves the several branches of the government within their due limits; for the people where they are as vigilant, and attentive to their rights as they ought to be, will be sure to take part against those who would usurp either the rights of the people, or the proper functions of a different agent; and, thus by their weight restore the constitutional balance. On the other hand, where such vigilance and attention to their just rights is wanting on the part of the people, the progress of usurpation is often as little perceived as that of a star, rising in the east whilst the sun is in the meridian. It reaches the zenith before the departure of day discovers its ascent. But whenever there is a due vigilance on the part of the people, not only the errors or vices of the administration, but any defects in the fundamental principles of the government are more readily discovered in a representative democracy, than in any other form of government. This sometimes produces parties; but they are never violent until a general spirit of encroachment, or of corruption, is discovered to exist in the public functionaries and agents; then indeed more violent parties arise, and such as may endanger the public happiness. But they are engendered, and fostered by the government, and not as is falsely supposed, by the people. The latter are always more disposed to submission, than to encroachment, and often distrust their own judgments rather than suspect the integrity of their representative, or agent: a delusion from which they seldom recover until it's almost too late.

If any possible device can ensure happiness to the state, and security to the individual, it must be the establishment of this important principle of responsibility in the public agents; and its union with that other important principle, the separation and division of the powers of the government. Bold and desperate must that representative be who dares openly to violate his duty, when he knows himself amenable to the people for such a breach of trust. And wicked and corrupt must be that administration, all the parts of which unite in one conspiracy against the peace and happiness of the people collectively, and the security of every individual of the community.

The limitation of power; the frequency of elections, by the body of the people; the capacity of every individual citizen to be elected to any public office, to which his talents and integrity may recommend him, and the responsibility of every public agent to his constituents, the people, are the distinguishing features of a representative democracy; and whilst the people preserve a proper sense of the value of such a form of government, will effectually guard it against the snares, intrigues, and encroachments of its counterfeit, and most dangerous enemy, aristocracy; of which we shall now proceed to speak.

SECTION VIII.

An aristocracy is that form of government in which the supreme power is vested in a small number of persons. It may be absolute, or limited; absolute, where it is not founded in the consent and compact of the society, over which the government is established; or limited, where that consent has been given, and the constitution and its powers have been fixed, and limited, at the time of such consent; but in which the other important characters of a representative democracy have not been preserved. It may likewise be temporary; as where the members of the supreme council, or senate sit there only for a certain term and then retire to their former condition; or perpetual, during their lives. It may likewise be hereditary; where the representatives of certain families (distinguished by the flattering epithet of the well-born,) are senators by birth, or elective, where either at certain periods the whole senate is chosen, and vacancies are supplied by election. And this election may be either popular as where the body of the people choose the person whom they may think proper to advance to the senatorial dignity; which is also called creation, where the person so chosen is advanced from the plebeian to the senatorial order: or it may be made by the whole senatorial order, from among themselves; or by the senate itself, out of the members of the senatorial order in which case it has been styled co-optation: or by the senate itself out of the order of plebeians; in which case as in one before mentioned, it obtains the name of creation.

This form of government is capable of such an approximation, and resemblance, in its external form, to a representative democracy that the one is frequently mistaken for the other. The discriminating features of a representative democracy, as we have before observed, are the limitation of power; the frequency of elections, by the whole body of the people; the capacity of every citizen of the state to be elected to any public office, to which his talents and integrity may recommend him; and the responsibility of the public agent to the people, for his conduct. If all, or either of these characters be wanting in the constitution of the state, it is an aristocracy, though it should be founded upon the consent of the people, if either of these characters be wanting in the mode of administering the government, it then becomes an aristocracy founded upon fraud and usurpation. Seldom has such a government failed to spring up, from the immediate ruins of monarchy: never, perhaps, has it hitherto failed to undermine and subvert a government founded on the principles of a democracy. There is not in nature a spirit more subtle than aristocracy; nothing more unconfinable; nothing whose operations are more constant, more imperceptible, or more certain of success; nothing less apt to alarm in infancy; nothing more terrible at maturity.

> Malum bud non aliud velocius ullum;
> Mobilitate yiget, vousque acquirit eundo;
> Parva mety primo; mox sese attollit in auras;
> Ingrediturque solo et caput inter nubila condit.
>
> VIRGIL

In aristocracies where the whole power is lodged in a senate, or council of men of eminent stations or fortunes, one may sometimes expect sufficient wisdom and political abilities to discern and accomplish whatever the interest of the state may require. But there is no security against factions, seditions, and civil wars; much less can this form secure fidelity to the public interest. The views of a corrupt senate will be the aggrandizing of themselves, their families, and their posterity, by all oppressions of the people. In hereditary senates these evils are certain; and the majority of such bodies may even want a competent share of talents to discharge the duties of their stations. Among men born in high stations of wealth and power, ambition, vanity, insolence, and an unsociable contempt of the lower orders, as if they were not of the same species, or were not fellow-citizens with them, too frequently prevail. And these high stations afford many occasions of corruption, by sloth, luxury, and debauchery, the general fore-runners and attendants of the barest venality. An unmixed hereditary aristocracy, if not the worst, must be among the very worst forms of government, since it engenders every species of evil in a government, without producing any countervailing benefit, or advantage.

In a council of senators elected for life, by the people, or by any popular interest, there is more reason to expect both wisdom and fidelity, than in the case of an hereditary aristocracy: but here the cogent tie of responsibility is wanting; and without that, the ambitious views of enlarging their powers, and their wealth, will supercede all ideas of gratitude, or fidelity to those to whom they owe their elevation.

When new members are admitted into the senatorial order by an election, in which the right of suffrage is confined to such as have already obtained an admission into that order; or where the right of admission into the senate itself is vested in that body; the senate will infallibly become a dangerous cabal, (Without any of the advantages desirable in civil polity,) and attempt to make their office hereditary. When senators are entitled to the privileges of that station in consequence of possessing a certain degree of wealth, the burdens of the state will, without exception, be, thrown upon the poorer classes of the people. Thus aristocracy, whatever foundation it may be raised upon, will always prove a most iniquitous and oppressive form of government.

In absolute monarchies, and in perfect democracies, the seeds of aristocracy are contained in wealth; but they do not germinate so long as these governments remain unmixed: for power is not attached to riches in the former, they being hidden from the sight there, least they should tempt the grasp of the sovereign: in the latter, they minister to domestic luxury, or furnish the means of secret, corruption only. The moment that wealth becomes influential, the principle of democracy is corrupted; when it is allied with power, the democracy itself is subverted; when this alliance becomes hereditary in any state, the democratic principle may be regarded as annihilated.

But the most easy and successful mode in which an aristocracy commences, or advances, consists in the secret and gradual abuse of the confidence of the people, in a representative democracy. Slight, and sometimes even imperceptible, innovations, occasional usurpations, founded upon the pretended emergency of the occasion: or upon former unconstitutional precedents; the introduction of the doctrines of constructive grants of power: of the duty of self-preservation in a government, however constituted, or however limited; of the right of eminent domain, (or in other words, absolute power,) in all governments; these, with the stale pretence of the dangers to be apprehended from the giddy multitude in democratic governments, and a thousand other pretexts and arguments of the same stamp, form the ladder by which the agents of the people mount over the heads of their constituents, and finally ascend to that pinnacle of authority and power, from whence they behold those who have raised them with contempt, and treat them with indignation and insult. The only preventive lies in the vigilance of the people. Where the people are too numerous, or too much dispersed to deliberate upon the conduct of their public agents, or too supine to watch over that conduct, the representative will soon render himself paramount to, and independent of, his constituents; and then the people may bid a long farewell to all their happiness.

The first form of government established at Venice, was founded upon principles perfectly democratic. Magistrates were chosen by a general assembly of the people; and their power continued only for one year. This simple form of government (we are told by Doctor Moore,[12] whose inquiries and researches upon this subject afford an useful, and an awful lesson to all democratic states;) remained uncorrupted for one hundred and fifty years. Upwards of three hundred years were afterwards employed in gradual, and almost imperceptible changes in the government, and encroachments upon the rights of the people, before that system of terror, which finally rendered the Venetian government the most tyrannical and formidable to its own citizens that the world has ever known, was completed by the establishment of the state inquisition. From that period the most complete despotism hath with unremitting

12. Travels into Italy.

rigor been exerted not only over the actions, but over the minds, of every citizen of that miserable state. A word, a look, nay silence itself, may be interpreted to be treasonable, in a government whose maxim is, "that it is better that an innocent person should suffer from an ill grounded suspicion, than the government should be endangered by any scrutiny into its conduct."

Should it be inquired how such important changes can possibly be effected where the supreme power is vested in the people, as in the American States, we may give the answer in the words of De Lolme.[13] The combination of those who share either in the actual exercise of the public power, or in its advantages, do not allow themselves to sit down in inaction. They wake, while the people sleep. Entirely taken up with the thoughts of their own power, they live but to increase it. Deeply versed in the management of public business, they see at once all the possible consequences of measures. And, as they have the exclusive direction of the springs of government, they give rise, at pleasure, to every incident that may influence the minds of a multitude who are not on their guard; ever active in turning to their advantage every circumstance that happens, they equally avail themselves of the tractableness of the people during public calamities, and its heedlessness in times of prosperity. By presenting in their speeches arguments and facts, which there is no opportunity of examining, they lead the people into gross, and yet decisive errors. In confirmation of these observations he cites two instances from the history of his own country, which have occurred within the present century; and which may serve to show how slight a movement of the political machine, may effect a total change in its operations. In Geneva in the year 1707 a law was enacted that a general assembly of the people, should be held every five years to treat of the affairs of the republic, but the magistrates who dreaded those assemblies soon obtained from the citizens themselves, the repeal of the law; and the first resolution of the people, in the first of these periodical assemblies, in the year 1712, was to abolish them forever. The profound secrecy with which the magistrates

13. De Lolme's Constitution of England.

prepared their proposals to the citizens on that subject, and the sudden manner in which the latter, when assembled, were acquainted with it, and made to give their votes upon it; and the consternation of the people when the result was proclaimed has confirmed many in the opinion that some unfair means were used. The whole transaction has been kept secret to this day: but the common opinion is, that the magistrates had privately instructed the secretaries in whose ear the citizens were to whisper their suffrages; when a citizen said "*approbation*," he was to be considered as approving the proposal of the magistrates; when he said "*rejection*," it was to be considered that he meant to reject the periodical assemblies.... In the year 1738 the citizens enacted at once into laws a small code of forty-four articles, by one single line of which they bound themselves forever to elect the four syndics, or chiefs of the council of twenty-five out of the members of the same council; whereas they were before free in their choice. They, at that time, suffered the word approved to be slipped into a law; the consequence of which was to render the magistrates absolute masters of the legislature. So watchful, so active, so preserving, so noxious, so incompatible with the principles of a democratic government, are those of aristocracy, that we may venture to pronounce it the most dangerous enemy to a free government. If a single germ of aristocracy, be once ingrafted upon a republican government, the stock will soon cease to bear any other branches. In an aristocracy, says Montesquieu, the republic is in the body of the nobles; and the people are nothing at all.

SECTION IX.

Monarchy is that form of government in which all the parts of the supreme power are committed to one person. And such a government may be either despotic, absolute, and unlimited; or limited. In the former case the administration is vested altogether in the prince, without any check, or restriction whatsoever. In this government, according to Montesquieu, the prince is *all in all*. The people were all equal, and their equality is the most abject slavery. The principle of this kind of government is fear generated in ignorance. Submission constitutes the only security, which the people enjoy: and the safety of the tyrant is alike the result of their terrors, and their ignorance.

In this government the will of the prince is the only law, manners and customs, says Montesquieu, supply the place of general laws, and the will of the prince constitutes the law in particular cases. Hence in a despotic government there are no laws which can be properly so called: laws are established; manners are inspired; these proceed from a general spirit, those, from a particular institution. It is a capital maxim, that the manners and customs of a despotic empire should never be changed; for nothing would more speedily produce a revolution.

In China, the fundamental laws of the empire are spoken of; the emperor presumes not to change them; but on particular occasions he dispenses with them. They are binding upon all the world but himself; and so far binding even upon him, that he leaves them to his successor, to dispense with, as he had done before him.

A limited monarchy (if indeed such a form of government can be anywhere found) is one where by some original laws in the very constitution or conveyance of power, the quantity of it is determined, and limits set to it, with reservations of certain public rights of the people, not entrusted to the prince; and yet no court or council, constituted which does not derive its power from him. How far the government established over the Israelites in the person of Saul .... when Samuel their prophet "told the people the manner of the kingdom, and wrote it in a book and laid it up before the Lord," may have furnished a model for this species of monarchy, is foreign from our present inquiry.

Baron Montesquieu distinguishes that species of monarchy in which there are intermediate, subordinate, and dependent powers, likewise, from the absolute or despotic kind, above-mentioned; yet he acknowledges that even in this, the prince, is the source of all power, civil and political, but that he governs by fundamental laws. "And these," says he, "necessarily suppose the intermediate channels through which the power flows. The most natural, intermediate, and subordinate power is that of the nobility. No nobility, no monarch; but there may be a despotic prince."

But I incline to refer this latter form of government to the class of mixed governments, rather than to the simple monarchical form. It partakes, however, of both; wherever the prince alone is the source of all power, the government is really absolute, in spite of forms. Though the establishment of different ranks, and orders may vary the condition of the people, whereby the burdens of government are unequally borne, yet this does not alter the nature of the government, unless there be some certain powers annexed to those different ranks, or some of them, which may on certain occasions control or check the administration of the monarch. Where no such incidental powers exist, the government is still absolute in the person of the prince: and wherever they do exist, their existence constitutes a mixed government. In Spain, since the suppression of the cortes, the monarchy is absolute; yet there is in Spain a splendid nobility, whose condition is far above the rest of the people, but who, possess no power in respect to the operations of the government. In France, before the late revolution; in Russia, in Prussia, and in Sweden under the government of its late monarch, this was also the case. In all these countries the prince is supposed to govern by fixed laws; yet in all of them, I apprehend he was absolute. In England, the nobility form a separate branch of the supreme legislature; the power of the crown is according to the theory of that government, limited thereby; and this constitutes the English government, what is ordinarily styled, a limited monarchy, but more properly a mixed government. Baron Montesquieu, at the same moment that he is speaking of that species of monarchy in which there are intermediate, subordinate, and dependent powers, subjoins; "that the prince is the source of all power political and civil." I am at a loss to conceive how the power of such a prince can be said to be limited. He considers indeed the ecclesiastical power in Spain and Portugal, as forming a carrier against the torrent of arbitrary power in those countries: but the ecclesiastical power can scarcely be considered as a dependent power on the crown in either of these kingdoms. It for a long time maintained a superiority over the civil power, in those, and most other countries in Europe; and even at this day, it might hazard a revolution in either of those two kingdoms, if the monarch should attempt to treat it as a subordinate, dependent power.

It must, however, be confessed, that there is a wide difference between those governments, where liberty hath never been known to exist, or has been long banished, as in Turkey, and in most of the Asiatic, and African states, and those, where absolute authority hath been acquired by gradual usurpations, or violent exertions, made at particular epochs, to suppress those branches of the government, which, in mixed governments, are stripped to form some check upon the supreme executive authority, as was the case in the suppression of the cortes, or assembly of the nobles, in Spain, by Charles V. Of the states general, and provincial parliaments, in France, by Louis XIII. And of the diet of the States, and the senate of Sweden, by the late king Gustavus III. In these last cases, the laws relating to property being previously established, and the privileges of the several orders and ranks of persons, understood, and admitted by general custom, and implied consent, the assumption of power by the prince, was directed to the abolition of public, rather than private rights. In such states, the business of legislation is ordinarily confined to a single subject, that of revenue. The ancient laws on all other subjects remaining unaltered, the people seem to possess some rights: whereas in the Turkish and Asiatic governments, the subject is held to be the slave of the sovereign and his property is held at his master's will. In the European monarchies, on the other hand, the higher orders, or nobility often, posses very extensive powers over the commonalty, or peasantry, as they are frequently styled, without interfering with, or in any manner diminishing the authority of the government over either; but, on the contrary, strengthening and supporting it on every occasion, where its oppressions might incline the people to resistance, if they possessed the means of making it. And this may serve to explain the maxim, "no nobility, no monarch." The foundations of this species of monarchy are to be sought for, in the ancient feudal governments, the prince having by degrees usurped, and annihilated all those privileges which might possibly interfere with his own authority; yet leaving the nobility in possession of such as might enable them to maintain a superiority over the people, without danger to the throne. Such was the state of France under Louis XIV, and his successors.

If this kind of monarchy be considered as limited, it proceeds not so much from the nature of the government, as from the character of the nation, previous to its establishment. If the prince from an apprehension of rousing that spirit of liberty, which has been smothered, rather than extinguished, pursues moderate measures, the people are flattered into a notion, that this circumstance is owing, equally, to the excellence of their government, and, to the benignity of their monarch. The distinction between the character of the prince, and the nature of the government, is soon lost sight of. Hence that profound veneration, that enthusiastic predilection for their own government, which is found almost universally, to prevail in all nations. The moderation of Augustus Caesar, after he was established in the empire of Rome, contributed not less to the annihilation of the spirit of liberty, in the nation, than his own previous tyranny, and that of his successors, did, to the enjoyment of it. The same moderation in the late king of Sweden's administration, after subverting the constitution, was calculated to obliterate the remembrance of that transaction, and even to persuade the nation that they were more free, than before he became absolute. His posterity will probably evince to them the change in their condition.

This species of monarchy being usually founded upon usurpation, rather than conquest, the prince does not always exert his authority to the utmost extent; but reserves such an exercise of it for extraordinary emergencies. When they occur, and the people feel new oppressions, if the spirit of liberty be not wholly extinguished among them, such oppressions are regarded as usurpations. From hence it happens that these governments are neither so durable, nor so tranquil, as those more rigorous despotisms, which are founded in conquest, and in which the spirit of liberty has been long since annihilated. In these last, the people, being already reduced to the most abject slavery, are incapable of distinguishing between one act of tyranny and another: they are divested of all power of resistance; and therefore acquiesce in any new burdens, which their cruel task-masters may impose, without presuming to murmur, or to complain but where the people are not yet reduced to such an abject state, a series of oppressions, heaped upon them from time to time, irritate and inflame their minds, much more than such an instantaneous accumulation of injuries, as would amount to a total privation of liberty at once. Reiterated oppressions, though comparatively light, have often the same effect as superficial wounds; a number of which are often more painful than a single one, that is mortal. The irritation of temper among the people, thus produced, generally manifests itself by open opposition, with the first favorable occasion; the suppression of such an opposition renders the government more absolute, despotic, and tyrannical: on the other hand its success overturns, or changes the nature of, the government. Such appears to have been the origin and progress of the late revolution in France.[14]

The distinction of ranks in this kind of government contributes not, as we have already observed, to impose any check upon the government, in favor of the people, in general. The nobility, are, according to Montesquieu, at once the slaves of the monarch, and the despots of the people. Their privileges have no relation to the government, otherwise than to exempt them from the utmost severity of those oppressions, which are indiscriminately heaped upon the lower orders; but they are great, as they respect the lower orders. An admission into the higher class gains an exemption from that intermediate oppression, which these orders exercise over the inferior ranks of the people. This produces a stimulus which Montesquieu has dignified with the epithet honour; which, as he informs us, is the vital principle of this kind of monarchy, and excites men to aspire to preferments, and to distinguishing titles. The term honour, thus understood, conveys no very favorable impression to the ear of a republican.

14. St. Etienne. *Editor's note:* Tucker here is citing a person who expressed the ideas of St. Etienne.

As, in a simple monarchy, the nation is as it were concentrated in the person of the prince, the lustre of the throne is often mistaken for the prosperity of the nation. Does a prince maintain an immense army in his territories; are the ports of his dominions filled with a powerful navy; does he not only inspire his neighbors with the terror of his arms, but even overawe remote nations by the greatness of his power: is he always on the watch from some specious cause, or pretext for a quarrel; does he ransack the records of nations to discover some obsolete claim to their territories; does he seize upon the dominions, or usurp the sovereignty of some weaker state; doth he carry fire and sword into every quarter; doth desolation mark the footsteps of his ambition; and the misery, or extermination of the human race point out the progress of his success? Such a prince hath arrived at the pinnacle of glory: and his frauds, avarice, injustice, cruelties, usurpation, and tyranny, are lost amidst the lustre of his diadem; and together with the groans, execrations and curses of the victims to his ambition, are consigned to oblivion by the partial pen of the historian. . . . Let the most partial admirers of the most renowned princes of antiquity, or of modern ages call this an exaggerated picture of a flourishing monarchy! In a mixed hereditary monarchy the features may be somewhat softened: but they are still the features of an enemy to the human race, if we may judge from some of the fairest examples of that species of government.

SECTION X.

From an union of the principles of these three simple forms of government, or the combination of any two of them, arises what political writers denominate a mixed, or complex form of government. These complex forms are innumerable, according as monarchy, either hereditary or elective, is combined with some of the several sorts of aristocracies, or democracies, or with both. And further important diversities may arise according as the several essential parts of the supreme power are entrusted, differently, with the prince, the senate, or the popular assembly; or according to the mode in which the prince, or either of those co-ordinate assemblies may themselves, be constituted. As whether the prince, or the members of the senate, be hereditary or elective, and if elective, for what periods, and out of what bodies, they may be elected; and by whom, and in what manner such election may be made. And again, by whom the popular assemblies shall be elected; for what periods; and whether any, and what qualifications in respect to estate, shall be required either in the electors, or in the representative.

Political writers seem to have differed in opinion respecting these kinds of mixed governments; for whilst some of them appear to regard such forms of government as corruptions of the simple forms, others have bestowed the most exalted encomiums on them, as uniting the advantages, and avoiding the inconveniences inseparable from each of them, singly. It is obvious, says Doctor Hutchinson,[15] that when by any plan of polity these four advantages can be obtained, wisdom in discerning, the fittest measures for the general interest; fidelity, with expedition and secrecy in the determination and execution of them; and concord, and unity; a nation must have all that happiness which any plan of polity can give it, as sufficient wisdom in the governors will discover the most effectual means, and fidelity will choose them by expedition and secrecy, they will be most effectually executed, and unity will prevent one of the greatest evils, civil wars, and seditions. The great necessity of taking sufficient precaution against the mischiefs of factions and civil wars, leads most writers in politics to another obvious maxim, viz. that the several parts of the supreme power if they are lodged by any complex plan in different subjects, some granted to a prince, others to a senate, and others to a popular assembly, there must in such case be some *nexus imperii*, or political bond, that they may not be able, or incline to act separately, and in opposition to each other. Without this, two supreme powers may be constituted in the same state, which may give frequent occasions to civil wars. This would be the case if both the sen-

15. Moral Philosophy.

ate and popular assembly, claimed, separately, and independently, the legislative power: as it happened in Rome, after the tribunes held assemblies of the plebeians, without authority of the senate, and obtained that the decrees of the plebeians should have the force of laws, while the senate insisted upon the like force to their decrees. The like was the case in many nations of Europe, while the ecclesiastical state pretended to make obligatory laws, and exercise certain jurisdictions, independently of the civil. If therefore the several essential parts of the supreme power are distributed among different persons, or courts, they must have a strong bond of union. If a prince has the executive, and the power of peace and war, while another body has the legislative, the power of raising tributes must be at least necessarily shared with the legislative council, that it never may be the prince's interest to make war without their concurrence: and the prince must have a share in the legislative. Without such bonds, laws might be enacted which the prince would not execute, or wars entered into which the nation would not support.... But there is no such necessity, adds the same writer, that all the parts of the supreme power should be committed either to one person, or to one council: And the other interests of the state may require that they should be divided.

It is evident, from the case here supposed, that this ingenuous writer had the British constitution (in which there is an hereditary prince, in whom the supreme executive authority, including the power of peace and war, is vested,) in his eye, when he wrote this passage, evidently calculated to justify that principle in the British constitution, that the regal character must possess some share in the legislature; as otherwise it might happen, that laws might be enacted, which he, being responsible to no one for his conduct, would not execute. That constitution must indeed be radically defective, where the executive authority may safely refuse to execute the law. But it may be doubted whether this defect is at all remedied, by allowing the executive magistrate, not only an absolute negative over every act of the legislature, but in fact an initiative authority within the legislature itself: and this initiative has been so long sanctioned by practice, that it is now considered as the peculiar province of the principal minister of the crown,[16] to bring forward every specific proposition for a tax that may be made in the house of commons; to whom the initiative right, in this case, is said to belong, exclusively not only of the crown, but even of the house of lords, or second branch of the legislature. But to return to our subject.

Dr. Hutchinson concludes, that none of the simple forms can be safe for a society. That if those deserve to be called the regular forms which are wisely adapted to the true ends of civil polity, all the simple forms are to be called rather rude and imperfect. That complex forms, made up of all three, will be found the best, and most regular, according to the general doctrine; both of ancients and moderns.

It was observed in another place, that governments may be variously modified upon the democratic principle: and it is perhaps susceptible of proof, that a representative democracy is more capable of such a modification, as may unite all the real advantages of the three simple forms of government, without hazarding the inconveniences actually inseparable from either, singly, than any other state, or body politic whatsoever.

The professed design, and obvious advantages of these mixed governments, is said to consist in the union of the public virtue and goodness of intention, to be found in popular assemblies, with the superior wisdom usually ascribed to a select council, composed of the most experienced citizens; and the strength, energy, and union of a government committed to the hands of a single person's influence.

The benefits of the democratic, or popular branch, strictly speaking, may be preserved by a popular assembly, chosen annually, by the people of convenient districts, in fair and equal proportions, from among themselves; wherein the right of electing, and of being elected, shall be extended to every citizen having a sufficient evidence of a permanent common interest with, and attachment to the community: which assembly should possess the initiative right in the establishment of all laws, and more especially such as may impose or create any burden upon the state or its citizens. To preserve this branch from falling under the influ-

16. Blackstone's Commentaries.

ence of men of wealth, an agrarian system should be established, to prevent the accumulation of wealth in the hands of a few, and the establishment of patronage and dependence among the yeomanry or farmers, by reducing them from the state of absolute proprietors of their farms, to that of tenants, or vassals, over whom, their rich landlords may acquire a kind of feudal authority and control. The best mode of obviating such an accumulation seems to be the partibility of estates among all the children, or collateral relations of persons dying intestate, and the absolute prohibition of all perpetuities in lands. If the members of this assembly be rendered incapable of holding, or accepting any lucrative office which may be created by the legislature, or filled by the choice of any other department of the government, their purity, integrity, and independence, will be unimpaired and unsuspected. They will not impose burdens which they must share in bearing, nor will they create offices, and increase emoluments, of which no part can arrive to themselves. They will not forfeit the confidence of their constituents by an abuse of the power confided to them, nor will they desire to extend those powers which another may be called upon the next year to exercise in their stead. If they have the power of nomination to office, in some of the more important ministerial and judiciary departments, in such mode as to give to the senate the power of selecting a smaller number from the whole number of persons nominated; and to the executive department, the final choice between those whom the senate may prefer; it might be expected that offices filled in such a mode, would be bestowed on persons eminent for their integrity, capacity, and diligence. If they were vested with a kind of censorial power likewise, or the right of impeaching such of the public agents as may betray their trust, and endanger the public happiness, such an assembly might be supposed to unite in it all the advantages which could be expected from a general assembly of the people in a democratic state.

If there be a second council, composed of fewer members, more advanced in age, and chosen from larger districts, by electors chosen for that especial purpose in the smaller districts by the people themselves, such a council may be presumed likely to possess more wisdom than any hereditary counsellors, and as much, both of wisdom, integrity, and of weight among the people, as any similar council constituted in any other mode; if one third, or one fourth, of the members should in continual rotation go out, every third or fourth year, there would always remain a sufficient number who may be supposed to have acquired an intimate acquaintance with the nature of the business they would have to transact; whilst the short period of three or four years at the end of which they must vacate their seats, and either return to the level of the rest of their fellow citizens, or owe their reelection to a general approbation of their conduct, would induce them constantly to bear in mind their duty to the public.... If no personal privileges were annexed to their station, and they, as well as the members of the popular assembly, were incapable of election to any other office; it would insure an honest independence of conduct, unswayed by hopes, and unawed by fears, from any other branch of the government. If to such a council every act of the initiative or popular assembly, were necessarily submitted for their amendment, approbation, or rejection, it might be presumed that no laws would be enacted, the nature and consequence of which had not been fully considered and digested, before they should become obligatory upon the people. If in those cases where the popular assemblies might have the power of nomination to office, the character of those recommended by popular favour were to undergo a scrutiny in such a council, and the number of candidates were reduced to two, or at most three, out of whom the final appointment should be made, the demagogues of faction would probably be excluded from office, in favor of those citizens, whose virtues and talents might give them a just title to a preference. A senate thus constituted, and restricted, might also, perhaps, be safely entrusted with the power of trying impeachments; in those cases, at least, where a member of the supreme judicial court, should incur the notice of the censorial power of the popular assembly: In all other cases, I should presume, that the judicial courts, would be the proper tribunals for such trials. In no simple aristocracy could a council as wise, as virtuous, and as faithful, be found.

The regal, or executive power of the state, might upon the same principles be lodged either in the hands of a single magistrate; or in such a magistrate with the advice and consent of a council, composed of a few select citizens, eminently distinguished for their fidelity, patriotism, wisdom, and experience, in the affairs of the state. The best mode of choosing such an executive body would probably be, by electors chosen from among the people, in several convenient districts, whose power should extend to that business, alone. If the chief magistrate be chosen in this manner, and for a short period; if after a certain period he be ineligible, for some years; if his council, (where such is assigned him) be composed of persons chosen in a similar manner, and going out by rotation at the end of two or three years, after their election; if they be precluded from any other lucrative office, during the period for which they may be elected; if they be liable to the censorial power of the popular assembly, and when removed from office return to the condition of private citizens; such an executive, on all necessary occasions, would possess all the energy, secrecy, unanimity, and dispatch to be found in a monarchy, without any danger of becoming the tyrants of the people, instead of their servants and agents. And a government so constituted would probably unite in itself every advantage which theorists ascribe to any complex, or mixed form of government whatsoever.

But such a government would be a REPRESENTATIVE DEMOCRACY, and not a *mixt government*, of that nature which those writers prefer. For it is the essence of this latter species of government, that the several powers, which, together, share the administration, or as it is ordinarily called, the supreme power, or sovereignty, should be, (in theory, at least) entirely independent of each other. Thus in England, we are told that "the legislature of the kingdom (in which the absolute rights of sovereignty, (or *jura summi imperii*) are said to reside) is entrusted to three distinct powers, entirely independent of each other; viz. the king, in whom the supreme executive power is also lodged; the house of lords, composed of an aristocratical assembly of persons, selected for their piety, their birth, their wisdom, their valor, or their property; and thirdly, the house of commons, freely chosen from the people among themselves, which makes it a kind of democracy; as this aggregate body, actuated by different springs, and attentive to different interests, composes the British parliament, and has the supreme disposal of everything, there can no inconvenience be attempted by either of these branches," says judge Blackstone, "but will be withstood by one of the other two; each branch being armed with a negative power, sufficient to repel any innovation which it shall think inexpedient."

Such is the outline of the far-famed British constitution, as sketched by the masterly pen of judge Blackstone, whose able commentary, and high wrought panegyric, upon it; together with the elaborate researches, and encomiums of De Lolme; and the elegant eulogium of president Montesquieu, are well deserving the attentive perusal of the student. And, if to all these, the suffrage of a late exalted character in the government of the United States can afford any additional lustre, the British constitution may be selected, not only as the most perfect model of these kinds of mixed governments, but as the most stupendous monument of human wisdom.[17]

It would far exceed the proposed limits of this essay to enter into a minute examination of its structure, and to point out the essential difference between its theoretical excellencies, and its practical defects, corruptions, and radical departures from those very principles, which have been supposed to constitute that superiority and preeminence, which these and other writers have ordinarily ascribed to it. But the following observations from the pen of a native, whose style and manner evince a superiority both of genius and discernment, whilst they leave no doubt upon the mind, that he had seen and felt all that he describes, may lead us to conclude, that the practical abuses, corruptions, and oppressions of that government, are at least equal to the theoretical preeminence of its constitution.

"It is perhaps susceptible of proof," says this nervous writer,[18] "that these governments of balance and control have never existed but in the

17. *Editor's note:* In referring to "the suffrage of a late exalted character," Tucker means the election of John Adams, a notorious admirer of the British constitution, as president.

18. Mackintosh's Defence of the French Revolution.

visions of theorists. The fairest example will be the constitution of England. If it can be proved that the two members of the legislature who pretend to control each other are ruled by the same class of men, the control must be granted to be imaginary. That opposition of interest which is supposed to preclude all conspiracy against the people can no longer exist. That this is the state of England, the most superficial observation must evince. The great proprietors, titled and untitled, possess the whole force of both houses of parliament, that is not immediately dependent on the crown. The peers have a great influence in the house of commons. All political parties are formed by a confederacy of the members of both houses. The court party by the influence of the crown, acting equally in both, supported by a part of the independent aristocracy: The opposition by the remainder of the aristocracy, whether commoners, or lords. Here is every symptom of collusion: no vestige of control. The only case where it could arise, is where the interest of the peerage, is distinct from that of the other great proprietors."

"Who can, without indignation," adds the same writer, "hear the house of commons of England called a popular representative?[19] A more insolent and preposterous abuse of language is not to be found in the vocabulary of tyrants. The criterion that distinguishes laws from dictates, freedom from servitude, rightful government from usurpation, the law being an expression of the general will is wanting. This is the grievance which the admirers of the revolution in 1688, desire to remedy according to its principles. This is that perennial source of corruption, which has increased, is increasing, and ought to be diminished. If the general interest is not the object of the government, it is, it must be, because the general will does not govern. We are boldly challenged to produce our proofs: our complaints are asserted to be chimerical, and the excellence

---

19. Burgh's Political Disquisitions: "It was reckoned, there were 232 members of the first parliament of George the first who had places, pensions, or titles: besides a great many brothers, and heirs apparent, of the nobility, or persons otherwise likely to be under undue influence; the number of which was not below fifty, which added together makes 282. A frightful majority on the side of the court. And there is no reason to suppose the Augean stable is generally cleaner, now, than it was then."

of our government is inferred from its beneficial effects. Most unfortunately for us, most unfortunately for our country, these proofs are too ready, and too numerous. We find them in that monumental debt, the bequest of wasteful, and profligate wars, which wrings from the peasant something of his hard-earned pittance which already has punished the industry of the useful and upright manufacturer, by robbing him of the asylum of his house, and the judgment of his peers; to which the madness of political quixotism adds a million for every farthing that the pomp of ministerial empyricism pays; and which menaces our children with convulsions and calamities, of which no age has seen the parallel. We find them in the bloody roll of persecuting statutes that are still suffered to stain our code; a list so execrable, that were there no monument to be preserved of what England was in the eighteenth century, but her statute-book, she might be deemed still plunged in the deepest gloom of superstitious barbarism. We find them in the ignominious exclusion of great bodies of our fellow citizens from political trusts, by tests which reward falsehood, and punish probity, which profane the rites of the religion they pretend to guard, and usurp the dominion of the God, they profess to receive. We find them in the growing corruptions of those who administer the government, in the venality of a house of commons which has become only a cumbrous and expensive chamber for registering ministerial edicts.... in the increase of a nobility arrived to a degradation, by the profusion and prostitution of honors, which the most zealous partisans of democracy would have spared them. We find them, above all, in the rapid progress which has been made to silence the great organ of public opinion, the Press, which is the true control on ministers and parliaments who might else, with impunity, trample on the impotent formalities, that form the pretended bulwark of our freedom.... The mutual control, the well-poised balance of the several members of our legislature, are the visions of theoretical, or the pretexts of practical politicians. It is a government not of check, but of conspiracy ...a conspiracy which can only be repressed by the energy of popular opinion."

If this be a true picture of the government of Great Britain (and whether it is or not, I shall leave it to others to inquire and determine,) the epoch can not be far distant, which Judge Blackstone hints at in the introduction of his commentaries. "If ever it should happen," says that enlightened author, "that the independence of any one of the three branches of the legislature should be lost, or that it should become subservient to the views of either of the other two, there would soon be an end of the constitution." In which case, according to Sir Matthew Hale,[20] the subjects of that kingdom are left without all manner of remedy.

Such, then, being this history of the British constitution, the most perfect model of these mixed governments, (as agreed on all hands by their admirers, and advocates,) that the world ever saw, we may apply to them generally, the observations of an excellent politician[21] of the last century. "If all the parts of the state do not with their utmost power promote the public good; if the prince has other aims than the safety and welfare of his country; if such as represent the people do not preserve their courage and integrity; if the nation's treasure is wasted; if ministers are allowed to undermine the constitution with impunity; if judges are suffered to pervert justice, and wrest the law; then is a mixed government the greatest tyranny in the world: it is *tyranny established by law*; and the people are bound in fetters of their own making. A tyranny that governs by the sword, has few friends but men of the sword; but a legal tyranny (where the people are only called to confirm iniquity with their own voices) has on its side the rich, the timid, the lazy, those that know law, and get by it, ambitious churchmen, and all whose livelihood depends upon the quiet posture of affairs: and the persons here described compose the influencing part of most nations; so that such a tyranny is hardly to be shaken off."

SECTION XI.

I cannot better conclude what relates to the several kinds of government of which we have been speaking, whether simple, or complex, than by a summary of their several characters, corruptions, and transitions from

20. Of Parliaments.
21. Sir William Devanant.

one to another, for which I am indebted to the pen of a most intimate friend,[22] from who I have borrowed several passages in the preceding part of this essay.

"In a democratical government all authority is derived from the people at large, held only during their pleasure, and exercised only for their benefit. The constitution is a social covenant entered into by express consent of the people upon the footing of the most perfect equality with respect to civil liberty. No man has any privilege above his fellow citizens, except whilst in office, and even then, none but what they have thought proper to vest in him solely for the purpose of supporting him in the effectual performance of his duty to the public.

"In every other form of government, authority is acquired more by usurpation than by appointment of the people; it serves to give dignity and grandeur to a few, and to degrade the rest and it is exercised more for the benefit of the rulers, than of the nation. The constitution is established upon a compromise of differences between two or more contending parties, each according to the means it possesses, extorting from the other every concession that can possibly be obtained, without the smallest regard to justice, or the common rights of mankind. It is a truce, by which the people are always compelled to surrender some, and generally a very large portion of their freedom; and of course they have a right to reclaim it, whenever more favorable circumstances put it in their power. If the prince, at the head of an armed force, reduces them to unconditional submission, he becomes a despotic monarch, and the people are in the most deplorable state of slavery. They have no longer the presumption to imagine themselves created for any other purpose than to be subservient to his will, and to administer to his pleasures and ambition. They even think it an honor to be made the base instruments of his tyranny. They look up to him with a reverential awe surpassing what they feel for the almighty parent of the universe. Such is the servility of man degraded by oppression.

22. T. T. T., formerly a delegate in congress from South Carolina, and afterwards a member of the house of representatives in congress, from the same state. *Editor's note:* Tucker here refers modestly to his brother, Thomas Tudor Tucker, author of the next eight paragraphs.

"If the people retain still some resources which may render the issue of the contest doubtful, the prince for his own safety, most humanely grants them some privileges, and is then a limited monarch. They are often deluded into an opinion, that what liberties they enjoy are entirely derived from his bounty; and taught to consider themselves as the happiest of mankind in having a sovereign who graciously condescends to allow them the possession of what happily he had not the power to wrest out of their hands.

"A despotic government is often both quiet and durable, because the tyrant having an army at command, is thereby enabled to keep the people in awe and subjection, and to deprive them of all opportunity of communicating their complaints, or deliberating on the means of relief. Conspiracies happen often among the troops, the reigning prince is murdered, or dethroned, but another tyrant takes his place, and the nation remains in peaceable servitude, scarcely sensible of the revolution.... When the government is less despotic, the people have more both of power and inclination to resist oppression. They are not so thoroughly stripped of the means of defense, they have more opportunity of concerting measures, and their mental faculties retain more of their natural activity. Such a government must generally be contentious and changeable. The rulers can not be long satisfied with a limitation of prerogative, or the people with the abridgment of their privileges. The same is also true in all mixed governments, the component, or balancing powers being ever at variance, until corruption, intrigue, or faction, establishes in one branch, a permanent superiority and influence over the others, or finally destroys them.

"Often it happens that the contest for power is between the prince and nobles, the people having been previously enslaved. In this case the form of government is variable so far as relates to the prince and nobility; but the slavery of the people is lasting. This happens in all feudal governments.

"Sometimes the dispute is between the bulk of the people, and a few leading men, who having been honored with the confidence of their fellow-citizens betray their trust, grasp at power, and endeavor to establish themselves in permanent superiority. Their success constitutes an aristocracy, which is generally a most oppressive government, although often for the sake of blinding the people, it is dignified with the name of a republic. Indeed every constitution that has hitherto existed under that name, has partaken more or less of the nature of an aristocracy; and it is this aristocratical leaven that has generally occasioned disorders and tumults in every republican government; and has so far brought the name into disrepute, (even in America, where the sovereignty is confessedly in the people,) that it is becoming a received opinion, that a commonwealth, in proportion as it approaches to democracy, wants those springs of efficacious authority, which are necessary to the production of regularity and good order, and degenerates into anarchy and confusion. This is commonly imputed to the capricious humor of the people, who are said to run riot with too much liberty, to be always unreasonable in their demands, and never satisfied, but when ruled with a rod of iron.

"These are the common place arguments against a democratic constitution. They are the pleas of ambition to introduce aristocracy, monarchy, and every species of tyranny and oppression. Unfortunate indeed for the liberties of mankind, if it be true, that to render them orderly, it is necessary to render them slaves. However generally this position may have been admitted, we may venture to deny that it is an inference fairly drawn from experience. Without better proof than has been adduced, we cannot justly admit that the people at large are capricious or unreasonable, or that a democratic government will be productive of disorder or tumult. The blame in such cases is indeed generally laid on the people, but it is easy to see that the charge is unjust. So far from being unreasonable in their demands, there is perhaps no one instance in history, where they have ventured at once to push their claims to the full extent of reason, and to make an ample demand of justice. They rarely complain at once of more than one or two grievances. When these are removed, they become sensible of others. In proportion as they acquire more freedom, they gain more strength of mind, and independence of spirit. They see further into the nature and extent of their own rights, and call louder for a restoration of them. This is called turbulence and caprice, but is in reality only a requisition of justice; which being either refused, or but partially and unwillingly granted, it is to the oppressors, and not the oppressed, that the mischief is to be imputed.

"It is thus, I apprehend, and not otherwise," continues the same writer, "that a government approaching to democracy is apt to be disorderly. The people have a right to complain, so long as they are robbed of any portion of their freedom; and if their complaints are not heard, they have a right to use any method of enfranchising themselves. On the contrary, I am inclined to believe, that in general the people are pretty easily satisfied when no injustice is intended towards them; and if it be allowed to reason *a priori* in such a case, I conclude that a real democracy, as it is the only equitable constitution, so it would be of all the most happy, and perhaps, of all the most quiet and orderly."

I shall conclude this summary with remarking, that if ever there was a country in which a fair experiment could be made of the efficacy, advantages, duration, and happiness to be derived from a democratic government, that country is United America.

SECTION XII.

Political bodies, whether great or small, if they are constituted by a people formerly independent, and under no civil subjection, or by those who justly claim independence from any civil power they were formerly subject to, have the civil supremacy in themselves, and are in a state of equal right and liberty with respect to all other states, whether great or small. No regard is to be had in this matter to names; whether the body politic be called a kingdom, an empire, a principality, a dukedom, a country, a republic, or free town. If it can exercise justly all the essential parts of civil power within itself independently of any other person or body politic, and no other hath any right to rescind or annul its acts, it has the civil supremacy, how small soever its territory may be, or the number of its people, and has all the rights of an independent state.[23]

23. Hutchinson's Moral Philosophy.

This independence of states, and their being distinct political bodies from each other, is not obstructed by any alliance or confederacies whatsoever, about exercising jointly any parts of the supreme power; such as those of peace and war, in leagues offensive and defensive. Two states, notwithstanding such treaties, are separate bodies and independent.[24]

They are then, only, deemed politically united when some one person, or council, is constituted with a right to exercise some essential powers for both, and to hinder either from exercising them separately. If any person or council is empowered to exercise all these essential powers for both, they are then one state: such is the state of England and Scotland, since the act of union made at the beginning of the eighteenth century, whereby the two kingdoms were incorporated into one, all parts of the supreme power of both kingdoms being henceforward united and vested in the three estates of the realm of Great Britain: by which entire coalition, though both kingdoms retain their ancient laws and usages in many respects, they are as effectually united and incorporated, as the several petty kingdoms, which composed the heptarchy, were before that period.

But when only a portion of the supreme civil power is vested in one person, or council for both, such as that of peace and war, or of deciding controversies between different states, or their subjects, whilst each state within itself exercise other parts of the supreme power, independently of all the others; in this case they are called *systems of states*: which Burlamaqui defines to be an assemblage of perfect governments, strictly united by some common bond; so that they seem to make but a single body with respect to those affairs which interest them in common, though each preserves its sovereignty full and entire, independently of all the others. . . . And in this case, he adds, the confederate states engage to each other only to exercise with common consent, certain parts of the sovereignty, especially those which relate to their mutual defense, against foreign enemies. But each of the confederates retains an entire liberty of exercising as it thinks proper, those parts of the sovereignty, which are not mentioned in the treaty of union, as parts that ought to be exercised

24. Vattel.

in common. And of this nature is the American confederacy, in which each state has resigned the exercise of certain parts of the supreme civil power which they possessed before (except in common with the other states included in the confederacy) reserving to themselves all their former powers, which are not delegated to the United States by the common bond of union.

A visible distinction, and not less important than obvious, occurs to our observation in comparing these different kinds of union. The kingdoms of England and Scotland are united into one kingdom; and the two contracting states by such an incorporate union are, in the opinion of Judge Blackstone, totally annihilated, without any power of revival; and a third arises from their conjunction, in which all the rights of sovereignty, and particularly that of legislation, are vested. From whence he expresses a doubt whether any infringements of the fundamental and essential conditions of the union, would of itself dissolve the union of those kingdoms, though he readily admits, that in the case of a *federate* alliance, such an infringement would certainly rescind the compact between the confederate states. In the United States of America, on the contrary, each state retains its own antecedent form of government; its own laws, subject to the alteration and control of its own legislatures, only; its own executive officers, and council of state: its own courts of judicature, its own judges; its own magistrates, civil officers, and officers of the militia; and, in short, its own civil state, or body politic, in every respect whatsoever. And by the express declaration of the twelfth article[25] of the amendments to the constitution, the powers not delegated to the United States by the constitution, or prohibited by it to the states, are reserved to the states respectively, or to the people. In Great Britain, a new *civil state* is created by the annihilation of two antecedent civil states; in the American States, a general *federal* council, and administrative, is provided, for the joint exercise of such of their several powers, as

25. *Editor's note:* Here and throughout his constitutional essays, Tucker refers to the Tenth Amendment as "the twelfth article of the amendments to the constitution." Apparently he was counting the twelve amendments originally proposed by the first Congress, two of which, however, were never ratified by a sufficient number of states.

can be more conveniently exercised in that mode, than any other; leaving their *civil state* unaltered; and all the other powers, which the states antecedently possessed, to be exercised by them, respectively, as if no union, or connection were established between them.

The ancient Achaia seems to have been a confederacy founded upon a similar plan; each of those little states had its distinct possessions, territories, and boundaries, each had its senate, or assembly, its magistrates and judges; and every state sent deputies to the general convention, and had equal weight in all determinations. And most of the neighboring states, which, moved, by fear of danger, acceded to this confederacy, had reason to felicitate themselves. The republic of Lycia was a confederacy of towns, which they ranged into three classes, according to their respective importance. To the cities of the first rank, they allowed three votes, each, in the general council; to those of the second two, and to those of the third one.... The assembly of the Amphictyons, that assembly whose councils enabled Greece to withstand the power of the Persian monarchy, and whose decisions were held in such veneration that their sentences were seldom, or never, disputed, was composed of deputies from the several states of Greece, in number twelve, each of which sent to this grand council one, two, or three delegates, according to their respective importance. The Helvetic confederacy consists in the union of several republics. They have a common assembly, in which all matters interesting to the whole community are debated: whatever is there determined by a majority, binds the whole; they all agree in making peace, and declaring war; and the laws and customs, which prevail throughout the Swiss cantons, are, excepting the difference of religion between the Protestant, and Popish cantons, nearly the same. There are, however, some important differences both in constitution, and administration.

The United Provinces of the Netherlands before their late revolution, maintained a common confederacy; each province possessing a constitution and internal government of its own, independent of the others: this government is called the states of that province; and the delegates from them formed the states-general, in whom the sovereignty of the whole confederacy was vested; but though a province might send two or more delegates, yet such province had no more than one voice in every resolution; and before that resolution could have the force of a law, it must have been approved by every province. . . . The council of state consisted likewise of deputies from the several provinces; but its constitution was different from that of the states-general; it was composed of twelve deputies, (some of the states sending two, and some one, only), who voted by persons, and not by provinces, as in the states-general. Their business was to prepare estimates, and ways and means, for raising the revenue, as well as other matters that were to be laid before the states-general.

It is very probable, says the president Montesquieu, that mankind would have at length been obliged to live constantly under the government of a single person, had they not contrived a constitution, (such as we are now speaking of) that has all the internal advantages of a republican, together with the external force of a monarchical, government. It was these associations, he adds, that contributed so long to the prosperity of Greece. By these the Romans attacked the universe, and by these only the universe withstood their power; for when Rome was arrived, to her highest pitch of grandeur, it was the associations beyond the Danube, and the Rhine, associations formed by terror, (such was the foundation of the American confederacy) that enabled the barbarians to resist her.

A confederate government, according to the same author, ought to be composed of states of the same nature, especially of the republican kind. The spirit of monarchy is war and the enlargement of empire and dominion: Peace and moderation is the spirit of a republic. These two kinds of government cannot naturally subsist in a confederate republic. Greece was undone as soon as the kings of Macedon obtained a seat among the Amphictyons. The confederate republic of Germany, composed of princes and free towns, subsists by means of a chief, who is in some measure the magistrate, and in some the monarch of the union.

These confederacies by which several states are united together by a perpetual league of alliance, are chiefly founded upon this circumstance, that each particular people choose to remain their own masters, and yet are not strong enough to make head against a common enemy. The purport of such an agreement usually is, that they shall not exercise some part of the sovereignty there specified, without the general consent of each other. For the leagues to which these systems of states owe their rise seem distinguished from others (so frequent among different states) chiefly by this consideration; that in the latter, each confederate people determine themselves by their own judgment to certain mutual performances, yet so that in all other respects they design not in the least to make the exercise of that part of the sovereignty, whence those performances proceed, dependent on the consent of their allies, or to retrench anything from their full and unlimited power of governing their own states. Thus we see that ordinary treaties propose, for the most part as their aim, only some particular advantage of the states thus transacting; their interests happening at present to fall in with each other; but do not produce any lasting union as to the chief management of affairs.[26] Such was the treaty of alliance between America and France in the year 1778, by which among other articles it was agreed, that neither of the two parties should conclude either truce or peace with Great Britain without the formal consent of the other first obtained; and whereby they mutually engaged not to lay down their arms until the independence of the United States should be formally or tacitly assured by the treaty or treaties which should terminate the war. Whereas in these confederacies of which we are now speaking, the contrary is observable; they being established with this design, that the several states shall forever link their safety one with another, and, in order to this mutual defense, shall engage themselves not to exercise certain parts of their sovereign power, otherwise than by a common agreement, and approbation. Such were the stipulations, among others, contained in the articles of confederation and perpetual union between the American states, by which it was agreed, that no state should without the consent of the United States in congress

26. Puffendorf.

assembled send any embassy to, or receive any embassy from, or enter into any conference, agreement, alliance, or treaty with, any king, prince, or state: nor keep up any vessels of war, or body of forces, in time of peace; nor engage in any war, without the consent of the United States in congress assembled, unless actually invaded; nor grant commissions to any ships of war, or letters of marque and reprisal, except after a declaration of war, by the United States in congress assembled, with several others: yet each state respectively retains its sovereignty, freedom, and independence, and every power, jurisdiction and right which is not expressly delegated to the United States in congress assembled. The promises made in these two cases here compared run very differently: in the former thus: "I will join you in this particular war, as was a confederate and the manner of our attacking the enemy shall be concerted by our common advice; nor will we desist from the war, till the particular end thereof, the establishment of the independence of the United States be obtained." In the latter thus: "none of us who have entered into this alliance will make use of our right, as to the affairs of war and peace, except by the general consent of the whole confederacy." We observed before, that these unions submit only some certain parts of the sovereignty to mutual direction. For it seems hardly possible that the affairs of different states should have so close a connection, as that all and each of them should look on it as their interest to have no part of the chief government exercised without the general concurrence. The most convenient method, therefore, seems to be that the particular states reserve to themselves all those branches of the supreme authority, the management of which can have little or no influence, on the affairs of the rest.[27] Thus the American states, have reserved to themselves the uncontrolled right of framing, establishing, and revoking their civil laws, and the administration of justice according to them, in all cases whatsoever, in which they have not specifically consented to the jurisdiction of the United States. But as to all affairs, on which the safety, peace, and happiness of

27. Ibid.

the federal union, hath a joint dependence, these say Puffendorf, ought in reason to be adjusted by a common constitution. This does not, however, says Barbeyrac, hinder but each confederated state may provide for its particular safety, by repressing its rebellious subjects. And herewith the present constitution of the United States fully agrees. For although congress are bound to guarantee to every state in the union a republican form of government, and to protect each of them against invasion; and also against domestic violence; yet this last is only to be done where the legislature, or executive of the state (where the legislature cannot be convened) shall make the application. Nor does any thing in the constitution prohibit any state from keeping troops, or ships of war, except in time of peace; nor from engaging in war, if it be either actually invaded, or in such imminent danger as not to admit of delay. Yet where no such invasion, or imminent danger exists, the engaging in war, whether offensive or defensive; and after the peace, as the result and issue of war, are among those things, which cannot be undertaken, or adjusted, but by the common consent of the confederacy. To which we may add, with Puffendorf, taxes and subsidies as they contribute, and are necessary, to the mutual support; and alliances with foreign states, as they may promote the common safety. It falls under the same head of duties, that in case any dispute arise among the confederates themselves, the other members who are unconcerned shall immediately interpose their mediation, and not suffer the controversy to come to blows. Or the confederates may establish some common tribunal by which their differences may be decided, such as the Amphictyonic council among the Grecian states; or as the supreme court of the United States, which hath original jurisdiction by the federal constitution, in all cases of controversy between two or more states. As for those other matters, which seem not so necessary to be transacted in common, (among which Puffendorf reckons negotiations of traffic, such as taxes, for the particular use of any single state, the constituting of magistrates, the enacting laws, the power of life and death over their respective citizens, or subjects, the ecclesiastical authority, where such an authority is permitted, and the like; there is no reason, but that they may be left to the pleasure of each distinct government: though at the same time particular states ought to manage their privileges as that they shall cause no disturbance in the general union.... Whence it is evident, that one or more of the allies cannot be hindered by the rest, from exercising, according to their own judgment, such parts of the civil administration, as are not in the compact of union, referred to the common direction.[28] And this, with the exception of commercial treaties (which, for very cogent reason, were by the common consent surrendered by the respective states, to the general confederacy,) may be considered as sketching the general outline of the American union.

Since, in these systems, it is necessary that there should be a communication of certain affairs expressed in the compact of union; and since this cannot be conveniently done by letters; and since, even where this could be done, delays might be attended with great prejudice, or inconvenience to the confederacy, a determinate time and place ought to be settled for the holding assemblies and one or more persons appointed, who shall have power to call the states together, in case of any extraordinary business, which will admit of no delay. Though it seems a much more compendious method to fix a standing council, made up of persons deputed by the several confederates, who shall dispatch business according to the tenor of their commission; and, to whom the ministers of the confederacy in foreign parts, shall give an immediate account of their proceedings, and who shall treat with the ambassadors of other nations, and conclude business in the general name of the confederates; but shall determine nothing that exceeds the bounds of their commission. How far the power of this council of delegates extends, is to be gathered from the words of the compact itself, or from the warrant and under which they act. This is certain; that the power whatever it be, is not their own, but derived to them from those whom they represent; and although the decrees, which they publish, pass solely under their own name, yet the whole force and authority of them flows from the states,

28. Ibid.

themselves, by whose consent such a council hath been erected: so that the deputies are no more than ministers of the confederate states, and are altogether as unable to enjoin any thing by their own proper authority, as an ambassador is to command and govern his master.[29]

SECTION XIII.

The dissolution of these systems happens, when all the confederates by mutual consent, or some of them, voluntarily abandon the confederacy, and govern their own states apart; or a part of them form a different league and confederacy among each other, and withdraw themselves from the confederacy with the rest. Such was the proceeding on the part of those of the American states which first adopted the present constitution of the United States, and established a form of federal government, essentially different from that which was first established by the articles of confederation, leaving the states of Rhode Island and North Carolina, both of which, at first, rejected the new constitution, to themselves. This was an evident breach of that article of the confederation, which stipulated that those "articles should be inviolably observed by every state, and that the union should be perpetual; nor should any alteration at any time thereafter be made in any of them, unless such alteration be agreed to in the congress of the United States, and be afterwards confirmed by the legislatures of every state." Yet the seceding states, as they may be not improperly termed, did not hesitate, as soon as nine states had ratified the new constitution, to supersede the former federal government and establish a new form, more consonant to their opinion of what was necessary to the preservation and prosperity of the federal union. But although by this act the seceding states subverted the former federal government, yet the obligations of the articles of confederacy as a treaty of perpetual alliance, offensive and defensive, between all the parties thereto, no doubt remained; and if North Carolina and Rhode Island had never acceded to the new form of government, that circumstance,

29. Ibid.

I conceive, could never have lessened the obligation upon the other states to perform those stipulations on their parts which the states, who were unwilling to change the form of the federal government, had by virtue of those articles a right to demand and insist upon. For the inadequacy of the form of government established by those articles could not be charged upon one state more than another, nor had North Carolina or Rhode Island committed any breach of them; the seceding states therefore had no cause of complaint against them. On the contrary, these states being still willing to adhere to the terms of the confederacy, had the right of complaining, if there could be any right to complain of the conduct of states endeavoring to meliorate their own condition, by establishing a different form of government. But the seceding states were certainly justified upon that principle; and from the duty which every state is acknowledged to owe to itself, and its own citizens by doing whatsoever may best contribute to advance its own happiness and prosperity; and much more, what may be necessary to the preservation of its existence as a state.[30] Nor must we forget that solemn declaration to which every one of the confederate states assented . . . . that whenever any form of government is destructive of the ends of its institution, it is the right of the people to alter or abolish it, and to institute new government. Consequently whenever the people of any state, or number of states, discovered the inadequacy of the first form of federal government to promote or preserve their independence, happiness, and union, they only exerted that natural right in rejecting it, and adopting another, which all had unanimously assented to, and of which no force or compact can deprive the people of any state, whenever they see the necessity, and possess the power to do it. And since the seceding states, by establishing a new constitution and form of federal government among themselves, without the consent of the rest, have shown that they consider the right to do so whenever the occasion may, in their opinion require it, as unquestionable, we may infer that that right has not been diminished by any new compact which they may since have entered into,

30. Vattel.

since none could be more solemn or explicit than the first, nor more binding upon the contracting parties. Their obligation, therefore, to preserve the present constitution, is not greater than their former obligations were, to adhere to the articles of confederation; each state possessing the same right of withdrawing itself from the confederacy without the consent of the rest, as any number of them do, or ever did, possess. Prudence, indeed, will dictate, that governments established by compact should not be changed for light or transient causes; but should a long train of abuses and usurpations, pursuing invariably the same object, evince a design in any one of the confederates to usurp a dominion over the rest; or, if those who are entrusted to administer the government, which the confederates have for their mutual convenience established, should manifest a design to invade their sovereignty, and extend their own power beyond the terms of compact, to the detriment of the states respectively, and to reduce them to a state of obedience, and finally to establish themselves in a state of permanent superiority, it then becomes not only the right, but the duty of the states respectively, to throw off such government, and to provide new guards for their future security. To deny this, would be to deny to sovereign and independent states, the power which, as colonies, and dependent territories, they have mutually agreed they had a right to exercise, and did actually exercise, when they shook off the government of England, first, and adopted the present constitution of the United States, in the second instance.

Another case from which a dissolution of these confederacies may follow, may be, where from any accident, or want of concert among the confederate states, the legislative or executive authority of the federal government may happen to be suspended, so as that no legislature or executive magistrate can, for a long space of time, succeed to an exercise of the functions of the former. As if a majority of the states should refuse any longer to choose representatives, or to supply the vacancies in the senate, in either of these cases it would seem that the legislature would be destroyed; on the other hand, if it should happen that no president should be chosen at the period when a president ought to be elected, here there would be a suspension both of the legislature and the executive, inasmuch as the president is an essential constituent part of the legislative body, since all bills, before they become law, must be submitted to him for his approbation. Now whenever the administration of any government is wholly suspended, a dissolution of the government follows of course; for, as Mr. Locke observes, whenever there is no remaining power[31] within the community to direct the public force, or provide for the necessities of the public, there certainly is no government left; where laws cannot be executed at all it is all one as if there were no laws. And if this be a sufficient reason for the dissolution of *civil* government, the reason is much stronger why it should amount to a dissolution of a *federal* government, whose existence is infinitely of less consequence than the former. Civil society, and civil government its cement and support, may well subsist without the aid of federal government; but they are so intimately blended, with each other, that civil society is in danger, the moment that civil government is exposed to hazard: it may, indeed, survive for a little time; as the pulsations of the heart are known to continue after every other vital function is suspended; but if they be not speedily restored, the whole animal frame perishes together.

Intestine wars are another cause which must necessarily break these unions, unless upon the establishment of peace, the league be also revived. A man must be far gone in Utopian speculations, says the author of the Federalist,[32] who can seriously doubt, that if the American States should either be wholly disunited, or only united in partial confederacies, the subdivisions into which they might be thrown, would have frequent and violent contests with each other. And as the prevention of such contests, was among the most cogent reasons to induce the adoption of the union, so ought it to be among the most powerful, to prevent a dissolution of it.

Conquest, where the conqueror happens to possess himself of one or two, or more of the confederate states, is another mode by which these confederacies may be dissolved; for the conqueror in this case, acquires

31. On civil government.
32. Federalist, No. 6.

no manner of right, over those states that remain, nor can he demand to be admitted into the confederacy, by virtue of the league which engaged the conquered states to the others, for, says Puffendorf, the alliance must always be presumed to expire, when any one people are brought under a foreign yoke, or are made an accession of another kingdom, because the league being made between free states, considered in that capacity, whenever this condition fails, the league must fail with it. But the American confederacy did not act upon these principles, when the states of Georgia and South Carolina were actually conquered by the British arms, and the British government was reestablished in them. The rest of the confederates did not abandon them in this situation, but continued the contest until Great Britain agreed to acknowledge those states, as well as the rest of their confederates, free and independent states. An example which I trust the members of that confederacy will hold in reverence for ever, even, though the guarantee of a republican form of government contained in the present federal constitution should be wholly forgotten. On the other hand, these systems do more closely unite, and are incorporated into the same civil state, either, if all the confederates, by a voluntary submission, incorporate themselves together, under the entire rule and government of some one person, or council, in all things; as in the union between England and Scotland before mentioned; or if some one state, which hath the advantage of strength and power, reduces the rest to the condition of dependent provinces. And lastly, if some particular man invade the sovereign command, through the favor of the soldiers, the esteem of the commonalty, or the strength of a prevailing faction. From which last source more danger may be apprehended to the American Confederacy, than from all the rest.

SECTION XIV.

Having in the preceding section considered the several modes by which a system, or confederacy of states may be dissolved, I shall add a few words only concerning the dissolution of *civil* government, which, according to Mr. Locke,[33] and other writers, may happen either by conquest, and tearing up the roots of society at once, or by the public functionaries who are entrusted with the administration of the government, abusing, or betraying their trusts, and instead of consulting the happiness of the people, endeavoring to establish a model and form of government different from that which they have been entrusted to administer. All which may be summed up in the words of the American declaration of independence, "that whenever any form of government becomes destructive of those ends for which it is instituted, it is the right of the people to alter, or to abolish it, and to institute new government, laying its foundation on such principles, and organizing its powers in such form, as to them shall seem most likely to effect their happiness and safety. Prudence indeed will dictate that governments long established, should not be changed for light, or transient causes. But when a long train of abuses and usurpations, pursuing invariably the same object, evinces a design to reduce them under absolute despotism, it is their right, it is their duty, to throw off such government, and to provide new guards for their future security."

I shall now proceed to offer to the student a view of the constitution of the commonwealth of Virginia;[34] after which I shall go on to consider that of the United States, from which a more correct view will be obtained of the nature of the American governments, in general, than could be given in a general essay upon the nature of the several kinds of government.

33. On civil government, a work with which every American ought to be perfectly acquainted.

34. *Editor's Note:* Tucker's essay on the Virginia constitution is not included in this edition.

WORKS USED BY TUCKER

James Burgh, *Political Disquisitions, or an Enquiry into Public Errors Defects and Abuses.*

Jean Louis De Lolme, *The Constitution of England, in Which It Is Compared Both with the Republican Form of Government, and the Other Monarchies in Europe.*

Sir Matthew Hale, *Original Institution, Power, and Jurisdictions of Parliaments.*

Francis Hutchinson, *An Inquiry into the Origination of Our Ideas of Beauty and Virtue: Concerning Moral Good and Evil.*

John Locke, *Two Treatises on Civil Government.*

Sir James Mackintosh, *Vindiciae Gallicae: Defence of the French Revolution and Its English Admirers.*

Charles Louis de Secondat Montesquieu, *The Spirit of Laws.*

John Moore, *A View of Society and Manners in Italy.*

Thomas Paine, *The Rights of Man.*

Samuel, Baron von Pufendorf, *On the Law of Nature and of Nations.*

William Robertson, *History of Greece.*

Jean Jacques Rousseau, *The Social Contract.*

Zephaniah Swift, *A System of the Laws of the State of Connecticut.*

Emerich de Vattel, *Law of Nations.*

Samuel Williams, *The Natural and Civil History of Vermont.*

❧ View of the Constitution of the United States

HAVING in the preceding pages taken a slight view of the several forms of government, and afterwards examined with somewhat closer attention the constitution of the commonwealth of Virginia, as a sovereign, and independent state, it now becomes necessary for the American student to inquire into the connection established between the several states in the union by the constitution of the United States. To assist him in this inquiry, I shall now proceed to consider: First, the nature of that instrument, with the manner in which it hath been adopted; and, Secondly, its structure, and organization; with the powers, jurisdiction, and rights of the government thereby established, either independent of, or connected with, those of the state governments; together with the mutual relation which subsists between the federal, and state governments, in virtue of that instrument.

I. I am to consider the nature of that instrument by which the federal government of the United States, has been established, with the manner of its adoption.

The constitution of the United States of America, then, is an original, written, federal, and social compact, freely, voluntarily, and solemnly entered into by the several states of North-America, and ratified by the people thereof, respectively; whereby the several states, and the people thereof, respectively, have bound themselves to each other, and to the federal government of the United States; and by which the federal government is bound to the several states, and to every citizen of the United States.

1. It is a compact; by which it is distinguished from a charter, or grant; which is either the act of a superior to an inferior; or is founded upon some consideration moving from one of the parties, to the other, and operates as an exchange, or sale: but here the contracting parties, whether

considered as states, in their politic capacity and character; or as individuals, are all equal; nor is there any thing granted from one to another: but each stipulates to part with, and to receive the same thing, precisely, without any distinction or difference in favor of any of the parties. The considerations upon which this compact was founded, and the motives which led to it, as declared in the instrument itself, were, to form a more perfect union than theretofore existed between the confederated states; to establish justice, and ensure domestic tranquility, between them; to provide for their common defense, against foreign force, or such powerful domestic insurrections as might require aid to suppress them; to promote their general welfare; and to secure the blessings of liberty to the people of the United States, and their posterity.

2. It is a federal compact; several sovereign and independent states may unite themselves together by a perpetual confederacy, without each ceasing to be a perfect state. They will together form a federal republic: the deliberations in common will offer no violence to each member, though they may in certain respects put some constraint on the exercise of it, in virtue of voluntary engagements.[1] The extent, modifications, and objects of the federal authority are mere matters of discretion; so long as the separate organization of the members remains, and from the nature of the compact must continue to exist, both for local and domestic, and for federal purposes; the union is in fact, as well as in theory, an association of states, or, a confederacy.[2] The state governments not only retain every power, jurisdiction, and right not delegated to the United States, by the constitution, nor prohibited by it to the states, but they are constituent and necessary parts of the federal government; and without their agency in their politic character, there could be neither a senate, nor president of the United States; the choice of the latter depending mediately, and of the former, immediately, upon the legislatures of the several states in the union.

1. Vattel.
2. Federalist, No. 9.

This idea of a confederate, or federal, republic, was probably borrowed from Montesquieu, who treats of it as an expedient for extending the sphere of popular government, and reconciling internal freedom with external security, as hath been mentioned elsewhere. The experience of the practicability and benefit of such a system, was recent in the memory of every American, from the success of the revolutionary war, concluded but a few years before; during the continuance of which the states entered into a perpetual alliance and confederacy with each other. Large concessions of the rights of sovereignty were thereby made to congress; but the system was defective in not providing adequate means, for a certain, and regular revenue; congress being altogether dependent upon the legislatures of the several states for supplies, although the latter, by the terms of compact, were bound to furnish, whatever the former should deem it necessary to require. At the close of the war, it was found that congress had contracted debts, without a revenue to discharge them; that they had entered into treaties, which they had not power to fulfil; that the several states possessed sources of an extensive commerce, for which they could not find any vent. These evils were ascribed to the defects of the existing confederation; and it was said that the principles of the proposed constitution were to be considered less as absolutely new, than as the expansion of the principles contained in the articles of confederation: that in the latter those principles were so feeble and confined, as to justify all the charges of inefficiency which had been urged against it; that in the new government, as in the old, the general powers are limited, and that the states, in all unenumerated cases, are left in the enjoyment of their sovereign and independent jurisdictions. This construction has since been fully confirmed by the twelfth article of amendments,[3] which declares, "that the powers not delegated to the United States by the constitution, nor prohibited by it to the states, are reserved to the

3. *Editor's note:* Here, and throughout, Tucker, somewhat disconcertingly, refers to the Tenth Amendment as "the twelfth article of the amendments." At the time he wrote his lectures, there were twelve proposed amendments current, two of which, however, were never ratified.

states respectively, or to the people." This article was added "to prevent misconstruction or abuse" of the powers granted by the constitution,[4] rather than supposed necessary to explain and secure the rights of the states, or of the people. The powers delegated to the federal government being all positive, and enumerated, according to the ordinary rules of construction, whatever is not enumerated is retained; for, *expressum facit tacere tacitum* is a maxim in all cases of construction: it is likewise a maxim of political law, that sovereign states cannot be deprived of any of their rights by implication; nor in any manner whatever by their own voluntary consent, or by submission to a conqueror.

Some of the principal points mutually insisted on, and conceded, by the several states, as such, to each other, were, that representatives and direct taxes should be apportioned among the states, according to a decennial census; that each state should have an equal number of senators; and that the number of electors of the president of the United States, should in each state be equal to the whole number of senators and representatives to which such state may be entitled in the congress; that no capitation or other direct tax shall be laid, unless in proportion to the census; that full faith and credit shall be given in each state to the public acts, records, and proceedings of every other state; that the citizens of each state shall be entitled to all the privileges and immunities of citizens in the several states; that persons charged with treason, felony, or other crime, in one state, and fleeing from justice to another state, shall be delivered up, on demand of the executive authority of the state from which he fled; that no new state shall be formed or erected within the jurisdiction of any other state; nor any state be formed by the junction of two or more states, or parts of states, without the consent of the legislatures of the states concerned; that the United States shall guarantee to every state in the union a republican form of government, and shall protect each of them against invasion; and, on application of the legislature, or of the executive (when the legislature cannot be convened) against

---

4. *Editor's note:* Here Tucker quotes from the preamble of the congressional resolution proposing the amendments which became known as the "Bill of Rights."

domestic violence; that amendments to the constitution, when proposed by congress, shall not be valid unless ratified by the legislatures of three fourths of the several states; and that congress shall, on the application of two thirds of the legislatures of the several states, call a convention for proposing amendments, which when ratified by the conventions in three fourths of the states shall be valid to all intents and purposes, as a part of the constitution; that the ratification of the conventions of nine states, should be sufficient for the establishment of the constitution, between the states so ratifying; and lastly, by the amendment before mentioned, it is declared, that the powers not delegated to the United States by the constitution, nor prohibited by it to the states, are reserved to the states respectively, or to the people. Thus far every feature of the constitution appears to be strictly federal.

3. It is also, to a certain extent, a social compact; the end of civil society is the procuring for the citizens whatever their necessities require, the conveniences and accommodations of life, and, in general, whatever constitutes happiness: with the peaceful possession of property, a method of obtaining justice with security; and in short, a mutual defense against all violence from without. In the act of association, in virtue of which a multitude of men form together a state or nation, each individual is supposed to have entered into engagements with all, to procure the common welfare: and all are supposed to have entered into engagements with each other, to facilitate the means of supplying the necessities of each individual, and to protect and defend him.[5] And this is, what is ordinarily meant by the original contract of society. But a contract of this nature actually existed in a visible form, between the citizens of each state, respectively, in their several constitutions; it might therefore be deemed somewhat extraordinary, that in the establishment of a federal republic, it should have been thought necessary to extend its operation to the persons of individuals, as well as to the states, composing the confederacy. It was apprehended by many, that this innovation would be construed to change the nature of the union, from a confederacy, to a

5. Vattel.

consolidation of the states; that as the tenor of the instrument imported it to be the act of the people, the construction might be made accordingly: an interpretation that would tend to the annihilation of the states, and their authority. That this was the more to be apprehended, since all questions between the states, and the United States, would undergo the final decision of the latter.

That the student may more clearly apprehend the nature of these objections, it may be proper to illustrate the distinction between federal compacts and obligations, and such as are social by one or two examples. A federal compact, alliance, or treaty, is an act of the state, or body politic, and not of an individual; on the contrary, the social contract is understood to mean the act of individuals, about to create, and establish, a state, or body politic, among themselves. . . . Again; if one nation binds itself by treaty to pay a certain tribute to another; or if all the members of the same confederacy oblige themselves to furnish their quotas of a common expense, when required; in either of the cases, the state, or body politic, only, and not the individual is answerable for this tribute, or quota; for although every citizen in the state is bound by the contract of the body politic, who may compel him to contribute his part, yet that part can neither be ascertained nor levied, by any other authority than that of the state, of which he is a citizen. This is, therefore, a federal obligation; which cannot reach the individual, without the agency of the state who made it. But where by any compact, express, or implied, a number of persons are bound to contribute their proportions of the common expense; or to submit to all laws made by the common consent; and where, in default of compliance with these engagements the society is authorized to levy the contribution, or, to punish the person of the delinquent; this seems to be understood to be more in the nature of a social than a federal obligation. . . . Upon these grounds, and others of a similar nature, a considerable alarm was excited in the minds of many, who considered the constitution as in some danger of establishing a national, or consolidated government, upon the ruins of the old federal republic.

To these objections the friends and supporters of the constitution replied,[6] "that although the constitution would be founded on the assent and ratification of the people of America, ye that assent and ratification was to be given by the people, not as individuals composing one entire nation; but as composing the distinct and independent states, to which they respectively belong. It is to be the assent and ratification of the several states, derived from the supreme authority in each state, the authority of the people themselves.   The act, therefore establishing the constitution, will not," said they, "be a national but a federal act.

"That it will be a federal and not a national act, as these terms are understood by the objectors, the act of the people, as forming so many independent states, not as forming one aggregate nation, is obvious from this single consideration, that it is the result neither from the decision of a majority of the people of the union, nor from a majority of the states. It must result from the unanimous assent of the several states that are parties to it, differing no otherwise from their ordinary assent, than in its being expressed, not by the legislative authority, but by that of the people themselves. Were the people regarded in this transaction as forming one nation, the will of the majority of the whole people of the United States would bind the minority; in the same manner as the majority in each state must bind the minority; and the will of the majority must be determined either by a comparison of the individual votes; or by considering the will of the majority of the states, as evidence of the will of the majority of the people of the United States. Neither of these rules have been adopted. Each state in ratifying the constitution, is considered as a sovereign body, independent of all others, and only to be bound by its own voluntary act. In this relation then the new constitution will be a federal, and not a national, constitution.

"With regard to the sources from which the ordinary powers of government are to be derived. The house of representatives will derive its powers from the people of America, and the people will be represented

6. *Editor's note:* From this point to the end of section 3, Tucker quotes directly from The Federalist, No. 39.

in the same proportion, and on the same principle, as they are in the legislature of a particular state. So far the government is national, not federal. The senate, on the other hand, will derive its powers from the states, as political and co-equal societies; and these will be represented on the principle of equality in the senate, as under the confederation. So far the government is federal, not national. The executive power will be derived from a very compound source. The immediate election of the president is to be made by the states, in their political character. The votes allotted to them are in a compound ratio, which considers them partly as distinct and co-equal societies; partly as unequal members of the same societies. The eventual election again is to be made, by that branch of the legislature which consists of the national representatives: but in this particular act they are to be thrown into the form of individual delegations, from so many distinct and co-equal bodies politic. From this aspect of the government it appears to be of a mixed character, presenting at least as many federal, as national features.

"The difference between a federal and national government, as it relates to the operation of the government, is, by the adversaries of the plan of the convention, supposed to consist in this, that in the former the powers operate on the political bodies composing the confederacy in their political capacities; in the latter, on the individual citizens composing the nation in their individual capacities. On trying the constitution by this criterion, it falls under the national, not the federal character, though perhaps not so completely as has been understood. In several cases, and particularly in the trial of controversies to which states may be parties, they must be viewed and proceeded against in their collective and political capacities only. In some instances the powers of the federal government, established by the confederation, act immediately on individuals: in cases of capture, of piracy, of the post office, of coins, weights, and measures, of trade with the Indians, of claims under grants of land by different states, and, above all, in the cases of trials by courts martial in the army and navy, by which death may be inflicted without the intervention of a jury, or even of a civil magistrate; in all these cases the powers of the confederation operate immediately on the persons and interests of individual citizens. The confederation itself authorizes a direct tax to a certain extent on the post-office; and the power of coinage has been so construed by congress, as to levy a tribute immediately from that source also. The operation of the new government on the people in their individual capacities, in its ordinary and most essential proceedings, will, on the whole, in the sense of its opponents, designate it, in this relation, a national government.

"But if the government be national with regard to the operation of its powers, it changes its aspect again when we contemplate it in relation to the extent of its powers. The idea of a national government involves in it, not only an authority over the individual citizens, but an indefinite supremacy over all persons and things, so far as they are objects of lawful government. Among a people consolidated into one nation, this supremacy is completely vested in the national legislature. Among communities united for particular purposes, it is vested partly in the general, and partly in the municipal legislatures. In the former case, all local authorities are subordinate to the supreme; and may be controlled, directed, or abolished by it at pleasure. In the latter, the local or municipal authorities form distinct and independent portions of the supremacy, no more subject within their respective spheres to the general authority, than the general authority is subject to them within its own sphere. In this relation then the government cannot be deemed a national one, since its jurisdiction extends to certain enumerated objects, only, and leaves to the several states a residuary and inviolable sovereignty over all other objects. It is true that in controversies relating to the boundary between the two jurisdictions, the tribunal which is ultimately to decide, is to be established under the general government. But this does not change the principle of the case. The decision is to be impartially made according to the rules of the constitution; and all the usual and most effectual precautions are taken to secure the impartiality.

"If we try the constitution by its last relation, to the authority by which amendments are to be made, we find it neither wholly national, nor wholly federal. Were it wholly national, the supreme and ultimate authority would reside in a majority of the people of the union; and this authority would be competent at all times, like that of a majority of every national society, to alter or abolish its established government. Were it wholly federal on the other hand, the concurrence of each state in the union would be essential to every alteration that would be binding on all. The mode provided by the plan of the convention is not founded on either of these principles. In requiring more than a majority, and particularly in computing the proportion by states, not by citizens, it departs from the national, and advances towards the federal character; in rendering the concurrence of less than the whole number of states sufficient, it loses again the federal, and partakes of the national character.

"The proposed constitution, therefore, even when tested by the rules laid down by its antagonists, is in strictness neither a national nor a federal constitution, but a composition of both. In its foundation it is federal, not national; in the sources from which the ordinary powers of the government are drawn, it is partly federal, and partly national; in the operation of those powers, it is national, not federal; in the extent of them, it is federal, not national; and finally, in the authoritative mode of introducing amendments, it is neither wholly federal, nor wholly national."

4. It is an original compact; whatever political relation existed between the American colonies, antecedent to the revolution, as constituent parts of the British empire, or as dependencies upon it, that relation was completely dissolved and annihilated from that period.... From the moment of the revolution they became severally independent and sovereign states, possessing all the rights, jurisdiction, and authority, that other sovereign states, however constituted, or by whatever title denominated, possess; and bound by no ties but of their own creation, except such as all other civilized nations are equally bound by, and which together constitute the customary law of nations. A common council of the colonies, under the name of a general congress, had been established by the legislature, or rather conventional authority in the several colonies. The revolutionary war had been begun, and conducted under its auspices; but the first act of union which took place among the states after they became independent, was the confederation between them,

which was not ratified until March 1781, near five years from the commencement of their independence. The powers thereby granted to congress, though very extensive in point of moral obligation upon the several states, were perfectly deficient in the means provided for the practical use of them, as has been already observed. The agency and cooperation of the states, which was requisite to give effect to the measures of congress, not infrequently occasioned their total defeat. It became an unanimous opinion that some amendment to the existing confederation was absolutely necessary, and after a variety of unsuccessful attempts for that purpose, a general convention was appointed by the legislatures of twelve states, who met, consulted together, prepared, and reported a plan, which contained such an enlargement of the principles of the confederation, as gave the new system the aspect of an entire transformation of the old. The mild tone of requisition was exchanged for the active operations of power, and the features of a federal council for those of a national sovereignty. These concessions it was seen were, in many instances, beyond the power of the state legislatures, (limited by their respective constitutions) to make, without the express assent of the people. A convention was therefore summoned, in every state by the authority of their respective legislatures, to consider of the propriety of adopting the proposed plan; and their assent made it binding in each state; and the assent of nine states rendered it obligatory upon all the states adopting it. Here then are all the features of an original compact, not only between the body politic of each state, but also between the people of those states in their highest sovereign capacity.

Whether this original compact be considered as merely federal, or social, and national, it is that instrument by which *power is created* on the one hand, and *obedience exacted* on the other. As federal it is to be construed strictly, in all cases where the antecedent rights of a *state* may be drawn in question;[7] as a social compact it ought likewise to receive the same strict construction, wherever the right of personal liberty, of personal security, or of private property may become the subject of dis-

7. Vattel.

pute; because every person whose liberty, or property was thereby rendered subject to the new government, was antecedently a member of a civil society to whose regulations he had submitted himself, and under whose authority and protection he still remains, in all cases not expressly submitted to the new government. The few particular cases in which he submits himself to the new authority, therefore, ought not to be extended beyond the terms of the compact, as it might endanger his obedience to that state to whose laws he still continues to owe obedience; or may subject him to a double loss, or inconvenience for the same cause.

And here it ought to be remembered that no case of *municipal* law can arise under the constitution of the United States, except such as are expressly comprehended in that instrument. For the *municipal* law of one state or nation has no force or obligation in any other nation; and when several states, or nations unite themselves together by a federal compact, each retains its own municipal laws, without admitting or adopting those of any other member of the union, unless there be an article expressly to that effect. The municipal laws of the several American states differ essentially from each other; and as neither is entitled to a preference over the other, on the score of intrinsic superiority, or obligation, and as there is no article in the compact which bestows any such preference upon any, it follows, that the municipal laws of no one state can be resorted to as a general rule for the rest. And as the states, and their respective legislatures are absolutely independent of each other, so neither can any common rule be extracted from their several municipal codes. For, although concurrent laws, or rules may perhaps be met within their codes, yet it is in the power of their legislatures, respectively to destroy that concurrence at any time, by enacting an entire new law on the subject; so that it may happen that that which is a concurrent law in all the states today may cease to be law in one, or more of them tomorrow. Consequently neither the particular municipal law of any one, or more, of the states, nor the concurrent municipal laws of the whole of them, can be considered as the common rule, or measure of justice in the courts of the federal republic; neither hath the federal government any power to establish such a common rule, generally; no such power being granted by the constitution. And the principle is certainly much stronger, that neither the common nor statute law of any other nation, ought to be a standard for the proceedings of this, unless previously made its own by legislative adoption: which, not being permitted by the original compact, by which the government is *created,* any attempt to introduce it, in that or any other mode, would be a manifest breach of the terms of that compact.

Another light in which this subject may be viewed is this. Since each state in becoming a member of a federal republic retains an uncontrolled jurisdiction over all cases of *municipal* law, every grant of jurisdiction to the confederacy, in any such case, is to be considered as special, inasmuch as it derogates from the antecedent rights and jurisdiction of the state making the concession, and therefore ought to be construed strictly, upon the grounds already mentioned. Now, the cases falling under the head of *municipal law,* to which the authority of the federal government extends, are few, definite, and enumerated, and are all carved out of the sovereign authority, and former exclusive, and uncontrollable jurisdiction of the *states* respectively: they ought therefore to receive the strictest construction. Otherwise the gradual and sometimes imperceptible usurpations of power, will end in the total disregard of all its intended limitations.

If it be asked, what would be the consequence in case the federal government should exercise powers not warranted by the constitution, the answer seems to be, that where the act of usurpation may immediately affect an individual, the remedy is to be sought by recourse to that judiciary, to which the cognizance of the case properly belongs. Where it may affect a state, the state legislature, whose rights, will be invaded by every such act, will be ready to mark the innovation and sound the alarm to the people: and thereby either effect a change in the federal representation, or procure in the mode prescribed by the constitution, further "declaratory and restrictive clauses," by way of amendment thereto. An instance of which may be cited in the conduct of the Massachusetts legislature: who, as soon as that state was sued in the federal court, by an individual, immediately proposed, and procured an amendment to the constitution, declaring that the judicial power of the United States shall not be construed to extend to any suit brought by an individual against a state.

5. It is a written contract; considered as a federal compact, or alliance between the states, there is nothing new or singular in this circumstance, as all national compacts since the invention of letters have probably been reduced to that form: but considered in the light of an original, social, compact, it may be worthy of remark, that a very great lawyer, who wrote but a few years before the American revolution, seems to doubt whether the original contract of society had in any one instance been formally expressed at the first institution of a state.[8] The American revolution seems to have given birth to this new political phenomenon: in every state a written constitution was framed, and adopted by the people, both in their individual and sovereign capacity, and character. By this means, the just distinction between the sovereignty, and the government, was rendered familiar to every intelligent mind; the former was found to reside in the *people,* and to be unalienable from them; the latter in their *servants* and *agents*: by this means, also, government was reduced to its elements; its object was defined, its principles ascertained; its powers limited, and fixed; its structure organized; and the functions of every part of the machine so clearly designated, as to prevent any interference, so long as the limits of each were observed. The same reasons operated in behalf of similar restrictions in the federal constitution. Whether considered as the act of the body politic of the several states, or, of the people of the states, respectively, or, of the people of the United States, collectively. Accordingly we find the structure of the government, its several powers and jurisdictions, and the concessions of the several states, generally, pretty accurately defined, and limited. But to guard against encroachments on the powers of the several states, in their politic character, and of the people, both in their individual and sovereign capacity, an amendatory article was added, immediately after the government was organized, declaring; that the powers not delegated to the United States,

---

8. Blackstone.

by the constitution, nor prohibited by it to the states, are reserved to the states, respectively, or to the people. And, still further, to guard the people against constructive usurpations and encroachments on their rights, another article declares; that the enumeration of certain rights in the constitution, shall not be construed to deny, or disparage, others retained by the people. The sum of all which appears to be, that the powers delegated to the federal government, are, in all cases, to receive the most strict construction that the instrument will bear, where the rights of a state or of the people, either collectively, or individually, may be drawn in question.

The advantages of a written constitution, considered as the original contract of society must immediately strike every reflecting mind; power, when undefined, soon becomes unlimited; and the disquisition of social rights where there is no text to resort to, for their explanation, is a task, equally above ordinary capacities, and incompatible with the ordinary pursuits, of the body of the people. But, as it is necessary to the preservation of a free government, established upon the principles of a representative democracy, that every man should know his own rights, it is also indispensably necessary that he should be able, on all occasions, to refer to them. In those countries where the people have been deprived of the sovereignty, and have no share, even in the government, it may perhaps be happy for them, so long as they remain in a state of subjection, to be ignorant of their just rights. But where the sovereignty is, confessedly, vested in the people, government becomes a subordinate power, and is the mere creature of the people's will: it ought therefore to be so constructed, that its operations may be the subject of constant observation, and scrutiny. There should be no hidden machinery, nor secret spring about it.

The boasted constitution of England, has nothing of this visible form about it; being purely constructive, and established upon precedents or compulsory concessions betwixt parties at variance. The several powers of government, as has been elsewhere observed, are limited, though in an uncertain way, with respect to each other; but the three together are without any check in the constitution, although neither can be properly called the representative of the people. And from hence, the union of these powers in the parliament hath given occasion to some writers of that nation to stile it omnipotent: by which figure it is probable they mean no more, than to inform us that the sovereignty of the nation resides in that body; having by gradual and immemorial usurpations been completely wrested from the people.

6. It is a compact freely, voluntarily, and solemnly entered into by the several states, and ratified by the people thereof, respectively: freely, there being neither external, nor internal force, or violence to influence, or promote the measure; the United States being at peace with all the world, and in perfect tranquility in each state: voluntarily, because the measure had its commencement in the spontaneous acts of the state-legislatures, prompted by a due sense of the necessity of some change in the existing confederation: and, solemnly, as having been discussed, not only by the general convention who proposed, and framed it; but afterwards in the legislatures of the several states, and finally, in the conventions of all the states, by whom it was adopted and ratified.

The progress of this second revolution in our political system was extremely rapid. Its origin may be deduced from three distinct sources: The discontents of the army, and other public creditors; . . . . the decay of commerce, which had been diverted from its former channels; and the backwardness, or total neglect of the state-legislatures in complying with the requisitions, or recommendations of congress.

The discontents of the army had at several periods, during the war, risen to an alarming height, and threatened, if not a total revolt, at least a general disbandment. They were checked, or palliated by various temporary expedients and resolves of congress; but, not long before the cessation of hostilities, some late applications to congress, respecting the arrears of their pay and depreciation, not having produced the desired effect; an anonymous address to the army, couched in the most nervous language of complaint, made its appearance in camp; it contained a most spirited recapitulation of their services, grievances, and disappointments, and concluded with advising, "an appeal from the justice to the fears of government." The effects, naturally to have been apprehended from so animated a performance, addressed to men who felt their own injuries in every word, were averted by the prudence of the commander in chief;[9] and congress, as far as in them lay, endeavoured to do ample justice to the army; which was soon after entirely disbanded: but, as congress had not the command of any revenue, requisitions to the states were the only mode, by which funds for the discharge of so honorable a debt, could be procured. The states, already exhausted by a long and burdensome war, were either in no condition to comply with the recommendations of congress, or were so tardy and parsimonious in furnishing the supplies required, that the clamors against the government became every day louder and louder. Every creditor of government, of which there were thousands, besides the army now dispersed among the citizens, became an advocate for the change of such an inefficient government, from which they saw it was in vain to hope for satisfaction of their various demands.

But it is not probable that the discontents or clamors of the creditors of government, alone, would have been sufficient to effectuate a fundamental change in the government, had not other causes conspired to render its inefficiency the subject of observation and complaint, among another very numerous class of citizens...these were the commercial part of the people, inhabiting almost exclusively all the sea-ports, and other towns on the continent, and dispersed at small intervals through the whole country. The New-England states, in a great measure, dependent upon commerce, had before the war enjoyed a free trade with the West-India Islands, subject to the crown of Great-Britain; they had likewise maintained a very beneficial intercourse with the French Islands, from whence they drew supplies of molasses for their distilleries. The whale and cod-fisheries might be said to have been almost monopolized by them, on the American coast; at least the advantages they enjoyed for carrying on these branches of trade, bade fair to exclude every other

9. Had General Washington no other claim to the gratitude of his country, his conduct on that occasion, alone, would have entailed an unextinguishable debt of gratitude upon it, to all posterity.

nation from a competition with them on their native coasts. New-York and Pennsylvania had likewise the benefit of an advantageous fur-trade, through the channels lately occupied by the British posts, on the frontiers of the United States, which by the treaty of peace were to have been evacuated with all convenient speed. The possession of these being still retained, and the utmost vigilance exerted by the British government to prevent any communication with the Indian country; that very lucrative branch of the trade of the United States had been wholly diverted into the channel of Canada.... The ports of the English West-India Islands, which, it was expected would have been open to our vessels, as before the revolution, were, immediately after the conclusion of the peace, strictly prohibited to the American traders:.... those of the French islands were under such restrictions as greatly impaired the former advantageous intercourse with them:.... The protection formerly enjoyed under the British flag from the depredations of the corsairs of the Barbarian states, being now withdrawn, the commerce with the Mediterranean and the ports bordering thereupon, whither a great part of the produce of the fisheries, as well as the surplus of grain, was exported, was entirely cut off, from the danger of annoyance from those piratical states.... Great-Britain had, formerly, not only afforded a market for the whale oil, but had given a liberal bounty on it, both of which she now ceased to do, and no other country could be found to supply either of these advantages. Thus the sources of commerce in those states, were either dried up, or obstructed on every side, and the discontents prevailing among the newly liberated states, were little short of those of the Israelites in the wilderness.... Commotions in the northern states, seemed to threaten a repetition of the horrors of a civil war; these were ascribed to the inadequacy of the general government to secure or promote the interest and prosperity of the federal union: but whether their origin was not also to be ascribed to the administration of the state governments, is at least highly questionable.

The little regard which was paid to the requisitions of congress for money from the states, to discharge the interest of the national debt, and in particular that part due to foreigners, or foreign states, and to defray the ordinary expenses of the federal government, gave rise to a proposition, that congress should be authorized, for the period of twenty-five years, to impose a duty of five percent on all goods imported into the United States. Most of the states had consented to the measure, but the number required by the confederation could not be prevailed on to adopt it: New-York and Rhode-Island were particularly opposed to it. Thus a project which might perhaps have answered every beneficial purpose, proposed afterwards by the new constitution, was disconcerted, from the jealousy of granting a limited power for a limited time, by the same people, who, within three years after, surrendered a much larger portion of the rights of sovereignty without reserve.

In addition to this measure, congress in their act of April 18th, 1783, had proposed, that the eighth article of the confederation, which made the value of lands the ratio of contribution from the several states, should be revoked, and instead thereof the ratio should be fixed among the states, in proportion to the whole number of white inhabitants and three-fifths of all other persons, according to a triennial census. This proposition was agreed to in Virginia, but like the former, was not acceded to by a sufficient number of the states to form an article of the confederation.... Yet this ratio is precisely the same, which has been since fixed by the new constitution as the rate by which direct taxes shall be imposed on the several states.

The total derangement of commerce, as well as of the finances of the United States, had proceeded to such lengths before the conclusion of the year 1785, that early in the succeeding year commissioners were appointed by the state of Virginia, to meet such commissioners as might be appointed by other states, for the purpose of "considering how far an uniform system in the commercial regulations may be necessary to their common interests, and their permanent harmony; and to report to the several states such an act, relative to that object, as when unanimously ratified by them, would enable congress effectually to provide for the same." The commissioners assembled at Annapolis accordingly, in September 1786, but were met only by commissioners from four of the other twelve states.... They considered the number of states represented to be too few to proceed to business … but before they separated, wrote a letter to their constituents, recommending the appointment of deputies to meet in Philadelphia the succeeding May, for the purpose of extending the revision of the federal system to all its defects. … In pursuance whereof the legislature of Virginia passed an act, appointing seven commissioners to meet such deputies as may be appointed by other states, to assemble, as recommended, and join in "devising and discussing, all such alterations, and further provisions as may be necessary to render the federal constitution adequate to the exigencies of the union; and in reporting such an act for that purpose to the United States in congress, as when agreed to by them, and duly confirmed by the several states, would effectually provide for the same. Similar measures were adopted by all the states in the union, except Rhode Island: deputies assembled from all the other states; but instead of amendments to the confederation, they produced a plan for an entire change of the form of the federal government, and not without some innovation of its principles. The moment of its appearance all the enemies of the former government lifted up their voices in its favor. Party zeal never ran higher without an actual breach of the peace. Had the opposers of the proposed constitution been as violent as its advocates, it is not impossible that matters would have proceeded to some pernicious lengths: but the former were convinced that some change was necessary, which moderated their opposition; whilst the latter were animated in the pursuit of their favorite plan, from an apprehension that no other change was practicable. In several of the states, the question was decided in favor of the constitution by a very small majority of the conventions assembled to consider of its adoption. In North Carolina it was once rejected, and in Rhode Island twice: nor was it adopted by either, until the new government was organized by the ratifying states. Considerable amendments were proposed by several states; by the states of Massachusetts, South Carolina, Virginia, and New York, particularly. It was finally adopted by all the States, after having been the subject of consideration and discussion for a period little short of two years.

The form of ratification, and the amendments proposed by the convention of Virginia, were as follows:

"We, the delegates of the people of Virginia, duly elected, in pursuance of a recommendation of the general assembly, and now met in convention, having fully and fairly investigated and discussed the proceedings of the federal convention, and being prepared, as well as the most mature deliberation will enable us, to decide thereon, DO, in the name and behalf of the people of Virginia, declare and make known, that the powers granted under the constitution, being derived from the people of the United States, may be resumed by them, whenever the same shall be perverted to their injury or oppression; and that every power not granted thereby, remains with them and at their will: that therefore no right, of any denomination, can be cancelled, abridged, restrained, or modified by the congress, by the senate, or house of representatives, acting in any capacity, by the president, or any department or office of the United States, except in those instances where power is given by the constitution for those purposes: that among other essential rights, the liberty of conscience and of the press, cannot be cancelled, abridged, restrained, or modified by any authority of the United States.

"With these impressions, with a solemn appeal to the searcher of hearts for the purity of our intentions, and under the conviction, that whatsoever imperfections may exist in the constitution, ought rather to be examined in the mode prescribed therein, than to bring the union into danger by delay, with a hope of obtaining amendments previous to the ratification: we, the said delegates, in the name and in behalf of the people of Virginia, do, by these presents, assent to, and ratify the constitution recommended on the 17th day of September, 1787, by the federal convention for the government of the United States; hereby announcing to all those whom it may concern, that the said constitution is binding upon the said people, according to an authentic copy hereto annexed, in the words following:[10]

10. To this ratification was annexed a copy of the new constitution.

"The declaration of rights, and the amendments to the new constitution agreed by the convention of Virginia, to be recommended to the consideration of the congress which shall first assemble under the said constitution.[11]

RICHMOND, VIRGINIA

In Convention, June 27, 1788.

I. That there are certain natural rights, of which men, when they form a social compact, cannot deprive or divest their posterity; among which are the enjoyment of life and liberty, with the means of acquiring, possessing, and protecting property, and pursuing and obtaining happiness and safety.

II. That all power is naturally vested in, and consequently derived from, the people; that magistrates, therefore, are their trustees and agents, and at all times amenable to them.

III. That government ought to be instituted for the common benefit, protection, and security of the people; and that the doctrine of non-resistance against arbitrary power and oppression, is absurd, slavish, and destructive to the good and happiness of mankind.

IV. That no man or set of men are entitled to exclusive or separate public emoluments or privileges from the community, but in consideration of public services; which not being descendible, neither ought the offices of magistrate, legislator, judge, or any other public offices, to be hereditary.

V. That the legislative, executive, and judiciary powers of government, should be separate and distinct: and that the members of the two first may be restrained from oppression by feeling and participating the public burdens, they should, at fixed periods, be reduced to a private station .... return into the mass of the people, and the vacancies be supplied by certain and regular elections; in which all, or any part of the members to be eligible or ineligible, as the rules of the constitution of government, and the laws shall direct.

---

11. *Editor's note:* Here Tucker prints a twenty-item declaration of rights and twenty proposed amendments that Virginia attached to its ratification.

VI. That elections of representatives in the legislature ought to be free and frequent: and all men having sufficient evidence of permanent common interest with, and attachment to the community, ought to have the right of suffrage; and no aid, charge, tax, or fee, can be set, rated, or levied upon the people, without their own consent or that of their representatives so elected, nor can they be bound by any law to which they have not, in like manner, assented for the public good.

VII. That all power of suspending laws, or the execution of laws, by any authority without the consent of the representatives of the people in the legislature, is injurious to their rights, and ought not to be exercised.

VIII. That in all capital and criminal prosecutions, a man hath a right to demand the cause and nature of his accusation; to be confronted with the accusers and witnesses; to call for evidence, and be allowed counsel in his favor; and to a fair and speedy trial, by an impartial jury of his vicinage, without whose unanimous consent he cannot be found guilty, (except in the government of the land and naval forces); nor can he be compelled to give evidence against himself.

IX. That no freeman ought to be taken, imprisoned, or disseized of his freehold, liberties, privileges, or franchises, or outlawed, or exiled, or in any manner destroyed, or deprived of his life, liberty, or property, but by the law of the land.

X. That every freeman restrained of his liberty, is entitled to a remedy, to inquire into the lawfulness thereof, and to remove the same, if unlawful; and that such remedy ought not to be denied or delayed.

XI. That in controversies respecting property, and in suits between man and man, the ancient trial by jury is one of the greatest securities to the rights of the people, and ought to remain sacred and inviolable.

XII. That every freeman ought to find a certain remedy of recourse to the laws for all injuries and wrongs he may receive in his person, property, or character. He ought to obtain right and justice freely without sale, completely and without denial, promptly and without delay, and that all establishments or regulations, contravening these rights, are oppressive and unjust.

XIII. That excessive bail ought not to be required, nor excessive fines imposed, nor cruel and unusual punishments inflicted.

XIV. That every freeman has a right to be secure from all unreasonable searches and seizures of his person, his papers, and property; all warrants, therefore, to search suspected places, or seize any freeman, his papers or property, without information upon oath (or affirmation of a person religiously scrupulous of taking an oath) of legal and sufficient cause, are grievous and oppressive, and all general warrants to search suspected places, or to apprehend any suspected person, without specially naming or describing the place or person, are dangerous, and ought not to be granted.

XV. That the people have a right peaceably to assemble together to consult for the common good, or to instruct their representatives: and that every freeman has a right to petition, or apply to the legislature for a redress of grievances.

XVI. That the people have a right of freedom of speech, and of writing and publishing their sentiments; that the freedom of the press is one of the greatest bulwarks of liberty, and ought not to be violated.

XVII. That the people have a right to keep and bear arms; that a well regulated militia, composed of the body of the people, trained to arms, is the proper, natural, and safe defense of a free state. That standing armies in time of peace are dangerous to liberty, and therefore ought to be avoided, as far as the circumstances and protection of the community will admit; and that in all cases the military should be under strict subordination to, and governed by the civil power.

XVIII. That no soldier, in time of peace, ought to be quartered in any house, without the consent of the owner, and in time of war in such manner only as the laws direct.

XIX. That any person religiously scrupulous of bearing arms, ought to be exempted upon payment of an equivalent to employ another to bear arms in his stead.

XX. That religion, or the duty which we owe to our creator, and the manner of discharging it, can be directed only by reason and conviction, not by force or violence, and therefore all men have an equal, natural, and unalienable right to the free exercise of religion according to the dictates of conscience, and that no particular religious sect or society ought to be favored or established by law in preference to others.

AMENDMENTS TO THE NEW CONSTITUTION.

1. That each state in the union shall respectively retain every power, jurisdiction, and right, when it's not by this constitution delegated to the congress of the United States, or to the departments of the federal government.

2. That there shall be one representative for every thirty thousand inhabitants, according to the enumeration or census mentioned in the constitution, until the whole number of representatives amounts to two hundred; after which, that number shall be continued or increased as congress shall direct, upon the principles fixed in the constitution, by apportioning the representatives of each state to some greater number of people, from time to time, as population increases.

3. When congress shall lay direct taxes or excises, they shall immediately inform the executive power of each state, of the quota of such state, according to the census herein directed, which is proposed to be thereby raised; and if the legislature of any state shall pass a law which shall be effectual for raising such quota, at the time required by congress, the taxes and excises laid by congress shall not be collected in such state.

4. That the members of the senate and house of representatives shall be ineligible to, and incapable of holding any civil office under the authority of the United States, during the time for which they shall respectively be elected.

5. That the journals of the proceedings of the senate and house of representatives, shall be published at least once in every year, except such parts thereof relating to treaties, alliances, or military operations, as in their judgment require secrecy.

6. That a regular statement and account of the receipts and expenditures of all public money, shall be published, at least, once in every year.

7. That no commercial treaty shall be ratified without the concurrence of two thirds of the whole number of the members of the senate;

and no treaty ceding, contracting, or restraining, or suspending the territorial rights or claims of the United States, or any of them... or their, or any of their rights or claims to fishing in the American seas, or navigating the American rivers, shall be made, but in cases of the most urgent and extreme necessity; nor shall any such treaty be ratified, without the concurrence of three-fourths of the whole number of members of both houses respectively.

8. That no navigation law, or law regulating commerce, shall be passed without the consent of two thirds of the members present in both houses.

9. That no standing army, or regular troops, shall be raised or kept up in time of peace, without the consent of two-thirds of the members present in both houses.

10. That no soldier shall be enlisted for any longer term than four years, except in time of war, and then for no longer a term than the continuance of the war.

11. That each state respectively shall have the power to provide for organizing, arming, and disciplining its own militia, whensoever congress shall omit or neglect to provide for the same. That the militia shall not be subject to martial law, except when in actual service, in time of war, invasion, or rebellion; and when not in the actual service of the United States, shall be subject only to such fines, penalties, and punishments, as shall be directed or inflicted by the laws of its own state.

12. That the exclusive power of legislation given to congress over the federal town and its adjacent district, and other places, purchased, or to be purchased by congress, of any of the states, shall extend only to such regulations as respect the police and good government thereof.

13. That no person shall be capable of being president of the United States for more than eight years, in any term of sixteen years.

14. That the judicial power of the United States shall be vested in one supreme court, and in such courts of admiralty, as congress may, from time to time, ordain and establish in any of the different states: the judicial power shall extend to all cases in law and equity, arising under treaties made, or which shall be made, under the authority of the United States; to all cases affecting ambassadors, other foreign ministers and

consuls; to all cases of admiralty and maritime jurisdiction; to controversies to which the United States shall be a party; to controversies
between two or more states, and between parties claiming lands under
the grants of different states. In all cases affecting ambassadors, other
foreign ministers and consuls, and those in which a state shall be a party,
the supreme court shall have original jurisdiction; in all other cases
before mentioned, the supreme court shall have appellate jurisdiction,
as to matters of law only: except in cases of equity, and of admiralty and
maritime jurisdiction; in which, the supreme court shall have appellate
jurisdiction both as to law and fact, with such exceptions and under such
regulations as the congress shall make: but the judicial power of the
United States shall extend to no case where the cause of action shall have
originated before the ratification of this constitution; except in disputes
between states about their territory; disputes between persons claiming
lands under the grants of different states: and suits for debts due to the
United States.

15. That in criminal prosecutions no man shall be restrained in the
exercise of the usual and accustomed right of challenging or excepting to
the jury.

16. That congress shall not alter, modify, or interfere in the times,
places, or manner of holding elections for senators and representatives,
or either of them, except when the legislature of any state shall neglect,
refuse, or be disabled by invasion or rebellion to prescribe the same.

17. That those clauses which declare, that congress shall not exercise
certain powers, be not interpreted in any manner whatsoever to extend
the power of congress; but that they be construed either as making
exceptions to the specified powers, where this shall be the case; or otherwise, as inserted merely for greater caution.

18. That the laws ascertaining the compensation of senators and
representatives for their services, be postponed in their operation, until
after the election of representatives immediately succeeding the passing
thereof; that excepted, which shall first be passed on the subject.

19. That some tribunal, other than the senate be provided for trying
impeachments of senators.

20. That the salary of a judge shall not be increased or diminished

during his continuance in office, otherwise than by general regulations of salary, which may take place on a revision of the subject, at stated periods of not less than seven years, to commence from the time such salaries shall be first ascertained by congress.

And, the convention do, in the name and behalf of the people of this commonwealth, enjoin it upon their representatives in congress, to exert all their influence, and use all reasonable and legal methods to obtain a ratification of the foregoing alterations and provisions, in the manner provided by the fifth article of the said constitution; and in all congressional laws to be passed in the meantime, to conform to the spirit of these amendments, as far as the said constitution will admit.

Extract from the Journal,

JOHN BECKLEY,
Clerk of the Convention.

I have said that the constitution was ratified by the conventions of the several states, assembled for the purpose of considering the propriety of adopting it. As the tenor of the instrument imports that it is the act of the people, and as every individual may, to a certain degree, be considered as a party to it, it will be necessary to add a few words on the subject of representation, and of the power which a majority have to bind the minority.

The right of suffrage is one of the most important rights of a free citizen; and in small states where the citizens can easily be collected together, this right ought never to be dispensed with on any great political question. But in large communities, such a measure, however desirable, is utterly impracticable, for reasons too obvious to be dwelt upon: hence the necessity that the people should appoint a smaller and more convenient number to represent the aggregate mass of the citizens. This is done not only for the purposes of ordinary legislation, but in large states, and on questions which require discussion and deliberation, is the most eligible mode of proceeding, even where the vote of every individual of the nation should be desired. Therefore, when the convention at Philadelphia had made their report, the ordinary legislatures, with great propriety, recommended the appointment of state-conventions, for the sole and especial purpose of considering the propriety of adopting the constitution, thus proposed by the convention of the states. The deputies in most of the counties were chosen according to the prevailing sentiments of the people in favor of the constitution, the opinions of the candidates being generally previously known. It is much to be wished that this had been universally the case, since the will of the people would in that case have been unequivocally expressed.

The right of the majority to bind the minority, results from a due regard to the peace of society; and the little chance of unanimity in large societies or assemblies, which, if obtainable, would certainly be very desirable; but inasmuch as that is not to be expected, whilst the passions, interests, and powers of reason remain upon their present footing among mankind, in all matters relating to the society in general, some mode must be adopted to supply the want of unanimity. The most reasonable and convenient seems to be, that the will of the majority should supply this defect; for if the will of the majority is not permitted to prevail in questions where the whole society is interested, that of the minority necessarily must. The society therefore, in such a case, would be under the influence of a minority of its members, which, generally speaking, can on no principle be justified.

It is true there are cases, even under our own constitution, where the vote of a bare majority is not permitted to take effect; but this is only in points which have, or may be presumed to have, received the sanction of a former majority, as where an alteration in the constitution is proposed. In order, therefore, to give the greater stability to such points, they are not permitted to be altered by a bare majority: in cases also which are to be decided by a few, but which may, nevertheless, affect a variety of interests, it was conceived to be safest to require the assent of more than a bare majority; as, in concluding treaties with foreign nations, where the interests of a few states may be vitally affected, while that of a majority may be wholly unconcerned. Or, lastly, where the constitution has reposed a corresponding trust in different bodies who may happen to disagree in opinion; as, where the president of the United States shall return a bill to congress with his reasons for refusing his assent to it; in all these cases more than a bare majority are required to concur in favor of any measure, before it can be carried into complete effect.

7th. It is a compact by which the several states and the people thereof, respectively, have bound themselves to each other, and to the federal government.

Having shown that the constitution had its commencement with the body politic of the several states; and, that its final adoption and ratification was by the several legislatures referred to, and completed by conventions, especially called and appointed for that purpose, in each state; the acceptance of the constitution was not only an act of the body politic of each state, but of the people thereof respectively, in their sovereign character and capacity: the body politic was competent to bind itself so far as the constitution of the state permitted; but not having power to bind the people, in cases beyond their constitutional authority, the assent of the people was indispensably necessary to the validity of the compact, by which the rights of the people might be diminished, or submitted to a new jurisdiction, or in any manner affected. From hence, not only the body politic of the several states, but every citizen thereof, may be considered parties to the compact, and to have bound themselves reciprocally to each other, for the due observance of it; and, also to have bound themselves to the federal government, whose authority has been thereby created, and established.

8. Lastly. It is a compact by which the federal government is bound to the several states, and to every citizen of the United States.

Although the federal government can, in no possible view, be considered as a party to a compact made anterior to its existence, and by which it was, in fact, created; yet as the creature of that compact, it must be bound by it, to its creators, the several states in the union, and the citizens thereof. Having no existence but under the constitution, nor any rights, but such as that instrument confers; and those very rights being in fact duties; it can possess no legitimate power, but such as is absolutely necessary for the performance of a duty, prescribed and enjoined by the constitution. Its duties, then, become the exact measure of its powers; and wherever it exerts a power for any other purpose, than the performance of a duty prescribed by the constitution, it transgresses its proper limits, and violates the public trust. Its duties, being moreover imposed for the general benefit and security of the several states, in their politic character; and of the people, both in their sovereign, and individual capacity, if these objects be not obtained, the government will not answer the end of its creation: it is therefore bound to the several states, respectively, and to every citizen thereof, for the due execution of those duties. And the observance of this obligation is enforced, by the solemn sanction of an oath, from all who administer the government.

The constitution of the United States, then being that instrument by which the federal government hath been created; its powers defined, and limited; and the duties, and functions of its several departments prescribed; the government, thus established, may be pronounced to be a confederal republic, composed of several independent, and sovereign democratic states, united for their common defense, and security against foreign nations, and for the purposes of harmony, and mutual intercourse between each other; each state *retaining an entire liberty* of exercising, as it thinks proper, all those parts of its sovereignty, which are not mentioned in the constitution, or act of union, as parts that ought to be exercised in common. It is the supreme law of the land, and as such binding upon the federal government; the several states; and finally upon all the citizens of the United States.... It can not be controlled, or altered without the express consent of the body politic of three fourths of the states in the union, or, of the people, of an equal number of the states. To prevent the necessity of an immediate appeal to the latter, a method is pointed out, by which amendments may be proposed and ratified by the concurrent act of two thirds of both houses of congress, and three fourths of the state legislatures; but if congress should neglect to propose amendments in this way, when they may be deemed necessary, the concurrent sense of two thirds of the state legislatures may enforce congress to call a convention, the amendments proposed by which, when ratified by the conventions of three fourths of the states, become valid, as a part of the constitution. In either mode, the assent of the body politic of the states, is necessary, either to complete, or to originate the measure.

Here let us pause a moment, and reflect on the peculiar happiness of the people of the United States, thus to possess the power of correcting whatever errors may have crept into the constitution, or may hereafter be discovered therein, without the danger of those tremendous scenes which have convulsed every nation of the earth, in their attempts to ameliorate their condition; a power which they have already more than once successfully exercised. "Americans," says a writer whom I have before quoted, "ought to look upon themselves, at present, as almost the sole guardians and trustees of republican freedom: for other nations are not, as we are, at leisure to show it in its true and most enticing form. Whilst we contemplate with a laudable delight, the rapid growth of our prosperity, let us ascribe it to its true cause, the wholesome operation of our new political philosophy. Whatever blessings we enjoy, over and above what are to be found under the British government, whatever evils we avoid, to which the people of that government are exposed; for all these advantages are we indebted to the separation that has taken place, and the new order of things that has obtained among us. Let us be thankful to the parent of the universe, that he has given us, the first enjoyment of that freedom, which is intended in due time for the whole race of man. Let us diligently study the nature of our situation, that we may better know how to preserve and improve its advantages. But above all, let us study the genuine principles of DEMOCRACY, and steadily practice them, that we may refute the calumnies of those who would bring them into disgrace.

"Let us publish to the world, and let our conduct verify our assertions, that by democracy we mean not a state of licentiousness, nor a subversion of order, nor a defiance of legal authority. Let us convince mankind, that we understand by it, a well ordered government, endued with energy to fulfill all its intentions, to act with effect upon all delinquents, and to bring to punishment all offenders against the laws: but, at the same time, not a government of usurpation; not a government of prescription; but a government of compact, upon the ground of equal right, and equal obligation; in which the rights of each individual spring out of the engagement he has entered into, to perform the duties required of him by the community, whereby the same rights in others, are to be maintained inviolate."[12]

That mankind have a right to bind themselves by their own voluntary acts, can scarcely be questioned: but how far have they a right to enter into engagements to bind their posterity likewise? Are the acts of the dead binding upon their living posterity, to all generations; or has posterity the same natural rights which their ancestors have enjoyed before them? And if they have, what right have any generation of men to establish any particular form of government for succeeding generations?

The answer is not difficult: "Government," said the congress of the American States, in behalf of their constituents, "derives its just authority from the consent of the governed." This fundamental principle then may serve as a guide to direct our judgment with respect to the question. To which we may add, in the words of the author of Common Sense, a law is not binding upon posterity, merely, because it was made by their ancestors; but, because posterity have not repealed it. It is the acquiescence of posterity under the law, which continues its obligation upon them, and not any right which their ancestors had to bind them.

Until, therefore, the people of the United States, whether the present, or any future generation, shall think it necessary to alter, or revoke the present constitution of the United States, it must be received, respected, and obeyed among us, as the great and unequivocal declaration of the will of the people, and the supreme law of the land.

II. I shall now proceed to the second branch of our inquiry; namely; the structure and organization of the federal government of the United States, with its powers, jurisdiction, and rights, as established by the constitution of the United States, either independent of or connected with, those of the state governments, respectively; together with the mutual relation which subsists between the federal and state governments in virtue of that instrument.

And, here, we may be permitted shortly to repeat some former obser-

---

12. *Editor's note:* Tucker does not identify the writer here any further, possibly because it was his brother, Thomas Tudor Tucker, whom he had quoted in earlier essays.

vations: That, when the whole body of the people are possessed of the supreme power in the state, it is a democracy. That in such a government, the people are in some respects the sovereign, and in others, the subject. That, in the establishment of the constitution or fundamental law by which the state is to be governed, and in the appointment of magistrates, they are the sovereign: when the constitution of the state is fixed, the government organized, and the magistrates are appointed, every citizen is bound to obedience to the sovereign will thus expressed, and consequently becomes a subject.

That, in a democracy, the people ought to do, themselves whatever they conveniently can; that, what they can not do of themselves, must be committed to the management of ministers chosen by themselves; that they are their trustees and agents; and that a government thus formed and organized, may be styled a REPRESENTATIVE DEMOCRACY. That, the choice of ministers may be made, either, personally, by the whole body of the people; or by their deputies, chosen for that especial purpose, and in whom they can repose a proper confidence.

That, a number of independent states may unite themselves by one common bond or confederacy, for the purposes of common defense and safety, and for the more perfect preservation of amity between themselves, without any of them ceasing to be a perfect, independent, and sovereign state, retaining every power, jurisdiction and right, which it has not expressly agreed shall be exercised in common by, the confederacy of the states, and not by any individual state of the confederacy.

In the commonwealth of Virginia, the constitution, which is the fundamental law of the republic, hath been shown to be the act of the people. The establishment of this constitution was an immediate act of sovereignty by them. They declared, that all power is vested in, and consequently derived from the people. That magistrates are their trustees and servants, and at all times amenable to them. That government is instituted for the common benefit, protection, and security of the people. That no man or set of men are entitled to exclusive or separate emoluments or privileges but in consideration of public services. That the people have a right to uniform government; and, that no free government, or the blessings of liberty, can be preserved to any people but by a firm adherence to justice, moderation, temperance, frugality, and virtue; and by frequent recurrence to fundamental principles.[13] This is the principle of democracy.

By the establishment of this constitution, without any dependence upon any foreign power, Virginia became an independent and sovereign state: her rights were naturally the same as any other state's. She might, therefore, perform every act, which any other sovereign state, however constituted, could perform: she was also equal to any other state, or nation, being sovereign and independent.[14]

In becoming a member of the federal alliance established between the American states, by the articles of confederation, she expressly retained her sovereignty and independence. The constraints put upon the exercise of that sovereignty, by those articles, did not destroy its existence.

We have already shown that this system was defective in not providing the means, for a certain and regular revenue; and, that the inefficiency of the system, in that, and perhaps in some other aspects, gave rise to the new constitution. Of the immediate causes, and the particular motives and reasons which may be supposed to have led to the adoption of this important measure, together with a short history of its origin, progress, and final consummation; as also, of the foundation, and general nature of the new instrument of union between the states, a short explanation has likewise been attempted; nevertheless, we shall not infrequently have occasion to recur to, and perhaps to repeat, the same points, already touched upon; that the student may more perfectly understand, and bear in mind the reasons for the several provisions contained in the constitution, and the subsequent amendments to it, which have been proposed and ratified, and now form a part of it.

In the new instrument of union, there is no express reservation, as in the former, of the sovereignty of the several states; a subject of considerable alarm, and discussion, among those who were opposed to every-

13. Virginia Bill of Rights.
14. Vattel.

thing that resembled, or might hazard, a consolidation of them. The advocates of the constitution answered, that "an entire consolidation of the states into one complete national sovereignty, would imply a complete subordination of all the parties; and whatever power might remain in them would be altogether dependent on the general will. But as the plan of the convention aims only at a partial union, the state governments will clearly retain all the rights of sovereignty, which they had before, and which are not by that act exclusively delegated to the United States. That this exclusive delegation, or rather this alienation of state sovereignty, would only exist in three cases; where the constitution in express terms grants an exclusive authority to the union; where it grants in one instance an authority to the union, and in another prohibits the states from exercising the like authority; and where it grants an authority to the union, to which a similar authority in the states, would be absolutely, and totally contradictory, and repugnant."[15] The same writer elsewhere adds, "that it is not a mere possibility of inconvenience in the exercise of some powers, but an immediate and constitutional repugnancy that can by implication alienate and extinguish a preexisting right of sovereignty." And further, that "the necessity of a concurrent jurisdiction in certain cases, results from the division of the sovereign power; and the rule that all authorities of which the states are not explicitly divested in favor of the union, remain with them in full vigor, is not only a theoretical consequence of that division, but is clearly admitted by the whole tenor of the instrument."[16] And this constitution, as we have already had occasion to remark, is now confirmed by the subsequent amendments to the constitution, Art. 12. The right of sovereignty, therefore, in all cases not expressly ceded to the United States by the constitution, or prohibited by it to the several states, remains inviolably, with the states, respectively. What powers are comprehended under this reservation, will form a part of our present inquiry.

The institutions of all well constructed governments, as we have

15. Federalist, No. 32.
16. Ibid.

before had occasion to remark, have regard to two distinct objects; their connections, intercourse, and commerce with other states, and nations; and, the administration of justice between individuals, the preservation of their own domestic peace, and that of their citizens, and the advancement and promotion of the general happiness and prosperity of all who put themselves under their protection. Where the form of government is *national*, it is the duty of the body politic of the state to attend to *all* these objects. But where the government is not national, but federal, a *division* of power necessarily results from such a form of government; and the connections, intercourse and commerce of the confederate republic, with foreign states and nations; and with each other, as sovereign and independent states, naturally fall under the jurisdiction of the federal government, whilst the administration of all their other concerns, whatsoever, as naturally, remains with the states forming the confederacy.

This distinction may be considered as marking out the grand boundary between the limits of federal and of state jurisdiction; but a more intimate union between the states, in certain respects, being thought desirable, this grand boundary has not been strictly adhered to in the federal constitution, but in some few instances the authority of the federal government has been extended beyond it; a remarkable instance of which occurs in the power granted to congress to make uniform laws on the subject of bankruptcies, throughout the United States; a regulation in the strictest sense, municipal, and not federal. These instances are, however, few, and being in derogation of the municipal jurisdiction of the several states, ought for reasons already given to be strictly construed.

With regard to the principles of the organization, and structure of the federal government, whenever it departs from those of a confederate republic, it appears to conform to those of a representative democracy. The representatives in congress are chosen immediately by the people: the president may be chosen in a manner very nearly approaching a popular election, as in this state; though in some others, the election is further removed from the people; or rather, may be considered as taken away from them by their own legislatures, as in some of the northern states. All officers of the government, including the president, are impeachable for misconduct in office, and on conviction may be removed, and otherwise punished. These are prominent features of a representative democracy. In the appointment of senators its type is federal: in the mode of appointing the judges, it has been regarded as "squinting at monarchy."[17]

The grand boundary which was noticed above, as marking the obvious limits between the federal and state jurisdictions, may be considered as allotting to the former, jurisdiction in all cases arising under the political laws of the confederacy, or such as relate to its general concerns with foreign nations, or to the several states, as members of the confederacy; and to the latter the cognizance of all matters of a civil nature, or such as properly belong to the head of municipal law; except in some few cases, where, by a special provision contained in the constitution either concurrent, or exclusive, jurisdiction is granted to the federal government. Of this distribution we shall endeavor to take a nearer survey.

The objects of the political laws of a state as mentioned by an eminent writer, are, first, to provide for the necessities of the nation.

To encourage labor and industry, to provide necessary workmen, to promote agriculture, to advance commerce, to establish an easy communication between the different parts of the state, to regulate the rates of money, are ranked among the first objects of a good government. To encourage education, the liberal arts, and sciences, justice and polity, and to fortify itself against attacks from without; to preserve peace, to support the dignity and equality of the nation, and to form advantageous connections, and a beneficial intercourse with other states and nations, may be considered as forming the aggregate of the political laws of a nation.[18] I say nothing of the advancement of piety and religion; the present age seems to doubt of the necessity of any connection between church and state.

The powers delegated to congress by art. 1. sect. 8. of the new consti-

17. Speech of the late Patrick Henry, Esq., in the Virginia convention.
18. Vattel.

tution; to the president and senate by art. 2. sect. 2. and 3. and to the judiciary by art. 3. sect. 2. may severally be arranged under one, or the other of these heads.

Of these powers some appear to be exclusively vested in congress, or some other department of the federal government; in others, the states certainly have concurrent, though perhaps subordinate, powers; in a third class is not easy to determine, the limits of either the state, or federal authority. The administration of justice between the citizens of the same state, appears to be left without reserve, (except in a few instances which will be particularly noticed, in the sequel) to the jurisdiction and control of the state governments.

Thus have we endeavored to trace the line of separation between the jurisdictions of the federal and the state governments:... it is however a broad line, extending like the ecliptic, sometimes on one side, and sometimes on the other, of our political equator: but let us examine it more minutely.

All the powers delegated by the people of the United States to the government, whether the federal, or that of the state, must fall under one of the four following heads.

I. Those exclusively granted to the federal government.

II. Those in which the state has unquestionably concurrent, though perhaps subordinate powers with the federal government.

III. Those where the concurrent authority of the state government is questionable; or controllable by congress.

IV. Those reserved to the states, exclusively.

These powers are either legislative, executive, or judiciary: we shall examine them under their respective heads.

I. The powers exclusively granted to the federal government.

Of these,

1. The legislative: or those vested in congress; that body being empowered,

    1. To borrow money on the credit of the United States.

    2. To regulate commerce

        1. With foreign nations;

        2. Among the several states; and

3. With the Indian tribes. The commerce between the individuals of the same state, being reserved to the state governments.

3. To coin money, regulate the value thereof, and the value of foreign coin.

4. To fix the standard of weights and measures. These last powers seem to be a necessary appendage to that of regulating commerce.

5. To provide for the punishment of counterfeiting the securities and current coin of the United States.

6. To constitute tribunals, under the federal government, inferior to the supreme court.

7. To define and punish,

   1. Piracies;

   2. Felonies on the high seas;

   3. Offenses against the law of nations.

8. And to declare the punishment of treason against the United States.

9. To declare war; grant letters of marque and reprisal; and make rules concerning captures on land and water.

10. To provide and maintain a navy, [in time of peace.]

11. To make rules for the regulation and government of the land and naval forces.

12. To raise and support armies, [in time of peace.]

It is at least doubtful whether any such power as that last mentioned, was intended to be entrusted to the government, except in case of eminent danger of hostility; at least beyond the necessary guards for forts, magazines, arsenals, &c. and even in these cases the constitution seems to have provided that the service should be performed by the militia of the United States.

13. To provide for calling forth the militia, when necessary to be employed in the service of the United States.

14. And for governing them when so employed.

15. To provide for organizing and disciplining the militia.

16. To exercise exclusive jurisdiction within the ten miles square, where the seat of government shall be permanently established; and in

forts, magazines, arsenals, dock-yards, and other places ceded for the use of the federal government.

17. To prescribe the manner in which the public acts, records and judicial proceedings of the states shall be proved, in order to their obtaining faith and credit in other states, and the effect thereof.

18. To establish an uniform rule of naturalization.

19. And to make all laws necessary and proper for carrying the powers vested in the federal government into execution.

2. The powers vested in the executive department of the government of the United States, are all exclusive of the authority of the state government.

These are,

1. To make treaties.

2. To appoint ambassadors, ministers, and consuls.

3. Judges of the supreme courts, and all other officers of the United States, except such as are vested by congress in the president alone, in the courts of law of the United States, or, in the heads of departments.

3. The judicial power of the United States seems to be exclusively vested in the tribunals of the federal government.

1. In all cases affecting ambassadors, other public ministers and consuls.

2. In all cases of admiralty and maritime jurisdiction.

3. In controversies between two or more states.

4. In controversies between a state, and any foreign state.

5. In all cases of impeachment against an officer of the federal government.

To which I shall add,

6. In controversies to which the United States are a party, and

7. In all trials for offenses against the constitution, or laws of the federal government.

In which two last cases, I am inclined to suppose, that congress are not restrained from vesting the cognizance of any case, comprehended under those heads, in the state courts, should they find it advisable so to do, especially in fiscal proceedings, and lesser offenses against the peace.

The preceding enumeration seems to comprehend all the cases applicable to our first head: we shall now proceed to consider.

II. Those in which the state has unquestionably concurrent, though perhaps subordinate powers, with the federal government.

Of these,

1. The legislature hath unquestionable power.
    1. To impose taxes, and duties;
    2. Excises, for the support of its own domestic establishment.
    3. Imposts, or duties on exports, if absolutely necessary for the purpose of executing its inspection laws.
    4. To establish post-offices, and
    5. Post roads, within its own precincts or territory, so that they do not contravene the establishments of the federal government.
    6. To promote the progress of science, and useful arts by securing to the authors and inventors the exclusive right, within the state, to their respective writings and discoveries.
    7. To provide for arming the militia of the state; and to call them forth when necessary for their internal defense.
    8. To train and keep troops, and
    9. Ships of war in time of war.
    10. And to engage in war, when actually invaded; or in such imminent danger as will not admit of delay.
    11. And to propose amendments to the federal constitution.

To these we may add, that the judicial power of the state must be presumed to possess concurrent, though perhaps subordinate powers with the courts of the United States in the following cases:

1. In controversies between the state, and
    1. The citizens of another state,

2. Foreign citizens, or subjects.[19]

2. Between citizens of different states; if the defendant reside within the state claiming jurisdiction.

3. Between citizens of the same state claiming lands within the state, under grants from different states.

In all which cases, there were neither express words, nor any necessary implication that the states should be abridged of the powers in these respects, which as states they must have possessed.... we must therefore refer these powers to the twelfth article of the amendments to the constitution of the United States.

It is no less true, that the federal government possessing powers of deciding in these cases, the decision of the federal judiciary, is according to the principles and nature of our government, paramount to that of the state judiciary. Causes instituted in the state courts are therefore liable to reexamination in the federal courts; and, perhaps in all these cases to removal in the manner pointed out by the act of congress.

III. Let us now take a short view of those powers, where the concurrent authority of the state government, either is questionable; or subject to the control of congress.

1. Congress being authorized to establish an uniform rule of naturalization, and uniform laws on the subject of bankruptcies throughout the United States, it may well be questioned how far the states can possess any concurrent authority, on these subjects.

If, however, a doubt should arise respecting the former, it might be presumed, that the rights intended to be conferred by this uniform rule of naturalization, should be, in general, confined to such as might be derived from the federal government, without infringing those rights which peculiarly appertain to the states. Thus a person naturalized pursuant to the laws of the United States, would undoubtedly acquire every

19. But now by the thirteenth article of the amendments [i.e., the Eleventh Amendment] to the C.U.S. the states have exclusive jurisdiction in these causes.

right that any other citizen possesses, as a citizen of the United States, except such as the constitution expressly denies, or defers the enjoyment of; and such as the constitution of laws of the individual states require on the part of those who are candidates for office under the authority of the states. Five years residence, for example, is required by the laws of Virginia, before any naturalized foreigner is capable of being elected to any office under the state. It is presumable that his being naturalized under the laws of the United States would not supercede the necessity of this qualification.

In respect to bankruptcies it may be questioned whether the power of congress extends to cases arising between citizen and citizen of the same state, since their power does not extend to the internal or domestic commerce of the state, as we have already shown. Yet, on the other hand it may with great strength of reasoning be insisted, that here is a special case in which the power of the federal government extends to internal as well as foreign commerce; and that a contrary construction would probably defeat the constitution, which could not prescribe an uniform rule, without comprehending such cases as well as others.

2. The following powers appear to be vested in the federal government, but may be also exercised by the states, with the consent of the congress, viz.

    1. To lay imports or duties on goods imported into any state from a foreign state.

    2. To lay and duty of tonnage.

    3. To keep troops, or

    4. Ships of war, in time of peace.

    5. To enter into any compact or agreement with any other state, or,

    6. With any foreign power.

    7. To engage in war when not actually invaded, or in such imminent danger as will not admit of delay.

This finishes the actual enumeration of the powers granted to the federal government, except what relates to the ceded territory, and the erection of new states, and some of the provisions which do not seem necessary to be recapitulated here, though we shall have occasion to notice them hereafter. There remains only to mention,

IV. The powers reserved to the states exclusively,

The twelfth article of the amendments to the constitution of the United States, declares, that the powers not delegated to the United States by the constitution, nor prohibited by it to the states, are reserved to the states respectively, or to the people.

The powers absolutely prohibited to the states by the constitution, are, shortly, contained in article 1. section 10, viz.

1. No state shall enter into any treaty, alliance or confederation.

2. Nor grant letters of marque and reprisal.

3. Nor coin money.

4. Nor emit bills of credit.

5. Nor make any thing but gold and silver coins a tender in payment of debts.

6. Nor pass any bill of attainder.

7. Nor any expost facto law.

8. Nor any law impairing the obligation of contracts.

9. Nor grant any title of nobility.... Concerning all which, we shall make some few observations hereafter.

All other powers of government whatsoever, except these, and such as fall properly under the first or third heads above-mentioned, consistent with the fundamental laws, nature, and principle of a democratic state, are therefore reserved to the state governments.[20]

From this view of the powers delegated to the federal government, it will clearly appear, that those exclusively granted to it have no relation to

20. "The powers delegated by the proposed constitution of the federal government, are few and defined. Those which are to remain in the state governments are numerous and indefinite. The former will be exercised principally on external objects, as war, peace, negociation and foreign commerce; with which last, the power of taxation will for the most part be connected. The powers reserved to the several states, will extend to all the objects, which in the ordinary course of affairs, concern the lives, liberties, and properties of the people; and the internal order, improvement, and prosperity of the state." Federalist, No. 45.

the domestic economy of the state. The right of property, with all its train of incidents, except in the case of authors, and inventors, seems to have been left exclusively to the state regulations; and the rights of persons appear to be no further subject to the control of the federal government, than may be necessary to support the dignity and faith of the nation in its federal or foreign engagements, and obligations; or its existence and unity as the depositary and administrator of the political councils and measures of the united republics.... Crimes and misdemeanors, if they affect not the existence of the federal government; or those objects to which its jurisdiction expressly extends, however heinous in a moral light, are not cognizable by the federal courts; unless committed within certain fixed and determinate territorial limits, to which the exclusive legislative power granted to congress, expressly extends. Their punishment, in all other cases, exclusively, belongs to the state jurisprudence.

The federal government then, appears to be the organ through which the united republics communicate with foreign nations, and with each other. Their submission to its operation is voluntary: its councils, its sovereignty is an emanation from theirs, not a flame by which they have been consumed, nor a vortex in which they are swallowed up. Each is still a perfect state, still sovereign, still independent, and still capable, should the occasion require, to resume the exercise of its functions, as such, in the most unlimited extent.

But until the time shall arrive when the occasion requires a resumption of the rights of sovereignty by the several states (and far be that period removed when it shall happen) the exercise of the rights of sovereignty by the states individually, is wholly suspended, or discontinued, in the cases before mentioned: nor can that suspension ever be removed, so long as the present constitution remains unchanged, but by the dissolution of the bonds of union. An event which no good citizen can wish, and which no good, or wise administration will ever hazard.

Let us now take a view of the federal and state constitutions, and examine the structure and organization of the government, arising from their mutual connection, and the distribution of power among the several branches or departments of each, respectively.

The powers of government, both by the federal and state constitution, are distributed under three heads, the Legislative, Executive, and Judiciary; and these three departments the state constitution expressly declares shall be separate and distinct, so that neither exercise the powers properly belonging to the other. We shall nevertheless find that the constitution itself has in many respects blended them; assigning to the legislative body, duties, which, in strictness, belong to the executive; as in the appointment of the officers of government, &c. Yet this is undoubtedly conformable to the nature of a democracy in this, that the appointments is vested in the immediate representatives of the people. The constitution of the United States seems upon the same principle to have vested congress, in whom the legislative power is reposed, with powers absolutely foreign from the exercise of legislation, strictly speaking; but which will appear upon a scrutiny to have been more safely and beneficially entrusted to that department, than they could have been to any other whatsoever. Yet these deviations from the fundamental maxims of the government are to be construed strictly, and not made use of as precedents to justify others, where the constitution by its silence must be presumed to have referred it to that head under which it properly falls.

In the course of this investigation, we shall have occasion to inquire into the constituent parts of these several departments; with the mode of constituting them; the periods for which they are chosen; their respective qualifications, duties, and privileges; with the manner of removing them from, and punishing them for, any misconduct in office.

We shall begin with the federal government.

I. Of the congress.

1. The first article of the federal constitution, declares, that all legislative powers therein granted shall be vested in a congress of the United States, which shall consist of a senate and house of representatives. These, therefore, are the constituent parts of the federal legislature.

2. & 3. The next section prescribes the manner in which the last of

these bodies shall be chosen, that is to say, every second year, by the people of the several states; the qualifications of the electors being the same as that of electors of the most numerous branch of the state legislature.

The same article provides that representatives and direct taxes shall be apportioned among the several states according to their respective numbers, to be determined by adding to the whole number of free persons, including those bound to service for a term of years, and excluding Indians not taxed, three fifths of all other persons; according to an actual enumeration to be made every ten years: but the number of representatives is limited to one for every thirty thousand persons.

This mode of ascertaining the number of representatives, and the inseparable connection thereby established between the benefits and burdens of the state, seems to be more consonant with the true principles of representation than any other which has hitherto been suggested. For every man, in his individual capacity, has an equal right to vote in matters which concern the whole community: no just reason therefore can be assigned why ten men in one part of the community should have greater weight in its councils, than one hundred in a different place, as is the case in England, where a borough composed of half a dozen freeholders, sends perhaps as many representatives to parliament, as a county which contains as many thousands; this unreasonable disparity appears to be happily guarded against by our constitution. It may be doubted indeed how far the apportionment of the numbers, as it respects slaves, is founded upon the principles of perfect equality; and if it be not, it may be a further question whether the advantage preponderates on the side of the states that have the most, or the fewest slaves amongst them; for, if on the one hand it be urged, the slaves are not in the rank of persons, being no more than goods or chattels, according to the opinion of the Roman jurists, and consequently not entitled to representation, it may be answered that the ratio of representation and taxation being the same, this additional weight in council is purchased at an expense which secures the opposite party from the abuse of it in the imposition of burdens on the government. On the other hand, it must be remembered, that the two fifths of this class of people who are not represented, are by that means exempted from taxation. An exemption which probably took its rise from the unprofitable condition of that proportion of the number of slaves.

The times, places and manner of holding elections for representatives and senators, shall be prescribed in each state by the legislature; subject nevertheless to such alterations as congress may make, except as to the places of choosing senators.

It cannot be denied, that this article vests a power in congress, the exercise of which, if not really dangerous to the liberties of the states, may at least interrupt their tranquility, unless dictated by the utmost wisdom and discretion. In some of the states the vote is conducted by ballot, in others *viva voce*. In some the members are chosen by a general ticket or ballot of the whole state; in others the representatives are chosen by districts. Without entering into the discussion of the preference due to either of these modes, we may venture to pronounce that the states respectively will be tenacious of that to which their own constitution or laws may have given the preference: any attempt to render the manner of election uniform must therefore inevitably produce discontents among the states. Hitherto the congress has wisely left this article to the direction of the state governments. The manner of proceeding in this state, as established by the act of 1788, (V.L.) c. 2. amended by the act of 1792. c. 1, is shortly, as follows.

The act divides the states into as many districts, as there are representatives to be chosen, and directs that the persons qualified by law to vote for members to the house of delegates, in each county composing a district, shall assemble at their respective court houses, on the third Monday in March, (now altered by the act of 1798. c. 14. to the fourth Wednesday in April) in every second year, and then and there vote for a proper person as a representative in congress. The election to be conducted by the high sheriff, or in case of sickness or inability to attend, one of his deputies, in the same manner as the elections for delegates, except that as no determination is to be had by view, but only by the polls, the votes being publicly taken *viva voce*. Immediately after the closing of the poll, the clerk having first signed the same and made oath to the truth thereof, is to deliver it to the sheriff; the sheriffs of the respective counties in the district shall within seven days thereafter, assemble at the court house of the county first named in the district, compare their respective polls, and return the person having the greater number of votes, or in case of an equality of votes, giving their own votes. Duplicates of such return under the hands and seals of the sheriffs are to be sent one to the governor, the other to the representative elected, with ten days thereafter under the penalty of 100$, and poll book under a similar penalty are to be returned again to the clerk of the counties respectively. The governor is moreover required to transmit to congress without delay the returns made to him. The act further provides that no person shall, during the same election, vote more than once for the same candidate; under the penalty of one hundred dollars. This provision was made to prevent persons voting in several counties within the same district.

The representatives by this bill are chosen immediately by the people, in a public manner, by the electors within an aggregate number of counties composing a district. The person chosen seems to be strictly the delegate of those by whom he is chosen, and bound by their instructions whenever they think proper to exercise the right. This principle has been denied by the British writers on their own government, and a deference to the maxims of that government probably prevented the decision of the question, when agitated in congress in the form of an article to a proposed bill of rights: but if the maxim be true, that all power is derived from the people; that magistrates are their trustees and servants, and at all times amenable to them for their conduct, it seems impossible to withhold our assent from the proposition, that in a popular government the representative is bound to speak the sense of his constituents upon every subject, where he is informed of it. The difficulty of collecting the sense of the people upon any question, forms no argument against their right to express that sense when they shall think proper so to do. Otherwise, by whatever denomination the government may be called, it is a confined aristocracy, in which the people have nothing more to do than to choose their rulers, over whose proceedings, however despotic, and repugnant to the nature and principles of the fundamental laws of the state, they have no control. It will be answered, that the power of removing and punishing is not denied by this doctrine, I answer, that the power of preventing offenses against the commonwealth, is to be preferred to that of punishing offenders; and if the government is virtually in the people, it ought to be so organized, that whenever they choose to exercise the right of governing, they may do it without destroying its existence. Corruption and mal-administration, unchecked, may drive them to a resumption of all the powers which they have entrusted to the government, and bring on tumults and disturbances which will end only with its final dissolution: an event to be apprehended in all governments, but particularly in democracies, since dissatisfaction towards the administration may produce a desire of change in the constitution itself; and every change by which the government is in the smallest degree removed from its republican nature and principle, must be for the worse. This danger is effectually avoided by the principle here contended for. The aggregate of mankind understand their own interest and their own happiness better than any individual: they never can be supposed to have resigned the right of judging for themselves to any set of men whatsoever; it is a right which can never be voluntarily resigned, though it may be wrested from their hands by tyranny, or violated by the infidelity and perfidy of their servants.

When vacancies happen in the representation from any state, the executive authority thereof, shall issue writs of election to fill the vacancies.

The manner of electing senators is much shorter, being vested in the legislatures of the several states; each state being entitled to two senators, whose periods of service are six years, and each senator is entitled to one vote.

The election of representatives we have seen, is by a mode strictly popular. Had the distinction of states been entirely done away, there could have been no good reason assigned, perhaps, why the election of senators should not have been assimilated thereto, at least in respect to numbers, since in a government where all parts are equal, no preference under any pretext whatsoever ought to be allowed to any one part, over the rest. Why then should Rhode Island and Delaware have as many representatives in the senate as Virginia and Massachusetts, which contain ten times their respective numbers? It has been answered, the senate are chosen to represent the states in their sovereign capacity, as moral bodies, who as such, are all equal; the smallest republic, as a sovereign state, being equal to the most powerful monarchy upon earth. As states, then, Rhode Island and Delaware are entitled to an equal weight in council on all occasions, where that weight does not impose a burden upon the other states in the union. Now as the relation between taxation and representation, in one branch of the legislature, was fixed by an invariable standard, and as that branch of the legislature possesses the exclusive right of originating bills on the subject of revenue, the undue weight of the smaller states is guarded against, effectually, in the imposition of burdens. In all other cases their interests, as states, are equal, and deserve equal attention from the confederate government. This could no way be so effectually pro-vided for, as in giving them equal weight in the second branch of the leg-islature, and in the executive whose province it is to make treaties, &c.... Without this equality, somewhere, the union could not, under any pos-sible view, have been considered as an equal alliance between equal states. The disparity which must have prevailed, had the apportionment of rep-resentation been the same in the senate as in the other house, would have been such as to have submitted the smaller states to the most debasing dependence. I cannot, therefore, but regard this particular in the consti-tution, as one of the happiest traits in it, and calculated to cement the union equally with any other provision that it contains.

This body is not, like the former, dissolved at the end of the period for which its members were elected; it is a permanent, perpetual body; the members, indeed, are liable to a partial change every two years, the senate being divided into three classes, one of which is vacated every sec-ond year, so that a total change in the members may be made in six years, but cannot possibly be effected, without the intervention of death, in less time.... According to the arrangements of the classes actually made, both the senators from the same state shall never vacate their seats at the same time; a provision which certainly has its advantages, as no state is there-by in danger of being not represented at any time.

This mode of constituting the senate, seems liable to some important objections.[21] The perpetuity of the body is favorable to every stride it may be disposed to make towards extending its own power and influence in the government: a tendency to be discovered in all bodies, however constituted, and to which no effectual check can be opposed, but frequent dissolutions and elections. It is no satisfactory answer to this objection, that the members are removable, though the body itself be perpetual. The change, even were the members ineligible a second time, would be too gradual, to effect any counterpoise to this prevailing principle.

It has been insisted that the perpetuity of this body, is the only security to be found in the constitution against that instability of councils and of measures which has marked the proceedings of those states, where no such check is provided by the constitution.[22] To which it may be answered, that every newly established government must be a government of experiment.... The design of a machine may appear correct, the model perfect, and adapted to all the purposes which the original inventor proposed: yet a thousand defects may be discovered when the actual application of its powers is made, and, many useful improvements, in time, become obvious, to the eyes of a far less skillful mechanic. Their success and perfection must, however, still depend upon actual experiment, and that experiment may suggest still further improvement. Are we to reject these because they did not occur to the first projector, though evidently growing out of his original design? Or, if on the other hand we have unwarily adopted that as an improvement, which experiment shall evince to be a defect, shall we be so wedded to error as to persist in the practice of it, for no better reason than that we have once fallen into it.

In case of vacancies in the office of senator, the executive of the state are authorized to make a temporary appointment until the next meeting of the legislature, who are then to fill the vacancy.

4. The qualifications of the members of these bodies respectively, are,

21. See Federalist, No. 62.
22. Ibid.

that both senators and representatives should have been citizens of the United States, the former nine, and the latter seven years, and be citizens also of that state for which they shall be chosen, at the time of their election; to which the law of the state adds, that a representative should be a free holder and resident of the district for which he is chosen: a wise provision and perfectly consonant with the principles of representation, which should be made from the body of the people with whom the representative must be presumed to have a common interest, but which perhaps may be rendered nugatory, by the constitution which imposes no such condition, and which makes each house the judge of the qualifications, as well as of the elections and returns of its own members. The constitution further requires that a representative should be twenty-five, and a senator thirty years of age, to which may be added that no person holding any office under the United States shall be a member of either house during his continuance in office.

So much for the qualifications of the members of congress, to which we may subjoin their incapacities, as individuals, during the period for which they are elected; these are shortly an incapacity of being appointed to any civil office under the United States, which shall have been created or the emoluments thereof increased during their time. An admirable provision against venality, but which, it is to be feared, is not sufficiently guarded to prevent evasion. And to preclude undue influence on the part of the federal government over that of the commonwealth, it is provided by a law of the state, that the members of congress shall be ineligible to, and incapable of holding any seat in either house of assembly, or any legislative, executive, or judicial office, or other lucrative office whatsoever, under the government of this commonwealth: and this last provision is by the same act extended to all persons holding any legislative, executive, judicial or other lucrative office whatsoever under the United States, with a proviso in favor of militia officers, and county court magistrates.

5. Senators and representatives during their attendance in congress, as also in travelling to and returning from the place of their session, are privileged from arrest in all cases, except treason, felony, and breach of the

peace, and no speech or debate in either house can be questioned in any other place. They are also entitled to a compensation for their services, to be ascertained by law, and paid out of the treasury of the United States.

These are all the personal privileges which the constitution gives to the members of the federal legislature. And here I shall transcribe the words of one of its former members on a similar occasion....."The members of the legislature ought certainly to have no privilege but what is demonstrably essential to the freedom, and welfare of their constituents. The state is not made to dignify its officers, but the officers to serve the state. The dignity of a commonwealth does not consist in the elevation of one, or a few, but in the equal freedom of the whole. The privileges of the legislature ought to be defined by the constitution, and should be fixed as low as is consistent with the public welfare."[23]...This is the point which the constitution appears to have had in view, and every happily to have attained; and it is to be sincerely wished, the question may never arise whether they ought to have been more, or less, limited.

Thus much for the privileges of the members; each house has moreover its own distinct privileges and powers; those of the house of representatives are,

1. To choose their own speaker, and other officers.

2. To originate all bills for raising a revenue; but the senate may propose, or concur with amendments, as on other bills.

3. This house also possesses the sole power of impeachment. These are all its exclusive privileges.

The vice-president of the United States is, by virtue of his office, president of the senate; but has no vote unless they be equally divided.

This power may at first view appear to be of no great consequence: it is however of the utmost importance; and the occasions on which it is said to have been exercised, will demonstrate the necessity of leaving it, as seldom as possible, to its full scope.[24] In fact this part of the constitu-

---

23. *Editor's note:* Here again, the unidentified writer is probably Thomas Tudor Tucker.

24. In the first session of the second Congress, the house of representatives passed a bill apportioning the number of representatives in the ratio of one for every thirty thou-

tion gives a decided influence in the legislature to that part of the United States from which the vice-president shall be elected. He has eventually a veto, without being obliged to assign his reasons for it; it is otherwise with the president. But to return to the senate.

1. In case of the absence of the vice-president, or of his exercising the office of president of the United States, they may choose a president pro tempore.... they have also a right of choosing all their other officers.

2. The senate have the sole power of trying impeachments. A most inordinate power, and, in some instances, utterly incompatible with their other functions, as we shall hereafter have occasion more fully to demonstrate.

3. The senate likewise constitute a part of the executive department .... the examination of which part of their constitution we shall take up under its proper head.

Exclusive of these privileges which the two houses possess, as contradistinguished from each other, each house possesses the right of determining the rules of its own proceedings; of punishing its members for disorderly behavior; and of expulsion, provided two-thirds concur therein.

What further powers or privileges the several houses of congress may constitutionally possess, has now become a question of no small importance. The great Bacon observes,[25] "that as exception strengthens the force of a law, in cases not excepted, so enumeration weakens it, in cases not enumerated." The powers vested in congress, the privileges of the members, and of each house, are severally enumerated in the constitution; not made exceptions from general powers, not enumerated. Consequently it would appear that they were not capable of extension, beyond the letter of the constitution itself. The twelfth article of the

---

sand. The Senate were equally divided upon this bill. Some of the members, though momently expected, being absent, the question was put, and carried by the decision of the vice president against the bill. If ever a case could be named under the constitution which seemed to belong solely to the representatives to determine, it was this. *Editor's note:* For Tucker, as for all good Virginia Republicans, John Adams was guilty of monarchical aspirations.

25. On the advancement of learning.

amendments to the constitution seems also not to favor a constructive extension of the powers of the federal government, or any department thereof; yet a case has occurred, which shows that the house of representatives have put a different construction on their powers. . . . On the 28th day of December, 1795, on information given by several members in their places (not upon oath,) of an attempt to corrupt them made by one Robert Randall, it was "resolved, that Mr. Speaker do issue his warrant directed to the sergeant at arms attending this house, commanding him to take into custody, wherever to be found, the body of the said Robert Randall, and the same in his custody to keep, subject to the further order and direction of the house."

"A warrant, pursuant to the said resolution, was accordingly prepared, signed by Mr. Speaker under his seal, attested by the clerk, and delivered to the sergeant, with order forthwith to execute the same, and make due return thereof to the house." The next day Randall was brought before the house in custody. He was detained in custody from that time to the 6th day of January, when a motion was made and seconded, that the house do come to the following resolution:

"Whereas any attempt to influence the conduct of this house, or its members, on subjects appertaining to their legislative functions, by motives other than the public advantage, is a high contempt of this house, and a breach of its privileges: and whereas it does appear to this house, by the information on oath of sundry members, and by the proceedings thereon had before the house, that Robert Randall did attempt to influence the conduct of the said members, in a matter relating to their legislative functions, to wit, the sale of a large portion of the public property, by motives of private emolument to the said members, other than, and distinct from the public advantage: therefore,

"Resolved, That the said Robert Randall has thereby committed a high contempt of this house, and a breach of its privileges.

"The previous question thereon was called for by five members, to wit . . . . shall the main question, to agree to the said resolution, be now put?

"And on the question . . . . shall the said main question be now put?

"It passed in the negative.

"A motion was then made and seconded, that the house do come to the following resolution:

"Resolved, that it appears to this house, that Robert Randall has been guilty of a contempt to, and a breach of the privileges of this house, by attempting to corrupt the integrity of its members, in the manner laid to his charge.

"And on the question thereupon,

"It was resolved in the affirmative, Yeas, 78. Nays, 17.

"Another motion was then made and seconded, that the house do come to the following resolution:

"Resolved, that the said Robert Randall be brought to the bar, reprimanded by the speaker, and committed to the custody of the sergeant at arms, until the further order of this house.

"And on the question thereupon,

"It was resolved in the affirmative.

"Pursuant thereto, the said Robert Randall was brought to the bar in custody, reprimanded by Mr. Speaker, and remanded in custody of the sergeant at arms, until further order of the house.

"The 18th of January, the house proceeded to consider the petition of Robert Randall, praying to be released from the imprisonment to which he is subject, by the order of this house, which lay on the table: whereupon,

"Resolved, That Robert Randall be discharged from the custody of the sergeant at arms, upon the payment of fees.... Proceedings of the house of representatives of the United States, in the case of Robert Randall and Charles Whitney.... Published by order of the house of representatives."

Upon these proceedings a few remarks may not be deemed impertinent in this place.

1. By the amendments to the constitution, no person shall be deprived of life, liberty, or property, without due process of law.

Due process of law as described by Sir Edward Coke, is by indictment or presentment of good and lawful men, where such deeds be done in due manner, or by writ original of the common law. Due process of law must then be had before a judicial court, or a judicial magistrate. The judicial power of the United States is vested in one supreme court, and such inferior tribunals, as congress may establish, and extends to all cases in law and equity, arising under the constitution, &c. In the distribution of the powers of government, the legislative powers were vested in congress.... the executive powers (except in the instances particularly enumerated,) in the president and senate. The judicial powers (except in the cases particularly enumerated in the first article) in the courts: the word *the*, used in defining the powers of the executive, and of the judiciary, is with these exceptions, co-extensive in its signification with the word *all*: for all the powers granted by the constitution are either legislative, and executive, or judicial; to keep them for ever separate and distinct, except in the cases positively enumerated, has been uniformly the policy, and constitutes one of the fundamental principles of the American governments.

2. It will be urged, perhaps, that the house of representatives of the United States is, like a British house of commons, a judicial court: to which the answer is, it is neither established as such by the constitution (except in respect to its own members,) nor has it been, nor can it be so established by authority of congress; for all the courts of the United States must be composed of judges commissioned by the president of the United States, and holding their offices during good behavior, and not by the unstable tenure of biennial elections.

3. The amendments to the constitution expressly provide, "that no warrant shall issue but upon probable cause supported by oath or affirmation." The speaker's warrant for apprehending Randall was not supported by either: for the word affirmation must be understood as such a solemn asseveration by persons religiously scrupulous of swearing, as amounts in judicial proceedings to an oath, in point of obligation and penal consequences, and not to a bare assertion, however positive, made in any other manner. That the information of the members was made in the solemn manner before mentioned, or that their oath was dispensed with on account of religious scruples, cannot be presumed, since they were all sworn to their several declarations on the fourth of January, and not before.

4. The amendments to the constitution expressly provide, that no person shall be held to answer to a capital, or otherwise infamous crime, unless on presentment, or indictment of a grand jury. Randall's offense was certainly an infamous crime, for which he deserved exemplary punishment. On the twenty-ninth of December, being brought to the bar in custody, it was demanded of him, whether he did admit or deny the truth of the charge against him; to which he answered, that he was not prepared to admit or deny the same. On the fourth of January, being again brought to the bar in custody, it was demanded of him by Mr. Speaker what he had to say in his defense; to which he answered, that he was not guilty. Here then Randall was held to answer for an infamous crime, without indictment or presentment of a grand jury.

5. The constitution provides, that the trial of all crimes, except in cases of impeachment, shall be by a jury.

After the prisoner had pleaded not guilty, and made an application to the house that the information might be sworn to, the house (after some preliminary proceedings) "resumed the hearing of his trial, and made some progress therein"; the next day they resumed it; and resolved to "proceed to a final decision on the said case" the next day.

6. The amendments to the constitution provide, that in all criminal prosecutions, the accused shall enjoy the right to a speedy and public trial by an impartial jury of the state and district where the crime shall have been committed.

On the sixth of January the house proceeded to a final decision on the case of Robert Randall.

Five members of the house were his accusers, triers, and judges; four of these voted him guilty; the fifth voted with the minority; whether, as not conceiving him guilty, or as not conceiving the house to be a proper tribunal to condemn him, (both questions being blended in the resolution), does not appear.... Was this a trial by an impartial jury? Again,

By the amendments to the constitution, the jury should be from the state and district in which the crime was committed. The triers were composed of members, *huc undique collatis.*

Each house is moreover the judge of the elections, returns, and qualifications of its own members, as we have before observed; a majority of each is requisite to form a quorum to do business; a provision of no small importance, since otherwise it is possible that the concerns of the nation might be decided by a very small portion of its representatives; if, as has been done in other assemblies, the quorum were left to the decision of the body itself. In England, where there are near six hundred members in the house of commons, the number of 45 constitutes a quorum to do business. Is it possible that the nation can be represented by that number, whilst the elections stand upon their present footing? But although it requires a majority of the house of representatives, or the senate, to do the business of the nation, a smaller number may adjourn from day to day, and compel the attendance of absent members.

Each house is moreover required to keep a journal of its proceedings, and from time to time to publish the same; excepting such parts as may in their judgments require secrecy; a provision evidently calculated to defeat the salutary purposes of the former part of the rule; since every measure which intrigue may dictate, or cabal enforce, may thus be hid from the public eye, by being consigned to the secret journals; an expedient too obvious to be neglected whenever it may be found advisable.

The yeas and nays of the members of either house, on any question, shall, at the desire of one-fifth of those present, be entered on the journal. Any member of the house of lords in England may enter his protest on the journals of the house, but the commons possess no such privilege. In a representative government, it is of the utmost consequence that the people should be informed of the conduct of their delegates individually, as well as collectively. This purpose is fully answered by the rule here spoken of. But to prevent a call of the yeas and nays too frequently, as is said to have been practiced in the former congress, the constitution has set some reasonable limits to the exercise of this power, by requiring that at least one-fifth of the members present should concur in the expediency of it.

To prevent those inconveniences which might arise from the national legislatures omitting to assemble as often as the affairs of the nation require, the constitution provides, that congress shall assemble, at least once a year, and fixes the period of assembling to the first Monday of December, unless they shall by law appoint another day. It likewise vests the president of the United States with the power of convening them, or either house, on extraordinary occasions.

Lastly, to prevent the evils which might result from the want of a proper concert and good understanding between the houses, it is provided, that neither house, during the session of congress shall, without consent of the other, adjourn for more than three days, nor to any other place than that in which the two houses shall be sitting. And further to guard against any inconvenience which might result from their disagreement, it is provided, that in such case the president may adjourn them to any time he shall think proper. This is the only instance in which the constitution permits an interference with the duration of the session, on the part of the executive; and we have already seen, that though the power of convening the congress is entrusted, on extraordinary occasions, to the president of the United States, yet he has none to prevent, or even retard their assembling, at any time, by their own adjournment, or at certain stated periods fixed by law, or by the constitution.

The duration of congress is necessarily limited to two years, the period for which the house of representatives is chosen. The period of its commencement seems to have been fixed to the fourth day of March, the day on which the first congress assembled, and that of its expiration to the third of that month biennially.... It is incapable of any other mode of termination, there being no power in any part of the government to dissolve it. By these wise and salutary provisions, it is effectually guarded against every possible encroachment on its independence. Very different from the constitution of the British parliament, since the crown may, at any time, put an end to a session by a prorogation, or to the existence of a parliament by a dissolution.

The president of the United States may be considered *sub modo,* as one of the constituent parts of congress, since the constitution requires that every bill, order, resolution, or vote, to which the concurrence of the senate and house of representatives may be necessary (except on a question of adjournment) shall be presented to him: if he approve he shall sign it, but if not he shall return it with his objections to that house in which it shall have originated, who shall enter the objections at large on their journal, and proceed to reconsider it. If after such reconsideration two thirds of that house agree to pass it, it shall be sent, together with the objections to the other house, by which it shall likewise be reconsidered, and if approved by two thirds of that house shall become a law. In all such cases the yeas and nays shall be entered on the journals of both houses. If any bill, &c. be not returned by the president within ten days, Sundays excepted, unless in case of adjournment, whereby the return is prevented, it shall nevertheless be a law &c.

This closes our hasty sketch of the constituent parts of the congress of the United States, with a short view of the duration and the outlines of the distinct powers, and privileges of both houses, as also of the individuals who compose them. Before we proceed to the investigation of the powers of the whole body thus formed, let us compare some of its most distinguished features, with those of the two houses of the British parliament, long held in idolatrous veneration, as a palladium of political freedom which some partial deity had bestowed upon that favorite nation, and presenting a model of perfection which the combined wisdom of nations, and of ages, could but faintly imitate, and never equal. We shall occasionally resume this comparison at different periods of our inquiry, in order to assist the student in the application of what he will meet with in authors on the subject of that far famed constitution, to the more recent institutions of our own.

In the course of this investigation I shall select those parts of the constitution of the British parliament, which in the opinion of one of its ablest advocates,[26] constitutes its superior excellence, and not infrequently quote his opinions in his own words. To these I shall occasionally oppose the sentiments of later writers of his own country, on the same subject; the maxims of our own government, or the adaptation of those of the British government to the constitution of the United States: by these means I apprehend a fair comparison of their respective merits,

26. *Editor's note:* Tucker is here referring to Blackstone.

as tending to promote the liberty and general happiness of the community, may be made.

I. The constituent parts of the British parliament, are, the house of commons, the house of lords, and the king, sitting there in his royal political capacity, in the union of which three estates the body politic of the kingdom consists. Analogous to which, though very differently constituted, we have seen the house of representatives and senate of the United States, and *sub modo* the president of the United States forming the general congress, or the supreme political legislature of the federal government. Thus far the great outlines of both governments appear to run parallel: they will however upon a nearer scrutiny be found frequently to diverge. We shall begin with the house of commons, which forms the democratical part of the British constitution.

"In a free state" says the author of the commentaries "every man who is supposed a free agent, ought to be in some measure his own governor, and therefore a branch at least of the legislative power should reside in the whole body of the people. In so large a state as Britain, therefore, it is very wisely contrived that the people should do that by their representatives, which it is impracticable to perform in person; representatives, chosen by a number of minute and separate districts, wherein all the voters are, or easily may be, distinguished." He adds, elsewhere, "In a democracy there can be no exercise of sovereignty, but by suffrage, which is the declaration of the people's will. In all democracies, therefore, it is of the utmost importance to regulate by whom and in what manner the suffrages are to be collected. In England where the people do not debate in a collective body, but by representation, the exercise of this sovereignty consists in the choice of representatives."

Such are the principles laid down by this distinguished writer, from whence one would be led to conclude that the elections for members of the house of commons were regulated in a manner as conformable thereto as possible. That where there was an equality of right, an equality of representation would also be found; and that the right of suffrage would be regulated by some uniform standard, so that the same class of men should not possess privileges in one place, which they are denied in another.

1. By equality of representation, it will be understood, that I mean the right which any given number of citizens possessing equal qualifications in respect to the right of suffrage, have, to an equal share in the councils of the nation by their representatives, as an equal number of their fellow citizens in any other part of the state enjoy.

In England and in Wales there are fifty-two counties, represented by knights, elected by the proprietors of lands; the cities and boroughs are represented by citizens and burgesses, chosen by the mercantile part, or supposed trading part of the nation.... The whole number of English representatives, is 513 and of Scots, 45. The members of boroughs now bear above a quadruple proportion to those for counties: from whence one would, at first, be apt to conclude, that the population or at least the number of electors in the counties were equal; and, that the boroughs were at least four times as populous as the counties, collectively. The former of these suppositions would be perfectly unfounded in truth; the latter perhaps may approach nearer to it. In truth, were the latter supposition well founded, the equality of representation would not be much advanced by it.... In London which is supposed to contain near a seventh part of the number of the inhabitants of all England, they are entitled to four members only in parliament. The inconsiderable borough of Melcomb Regis in Dorsetshire sends as many. Manchester and Birmingham, two large populous, flourishing, manufacturing towns, have no representative, whilst the depopulated borough of Old Sarum, without a house or an inhabitant, is the vehicle through which two members obtain their seats in parliament; a representation equal to that of the most populous county.

Many other corresponding instances might be adduced to prove the inequality of representation; but they are unnecessary.... In America the representation is in exact proportion to the inhabitants. Every part of the states is therefore equal represented, and consequently has an equal share in the government. Here the principle that the whole body of the

people should have a share in the legislature, and every individual entitled to vote, possess an equal voice, is practically enforced.... In England
it is a mere illusion.

It is but justice to acknowledge that attempts have repeatedly been
made, to effect a reform in this part of the British constitution: the voice
of the nation has more than once loudly demanded it.... but their
rulers, like the god Baal, have been otherwise employed; or deaf, or per-
adventure asleep, and could not be awaked.

2. As to the right of suffrage in the individual, nearly the same principle seems to prevail in respect to the qualification in lands, in both
countries; and the different manner of ascertaining it, is not sufficient
to require any remark. I shall only observe that copy-holders, whose
interest, in almost every other respect in their lands, seem to be equal to
that of a free-holder, (at least, such as have inheritances in them) are not
admitted to the right of suffrage. The proportion of copy-holders for
life, or of inheritance, to the freehold tenants of the counties, I have never
heard estimated: it is, however, very considerable.

"The right of voting in boroughs is various," says Blackstone, "depending entirely on the several charters, customs, and constitutions of the
respective places, which has occasioned infinite disputes." It may vary no
less perhaps in the different states of America, but there is this advantage, that however various, there can be little room for doubts, or disputes on the subject. In Virginia the qualification to vote in boroughs, is
as fixed and invariable as in the counties. One principle however must
not be lost sight of, which perhaps should have come under the last head.
No borough can ever be entitled to a representative, whenever the number of inhabitants shall, for the space of seven years together, be less than
half the number of the inhabitants of any county in Virginia. In England
the boroughs retain the right of representation, as we have seen, even
after they have lost their inhabitants. Another circumstance respecting
them is no less notorious; though the right of suffrage is in the burgher,
the power of sending the member to parliament is in the lord of the soil;
a number of boroughs being private property, and the burghers, who are
tenants, bound to vote as their lord shall direct: the shadow of the right

of suffrage is all these burghers possess.... to the exercise of that right they are as much strangers, as to the pyramids of Egypt, or the ruins of Palmyra. It is scarcely possible that the electors of America should ever be degraded to a similar state of political mechanism.

3. The qualification of the members is the next object of our comparison. In England a knight of the shire must possess an estate in lands of the value of 600£ sterling, per annum, and a member for a borough of one half that value, except the eldest sons of peers; and of persons qualified to be knights of shires, and members of the two universities.

This at first view appears to be a proper and necessary precaution, as far as it extends, to secure the independence of the members of that branch of the legislature. But this argument is neither conclusive in fact, nor even in theory. Neither of these sums is an adequate support for a man moving in the rank of a member of the British parliament. Luxury has taken too deep root in the nation to authorize the supposition generally; and if it fails in general, it is of little avail that a few instances may be found of persons in that sphere, whose expenses do not exceed the requisite qualification in point of fortune. But if the principle be admitted that an independent fortune be necessary to secure the independence of the member in his legislative conduct, it would seem that the measure ought to be the same to all the members, since, according to the doctrine laid down by our author, a member though chosen by a particular district, when elected, serves the whole realm, the end of his election not being particular, but general. An equality of qualification should then have taken place; and if 600£ is necessary to secure the independence of the member, those who possess but half as much ought to be excluded; on the other hand, if 300£ be a competent sum for that purpose, how injurious must that law be to the rights of the citizen, which requires the qualification which is acknowledged to be sufficient for every good purpose, to be doubled. But a qualification in respect to estate is neither equally nor uniformly required; if the member elected should happen to be the eldest son of a peer, or of a person qualified to be knight of the shire; in either of these cases it is altogether dispensed with. The effect of this, as it respects the former of these classes of men, we shall speak of hereafter. As to the latter, it is sufficient to say, that presumption is allowed to supply the place of evidence; and both the exceptions prove the deviation from the general principle to have originated in the influence of the aristocratical interest of the nation.

In America no qualification in point of estate is required in the representative in congress by the constitution; and perhaps we may with some propriety insist that any such qualification would be not only unnecessary, but contrary to the true interests of their constituents. In England the interests of the crown, of the nobles, and of the people, are confessedly distinct and often diametrically opposite. In America all are citizens possessing equal rights in their civil capacities and relations; there are no distinct orders among us, except while in the actual exercise of their several political functions. When the member quits his seat, or the magistrate descends from the bench, he is instantly one of the people. The pageantry of office reaches not beyond the threshold of the place where it is exercised; and civil distinctions, privileges or emoluments independent of the office are interdicted by the principles of our government. To secure the independence of the members conduct, perhaps no previous qualification, in point of estate may be requisite; though such a qualification might for another reason have been not improper: that by sharing in the burdens of government, he might be restrained from an undue imposition of them upon his constituents. The law of the state indeed requires that the representative should be a freeholder, as well as a resident in the district; but both these provisions, as they require qualifications which the constitution does not, may possibly be found to be nugatory, should any man possess a sufficient influence in a district in which he neither resides nor is a freeholder, to obtain a majority of the suffrages in his favor. But how strong soever the reasons in favor of a qualification in point of estate might have been, on the grounds last spoken of, they were overbalanced probably by two considerations.

First, that in a representative government, the people have an undoubted right to judge for themselves of the qualification of their delegate, and if their opinion of the integrity of their representative will supply the want of estate, there can be no reason for the government to interfere, by saying, that the latter must and shall overbalance the former.

Secondly; by requiring a qualification in estate it may often happen, that men the best qualified in other respects might be incapacitated from serving their country. To which we may add, that the compensation which the members receive for their services, is probably such an equivalent, as must secure them from undue influence, or concessions from motives of interest.

A second qualification required by the British constitution is, that the person elected shall be of the age of twenty-one years at the time of his election: ours with more caution and perhaps with better reason, requires that he shall have attained to the age of twenty-five years.

These are all the positive qualifications, in which there appears to be any very material difference worth remarking. Of negative ones, those which relate to the incapacity of certain descriptions of placemen and pensioners in England, are limited to a very small part of the host of the former who depend upon the crown for support; and in respect to the latter only such pensioners as hold during the pleasure of the crown, are excluded. A list of placemen and pensioners in either the present or last parliament of England was published some years ago.... I do not recollect their exact number, but I can be positive that it exceeded two hundred. A number sufficient to secure the most unlimited influence in the crown: to these let us add the eldest sons of peers, and ask whether in a question between the commons and the nobility, it would be probable that they would give an independent vote, against the order in which they soon hoped to obtain a permanent rank and station.

Lastly, let me ask, if the conduct of those borough members who hold their seats by the appointment of members of the other house, or perhaps of their own, may reasonably be expected to be uninfluenced by the nod of their patrons? Can a house thus constituted be said to represent the people, the democratic part of the government? Can they be said to form a check upon the proceedings of the nobility, or the measures of the crown?[27] The question only requires to be understood, to be answered decidedly in the negative.

We have seen that no person holding any office under the United

27. Mackintosh's defence of the French revolution.

States, shall be a member of either house during his continuance in office; and that no member of congress shall during the time for which he was elected, be appointed to any civil office under the authority of the United States, which shall have been created, or the emoluments thereof increased during such time. These provisions appear to be more effectual to secure the independence of the members, than any qualification in respect to estate: but, they seem not to have been carried quite far enough.

In the course of this parallel, we have seen that every deviation in the constitution of the United States from that of Great Britain has been attended with a decided advantage and superiority on the part of the former. We shall perhaps discover, before we dismiss the comparison between them, that all its defects arise from some degree of approximation to the nature of the British government.

The exclusive privileges of the house of commons, and of our house of representatives, with some small variation are the same. The first relative to money bills, in which no amendment is permitted to be made by the house of lords, is modified by our constitution so as to give the senate a concurrent right in every respect, except in the power of originating them: and this upon very proper principles; the senators not being distinguished from their fellow citizens by any exclusive privileges, and being in fact the representatives of the people, though chosen in a different manner from the members of the other house; no good reason could be assigned why they should not have a voice on the several parts of a revenue bill, as well as on the whole taken together. The power of impeachment by the house of representatives corresponds, precisely with that of the British house of commons.

II. We are now to draw a parallel between the house of lords, and the senate of the United States, as a second constituent part of the national legislature; and could the parallel between them end there, it might have been said, that all the branches of our political legislature, were, like a well chosen jury, *omni exceptiono majores.*

The house of lords are to be considered in two distinct points of view. ... First, as representing a distinct order of men, with exclusive privileges annexed to their individual capacity, and secondly, as representing the nation.

1. As to the necessity of a distinct order of men in a state, with exclusive privileges annexed to the individual capacity, the author of the commentaries observes, "That the distinction of rank and honors is necessary in every well governed state, in order to reward such as are eminent for their public services, in a manner the most desirable to individuals, and yet without burden to the community; exciting thereby an ambitious, yet laudable ardor, and generous emulation, in others. A spring of action, which however dangerous or invidious in a mere republic, will certainly be attended with good effects under a monarchy. And since titles of nobility are thus expedient in the state, it is also expedient that their owners should form an independent and separate branch of the legislature. If they were confounded with the mass of the people, and like them only had a vote in electing representatives their privileges would soon be borne down and overwhelmed by the popular torrent, which would effectually level all distinctions."

The conclusion which evidently arises from the former part of this quotation, "that no mere republic can ever be a well governed state," inasmuch as honors and titles, the necessity of which, is here so pointedly urged, are dangerous and invidious in such a government, may be proved to be false, both from reasoning and example. But it will be time enough to controvert our author's conclusion, when the truth of the principle upon which it is founded is established. The British constitution, with him, is somewhat like the bed of *Procrustes*; principles must be limited, extended, narrowed, or enlarged, to fit it. If they are not susceptible of so convenient a modification, they are to be wholly rejected.... But to return:

The vital principle of mixed governments is the distinction of orders, possessing, both collectively and individually, different rights, privileges or prerogatives. In an absolute monarchy, a confirmed aristocracy, or a pure democracy, this distinction cannot be found. There being no distinction of orders, there can be no contention about rights, in either of these forms of government, so long as the government remains in the full vigor of its constitution. When either of these three forms of government departs from its intrinsic nature, unless it assumes one of the other instead thereof, it becomes a mixed government.... And this mixture may consist in the combination of monarchy with aristocracy, as in Poland; or with democracy, as in France, under its late constitution, as modelled by the national assembly, and ratified by the king; or, in the blending of the aristocratic and democratic forms, as was the case with the Roman republic after the establishment of the tribunes; or of all three, as in the British constitution. The existence of either of these combinations are said to form the constitution of the state, in all the governments of the world, except those of America, and France under its late constitution; in these the constitution creates the powers that exist: In all others, the existing powers determine the nature of the constitution. To preserve those existing powers in their full tone and vigor, respectively, it may be necessary that each should possess an independent share in the supreme legislature, for the reasons assigned by the author of the commentaries; but this no more proves the necessity of the order, in a well governed state, than the necessity of wings to the human body would be proved, by a critical dissertation, on the structure, size, and position, of those of the fabulous deities of antiquity.

Our author considers those rewards which constitute a separate order of men, as attended with no burden to the community; nothing can be more false than such a supposition. If the distinction be personal, only, it must be created at the expense of the personal degradation of the rest of the community, during the life of the distinguished person. If hereditary, this degradation is entailed upon the people: personal distinctions cannot be supported without power, or without wealth; these are the true supporters of the arms of nobility; take them away, the shield falls to the ground, and the pageantry of heraldry is trodden underfoot.[28] What character is less respected in England, than a poor Scotch lord, who is not one of the sixteen peers of that kingdom? That lord in his own clan, possesses comparative wealth and power sufficient among his humble dependents, to be looked up to as a Caesar in wealth, and a Caesar in authority.

28. George Nevil, duke of Bedford, was degraded by act of parliament, because of his poverty.

"A titled nobility," says a late distinguished English writer,[29] "is the most undisputed progeny of feudal barbarism. Titles had in all nations denoted offices; it was reserved for Gothic Europe, to attach them to ranks. Yet this conduct admits explanation, for with them offices were hereditary, and hence the titles denoting them become hereditary too. These distinctions only serve to unfit the nobility for obedience, and the people for freedom; to keep alive the discontent of the one and to perpetuate the servility of the other; to deprive the one of the moderation that sinks them into citizens, and to rob the other of the spirit that exalts them into freemen. The possession of honors by the multitude, who have inherited, but not acquired them, engrosses and depreciates these incentives and rewards of virtue." If these are the genuine fruits of that laudable ardor, and generous emulation, which give life and vigor to the community, and sets all the wheels of government in motion, heaven protect those whom it encounters in its progress.

But is there no stimulus to that laudable ardor and generous emulation which the commentator speaks of, to be found in a pure democracy, which may compensate for the absence of ranks and honors? Yes. VIRTUE; that principle which actuated the Bruti, a Camillus, and a Cato in the Roman republic, a Timoleon, an Aristides, and an Epaminondas among the Greeks, with thousands of their fellow citizens whose names are scarcely yet lost in the wreck of time. That principle whose operation we have seen in our own days and in our own country, and of which, examples will be quoted by posterity so long as the remembrance of American liberty shall continue among men.... "Virtue," says Montesquieu, "in a republic is a most simple thing; it is a love of the republic. Love of the republic in a democracy is a love of the democracy: love of the democracy is that of equality. The love of equality in a democracy limits ambition to the sole desire, to the sole happiness, of doing greater services to our own country than the rest of our fellow citizens.... But all cannot render equal services: hence distinctions arise here from the principle of equality, even when it seems to be removed, by signal services, or superior abilities."

29. Mackintosh on the French revolution.

This distinction, the only one which is reconcilable to the genius and principle of a pure republic, is, if we may reason from effect to cause,[30] the most powerful incentive to good government that can animate the human heart, with this advantage over those hereditary honors for which the commentator is so zealous an advocate, that the ambition excited by the former must of necessity be directed to public good, whilst the latter springing from self love, alone, may exist in the breast of a Caesar or a Cataline. A Franklin, or a Washington, need not the pageantry of honors, the glare of titles, nor the pre-eminence of station to distinguish them. Their heads like the mountain pine are seen above the surrounding trees of the forest, but their roots engross not a larger portion of the soil.

Equality of rights, in like manner, precludes not that distinction which superiority in virtue introduces among the citizens of a republic. Washington in retirement was equal, and only equal, in rights, to the poorest citizen of the state. Yet in the midst of that retirement the elevation of his character was superior to that of any prince in the universe, and the lustre of it far transcended the brightest diadem.

But even where it conceded that distinctions of rank and honors were necessary to good government, it would by no means follow that they should be hereditary; the same laudable ardor which leads to the acquisition of honor, is not necessary to the preservation of its badges; and these are all which its hereditary possessors, in general, regard. Had nature in her operations shown that the same vigor of mind and activity of virtue which manifests itself in a father, descends unimpaired to his son, and from him to latest posterity, in the same order of succession, that his estate may be limited to, some appearance of reason in favor of hereditary rank and honors might have been offered. But nature in every place, and in every age, has contradicted, and still contradicts this theory. The sons of Junius Brutus were traitors to the republic; the

---

30. The greatest characters the world has known, have risen on the democratic floor. Aristocracy has not been able to keep a proportionate place with democracy. The artificial noble shrinks into a dwarf before the noble of nature. Paine's Rights of Man.

emperor Commodus was the son of Antoninus the philosopher; and Domitian was at once the son of Vespasian, and the brother of Titus.

If what has been said be a sufficient answer to the necessity of the distinction of ranks and honors to the well government of a state, the commentator himself hath afforded an unanswerable argument against their expedience in a republic, by acknowledging them to be both dangerous and invidious in such a government. And herewith agrees the author of the Spirit of Laws, who informs us, that the principle of a democracy is corrupted, when the spirit of equality is extinct. The same admirable writer gives us a further reason why so heterogeneous a mixture ought not to have a place in any government where the freedom and happiness of the people is thought an object worthy the attention of the government. "A nobility," says he, "think it an honor to obey a king, but consider it as the lowest infamy to share the power with the people."

We are indebted to the same author, for the following distinguished features of aristocracy: "If the reigning families observe the laws, aristocracy is a monarchy with several monarchs: but when they do not observe them, it is a despotic state governed by a great many despotic princes. In this case the republic consists only in respect to the nobles, and among them only. It is in the governing body; and the despotic state is in the body governed. The extremity of corruption is when the power of the nobles becomes hereditary; they can hardly then have any moderation." Such is the picture of that order of men who are elevated above the people by the distinctions of rank and honors. When the subjects of a monarchy, they are the pillars of the throne, as the commentator styles them; or, according to Montesquieu, the tools of the monarch.... When rulers, as in an aristocracy, they are the despots of the people.... In a mixed government, they are the political Janizaries of the state, supporting and insulting the throne by turns, but still threatening and enslaving the people.

In America the senate are not a distinct order of individuals, but, the second branch of the national legislature, taken collectively. They have no privileges, but such as are common to the members of the house of representatives, and of the several state legislatures: we have seen that these privileges extend only to an exemption from personal arrests, in certain cases, and that it is utterly lost, in cases of treason, felony, or breach of the peace. They are more properly the privileges of the constituents, than of the members, since it is possible that a state might have no representative, and the United States no legislature, if the members might be restrained from attending their duty, by process issued at the suit of a creditor, or other person who might suppose he had cause of action against them. In England the privileges of the peerage are in some instances an insult to the morals of the people, the honor of a peer, on several occasions, being equivalent with the oath of a commoner. The exemption from personal arrests in civil cases is extended as well to his servant, as to the lord of parliament; to the injury of creditors, and the no small encouragement of fraud and knavery. And the statutes of *scandalum magnatum* hang *in terrorem* over the heads of those who dare to scrutinize, or to question the reality of those superior endowments which the law ascribes, to the immaculate character of a peer or peeress of the realm. Happy for America that her constitution and the genius of her people, equally secure her against the introduction of such a pernicious and destructive class of men.[31]

Secondly. We shall now consider the British house of lords, as representing the nation.

The superior degree of wisdom which is to be found in aristocracies, forms the principal argument in favor of this branch of the British legislature. Let us examine how far this requisite to national councils, is to be attained by the constitution of that house.

The house of lords is composed either of new made peers, or of such to whom that honor has been transmitted by hereditary right; we may admit, though the fact will hardly justify it, that the new made peers have a chance of being selected for their superior wisdom; nay that this is

31. An alien applying to be admitted to citizenship in the United States, who shall have borne any hereditary title, or been of any of the orders of nobility, in any other kingdome or state, must make an express renunciation thereof, in court, at the time of his admission. Laws of the U.S., 3rd Congress.

universally the case; the portion of wisdom thus acquired, even in the creative reign of George the third, could never be sufficient to counterbalance the large majority of hereditary peers, who affect to hold in great contempt the talents and learning of their new created brethren. The wisdom of this body rests then upon the chance of natural talents, with the advantages of education to improve and mature them. As to the latter, should we admit that a child, who, from the moment he is capable of making any observation, sees himself treated as a superior being, would have the same stimulus to improve, as one who is taught to consider the road to science as the only one which leads to distinction, no advantage could be claimed in favor of the hereditary legislator, unless it should be proved that the benefits of education are necessarily confined to that class of men.... The question rests then solely upon the mode by which the nobility become legislators, and here every argument against the transmission of talents and virtue in hereditary succession, recurs with accumulated force, the chance of this inheritance being confined by the laws to the eldest son.[32]

The senate of the United States, as we have seen, is composed of individuals selected for their probity, attachment to their country, and talents, by the legislatures of the respective states. They must be citizens of the states for which they are chosen.... their merits must be known, must have been distinguished, and respected. Age must have matured the talents, and confirmed the virtues which dawned with childhood, or shine forth with youth. Principles must have been manifested, and con-

---

32. The right of primogeniture to the inheritance of virtue and talents, has always appeared to be questionable, if we may draw our conclusion from the authority of the sacred scriptures. The first born son of the first man, was a murderer. The first born son of Abraham, (by a concubine it must be confessed,) was an outcast from society; his hand was against every man, and every man's hand against him.... The first born son of Isaac was, by the dispensations of the divine providence, postponed to his younger brother: the first born of Jacob went up into his father's bed, and defiled it: and the sceptre was transmitted to the race of Judah; the first born of Jesse, appeared worthy in the sight of the prophet, but he, with six of his brethren, was rejected in favour of David the youngest: and the first born of that same David, was by the same providence set aside in favour of Solomon his youngest son.

duct have evinced their rectitude, energy, and stability.... Equivocation of character can scarcely obtain admittance where the trust is important, elections rare, and limited to an individual, or, at most, to two. The whole number of senators are at present limited to thirty-two.... it is not probable that they will ever exceed fifty.... A late writer[33] has observed, that an assembly of Newtons, if they exceeded a hundred, would be a mob. The British house of peers consists of twice that number at the least, and may be increased, at the will of the prince, to any number....[34] The senators of America have the interest of a state to promote, or to defend. A British house of peers has the privileges of the order, the interests of the corporation of aristocracy, to advance. Their wisdom, their exertions, are directed to their own personal aggrandizement.... Those of an American senator can scarcely find an object, except the good of the nation, or of the individual state which he represents. A peer holds himself responsible to no one for his conduct; a senator is responsible to his constituents, and if he abuses their confidence, will be sure to be displaced, whilst the former hugs himself in the security and stability of his station. I say nothing of the bench of bishops. The independence of that body has been too frequently questioned to render them respectable, even in the eyes of their own nation, as a part of the legislature.

A member of the house of lords, may make another lord his proxy, to vote for him in his absence; a privilege which he is supposed to derive from sitting there in his own right; and not as one of the representatives of the nation. He may likewise, by leave of parliament enter his protest against any measure, analogous to which we have seen that the yeas and nays of either house of congress shall be called, if one fifth part of the members present concur therein.

The lord chancellor, or any other person appointed by the king's commission is speaker of the house of lords; and if none be so appointed, the house of lords may elect; and if the speaker be a lord of parliament he

33. Mackintosh.
34. The temporal peers of Great-Britain are said to amount to two hundred and twenty at this time.

may also give his opinion upon any question which the speaker of the commons cannot.... The vice president of the United States is in like manner speaker of the senate, but he is prohibited from voting unless the senate be equally divided. The necessity of providing for the case of a vacancy in the office of president doubtless gave rise to the creation of this officer: and for want of something else for him to do, whilst there is a president in office, he seems to have been placed, with no very great propriety, in the chair of the senate.

An idea probably originating from the tendency which we have sometimes discovered, to imitate the model of the British constitution. The casting vote, which this officer is entrusted with, (as was before observed,) is a very important trust, and ought to have been so modified as to leave the exercise of it, to as few cases as possible.... If a measure originates in the senate, indeed, it would seem to be less dangerous, to permit the exercise of this casting vote, than where it was made use of, to negative a measure, perhaps unanimously adopted by the other house, and upon which the senate have been divided merely from the absence of some of its members. This has actually happened once, on a very important occasion, as we have seen, and may happen again, on others equally interesting to the rights of the citizen.

3. The third constituent part of the British parliament, is the king, without whose assent no bill can pass into a law. The reason for this seems to be the protection of the *Jura Coronae* from the encroachments of the legislature, but this protection, says the Commentator, consists in the power of rejecting rather than resolving: in like manner we have seen, that the president of the United States, whom the executive power is entrusted, has a kind of suspensive veto.... not an absolute, but a qualified negative; and so qualified too, that no salutary measure can be so long delayed by his objection to it, if two thirds of both houses concur in the expediency. In England since the revolution, the royal negative, as to the practical and ostensible exercise of it, seems to be a mere fiction of the constitution, the influence of the crown in both houses, having always proved sufficient to prevent the obtrusion of any obnoxious bill upon the throne; as has been proved on more than one occasion. The

power of calling up any number of new lords, *ad libitum,* is a sufficient guarantee against the necessity of exercising this unpopular prerogative in the crown. But if that were to be found insufficient, a prorogation which puts an end to all matters depending in parliament would effectually answer the purpose.... And should the parliament upon being reassembled give any indications of reviving the offensive subject, a dissolution is sure to pave the way for a more complying body in the house of commons. The history of the present administration in England affords facts to justify what has here been offered.... In America the executive authority does not extend to the creating new members of the legislature: the president has no power of dissolution, or prorogation, nor even of adjournment, but in case of actual disagreement on that subject between the two houses. His assent if held longer than ten days exclusive of Sundays, is not necessary to the force of a law; and his negative, if it be exercised at all, must be notified within the same period to congress, together with his reasons in support of it: if they should be deemed insufficient for the rejection of the bill by two thirds of both houses, it will become a law without his approbation: which seems rather to have been intended as a precaution, provided by the constitution against the hasty passage of impolitic, or unconstitutional acts, than as an essential to the completion of a law; as we have before observed.

This concludes a short sketch of the constituent parts of the supreme legislatures of Great Britain and the United States, with a parallel between them, and the mutual checks and balances provided by the constitution of both countries against the possible encroachments of one of these constituent parts upon the rights of the other. A late English writer[35] of popular eminence, undertakes to prove that these governments of balance and control have never existed but in the vision of theorists. I leave the affirmative to be proved by the advocates for the British constitution, confessing that my own conviction inclines rather to the doctrines of the political heretic, than to those of the most orthodox supporters of the creed which he controverts. But before I quit the subject of

35. Mackintosh.

checks and balances, I shall say a few words on those required by the political situation, and provided by the constitution of the United States.

The territory of the United States extends along the seacoast from north to south, about one thousand miles, and westward from the coast about eight hundred, affording a variety of productions, and holding forth a variety of pursuits to the inhabitants, corresponding with that of climate, soil and situation.... To secure an equal representation of the interests of the individuals inhabiting this extensive country, united in one political bond, as to their correspondence and intercourse with the other nations of the globe, the house of representatives was constituted upon the principles of equality and reciprocity, between burdens and representation in the manner that we have already seen. But although the interests of the individuals might be common in many respects, throughout the United States, yet the territorial, as well as political division, constitution and laws of the several states, created or manifested a contrariety of interests between them, which all were perhaps equally tenacious of maintaining unimpaired. The territorial extent of Virginia being at least one hundred times as great as that of Delaware, and her representation in the proportion of nineteen to one, at present; the interest of the latter could never stand in competition with the former, if the whole legislature were composed of a single house constituted as the house of representatives is: but in the senate, Delaware, as a state; has an equal share in council with Virginia. Her separate interests are there put upon the same footing, with those of the largest states in the union, nor can she be oppressed, but in such a case as would render any other state liable to the same fate. This appears to me to be a wise and effectual balance. Should it fail, the suspensive negative of the president may counteract the machinations of an oppressive majority, in either, or both houses of congress by requiring, the concurrence of a larger proportion of both, than are likely to agree in any impolitic, unconstitutional, or partial measure. On the other hand should state interest prevail in the senate it would meet an effectual check in the house of representatives, where the number of members is not regulated by states, but by the right of suffrage. The influence of states on the latter house, can never be so great hereafter, as it was during the first and second congress, after the adoption of the constitution; that influence received a check from the negative of the president[36] which restored the constitution to its principles, and manifested the happy effects to be derived from a well organized government, so long as any part of it remains uninfluenced by partial or corrupt motives.

Before we dismiss our parallel, a short notice of some other points may not be improper. And first, the privileges of the parliament of England, and of its members, are indefinite, and depend upon their own construction of them when a new case occurs. In America the privileges of the members of congress are, as we have seen, defined, and I presume limited, by the constitution; and the powers of congress are equally prescribed thereby, whilst those of the British parliament have no constitutional limits whatsoever, "and if by any means a misgovernment should any way fall upon it, the subjects of the kingdom are left without all manner of remedy."[37] In America two methods are pointed out, by which any defects in the constitution may be remedied, and, should congress prove too corrupt to adopt the one, it is in the power of the state legislatures to enforce the other; besides the chance which frequent elections afford, of remedying an evil before it has taken root in the several branches of government too firmly to be eradicated. Frequent elections of the representatives of the people, have been justly esteemed one of the best securities to the liberties of the people. The most frequent elections of parliaments in England have been triennial.... they have been protracted to seven years, professedly says Blackstone; to prevent the great and continued expenses of frequent elections. Frequent elections would certainly offer the most effectual remedy for this evil, by diminishing that parliamentary influence which septennial elections tend to secure, and to secure which is the great object of election expenses. Whether biennial election

36. The bill for apportioning representatives among the states, was negatived by the president, as contrary to constitutional principles. A new bill was afterwards introduced and passed, there not being a majority of two thirds of either house, in favour of the former.

37. Blackstone.

of representatives to congress will be sufficiently frequent to secure the due dependence of the members upon their constituents, must be ascertained by experiment. I incline to think, that the reasons in favor of that period are at least equal to those against it: Every objection against its extension beyond the period assigned to the duration of our state legislature, must apply with accumulated force against the duration of the parliament of Great Britain. In England, the convening of the parliament, the continuance of the session, and the existence of the parliament depend on the pleasure of the crown. In America, the periods of election, convening, and duration of congress are fixed by the constitution or by law: the adjournments depend upon themselves, the executive have no control over any matter relative thereto, except in one instance before mentioned, and that must arise from a disagreement between the houses. In England, forty-five members constitute a house to do business, where the whole number consists of 558. In America there must be a majority of both houses to constitute a quorum.

The manner of conducting the business in congress is very similar to that observed in the British parliament. At the opening of the session, the president meets the congress in one or other of their chambers, and addresses them upon the general affairs of the union.[38] This address has generally received a separate answer from each house, which is presented by the whole house, to the president in his audience chamber, that is, at his own house. Every resolution to which the concurrence of the senate is necessary, must be laid upon the table on a day, preceding that, in which it is moved, unless, by express commission of the house. Petitions, memorials, &c. addressed to the house must be proceeded upon in like manner. Bills are introduced by motion for leave, or by order of the house on the report of a committee, and in either case a committee is appointed to prepare the bill. Revenue bills, as was observed elsewhere, must originate in the house of representatives; but the senate may orig-

---

38. *Editor's note:* Actually, in 1801 Jefferson had discontinued the "monarchical" practice of the president visiting the Congress in person, but had simply sent a written message. Jefferson's example was followed by every president until Woodrow Wilson.

inate any other bill, and may also propose, or concur to amendments, in revenue bills, as well as others. As the senate constitutes a part of the executive department, this power of origination must have a strong tendency to strengthen, and give activity to that branch of the government.[39] Every bill receives three readings; but no bill can be twice read on the same day without special order of the houses. If upon the first reading of a bill it be opposed, the question put is, whether it shall be rejected; upon the second reading, the speaker states that it is ready for commitment or engrossment. The commitment may be either to a select committee or to the whole house. In a committee of the whole, the speaker quits the chair, and a chairman is appointed, who, when the committee rises, reports to the house the progress therein made. After commitment and report, a bill may be recommitted, or at any time after, before its passage. Previous to the third reading of a bill, it is ordered to be engrossed, or written in a fair round hand; when passed in the house of representatives, it is sent to the senate for concurrence. Bills, except for imposing taxes, may originate in either house. If an amendment be agreed to, in one house, and dissented to in the other, if either house request a conference, a committee is appointed in each house, to meet in the conference chamber, to state to each other, verbally, or in writing the reasons of their respective houses, for and against the amendment. After a bill has passed both houses it is enrolled on parchment, examined by a joint committee of both houses, signed by the speaker of the house of representatives, and president of the senate, and is then presented by the committee of enrolment to the president of the United States for his approbation: with an indorsement thereon, specifying in which house it originated, and the day of presentation is entered on the Journals of such house. If the president approve the bill, he signs it; it is then received from him by the secretary of state, recorded, and deposited among the rolls in his office; a copy of it is published in at least three of the public papers, and one printed copy is delivered to each senator and representative, and two others, duly authenticated, are sent to the executive authority of each state.

39. See De Lolme.

The same course is to be observed, where a bill is not returned by the president, within the time limited by the constitution, and thereby becomes a law: or, having been returned, reconsidered, and approved by two thirds of both houses, becomes law. The manner of proceeding in case a bill be not approved and signed by the president, has been already fully mentioned.

We shall now resume our inquiry into the powers the exercise of which, is by the constitution confided to the congress of the United States. Most of these we have had occasion to enumerate in the course of our examination into the distribution of power between the federal and state governments. This examination we shall now resume more at large; another object of our further inquiry will be, how, these powers are adjusted and to whom confided, in other governments, particularly that of Great Britain: this will lead us frequently to resume our parallel, and I trust, it will scarcely be found, that upon a fair comparison, the superiority can in any instance be denied to the constitution of the United States.

The powers of congress are the next subject to which our inquiries are to be directed; these are in general legislative; yet in some few instances; they extend also to other subjects, which fall under the executive department in most other nations.

1. Congress is authorized to lay and collect taxes, duties, imposts, and excises, to pay the debts, and provide for the common defense, and general welfare of the United States: but all duties, imposts, and excise shall be uniform throughout the United States; and no capitation, or other direct tax shall be laid, unless in proportion to the census, or enumeration, before directed to be taken: nor shall any tax or duty be laid on articles exported from any state.

The principle upon which the right of taxation is founded, is here shortly expressed; viz. "To pay the debts and provide for the common defense, and general welfare of the United States." For since the government is bound to defend the lives and fortunes of the citizen, which protection cannot be afforded, unless the government be furnished with adequate supplies for that purpose, it is but reasonable that the individual should, on his part, contribute his proper proportion thereof.[40] On the other hand, since the citizen is on no other account obliged to pay taxes, or undergo any other public burden, but as they are necessary to defray the expenses of the state, it ought to be the singular care of the government to draw no further supplies than the exigencies of the public require; and to see likewise that the citizens be as little as possible incommoded with the charges they are forced to put them to; and moreover, that the public impositions be laid in just and fair proportions, without favoring and exempting of one, to the defrauding or oppression of another. Such are the principles which the constitution establishes, by requiring that direct taxes should be "according to the census"; and that indirect taxes, viz. duties, imposts, and excises should be "uniform" throughout the United States.

The distinction which the constitution thus creates between direct taxes, and others, renders an inquiry into the grounds and nature of that distinction particularly interesting.

The author of the treatise upon political economy defines a tax, to be "a certain contribution of fruits, service, or money imposed upon the individuals of a state."[41] He adds; "this definition may include, in general, all kinds of burdens which can possibly be imposed, whether under the name of tribute, tithe, tally, impost, duty, gable, custom, subsidy, excise, or any other."

As this definition includes the several species of burdens which the congress are authorized to impose, it may be proper to see in what manner the same author distinguishes them.... This he does into three classes: 1. Those upon alienation, which he calls proportional: 2. Those upon possessions, which he calls cumulative, or arbitrary: 3. Those exacted in service, as in the militia, on the roads, &c.

1. A proportional tax is paid by the buyer, who intends to consume, at the time of the consumption; and is consolidated with the price of the commodity.

---

40. Spavan's Puffendorf.
41. Stuart's Political Economy.

Two requisites are necessary to fix this tax upon any one; first, he must be a buyer; secondly he must be a consumer.

Examples of this tax are all excises, customs, (viz. duties on imposts or exports) stamp duties, postage, coinage, and the like.

2. A cumulative or arbitrary tax may be known; 1. By the intention; which is, to affect the possessor in such a manner as to make it difficult for him to augment his income in proportion to the tax he pays: 2. By the object; when instead of being laid on any determinate piece of labor, or consumption, it is made to affect past, and not present, gains: 3. By the circumstances, under which it is levied; which imply no transition of property from hand to hand.

Examples of cumulative taxes, are land taxes, poll taxes, window taxes, duties upon coaches, servants, &c.

The taxes, duties, imposts, and excises, mentioned in the constitution of the United States, appear naturally to fall under a similar division, and the words direct, and indirect, may consequently be substituted for the terms cumulative and proportional, used by that author.

It is the nature of a cumulative (or direct tax) to affect the possessions, income, and profit, of every individual, without suffering it to be in their power to draw it back again in any way whatever. A proportional, (or indirect tax) on the contrary may be said to be paid voluntarily; being paid by a voluntary purchaser, who is also a consumer.

This distinction it is conceived may be illustrated by the following example: If a tax be laid upon wheels, so that every person in the state shall be liable to pay a certain sum in proportion to the number of carriages he has for his convenience; this, according to the author last mentioned, would be a cumulative, or direct tax; but if a similar tax be collected in the hands of the wheel-wright, it would be a proportional, or indirect tax: in the first case, he who pays the tax upon the carriages, which he keeps for his convenience, cannot possibly draw the tax back again, after he has once paid it, by any means whatever; in the second, the wheel-wright only advances the tax, but is repaid by the purchaser who buys it for his convenience: inasmuch as he advances the price of his wheels, in proportion to the duty or tax, he has paid upon them.

Supposing this to be the true distinction to be taken between direct and indirect taxes, a correspondent distinction in the mode of imposing the tax should be adopted; if, for example, the last mentioned tax is to be levied upon the person who uses the carriage for his convenience; this being a direct tax, the whole sum required to be raised thereby, must first be apportioned among the several states; but the tax itself, need not be uniform throughout the state; if it be levied on the wheelwright, the tax becomes an indirect one, and must be uniform throughout the states; but there need not be any previous apportionment of the quotas of the several states.[42]

Whilst the constitution of the United States was under consideration, objections were offered in this state, and in some others, against the power of direct taxation, thereby granted to congress. One of the amendments proposed by the convention of this state, was, "That when congress shall lay direct taxes or excises, they shall immediately inform the executive power of each state, of the quota of such state according to the census by the constitution directed, which is proposed to be thereby raised; and if the legislature of any state shall pass a law, which shall be effectual for raising such quota, at the time required by congress, the taxes and excises laid by congress shall not be collected in such state." This amendment was passed over in silence by congress; but the exercise of the right of direct taxation, which it was intended to qualify, has never yet been exerted; and probably will not, so long as any other expedient can be fallen upon to raise money for the support of the government.[43] Not only Virginia, but Massachusetts, South-Carolina, New-York,

---

42. The preceding investigation of this subject, was made about two years before congress passed the act imposing duties upon carriages for the conveyance of persons. The tax was opposed in Virginia as unconstitutional, because the sum to be raised was not first apportioned among the states. A suit was brought in the federal court in Virginia; the judges were divided in opinion, and the case, by consent, was carried to the supreme federal court; it was there decided that the tax was not correct; and consequently that no apportionment was necessary. United States vs. Hylton. The editor's reasoning upon this subject, must therefore be regarded by the student as merely hypothetical, and speculative.

43. Direct taxes have been more than once proposed in congress: but the strenuous opposition to them leaves reason to believe that a *maritime* war, alone, will overcome

and North-Carolina, concurred in expressing a disapprobation of this part of the constitution. It may, however, be doubted, whether there is as much reason for the objection, as the concurring sense of five such considerable states induces a supposition that there may be in its favour. The power of taxation seems indispensably necessary to constitute an efficient government, and appears inseparable from the right of deciding upon any measure, which requires the aid of taxes, to carry it into effect. By the same article of the constitution we shall find, that congress have power to declare war, and to raise and support armies. What could this declaration avail without the further power of procuring the means for their support? The effects of paper-emissions, lotteries, loan-offices, impressments, and requisitions from the states, the occasional expedients, and ultimate resources of a feeble confederacy, had been sufficiently seen, and felt during the revolutionary war. How often were the sinews of government unstrung; how often were its operations stopped in the most critical conjunctures; how few of them were carried into vigorous effect, from the imbecility of the federal government, and the deranged state of the finances of the union?.... Nor is the mode proposed by the amendment, altogether free from objection: the states might pass laws apparently effectual, for the purpose of raising the sum required, and yet the execution of those laws be so retarded by the delinquency of collectors, as to render the suspension of the act of congress a matter no longer reconcilable to the pressing emergencies of the government. In this case, the government must either be deprived of its resources, or the citizens be doubly burdened. Was there an instance where the requisitions of the revolutionary congress were strictly complied with, both as to the time of payment, and the quantum required? Were not arrears upon arrears continually the subject of their demands from the respective states? If this was the case during the struggle for independence, what may not be apprehended upon other occasions? It will be alleged, perhaps, that the

---

the repugnance to them. Happy for America, if this repugnance should always operate so strongly, as to make her avoid such an occasion for them.

But since the preceding was written, congress have imposed a direct tax of two million dollars.

quotas of the several states were not adjusted upon equal principles by the confederation: that each state supposed, and even complained, that it had already contributed more than its proper quota; and that this may well account for their tardiness in complying with the requisitions of congress. This, it is true, was the ostensible excuse with most of them: but it is no less true that the states who were under-rated, or who were actually in arrears, were not less positive, or vehement, in their complaints of the inequality of the burden, than those who had reason and justice on their side; consequently they were not less tardy in complying with any new requisition. If the experience of former evils ought to make us wise, the United States have surely derived sufficient information from this source.

It is observable, that the objection only goes to the exercise of the right of direct taxation; and the imposition of excises; all other indirect modes of taxation seem to be given up without a question: but if the necessity of investing congress with a power to impose taxes be admitted, it may be questioned, whether more numerous, and important objections may not be offered against indirect, than direct taxation, as a source of revenue in a free state. If, on the one hand, indirect taxation may be considered as least burdensome in the mode of collection, on the other hand it may be remarked, that the increase of burden upon the consumer, who ultimately pays every indirect tax, is probably more than an equivalent for this convenience; which is moreover fully counterbalanced by that unavoidable inequality of burdens, resulting from indirect taxes, which it should be the object of direct taxation to avoid. Indeed, if equality of taxation be desirable, the only mode by which it can be obtained, seems to be by direct taxes, imposed in the mode prescribed by the constitution. It was, perhaps, impracticable to fix the ratio of direct taxes, in any just proportion, by reference to any particular species of property, even land, that kind of property, which, of all others, is most susceptible of such an adjustment, being of very unequal value, although perfectly equal in quality and produce, in different parts of the United States. And this circumstance, alone, appears to afford a sufficient reason against uniformity, in the imposition of direct taxes. The attempt was made under the confederation to apportion the burdens of the union among the states, according to the value of all lands within each state, granted to, or surveyed for any person, with the buildings and improvements thereon. But congress, by their act of April 18, 1783, proposed to the states to rescind that part of the articles of confederation, and in lieu thereof, to adopt precisely the same mode which the present constitution establishes. A bill to that effect was passed in this state; but whether the proposal was favorably received by the other states, I am not informed. It appears then to be somewhat extraordinary, that the opposition to direct taxation was so strong in Virginia, where the proportion proposed, had already received the approbation of her legislature. A proportion established by reference to labor, the original source of wealth, may be considered as the best medium, by which to ascertain the rate of actual wealth; and if it be remembered, that two-fifths of the slaves in the southern states are thrown out of the calculation, we should conclude that they could not reasonably be dissatisfied with the ratio thereby established.[44]

One of the objections to the power of direct taxation most strongly insisted on, was, that a representative of Massachusetts, or Georgia, could not be a proper judge of the most fit objects of taxation in Virginia; this objection, however, the constitution seems to have guarded against effectually, by requiring that the sum to be raised by direct taxes should be apportioned among the several states in the first instance. What motive, then, could a representative from Massachusetts, or from Georgia, have for opposing any mode of raising the tax in Virginia, which might be proposed by the representatives from that state? As the sum to be contributed by the state would be previously fixed, it could neither be augmented nor diminished by the mode of collection: of this, the members from the several states might be considered as the best judges, respectively. Uniformity not being required by the constitution to be observed in the imposition of direct taxes, the tax in New-England might be a poll-tax, in Pennsylvania a land-tax, and in South Carolina a tax on slaves, if those modes, respectively, should be recommended by the rep-

44. See Federalist, No. 44.

resentatives of those states, without either violating the constitution, or disadvantage to any other state. In the imposition of such taxes, therefore, congress might pursue the system of each state, respectively, within that state.[45] The inequality of indirect taxes, among states, as well as among individuals, is perfectly unavoidable. It may in time become so great as to shift all the burdens of government from a part of the states, and to impose them, exclusively, on the rest of the union. The northern states, for example, already manufacture within themselves, a very large proportion, or perhaps the whole, of many articles, which in other states are imported from foreign parts, subject to heavy duties. They are consequently exempted, in the same proportion, from the burden of duties paid on these articles. Hence a considerable inequality already exists between the contributions from the several states; this inequality daily increases, and is indeed daily favored, upon principles of national policy: for whenever any species of manufacture becomes considerable in the United States, it is considered proper to impose what are called protecting duties, upon foreign articles of the same kind. Nor does the matter rest here; for several American manufactures are now subject to an excise: this species of tax, though advanced by the manufacturer, is paid by the consumer, as has been already shown: consequently, the duty upon every excised commodity is in fact paid by the state where it is consumed, whilst the manufacturing state is not only exempt from the burden, but enriched by it.[46] This inequality is not otherwise to be avoided but by direct taxes. The same disproportion also obtains among individuals of the same state; where it operates as a tax on luxury, it may be considered in a beneficial light; but there are a thousand instances where a tax upon consumption will produce an inequality of burdens, though the tax should operate only upon the necessaries, and not the luxuries of life: a person in health may dispense with many comforts which a sick man stands in the utmost need of; he can better afford to pay a tax on

45. See Federalist, No. 36.

46. *Editor's note:* Tucker here anticipates the Southern complaints against the protective tariff, which came to a head in the early 1830s.

what he consumes; but the sick man must either pay an additional tax, or perish because he cannot afford it. Indirect taxes, therefore, not infrequently impose the burden upon those who are least able to sustain it; a direct tax on the contrary may always be apportioned according to the means of defraying it.

It seems agreed among political writers, that another objection to indirect taxes arises from the tax being so interwoven with the price, that the consumer blends them together, and is thus rendered ignorant of the burdens imposed upon him by the government. This is conceived to be peculiarly dangerous in a free government, and utterly incompatible with that responsibility, which ought to subsist between the representative and his constituents; whose burdens are thus imperceptibly increased, to the great hazard of their liberties, whenever the government shall thus insensibly acquire an independent revenue; the source and amount of which may be equally unknown to the generality of the people. If, for example, a duty of 10 *per cent. ad valorem,* be imposed upon any foreign article imported, or upon any domestic manufacture made for sale in the United States, the duty is in a very few years entirely forgotten, being wholly lost in the price of the article, in the consumer's estimation; an additional 5 *per cent.* is laid; this, like the former, is equally forgotten, and blended with the price in a few years more. This may be repeated at no very distant periods, till the duty is doubled, trebled, or quadrupled, and the effect still be the same: in another generation the same experiment may be repeated with like success, and each succeeding generation undergo the like additional burdens, until it would require the most consummate skill in political arithmetic to calculate the amount; whereas, if direct taxes were increased in the like proportion, every individual would at once perceive from what source this additional burden arose, and would be led to inquire for what reason he was subjected to it. Hence it would seem to be the interest of every freeman, in a free state, that his taxes should be imposed in such manner as to be subject to his immediate observation; since whatever inconvenience he may thereby sustain, must be amply recompensed by the security thus afforded to his liberty.

The power of imposing direct taxes, excises, and duties, except on imports or exports, is one of those, in which, according to our distribution, the United States and the individual states possess concurrent authority. It was apprehended by the opposers to the constitution, that this power in the congress would, like Aaron's rod, swallow up that of the state legislatures.[47] The government must be wholly corrupted whenever this happens; so long as the taxes imposed by the federal legislature are limited to constitutional purposes, it is impossible that the states should be without a revenue sufficient to support their civil lists. Beyond that object, so long as the federal government is properly administered, the states can have no urgent occasion for any revenue.[48]

The abuse of the powers of government should be guarded against by the constitution as far as possible. The purposes for which any grievous tax can, with any shadow of necessity, be imposed by the federal legislature, must be the raising and supporting armies. Appropriations for that purpose are limited to two years. The duration of congress is limited to the like period. Would not a new election strike at the root of the evil? If it should not, the people must resort to first principles. Even annual elections would probably be an insufficient protection against such a total depravity, as could not be curbed by these provisions in the constitution.

Excises, the second branch of revenue which created an alarm in the minds of the opposers of the constitution, are defined to be an inland imposition, usually paid upon the retail sale of a commodity. It appears, however, that they are generally imposed on manufactures, and paid by

47. "Though the law for laying a tax for the use of the United States would be supreme in its nature, and could not legally be opposed or controled, yet a law for abrogating or preventing the collection of a tax laid by the authority of a state, unless upon exports or imports, would not be the supreme law of the land, but an usurpation of power not granted by the constitution.... The inference upon the whole is, that under the proposed constitution the individual states would retain an independent and uncontrolable authority to raise revenue to any extent, of which they may stand in need, by every kind of taxation, except duties on exports and imports." Federalist, No. 33.

48. "As to the suggestion of double taxation, the answer is plain. The wants of the union are to be supplied in one way or another: if it be done by the authority of the federal government, it will not be done by that of the state governments. The quantity of taxes to be paid by the community must be the same in either case." Ibid.

the manufacturer, who advances the price of his commodity in proportion. The author of the commentaries on the laws of England acknowledges, that the rigor and arbitrary proceedings of excise laws, seems hardly compatible with the temper of a free nation. . . . This observation, founded on the experience of a nation whose accumulated debts, financial embarrassment may have driven them to its adoption, it might have been expected, would have cooperated with the clamors of a considerable part of the union, against the admission of such a principle of taxation into the constitution, to deter congress from an immediate resort to an experiment of its effects upon the minds of their constituents. It is said that this mode of taxation is familiar to the New England states, and that it is by no means obnoxious to the people there. This circumstance probably paved the way for its reception in congress; in this state it was a perfect novelty, and was made the subject of one of the amendments, proposed to the constitution. The arguments in favor of this, as an economical mode of taxation, abstractedly considered, appear to be much in its favor; it being alleged, that the charges of levying, collecting, and managing the excise duties in England, are considerably less in proportion, than in any other branches of the revenue. This may be true in a country abounding in manufacturing towns; but in a country where the objects of the excise are few, and those dispersed over an immense tract of country, it is perhaps demonstrable from the number of salaried officers employed in the collection, that a smaller portion of the excise, than of any other tax goes into the treasury of the United States. The giving salaries to these officers is an irrefragable proof of this position: for if the tax to be collected were so considerable, as that a moderate percentage would afford a sufficient compensation to the collectors, for their trouble, there would be no need of resorting to salaries, which may perhaps amount to fifteen, or twenty percent, in some places, and in others, prove almost commensurate with the tax itself. On the other hand, it must be acknowledged, that the excise contributes in some measure to restore the balance arising from the inequality produced by duties on foreign imports; and this, not only among individuals, but in a small degree among the states; the manufacturing states being thereby subject to some portion of the tax on consumption: but this last benefit can only last so long as each state shall manufacture for its own consumption, only; and it will be entirely lost, and even become doubly oppressive, whenever the manufactures of one part of the union, are exported from thence and consumed in the other states. Excises will then operate as the most burdensome species of impost, on those part of the union, where consumption takes place.

Duties and imposts, in their common acceptation mean those taxes which merchants are compelled to pay upon merchandise imported, or exported, from any state, and which have in many countries obtained the general name of customs; probably from the usual and constant demand made of them for the use of the princes, state, or government. But in the constitution of the United States they seem to have obtained a more extensive signification, and were probably intended to comprehend every species of tax, or contribution, not included under the ordinary terms, taxes and excises. Taken in the general and comprehensive sense, the states respectively possess the power of imposing them, concurrently with the federal government, with the single exception of customs, or duties upon imports or exports; the right of imposing which, is either exclusively vested in the congress of the United States, or can only be exercised by the respective states with the assent of congress, except what may be absolutely necessary for executing their inspection laws; and the net produce of all duties and imposts laid by any state on imports or exports, shall be for the use of the treasury of the United States; and all such laws are subject to the revision and control of the congress; nor can any state without the consent of congress lay any duty on tonnage. Frequent instances have occurred where the assent of congress has been given to acts of the state legislatures, made for especial purposes, such as erecting piers, appointing health officers, deepening the navigation.

In February 1781, the congress of the United States made a proposal to the several states to authorize congress to impose a duty of five percent *ad valorem,* on certain goods, wares and merchandise, (such as wines and ardent spirits, &c.) and on all prizes and prize goods, which might be imported, or brought, into the United States. The legislature, at their next session, passed an act, in conformity thereto. Several of the states as was afterwards alleged, neglected to pass similar laws, and their unanimous consent was requisite, under the existing articles of confederation, to give effect to such an important change in the system; in consequence of which, the act of this state was suspended, by a law passed at the ensuing session, until the several states in the union should concur in adopting the measure: it has been said that the non-concurrence of a single state, (and that, one of the smallest in the union,) prevented the proposition from taking effect; but this not the reason, assigned by the legislature of this state, for repealing their act of assent. An ill timed jealousy at that period had crept into the legislature, who declared by their act of October, 1782, c. 137. "That the permitting any power, other than the general assembly of the commonwealth to levy duties or taxes upon the citizens of this state, within the same, is injurious to its sovereignty, and may prove destructive of the rights and liberties of the people"; for which reason they repealed the act of the preceding year, by which the concurrence of the state was yielded to the proposed measure. In the month of April 1783, the proposition was new modelled by congress, and again presented to the states, for their assent and concurrence; and was a second time acceded to by the state of Virginia, in the month of October, in the same year, but, with a suspending clause, until the other states, in the union, should likewise, concur in the proposed concession. The preamble to this act recites, that congress had recommended to the several states as indispensably necessary to the restoration of public credit, and to the punctual and honorable discharge of the public debt, to invest the United States in congress assembled with a power to levy, for the use of the United States, certain duties upon goods imported into the said states from any foreign part, for the period of twenty-five years. The powers thereby granted were moreover guarded by a number of provisoes and restrictions, and limited to a period, barely sufficient to answer the purpose of reviving the confidence of the creditors of the union. . . . Yet this measure like the former, miscarried for the want of the unanimous concurrence of the states, so cautious were they at that time, in their con-

cessions of power to the federal government. It was at this session, likewise, (Oct. 1783,) that the legislature of Virginia, passed an act to authorize the congress of the United States to adopt certain regulations
respecting the British trade; the object of which was to authorize that
body to prohibit the importation of the growth or produce of the British
West-India Islands, in British vessels; or, to adopt any other mode which
might most effectually tend to counteract the designs of Great Britain,
with respect to the American commerce, so long as the growth or produce of any of the United States of America should be prohibited from
being carried to those islands, by any other than British subjects, in
British built ships, owned by British subjects, and navigated according to
the laws of that kingdom. This measure, which, if it had been adopted
would have operated to the exclusive benefit of the navigating states, likewise failed, from the same causes as the two former. When peace was
concluded with Great Britain a commercial rivalship very soon began to
manifest itself among the several states, but between none more remarkable than Maryland and Virginia, to both which the waters of the Chesa-
peake, and the Potomac, were as a common highway. Scarcely a session
of the general assembly passed over in either state, without some change
in the duties upon imports, and tonnage, with a view to counteract some
law, or regulation, of the other. Various attempts were made to produce
an uniformity in their custom-house systems, but without effect. At this
period, likewise, the inefficiency of the federal government began to
excite loud clamors, as we have had occasion to mention, elsewhere. The
want of an uniform system of commercial regulations, among the states,
and the total want of funds, in the hands of congress, for the discharge of
the continental debt, as well foreign, as domestic, convinced every one of
the propriety of investing congress with power over these subjects, and
gave rise to the measures already mentioned elsewhere. Hence, no opposition was ever made, to these branches of the authority of congress,
when the question respecting the adoption of the constitution of the
United States was agitated.

All duties and imposts (as contradistinguished from direct taxes) and
all excises, as we have seen, must be uniform throughout the United

States, by which means the principle of equality, as far as the nature of the subject will admit, is still adhered to in the constitution. A candid review of this part of the federal constitution, cannot fail to excite our just applause of the principles upon which it is founded. All the arguments against it appear to have been drawn from the inexpediency of establishing such a form of government, rather than from any defect in this part of the system, admitting that a general government was necessary to the happiness and prosperity of the states, individually. This great primary question being once decided in the affirmative, it might be difficult to prove that any part of the powers granted to congress in this clause, ought to have been altogether withheld: yet being granted, rather as an ultimate provision in any possible case of emergency, than as a means of ordinary revenue, it is to be wished that the exercise of powers, either oppressive in their operation, or inconsistent with the genius of the people, or irreconcilable to their prejudices, might be reserved for cogent occasions, which might justify the temporary recourse to a lesser evil, as the means of avoiding one more permanent, and of great magnitude.

2. Congress have power to borrow money on the credit of the United States; a power inseparably connected with that of raising a revenue, and with the duty of protection which that power imposes upon the federal government. For, though in times of profound peace, it may not be necessary to anticipate the revenues of a state, yet the experience of other nations, as well as our own, must convince us that the burden and expense of one year, in time of war, may be more than equal to the revenues of ten years. Hence a debt is almost unavoidable, whenever a nation is plunged into a state of war. The least burdensome mode of contracting a debt is by a loan: in case of a maritime war, the revenues arising from duties upon merchandise imported, and upon tonnage, must be greatly diminished. Had not congress a power to borrow money, recourse must be had to direct taxes in the extreme, or to impressments, lotteries, and other miserable and oppressive expedients. A system of revenue being once organized, and the ability of the states to pay their debts, being known, money may easily be procured on loan, to be repaid when

all the sources of revenue shall have regained their operation, and flow in their proper channel.

But while we contend for the power, let it not be supposed that it is meant to contend for the abuse of it. When used as a means of necessary defense, it gives energy, vigor and dispatch to all the measures of government; inspires a proper confidence in it, and disposes every citizen to alacrity and promptitude, in the service of his country. By enabling the government punctually to comply with all its engagements, the soldier is not driven to mutiny for want of his subsistence, nor the officer to resign his commission to avoid the ruin of himself, and his family. By this means also, the pressure and burden of a war, undertaken for the benefit of posterity, as well as the present generation, may be in some degree alleviated, and a part of the burden transferred to those who are to share the advantage. On the other hand, where loans are voluntarily incurred, upon the principle that public debt is a public blessing, or to serve the purposes of aggrandizing a few at the expense of the nation, in general, or of strengthening the hands of government, (or more properly those of a party grasping at power, influence and wealth,) nothing can be more dangerous to the liberty of the citizen, nor more injurious to remotest posterity, as well as to present generations.

Congress had power, under the former articles of confederation, to borrow money upon the credit of the United States, and to pledge their faith for the repayment. But not possessing any revenue independent of the states, their loans were obtained with difficulty, and, very rarely in time to answer the purposes for which they were intended. The consequences of these, and other corresponding defects in the system, have been too frequently noticed to require a repetition of them in this place.

3. Congress have power to regulate commerce with foreign nations, and among the several states, and with the Indian tribes.

We have already had occasion to mention the state of foreign commerce, upon the conclusion of the peace with Great-Britain, and the conduct of the government of that nation in excluding our vessels from their ports in the West-India Islands. The proposition made by the state of Virginia to authorize congress to prohibit the importation of the growth or produce of those islands into the United States in British vessels, and even to adopt more energetic measures, by refusing the necessary supplies to those islands, if adopted, would probably have counteracted the designs of that politic nation: but, that fatal want of unanimity among the states, which at that period marked all their councils, defeated the proposal. The boldness of the measure on the part of Great-Britain, evinced a determination to secure her commercial advantages, even at the risk of the existence of her colonies; yet it is not to be imagined that she would have persevered in such a conduct towards her own colonies, if the United States had offered to retaliate her policy, by refusing them provisions, lumber, and other articles of the first necessity, unless they were admitted to send them thither in their own vessels, as well as in those of British subjects. For, independent of the injustice and inhumanity of such a conduct in the predominant state, the prosperity of the sugar colonies must have been of more consequence to Great-Britain, than the whole of the carrying trade between those islands and the United States. True it is, that it was pretended by the British ministry, and their adherents, that Nova Scotia and Canada could supply those islands, with every necessary formerly derived from the United States. But the bare admission of those articles from the United States, in any manner whatsoever, might be relied on as an unequivocal evidence that they had no confidence in the sufficiency of the resources which might be drawn from Canada or Nova Scotia; and experience is said to be strongly in favor of the opinion that those colonies cannot supply the sugar islands, either with provisions or lumber, in any degree proportionate to their necessities. The conduct of Great-Britain in declining any commercial treaty with America, at that time, was unquestionably dictated at first by a knowledge of the inability of congress to extort terms of reciprocity from her; and of that want of unanimity among the states, which, under the existing confederation, was a perpetual bar to any restriction upon her commerce with the whole of the states; and any partial restriction would be sure to fail of effect.

Having repeatedly noticed the defect of the former confederation, in respect to the regulation of the commerce between the several states, and the inconveniences resulting from it, I shall only mention one not yet touched upon: I mean the burdens which might be imposed by some of the states, on others, whose exports and imports must necessarily pass through them. Thus a duty on salt imported into Virginia, or on tobacco exported from thence, might operate very extensively as a taxation on the citizens of the western parts of North Carolina and Tennessee, to the exclusive emolument of the state of Virginia. So unreasonable an advantage ought not to prevail among members of the same confederacy, and without a power to control its burden somewhere, it would be impossible that it should not be exerted: the repetition of such exertions could scarcely fail to lay the foundation of irreconcilable jealousies, and animosities among the states. And it was evidently with a view to prevent these inconveniences, that the constitution provides that no state shall, without the consent of congress, lay any imposts, or duties on exports or imports, except what may be absolutely necessary for executing its inspection laws.

A direct consequence of this power of regulating commerce with foreign nations, and among the several states, is that of establishing ports; or such places of entry, lading, and unlading, as may be most convenient for the merchant on the one hand, and for the easy and effectual collection of the revenue from customs, on the other. In England, this is one of the branches of the royal prerogative, but is vested in the supreme federal legislature, and not in the executive, by the constitution of the United States.

Previous to the revolution the ports of Virginia were co-extensive with her tide waters. The ships anchored wherever their navigators thought proper, and discharged or took on board their cargoes, as suited their own convenience, or contributed to the saving of expense. Nothing could be more favorable to the practice of smuggling; and consequently the revenue was frequently defrauded with impunity. Nothing could be more unfavourable to the internal navigation by small vessels, although few countries possess greater advantages for its encouragement and promotion. The employment of a considerable number of these, would not only afford a nursery for seamen, but prove an actual mercantile saving

to the state, so long as commerce should be carried on in foreign bot-
toms, as was at that time pretty generally the case. The legislature became
sensible of these things, and in the year 1784, (May session, c. 32.) passed
an act, whereby ships and other vessels trading to this commonwealth,
from foreign parts, being the property of other than citizens of the commonwealth, were obliged to lade, and unlade at certain particular ports,
and no where else, within the commonwealth. The number of ports was
increased, by the act of 1786. c. 42. and the restrictions as to unloading
was extended to all vessels whatsoever, coming into the state; but any
vessel built within the United States, and wholly owned by any citizens
thereof, was permitted to take in her lading at any port or place within
the state. These acts underwent some further amendments by the acts
of 1787. c. 3, among which were some wholesome regulations respecting
river craft: but these appear to have been considered as repealed, by the
act of 1 cong. 1 sess. c. 11. sec. 22 and 23, on the subject of the coasting
trade. But the constitutionality of that act may perhaps be questioned,[49]
so far as it relates to vessels trading wholly within the limits of any particular state. The policy of the before-mentioned acts of this state,
appears to have been well founded: the effects begun to manifest themselves in the production of a greater number of river craft, than had ever
been known at any former period.... But the acts of congress, for the
establishment of ports, having extended the number for foreign ships to
fourteen, and even permitted them to proceed as far as the tide-water
flows in James' River, Rappahannock, and Potomac, these salutary regulations in the state laws, have undoubtedly been, in a great measure, frus-

49. The constitution of the United States does not authorise congress to regulate, or
in any manner to interfere with, the domestic commerce of any state. Consequently, a
vessel wholly employed in that domestic commerce, seems not to be subject to the control of the laws of the United States. Those laws may certainly provide for the punishment
of such persons, and confiscation of such vessels, as may be detected in giving aid and
assistance to any fraudulent commerce, either with foreign parts, or between the states;
they may also prescribe, or limit the terms and conditions, upon which vessels may be
permitted to trade with foreign parts, or with other states: but they seem to have no constitutional right to control the intercourse between any two or more parts of the same
state.

trated. It seems rather extraordinary, that on a subject of this nature, no regard should have been paid to the former policy of the state legislature, especially, as that policy was evidently favourable to the collection of the revenue arising from the customs.

A distinction between the admission of foreign ships, and those of our own confederacy, into the ports of the state, obviously appears to be proper to be made on other grounds. The navigation of our rivers was found, in the time of the revolutionary war, to be infinitely too familiar to our enemies, in consequence of the privilege before-mentioned, which had so long been enjoyed by the trading ships of Great Britain. A renewal of the same policy will probably produce the same consequences, whenever the occasion will permit. But if these reasons be not sufficiently cogent for restraining foreign ships to a few ports, and those as near to the sea as might be consistent with safety; the promotion of an internal domestic navigation, as a nursery for domestic seamen, appears of itself to be an object of sufficient importance to have engaged the attention of congress to this subject.

Another consequence of the right of regulating foreign commerce, seems to be the power of compelling vessels infected with any contagious disease, or arriving from places usually infected with them, to perform their quarantine. The laws of the respective states, upon this subject, were, by some persons, supposed to have been virtually repealed by the constitution of the United States. But congress have manifested a different interpretation of the operation of that instrument, and had passed several acts for giving aid and effect to the execution of the laws of the several states respecting quarantine. The last act upon the subject, 5. cong. c. 118, enjoins it as a duty upon the collectors, and other officers of the revenue, the masters and crews of the revenue-cutters, and the commanding officers of forts or stations upon the sea-coasts, duly to observe, and aid in the execution of those laws. Upon the like principle, I presume that the act of this commonwealth concerning wrecks, (1794. c. 6.) remains in force, until congress shall think proper to pass some law upon that subject. A contrary construction of the operation of the federal constitution in these and other similar cases, upon which congress may be authorized to legislate, but omit doing it, might be productive of infinite inconvenience and disorder.

The right of regulating foreign commerce, draws after it also, the right of regulating the conduct of seamen, employed in the merchant service; and by a continued chain, that of punishing other persons harboring or secreting them, as well on land, as elsewhere; and the act of 1. cong. 2 sess. c. 29, accordingly makes it penal in any person to harbor or secret any seaman regularly engaged in the service of any ship.

There seems to be one class of laws which respect foreign commerce, over which the states still retain an absolute authority; those, I mean, which relate to the inspection of their own produce, for the execution of which, they may even lay an impost, or duty, as far as may be absolutely necessary for that purpose: of this necessity it seems presumable, they are to be regarded as the sole judges. (C.U.S. Art. 1. Sec. 10 .) The article, indeed, is not altogether free from obscurity; but as no controversy has hitherto arisen upon the subject, it is not my intention to begin one.

But, this power of regulating commerce is qualified by some very salutary restrictions; for the constitution expressly declares, Art. 1. Sec. 9. "That no tax or duty shall be laid on articles exported from any state.... that no preference shall be given by any regulation of commerce, or revenue, to the ports of one state, over those of another; and that vessels bound to, or from, one state, shall not be obliged to enter, clear, or pay duties in another." These restrictions are well calculated to suppress those jealousies, which must inevitably have arisen among the states, had any tax or duty been laid upon any particular article of exportation; and, at the same time, to curb any disposition towards partiality in congress, should it at any time be likely to manifest itself.

An amendment to the constitution proposed by the convention of this state, and concurred in by that of North Carolina, was, "That no commercial treaty should be ratified without the concurrence of two-thirds of the whole number of the members of the senate.... And, that no navigation law, or law regulating commerce should be passed without the consent of two-thirds of the members present in both houses." It is somewhat remarkable, that the treaty of navigation and commerce concluded with Great Britain in the year 1794, notwithstanding the very general repugnance to it in almost every part of the United States, was, nevertheless, ratified precisely in the manner proposed by the first of these amendments. It appears that a proposition somewhat like the second, viz. "that no treaty should be binding upon the United States, which was not ratified by law," had been made in the general convention at Philadelphia, and rejected.[50] Nevertheless, the experience which we have had upon the subject of treaties, seems to recommend the adoption of some further precautions against the indiscreet use of this extensive power. On this subject we shall say something more hereafter.

The regulation of commerce with the Indian tribes, as distinguished from foreign nations, seems, in some degree, to be founded upon this principle, that those tribes which are not settled within the limits of any particular state, could only be regarded as tributary to the United States in their federal capacity; as to those who reside within the limits of particular states, it was thought necessary to unfetter them from two limitations in the articles of confederation which rendered the provision obscure, and perhaps contradictory. The power is there restrained to Indians not members of any of the states, and is not to violate or infringe the legislative right of any state within its own limits. What description of Indians were to be deemed members of a state, had been a question of frequent contention and perplexity in the federal councils. And how the trade with Indians, though not members of a state, yet residing within its legislative jurisdiction, could be regulated by an external authority, without so far intruding on the internal rights of legislation, seems altogether incomprehensible.[51]

4. Congress have power to establish an uniform rule of naturalization, and uniform laws on the subject of bankruptcies, throughout the United States.

As to the former of these powers; by the first articles of confederation

50. Message from the President of the U.S. to the House of Representatives, March 30, 1796.
51. Federalist, No. 42.

and perpetual union between the states, it was agreed, that the free inhabitants of each state, paupers, vagabonds, and fugitives from justice excepted, should be entitled to all privileges and immunities of free citizens in the several states; and the people of each state shall, in every other, enjoy all the privileges of trade and commerce. The dissimilarity of the rules of naturalization in the several states, had long been remarked as a fault in the system, and, as combined with this article in the confederation, laid a foundation for intricate and delicate questions. It seems to be a construction scarcely avoidable, that those who come under the denomination of free inhabitants of a state, (although not citizens of such state), were entitled in every other state to all the privileges of free citizens of the latter, that is, to greater privileges than they may be entitled to in their own state: our free negroes, for example, though not entitled to the right of suffrage in Virginia, might, by removing into another state, acquire that right there; and persons of the same description, removing from any other state, into this, might be supposed to acquire the same right here, in virtue of that article, though native-born negroes are undoubtedly incapable of it under our constitution: so that every state was laid under the necessity, not only to confer the rights of citizenship in other states, upon any whom it might admit to such rights within itself, but upon any whom it might allow to become *inhabitants* within its jurisdiction. But were an exposition of the term "inhabitants" to be admitted, which would confine the stipulated privileges to citizens alone, the difficulty would not be removed. The very improper power would still have been retained by each state, of naturalizing in every other state. In one state, residence for a short time conferred all the rights of citizenship; in another, qualifications of greater importance were required: an alien, therefore, legally incapacitated for certain rights in the latter, might, by previous residence only in the former, elude his incapacity; and thus the law of one state, be preposterously rendered paramount to the law of another, within the jurisdiction of such other. By the laws of several states, certain descriptions of aliens, who had rendered themselves obnoxious, and other persons whose conduct had rendered them liable to the highest penalties of the law, were laid under interdicts inconsistent, not only with the rights of citizenship, but with the privileges of residence, beyond the short period allowed by the treaty of peace with Great Britain. We owe it to mere casualty, that very serious embarrassments on this subject have not occurred. The constitution, and the several acts of naturalization passed by congress, have therefore wisely provided against them by this article, and by an explicit declaration contained in the law, that no person heretofore proscribed by any state, shall be admitted a citizen, except by an act of the legislature of the state in which such person was proscribed.

The federal court, consisting of judges Wilson and Blair, of the supreme court, and judge Peters, district judge in Pennsylvania, at a circuit court held for the district of Pennsylvania, in April, 1792; decided, "that the states, individually, still enjoy a concurrent jurisdiction upon the subject of naturalization: but that their individual authority cannot be exercised so as to contravene the rule established by the authority of the union: the true reason for investing congress with the power of naturalization (said the court,) was to guard against too narrow, instead of too liberal a mode of conferring the right of citizenship. Thus the individual states cannot exclude those citizens, who have been adopted by the United States; but they can adopt citizens upon easier terms, than those which congress may deem it expedient to impose."

But this decision seems to have been afterwards doubted by judge Iredel. And the act of 5 cong. c. 71. declares, that "no alien shall be admitted to become a citizen of the United States, or of any state, unless in the manner prescribed by that act." And by a subsequent act, passed 7 cong. chapter 28, it is also declared, that any alien, being a free white person, may become a citizen of the United States, or any of them on the conditions therein mentioned, "and not otherwise." These legislative expositions of the constitution do not accord with the judicial opinion above-mentioned. A very respectable political writer makes the following pertinent remarks upon this subject. [52] "Prior to the adoption of the constitution, the people inhabiting the different states might be divided into

52. See a letter of George Nicholas, Esq. on the Alien and Sedition laws.

two classes: natural born citizens, or those born within the state, and aliens, or such as were born out of it. The first, by the birth-right, became entitled to all the privileges of citizens; the second, were entitled to none, but such as were held out and given by the laws of the respective states prior to their emigration. In the states of Kentucky and Virginia, the privileges of alien friends depended upon the constitution of each state, the acts of their respective legislatures, and the common law; by these they were considered, according to the time of their residence, and their having complied with certain requisitions pointed out by these laws, either as denizens, or naturalized citizens. As denizens, they were placed in a kind of middle state between aliens and natural born citizens; by naturalization, they were put exactly in the same condition that they would have been, if they had been born within the state, except so far as was specially excepted by the laws of each state. The common law has affixed such distinct and appropriate ideas to the terms denization, and naturalization, that they can not be confounded together, or mistaken for each other in any legal transaction whatever. They are so absolutely distinct in their natures, that in England the rights they convey, can not both be given by the same power; the king can make denizens, by his grant, or letters patent, but nothing but an act of parliament can make a naturalized subject. This was the legal state of this subject in Virginia, when the federal constitution was adopted; it declares that congress shall have power to establish an uniform rule of naturalization; throughout the United States; but it also further declares, that the powers not delegated by the constitution to the United States, nor prohibited by it to the states, are reserved to the states, respectively or to the people. The power of naturalization, and not that of denization, being delegated to congress, and the power of denization not being prohibited to the states by the constitution, that power ought not to be considered as given to congress, but, on the contrary, as being reserved to the states. And as the right of denization did not make a citizen of an alien, but only placed him in a middle state, between the two, giving him local privileges only, which he was so far from being entitled to carry with him into another state, that he lost them by removing from the state giving them, the inconveniences which might result from the indirect communication of the rights of naturalized citizens, by different modes of naturalization prevailing in the several states, could not be apprehended. It might therefore have been extremely impolitic in the states to have surrendered the right of *denization,* as well as that of *naturalization* to the federal government, inasmuch as it might have operated to discourage migration to those states, which have lands to dispose of, and settle; since, it might be a disagreeable alternative to the states, either to permit aliens to hold lands within their territory, or to exclude all who have not yet completed their probationary residence within the United States, so as to become naturalized citizens, from purchasing, or holding lands, until they should have acquired all other rights appertaining to that character."

Here, another question presents itself: if the states, individually, possess the right of making denizens of aliens, can a person so made a denizen of a particular state, hold an office under the authority of such state? And I think it unquestionable that each state hath an absolute, and uncontrollable power over this subject, if disposed to exercise it. For every state must be presumed to be the exclusive judge of the qualifications of its own officers and servants: for this is a part of their sovereignty which they can not be supposed to have intended ever to give up. And if there be nothing in their constitutions, respectively, to the contrary, the legislature may unquestionably, by a general law, limit, or extend such qualifications, so far as they may think proper. The law of Virginia declares, "that all persons other than alien enemies, who shall migrate into this state, and give satisfactory proof by oath or affirmation that they intend to reside therein, and take the legal oath of fidelity to the commonwealth shall be entitled to all the rights, privileges and advantages of citizens, except that they shall not be capable of election or appointment to any office, legislative, executive or judiciary, until an actual residence in the state for five years thereafter; nor until they shall have evinced a permanent attachment to the state, by intermarrying with a citizen thereof, or of some one of the United States, or purchased lands of the value of three hundred dollars therein." Now although the act of congress may operate to repeal this act, so far as relates to the rights of naturalization, or, a state of perfect citizenship, under the constitution and laws of the union; yet, as it respects the rights which the state hath power to grant, such as holding lands, or an office under the sole, and distinct authority of the state, I see no reason to doubt that the law is as valid at this day, as it was before the adoption of the constitution of the United States.

The periods of residence, required by the several acts of congress before an alien can be admitted a citizen, have been various. The act of 1 congress, 2 session, c. 3, required two years only: this period was increased to five years, by the act of 3 congress, c. 85, which was still further extended to fourteen years, by the act of 5 congress, c. 71, but the act of, 7 cong. c. 28. has reduced it to five years, again. Any alien who shall have borne any hereditary title; or been of any order of nobility, in any other state, must renounce the same, on oath, at the time of his admission to take the oath of a citizen. A wise provision, the benefit of which it is to be hoped, may reach to the latest posterity.

There are few subjects upon which there is less practical information to be obtained in Virginia, than that of bankruptcies. The English statutes of Bankruptcy have never been regarded as in force, here; and the manner in which the commerce of the colony was conducted, before the revolution, by no means seemed to favor their adoption. In a commercial country, such as England, the necessity of good faith in contracts, and the support of commerce, oblige the legislature to secure for the creditors the persons of bankrupts. It is, however, necessary to distinguish between the fraudulent and the honest bankrupt: the one should be treated with rigor; but the bankrupt, who, after a strict examination, has proved before proper judges, that either the fraud, or losses of others, or misfortunes unavoidable by human prudence, have stripped him of his substance, ought to receive a very different treatment. Let his whole property be taken from him, for the benefit of his creditors; let his debt, if you will, not be considered as cancelled, till the payment of the whole; let him be refused the liberty of leaving his country without leave of his creditors, or of carrying into another nation that industry, which, under a penalty, he should be obliged to employ for their benefit; but what pretence can justify the depriving an innocent, though unfortunate man, of his liberty, as is said to be the practice in some parts of Europe, in order to extort from him the discovery of his fraudulent transactions, after having failed of such a discovery, upon the most rigorous examination of his conduct and affairs!

But, how necessary soever, bankrupt laws may be in great commercial countries, the introduction of them into such as are supported chiefly by agriculture, seems to be an experiment which should be made with great caution. Among merchants and other traders, with whom credit is often a substitute for a capital, and whose only actual property is the gain, which they make by their credit, out of the property of others, a want of punctuality in their contracts, may well be admitted as a ground to suspect fraud, or insolvency. But the farmer has generally a visible capital,[53] the whole of which he can never employ, at the same time, in a productive manner. His want of punctuality may arise from bad crops, unfavorable seasons, low markets, and other causes, which however they may embarrass, endanger not his solvency; his property is incapable of removal, or of that concealment, which fraudulent traders may practice with success; his transactions within the proper line of his occupation are few, and not liable to intricacy; whilst the merchant is perhaps engaged in a dozen different copartnerships, in which his name does not appear, and in speculations which it might require a life to unravel. To expose both to the same rigorous, and summary mode of procedure, would be utterly inconsistent with those maxims of policy, which limit laws to their proper objects, only. And accordingly, we find, that even in England, where the interests of commerce are consulted on all occasions, and where they are never sacrificed, (unless, perhaps, to ambition,) the bankrupt laws cannot affect a farmer, who confines himself to the proper sphere of his occupation; and the bankrupt law of the United States, 6 congress, 1 session, c. 19, is confined to merchants, or other persons,

---

53. In Virginia, farmers generally cultivate their own lands. It may be otherwise in the northern states.

actually using the trade of merchandise, by buying and selling in gross, or by retail, or dealing in exchange as a banker, broker, factor, underwriter, or marine insurer. Whilst the bankrupt laws are confined to such characters, and are resorted to, merely as a necessary regulation of commerce, their effect, in preventing frauds, especially where the parties or their property may lie, or be removed into different states, will probably be so salutary, that the expediency of this branch of the powers of congress, will cease to be drawn in question.

5. Congress have power to coin money, regulate the value thereof, and of foreign coin, and fix the standard of weights and measures.

By the former articles of confederation it was agreed that the United States in congress assembled, should have the sole and exclusive right and power of regulating the alloy and value of coin struck by their own authority, or by that of the respective states; and fixing the standard of weights and measures throughout the United States. By the present constitution the respective states are interdicted from coining money. All the powers mentioned in this clause are branches of the royal prerogative in England, but are with much greater propriety vested in the legislative department by the federal constitution. The history of England affords numberless instances, where this prerogative has been exercised to the great oppression of the subject. The power of debasing the value of the coin, at pleasure, has in fact been frequently used as an expedient for raising a revenue, and is accordingly reckoned as one of the indirect modes of taxation, by the author of the treatise on political economy: for if the government gives coin of an inferior standard, for purer coin of the same weight, as is generally done in these cases; or if it receives more for the coin, than the value of the bullion, and the expense of the coinage, as is likewise frequently practiced, the difference is an acquisition of revenue, paid by him who brings his bullion to the mint. According to the principles of our constitution, therefore, such a tax can not be imposed but by the representatives of the people.[54]

---

54. Consequently every bill for this purpose, or for any other by which a revenue may be raised, should originate in the house of representatives. Yet I am very much mistaken

Mr. Barrington, in his readings upon the English statutes, doubts whether the regulation of weights and measures be practicable, by law. He remarks, that in England it has been attempted by at least six different statutes, all of which have been ineffectual. He quotes an observation of Montesquieu's that it is the mark of a little mind in a legislature to attempt regulations of this kind. In England, perhaps, the attempt has not succeeded from some defect in the system. That proposed by Mr. Jefferson, when secretary of state, appears to be perfectly simple, and, I should apprehend, easily practicable: and the standard of measure, especially, may be obtained with a mathematical exactness sufficient for all the purposes of commerce, and even of arts and sciences.

It appears by the journals of the senate of the United States, March the 1st, 1791. "That a proposition had been made to the national assembly of France for obtaining a standard of measure, which shall at all times be invariable, and communicable to all nations, and at all times. That a similar proposition had been submitted to the British parliament: as the avowed object of these is to introduce an uniformity in the weights and measures of commercial nations; and as a coincidence of regulation by the government of the United States on so interesting a subject would be desirable, the senate resolved, that it would not be eligible at that time to introduce any alterations in the weights and measures of the United States."

6. Congress have power to provide for the punishment of counterfeiting the securities, and current coin of the United States.

––––––––––

if a recurrence to the early journals of the senate of the United States, would not prove, that the several acts for establishing the post-office; for regulating the value of foreign coins, and for establishing a mint, all originated in the senate. The reason of the acquiescence of the house of representatives on these occasions, probably was, that no revenue was intended to be drawn to the government by these laws: whereas strictly speaking, a revenue is raised by the act establishing the mint; equal to one half per centum, as an indemnification to the mint for the coinage: and in the case of the bill for establishing the post-office, there can be no room to doubt that it operates as a revenue law, and that, to a very considerable amount.

This power seems to be a natural incident to two others, of which we have before taken notice: the power of borrowing money on the credit of the United States, and that of coining money, and regulating the value thereof.

But congress appear to have extended the interpretation of this article much further than it might have been supposed it would bear: and possibly much further than the framers of the constitution intended. I allude to the act of 5 cong. c. 7 8, to punish frauds committed on the bank of the United States, which inflicts the penalty of fine and imprisonment, for forging or counterfeiting any bill or note, issued by order of the president, directors and company of the bank of the United States.

The right of congress to establish this company or corporation, with exclusive privileges, was warmly contested when the bill for establishing the bank was introduced into congress. 1 cong. 3 sess. c. 10. The same congress had at their first session agreed to an amendment of the constitution, declaring, that the powers not delegated to the United States, by the constitution, nor prohibited by it to the states, are reserved to the states respectively, or to the people. The advocates for the bill were challenged to produce the clause in the constitution which gave congress power to erect a bank. It nevertheless passed both houses. The president of the United States hesitated; it is said that he consulted his constitutional advisers upon the subject. That two of them were of opinion the bill was unconstitutional. It nevertheless, received his assent on the last day, that the constitution allowed him to deliberate upon it. Had he turned to the journals of convention (as on another occasion,) it has been confidently said, he would there have seen, that the proposition to authorize congress to establish a bank, had been made in convention and rejected: of this, he can not be supposed to have been ignorant, as he presided in the convention, when it happened; the journals of that body were then a secret, and in his keeping. If it was proper to resort to those journals to give a proper interpretation to the constitution in one instance, it surely was equally proper in the other; and if the rejection of one proposition in that body, was a sufficient reason for rejecting the same, when made by either house of congress, it seems difficult to assign a reason why the other should not have been treated in the same manner.[55]

If it were, in fact, an unconstitutional exercise of power in congress to pass a law establishing the bank, nothing can manifest the impropriety of over-stepping the limits of the constitution, more than the act which we have just noticed. It shows that the most unauthorized acts of government may be drawn into precedents to justify other unwarrantable usurpations.

7. Congress have power to establish post-offices, and post-roads. And this is one of those cases, in which I have supposed that the states may possess a concurrent, but subordinate authority, to that of the federal government. Concurrent, inasmuch, as there seems to be nothing in the constitution, nor in the nature of the thing itself, which may not be exercised by both, at the same time, without prejudice, or interference; subordinate, because wherever any power is expressly granted to congress, it is to be taken, for granted, that it shall not be contravened by the authority of any particular state. If, therefore, any state should find it necessary to establish post-offices on any road, which is not an established post-road, under the laws of the United States, there seems to be no constitutional objection to its doing so, until congress should think proper to exert its constitutional right to establish a communication by post, between the same places.... I put this case merely to show how far the exercise of these concurrent powers may be reconciled: it is much to be desired that a question of such delicacy may never occur between any state, and the federal government.

55. On the 24th of March, 1796, the house of representatives requested the president to lay before the house his instructions to Mr. Jay, together with the correspondence and other documents relative to the treaty with Great Britain, which he refused to do, upon the ground, that the house had no constitutional participation in the business of making treaties; to which he adds the following: "If other proofs than these, and the plain letter of the constitution itself be necessary to ascertain the point under consideration, they may be found in the journals of the general convention, which I have deposited in the office of the department of state. In those Journals, it will appear, that a proposition was made, that no treaty was binding on the United States which was not ratified by a law, and that the proposition was explicitly rejected."

The post-office, under proper regulations, is one of the most beneficial establishments which can be introduced by any government; by providing the means of intercourse between the citizens of remote parts of the confederation, on such a regular footing, as must contribute greatly to the convenience of commerce, and to the free, and frequent communication of facts, and sentiments between individuals. Hence the revenue arising from this source will always be more easily collected, and more cheerfully paid, than any other whatever. It appears, that notwithstanding the many unprofitable branches, into which the post-roads have been divided for the convenience of the people of the United States, there still remains a considerable sum that is annually brought into the federal treasury.

It seems reasonable that the product of this branch of the revenue should be, exclusively, applied to the extension of its benefits, until they shall completely pervade every part of the union.

8. Congress have power to promote the progress of science and useful arts, by securing for limited times to authors and inventors the exclusive right to their respective writings and discoveries.

This is another branch of federal authority, in which I presume the states may possess some degree of concurrent right within their respective territories; but as the security which the state could afford, would necessary fall short of that which an authority co-extensive with the union may give, it is scarcely probable that the protection of the laws of any particular state will hereafter be resorted to; more especially, as the act of 2 Cong. c. 55, declares, that "where any state before its adoption of the present form of government shall have granted an exclusive right to any invention, the party claiming that right, shall not be capable of obtaining an exclusive right under that act, but on relinquishing his right under such particular state, and of such relinquishment his obtaining an exclusive right under that act, shall be sufficient evidence." But this act does not appear to extend to copy-rights: the exclusive right to which is secured by an act passed, 1 Cong. 2 Sess. c. 15, amended by the act of 7 Cong. c. 36, for fourteen years; and if at the expiration of that term, the author being living, the same exclusive right shall be continued to him and his heirs, for other fourteen years. But the exclusive rights of other persons to their inventions, is limited to fourteen years, only, by the act first mentioned. Aliens, who have resided two years in the United States, are moreover entitled to the benefit of a patent for any new invention, by virtue of the act of 6 Cong. c. 25.

Whether it was under this clause of the constitution, or not, that the first secretary of the treasury grounded his opinion of the right of congress to establish trading companies, for the purpose of encouraging arts and manufactures;[56] or whether it was under this clause, that the establishment of a company for the discovery of mines, minerals, and metals, was contemplated by the authors of that scheme;[57] or whether it was from a conviction of the unconstitutionality of the proposition, in both cases, that neither of them took effect, I cannot presume to determine: but, certainly, if this clause of the constitution was relied upon, as giving congress a power to establish such monopolies, nothing could be more fallacious than such a conclusion. For the constitution not only declares the object, but points out the express *mode* of giving the encouragement; viz. "by securing for a limited time to authors and inventors, the exclusive right to their respective writings, and discoveries." Nothing could be more superfluous, or incompatible, with the object contended for, than these words, if it was, indeed, the intention of the constitution to authorize congress, to adopt any other mode which they might think proper.

9. Congress is moreover authorized to constitute tribunals inferior to the supreme court. (C.U.S. Art. 1. Sec. 8.) The third article of the constitution further declares, that the judicial powers of the United States shall be vested in one supreme court, and in such inferior courts, as congress may from time to time, ordain, and establish.... The establishment of courts, is in England, a branch of the royal prerogative, which has in that

56. See the report of Mr. Secretary Hamilton on this subject.

57. See the resolution of congress respecting the copper-mines on the south side of Lake Superior. April 16, 1800.... A bill for establishing a mine, mineral, and metal company, was brought into congress the next session, (as I have understood) but miscarried.

country been, from time to time, very much abused; as in the establishment of the famous courts of high-commission, and of the star-chamber; two of the most infamous engines of oppression and tyranny, that ever were erected in any country. "The judges of which (as the statute for suppressing the former declares) undertook to punish, where no law did warrant, and the proceedings, and censures of which were an intolerable burden upon the subject, and the means to introduce an arbitrary power and government." In England there are also courts of special-commission of *oyer and terminer,* (I do not here speak of the ordinary commissions of *oyer and terminer* and general goal of delivery, under which, courts are held by the judges of the courts of West-minister-hall, at the assizes, in every county,) occasionally constituted for the special purpose of trying persons accused of treason, or rebellion, the judges of which, are frequently some of the great officers of state, associated with some of the judges of West-minister-hall, and others, whose commission determines as soon as the trial is over. Most of the state trials, have been had before courts thus constituted: and the number of convictions and condemnations in those courts is a sufficient proof how very exceptionable such tribunals are: or rather how dangerous to the lives and liberties of the people, a power to select particular persons, as judges for the trial of state offenses, must be, in any country, and under any possible form of government. In these cases, the offense is not only in theory, against the crown and government, but often, in fact, against the person, authority, and life of the ruling monarch. His great officers of state share with him in danger, and too probably in apprehension, and resentment. These are the judges, he selects, and from their hands expects security for himself and them. Whilst the frailties of human nature remain, can such a tribunal be deemed impartial? Wisely, then, did the constitution of the United States deny to the executive magistrate a power so truly formidable: wisely was the supreme federal legislature made the depositary of the power of establishing courts, inferior to the supreme court; and most wisely was it provided, that the judges of those courts, when once appointed by the president with the advice of the senate, should depend only on their good behavior for their continuance in office, and be placed at once beyond the reach of hope or fear, where they might hold the balance of justice steadily in their hands.

These considerations induce a conviction in my mind, that this clause of the constitution does not authorize the establishment of occasional, or temporary courts, but courts of a permanent constitution and duration. Courts that could neither be affected in their conduct nor in the existence by the ferments or changes, of parties; and which might remain a monument to all posterity of the wisdom of that policy, which separates the judiciary from the executive and legislative departments, and places it beyond the influence or control of either.

These remarks are offered in this place, only for the sake of method; it will be our duty to give the subjects a fuller consideration elsewhere.

10. Congress have power to define and punish piracies and felonies committed on the high seas, and offenses against the law of nations.

The definition of piracies, says the author of the Federalist, might perhaps, without inconvenience, be left to the law of nations: though a legislative definition of them is found in most municipal codes. A definition of felonies on the high seas is evidently requisite, being a term of loose signification, even in the common law of England. The true ground of granting these powers to congress seems to be, the immediate and near connection and relation which they have to the regulation of commerce with foreign nations, which must necessarily be transacted by the communication on the high seas; and the right of deciding upon questions of war and peace, where the law of nations, is the only guide. Under this head, of offenses against the law of nations, the violation of the rights of ambassadors, as also of passports, and safe conducts is included. The act of 1 cong. 2 sess. c. 9, embraces the whole.

And here we may remark by the way, the very guarded manner in which congress are vested with authority to legislate upon the subject of crimes, and misdemeanors. They are not entrusted with a general power over these subjects, but a few offenses are selected from the great mass of crimes with which society may be infested, upon which, only, congress are authorized to prescribe the punishment, or define the offense. All felonies and offenses committed upon land, in all cases not expressly enumerated, being reserved to the states respectively. From whence this corollary seems to follow. That all crimes cognizable by the federal courts (except such as are committed in places, the exclusive jurisdiction of which has been ceded to the federal government) must be previously defined, (except treason,) and the punishment thereof previously declared, by the federal legislature.[58]

11. The power of declaring war, with all its train of consequences, direct and indirect, forms the next branch of the powers confided to congress; and happy it is for the people of America that it is so vested. The term war, embraces the extremes of human misery and iniquity, and is alike the offspring of the one and the parent of the other. What else is the history of war from the earliest ages to the present moment but an afflicting detail of the sufferings and calamities of mankind, resulting from the ambition, usurpation, animosities, resentments, piques, intrigues, avarice, rapacity, oppressions, murders, assassinations, and other crimes, of the few possessing power! How rare are the instances of a just war! How few of those which are thus denominated have had their existence in a national injury! The personal claims of the sovereign are confounded with the interests of the nation over which he presides, and his private grievances or complaints are transferred to the people; who are thus made the victims of a quarrel in which they have no part, until they become principals in it, by their sufferings. War would be banished from the face of the earth, were nations instead of princes to decide upon their necessity. Injustice can never be the collective sentiment of a people emerged from barbarism. Happy the nation where the people are the arbiters of their own interest and their own conduct! Happy were it for the world, did the people of all nations possess this power.

In England the right of making war is in the king. In Sweden it was otherwise after the death of Charles XII. Until the revolution in 1772, when from a limited monarchy, Sweden became subject to a despot.

---

58. See the opinion delivered by Judge Chase, in the federal circuit court of Pennsylvania, in the case of the United States vs. Worrel.

With us the representatives of the people have the right to decide this important question, conjunctively with the supreme executive who may, on this occasion as on every other, (except a proposal to amend the constitution,) exercise a qualified negative on the joint resolutions of congress; but this negative is unavailing if two thirds of the congress should persist in an opposite determination; so that it may be in the power of the executive to prevent, but not to make, a declaration of war.[59]

The several states are not only prohibited from declaring war, but even from engaging in it, without consent of congress, unless actually invaded, or in such imminent danger as will not admit of delay. This is certainly a very wise prohibition . . . . in fact, every barrier which can be opposed to the hasty engaging in war, is so much gained in favor of the interests of humanity. Upon the same principle it seems to be, that the states are likewise prohibited from granting letters of marque and reprisal: a measure which not infrequently precedes a declaration of war where individuals of one nation are oppressed or injured by those of another, and justice is denied by the state to which the author of such oppression or injury belongs. Did the several states possess the power of declaring war, or of commencing hostility without the consent of the whole, the union could never be secure of peace, and since the whole confederacy is responsible for any such act, it is strictly consonant with justice and sound policy, that the whole should determine on the occasion which may justify involving the nation in a war. The keeping up troops or ships of war in time of peace, is also prohibited to the several states upon the same principle. For these kinds of preparations for hostility are such as frequently may provoke, and even justify hostility on the part of other nations. But whenever war is actually declared, this prohibition ceases, and any state may adopt such additional measures for its own peculiar defense as its resources will enable it to do. The prohibition to emit bills

59. This is certainly the spirit of the constitution; but in the practical exercise of the functions of the president of the United States, it may be found to be in the power of that magistrate to *provoke,* though not to *declare* war. *Editor's note:* Here as elsewhere, Tucker seems remarkably prophetic.

of credit, must, however, infallibly narrow the means of recurring to these resources; a consequence which probably was not adverted to by the state conventions, as I do not recollect any amendments proposed on that subject.

The power of declaring war, with all its immediate consequences, was granted to congress under the former confederation, and nearly the same restrictions against engaging in war, keeping up troops and vessels of war in time of peace, were laid upon the individual states by the same instrument.

Among the amendments proposed by the convention of this state, and some others, to the constitution, there was one, "that no declaration of war should be made, nor any standing army or regular troops be raised or kept up, in time of peace, without the consent of two-thirds of the members present in both houses. And that no soldier should be enlisted for a longer term than four years, except in time of war, and then for no longer term than the continuance of the war." North-Carolina, as well as some other of the states, concurred in proposing similar amendments, but none has yet been made in this respect.

One of the most salutary provisions of the constitution, under this head, appears to be, that no appropriation of money to the use of an army, shall be for a longer term than two years.[60] Perhaps it would have been better to have limited such an appropriation to a single year. But inasmuch as no appropriation can be made for a longer time than the period affixed for the duration of congress, it will be in the power of the people, should the reasons of such an appropriation be disapproved by them, to remove their representatives, on a new election, from a trust which they may appear willing to betray. It is, therefore, to be hoped, that such a consideration will afford a sufficient check to the proceedings of congress, in regard to the raising and supporting armies. With

60. This restriction has proved illusory in practice; though congress are restricted from making any appropriation for the support of an army for more than two years, they have supposed themselves authorised to enlist an army for any period they may think proper, even in times of peace.

regard to a navy, the nature of such an establishment, to have any good effect, must be permanent. It would, therefore, have been extremely unwise to impose any prohibitions on that subject.

12. Congress has, moreover, power to provide for organizing, arming and disciplining the militia, and for governing such part of them as may be employed in the service of the United States, reserving to the states, respectively, the appointment of the officers, and the authority of training the militia, according to the discipline prescribed by congress.... C.U.S. Art. 1, Sec. 8.

The objects of this clause of the constitution, although founded upon the principal of our state bill of rights, Art. 8, declaring, "that a well regulated militia, composed of the body of the people trained to arms, is the proper, natural, and safe defense of a free state," were thought to be dangerous to the state governments. The convention of Virginia, therefore, proposed the following amendment to the constitution; "that each state respectively should have the power to provide for organizing, arming, and disciplining its own militia, whenever congress should neglect to provide for the same.".... A further amendment proposed, was, "that the militia should not be subject to martial law, except when in actual service, in time of war, rebellion, or invasion:... A provision manifestly implied in the words of the constitution. As to the former of these amendments, all room for doubt, or uneasiness upon the subject, seems to be completely removed, by the fourth article of amendments to the constitution, since ratified, viz. "That a militia being necessary to the security of a free state, the right of the people to keep, and bear arms, shall not be infringed.".... To which we may add, that the power of arming the militia, not being prohibited to the states, respectively, by the constitution, is, consequently, reserved to them, concurrently with the federal government. In pursuance of these powers, an act passed, 2 Cong. 1 Sess. c. 33, to provide for the national defense, by establishing an uniform militia throughout the United States; and the system of organization thereby established, has been carried into effect in Virginia, and probably in all the other states of the union.

Uniformity in the system of organization, and discipline of the militia, the constitutional defense of a free government is certainly desirable, and must be attended with beneficial effects, whenever the occasion may again require the cooperation of militia of the states respectively. The want of power over these subjects, was one of the defects of the former system of government under the confederation; and the consequent want of uniformity of organization, and of discipline, among the several corps of militia drawn together from the several states, together with the uncertainty and variety of the periods of service, for which those corps were severally embodied, produced a very large portion of those disgraces, which attended the militia of almost every state, during the revolutionary war; and, thus contributed to swell the national debt, to an enormous size, by a fruitless expense. By authorizing the federal government to provide for all these cases, we may reasonable hope, that the future operations of the militia of the confederated states, will justify the opinion, that they are the most safe, as well as most natural defense of a free state. An opinion, however, which will never be justified, if the duty of arming, organizing, training, and disciplining them, be neglected: a neglect the more unpardonable, as it will pave the way for standing armies; the most formidable of all enemies to genuine liberty in a state.

We have seen that the appointment of the officers of the militia, and the authority of training them, are expressly reserved to the states, by this article: this was considered as a most important check to any possible abuse of power in the federal government, whenever the aid of the militia should be required by it.

Notwithstanding this wise precaution in the constitution, the fifth congress appear to have disregarded it, by authorizing the president of the United States, to enlist and organize volunteers, or special corps of militia, whose officers HE was authorized to appoint, either by *his own authority,* or with the concurrence of the senate; they were likewise to be trained and disciplined in the manner which he should direct, and be liable to be called upon to do duty, at any time that he should judge proper, within two years after their acceptance, and be exempted, during the time of their engagement, from all militia duty, which might be required of them by the laws of the United States, or of any state, and

from every fine, penalty, or disability, provided to enforce the performance of any duty or service in the militia.... The number of these corps
was at first unlimited,[61] and the president was authorized to sell or lend
them artillery, small-arms, accoutrements, from the public arsenals.
L.U.S. 5 Cong. c. 64, Sec. 3, and c. 74.... As these select corps were not
called upon at the pleasure of the president, it seems impossible to view
them in any other light, than as a part of the militia of the states, separated by an unconstitutional act of congress, from the rest, for the purpose of giving to the president powers, which the constitution expressly
denied him, and an influence the most dangerous that can be conceived,
to the peace, liberty, and happiness of the United States.

13. Congress have power to declare the punishment of treason, against
the United States; but no attainder of treason shall work corruption of
blood, or forfeiture, except during the life of the person attainted. C.U.S.
Art. 3. Sec. 3. The act of 1 Cong. 2 Sess. c. 9. accordingly declares, that the
punishment shall be death, by hanging; and that no conviction or judgment for treason, shall work any forfeiture of estate. The constitution
itself declares, that treason against the United States shall consist only in
levying war against them, or in adhering to their enemies, giving them
aid and comfort: and that no person shall be convicted of treason, unless
on the testimony of two witnesses to the same overt act, or on confession
in open court.

The precise definition of treason, and the limitation of it to two cases,
only, both of which are clearly and explicitly described, at once evince
the prudence, caution, and wisdom, of the framers of the constitution, by
shutting the door (as far as human prudence, and human foresight,
could provide the means of doing so), against all possible cases of constructive treason. The many infamous acts of complying parliaments in
England, during the reigns of the Tudors and other tyrannical princes,
and the still more infamous and detestable decisions of servile and corrupt judges, from the days of Empson and Dudley, to those of the execrable Jefferies, must evince the necessity and propriety of such a

61. They were afterwards limited to 75,000 men.

limitation. From such corruption and servility, either in the legislature, or in the tribunals of justice, we may reasonably hope that this clause of the constitution will effectually guard and protect the United States. Nor should we forget, that the security of the citizen is still further ensured by that provision in the constitution, which declares that no person shall be convicted of treason, unless on the testimony of two witnesses to the same overt act, or on confession in open court. So that no extrajudicial confession, though proved by fifty witnesses, would, of itself, be evidence sufficient to convict a man upon a charge of treason. A provision which almost bids defiance of false witnesses.... The abolition of forfeiture, and of the corruption of blood, in cases of treason, is moreover a happy expedient for lessening the incentives, to prosecutions for treason, in corrupt governments. Rapacity is equally the cause and effect of tyranny. To curb every pretence for the exercise of it, should be the invariable object of a people forming a constitution. It is a monster that assumes a thousand shapes; of which the most odious, as well as the most terrible, is that, in which it attacks life, liberty and property, at the same time, and with the same weapons: its power is then irresistible.

14. Congress have power to exercise exclusive legislation, in all cases whatsoever, over such district, (not exceeding ten miles square) as may, by cession of particular states, and the acceptance of congress, become the seat of the government of the United States; and to exercise like authority over all places purchased by the consent of the legislature of the state; in which the same shall be, for the erection of forts, magazines, arsenals, dock-yards, and other needful buildings, C.U.S. Art. 1. Sec. 8.

The exclusive right of legislation granted to congress by this clause of the constitution, is a power, probably, more extensive than it was in the contemplation of the framers of the constitution to grant: such, at least, was the construction which the convention of Virginia gave to it. They, therefore, proposed an article as an amendment to the constitution, declaring, "that the powers granted by this clause, should extend only to such regulations as respect the police, and good government thereof." The states of New-York and North-Carolina proposed similar amendments; and one to the like effect was actually proposed in the senate of the United States, but shared the fate of many others, whose object was to limit the exercise of powers in the federal government.

I agree with the author of the Federalist,[62] that a complete authority at the seat of government was necessary to secure the public authority from insult, and its proceedings from interruption. But the amendment proposed by Virginia, certainly, would not have abridged the federal government of such an authority. A system of laws incompatible with the nature and principles of a representative democracy, though not likely to be introduced at once, may be matured by degrees, and diffuse its influence through the states, and finally lay the foundation of the most important changes in the nature of the federal government. Let foreigners be enabled to hold lands, and transmit them by inheritance or devise; let the preference to males, and the rights of primogeniture, be revived, together with the doctrine of entails, and aristocracy will neither want a ladder to climb by, nor a base for its support. Many persons already possess an extent of territory in the United States, not inferior to many of the German principalities: if they can be retained for a few generations, without a division, our posterity may count upon the revival of feudal principles, with feudal tenures.

The permanent seat for the government of the United States, has been established under the authority of an act passed 1 Cong. 2 Sess. c. 28, and 3 Sess. c. 17, upon the river Potomac, including the towns of Alexandria in Virginia, and Georgetown in Maryland. And the laws of Virginia (with some exceptions) were declared in force in that part of the ten miles square, which was ceded by Virginia, and those of Maryland in the other part, ceded by Maryland; and several other regulations were likewise established by two several acts, 6 Cong. 2 Sess. c. 15 and 24. An amendatory act passed also at the first session of the seventh congress, but the system does not appear to be as yet completely organized. It has been said, that it was in contemplation to establish a subordinate legislature, with a governor to preside over the district. But it seems highly questionable whether such a substitution of legislative authority is compati-

---

62. Federalist, No. 43.

ble with the constitution; unless it be supposed that a power to exercise exclusive legislation in all cases whatsoever, comprehends an authority to delegate that power to another subordinate body. If the maxim be sound, that a delegated authority cannot be transferred to another to exercise, the project here spoken of will probably never take effect. At present that part of the union is neither represented in the congress, nor in any state legislature; a circumstance, of which there seems to be some disposition to complain. An amendment of the constitution seems to be the only means of remedying this oversight.

15. Congress may admit new states into the union; but no new state shall be formed, or erected within the jurisdiction of any other state, nor any state be formed by the junction of two or more states, or parts of states, without the consent of the legislatures of the states concerned, as well as of congress.

In the articles of confederation it was agreed, that Canada, acceding thereto, and joining in the measures of the United States, should be admitted into the union; but no other colony should be admitted, unless such admission be agreed to by nine states. The eventual establishment of new states, within the limits of the territory of the United States, seems to have been overlooked by the compilers of that instrument. The inconvenience of this omission had been felt, and congress were, perhaps, led into an assumption of power not strictly warranted by the confederation, in the establishment of a government north-west of the Ohio. With great propriety, therefore, has the constitution supplied the defect. The general precaution that no new states should be formed without the concurrence of the federal authority, and that of the states concerned, is consonant to the principles which ought to govern, such transactions. The particular precaution against the erection of new states by the partition of a state without its consent, quiets the jealousy of the larger states; as that of the smaller is quieted by a like precaution against a junction of states without their consent. Under the authority of this article, the states of Vermont, Kentucky, and Tennessee, have been admitted into the union. And the boundaries of a new state have been lately established within the territory north-west of the Ohio, which, as soon as formed, is to be admitted as a member of the union, upon the same footing with the original states.

Congress, under the former confederation, passed an ordinance, July 13, 1787, for the government of the territory of the United States, north-west of the Ohio, which contained, among other things, six articles, which were to be considered as articles of compact between the original states, and the people and states of the said territory, and to remain unalterable, unless by common consent. These articles appear to have been confirmed by the sixth article of the constitution, which declares, that, all debts contracted, and engagements entered into before the adoption of the constitution, shall be as valid against the United States under the constitution, as under the confederation. The first of these articles secures the absolute freedom of religion: The second secures the benefit of the writ of *habeas corpus;* the trial by jury; judicial proceedings according to the course of the common law; the right of bail; the moderation of fines and of punishments; the right of personal security, and the right of private property; the sacredness of private contracts; and a proportionate representation of the people in the legislature. The third engaged for the encouragement of schools, and the means of education; and for good faith with the Indians, and the security of their persons and property from injury. The fourth stipulates, that the states formed in that territory shall forever remain a part of the American confederacy, &c. that they shall pay a part of the federal debt, and a proportional part of the expenses of government; that the legislatures of the new states shall never interfere with the primary disposal of the soil, by the United States in congress assembled; that no tax shall be imposed on lands the property of the United States; and that non-resident proprietors shall in no case be taxed higher than residents. That the navigable waters and carrying places shall be common high-ways, and forever free to all the citizens of the American confederacy, without any tax, impost, or duty therefor. The *sixth* article declares, that there shall be formed in the said territory, not less than three, nor more than five states; that whenever any of the states shall have sixty thousand free inhabitants, it will be admitted into the confederacy on an equal footing with the original states in all respects whatever, and be at liberty to form a permanent constitution and state government; provided the same be republican, and in conformity to the principles contained in those articles: and so far as can be consistent with the general interest of the confederacy, such admission shall be sooner allowed. The last articles stipulates that there shall be neither slavery, nor involuntary servitude, otherwise than in punishment of crimes; with a proviso, that persons escaping into the same from any state, where they may have been lawfully held to service, may be lawfully reclaimed and delivered up.

The ordinance further provides, that the estates both of resident and non-resident proprietors, shall descend to their children, or other next of kin, of a person dying intestate, in equal degree; and that there shall be no distinction between kindred of the whole and half blood; that the widow shall be endowed of one third part of the real and personal estate of her intestate husband, for life; and that this law, relative to descents and dower, shall remain in full force until altered by the legislature. That estates may be devised by will, and conveyed by lease and release, or by bargain and sale, by persons of full age, until the governor and judges should adopt other laws, as therein authorised. That the governor and judges, or a majority of them, shall adopt and publish, in the district, such laws of the original states, criminal and civil, as may be necessary, and best suited to the circumstances of the district, and report them to congress from time to time; which laws shall be in force until the organization of the general assembly therein, unless disapproved of by congress; but afterwards, the legislature might alter them as they should think fit. That the general assembly shall consist of the governor, a legislative council, and a house of representatives; that the governor shall be appointed by congress, every three years; that he shall have a negative upon all legislative acts; that he shall have power to convene, prorogue, and dissolve the general assembly; that the legislative council shall consist of five members, to continue five years in office, and to be appointed by congress, out of ten persons, residents and freeholders in the district, to be nominated by the house of representatives; that the governor and members of the council be removable by congress; that a house of representatives shall be chosen as soon as there shall be five thousand free male inhabitants of full age in the district, and consist of one member for every five hundred free male inhabitants, until the number shall amount to twenty-five, after which the number shall be regulated by the legislature; that the representatives thus elected, shall serve for two years. That a court of common law jurisdiction shall be appointed, to consist of three judges, who shall hold their offices during good behaviour. Such are the principal outlines of the temporary provisions made upon this subject, which, I presume, still remain in force in those parts of the territory, not included within the bounds of the new state, lately admitted as a member of the federal union. By the act of 1 Cong. c. 8, the president of the United States is authorised to nominate, and by and with the advice and consent of the senate, to appoint all officers, which, by that ordinance were to have been appointed by congress, under the confederation. And by the act of 6 Cong. c. 41, the territory was divided into two separate governments, one of which was called the Indiana territory, and a government established therein, in all respects similar to that provided by the above mentioned ordinance, except that the legislature thereof might be organized, notwithstanding there may not be five thousand free male inhabitants of full age therein. The act further declares, that nothing therein contained, shall be construed in any manner, to affect the government already in force, on the northwest of the Ohio river, further than to prohibit the exercise thereof within the Indiana territory.

By the act of 5 Cong. c. 45, authorizing the establishment of a government in the Mississippi territory, the president of the United States is authorized to establish therein a government, in all respects similar to that in the northwest territory, excepting and excluding that article of the ordinance of July 13, 1787 which declares, that there shall be neither slavery, nor involuntary servitude therein. The importation of slaves from foreign parts, is, nevertheless, prohibited, under the penalty of three hundred dollars upon the importer, and the slave is moreover entitled to freedom. Considering that the southern climate is in general favorable to negroes, and the difficulties which the number of them may in time create in some of the states; their dispersion is an object rather to be favored, perhaps, than discountenanced. Yet it is difficult to suppress a sigh, whenever we discover any measure which seems to favor the continuance of slavery among us.

16. Congress have power to dispose of, and make all needful rules and regulations respecting the territory, or other property belonging to the United States; and nothing in the constitution shall be so construed as to prejudice any claims of the United States, or of any state. C.U.S. Art. 3, Sec. 3.

During the revolutionary war, congress recommended to the several states in the union, having claims to waste and unappropriated lands in the western country, a liberal cession to the United States of a portion of their respective claims, for the common benefit of the union. In consequence of which, the state of Virginia ceded to the United States, for the common benefit of the whole confederacy, all the right, title, and claim which the commonwealth had to the territory northwest of the river Ohio, subject to the terms and conditions contained in her several acts of cession, viz. January 2, 1781 . . . Acts of October session, 1783. c. 18, and of December 30, 1778. One of the conditions of the latter act, being, that the said territory should be divided into not more than five, nor less than three states, whose boundaries are therein prescribed, of which we have already had occasion to make mention. It appears by a late document,[63] that the tract of country thus ceded, probably contains about 10,894,447, acres, within the line of the Indian boundary, of which 1,059,120, acres have been either located or set apart for military claims, 575,268, have been sold, or otherwise granted, and about 9,260,089, remained unsold on the first of November, 1801. The acts of 4 Cong. c. 29, and 6 Cong. c. 55, providing for the sale of these lands, contain many wise, and wholesome regulations, the principal of which, are, that they shall be laid out into townships six miles square, by north and south lines, according to the true meridian, and by others crossing them at right angles; that one

---

63. Report of the Secretary of the Treasury, Dec. 18, 1801.

half of those townships, taking them alternately, shall be subdivided into sections of six hundred and forty acres, which shall be numbered in order; that fair plats of these townships shall be made; that four sections at the center of every township, and every other section upon which a salt spring may be discovered shall be reserved for the use of the United States; that all navigable rivers shall be deemed, and remain public highways; and all lesser streams, and their beds shall become common to the proprietors of the lands on the opposite banks; and that no part of the lands shall be sold for less than two dollars per acre. A former secretary of the treasury estimated the value of these lands at twenty cents per acre, only.[64] Those which have been already sold pursuant to the act of congress, have averaged two dollars and nine cents; or, more than ten times that valuation. The celebrated Doctor Price, in his observations on the importance of the American revolution, recommends the reserving the whole, or a considerable part of these lands, and appropriating a certain sum annually to the clearing unlocated lands, and other improvements thereon; and computes that 100,000£ thus expended, with fidelity, would produce a capital of one hundred millions sterling, in about eighty years. This hint is probably worthy of attention to a certain extent: but it might well be questioned, whether, if the measure were adopted as far as he seems to have thought advisable, it might not lay the foundation of so large a revenue, independent of the people, as to be formidable in the hands of any government. To amass immense riches to defray the expenses of ambition when occasion may prompt, without seeming to oppress the people, has uniformly been the policy of tyrants. Should such a policy creep into our government, and the sales of land, instead of being appropriated to the discharge of former debts, be converted to a treasure in a bank, those who can at any time command it, may be tempted to apply it to the most nefarious purposes. The improvident alienation of the crown lands in England, has been considered as a circumstance extremely favorable to the liberty of the nation, by rendering

64. Report of Mr. Secretary Hamilton, to congress, January 19, 1795.

the government less independent of the people.[65] The same reason will apply to other governments, whether monarchial or republican: whenever any government becomes independent of the nation all ideas of responsibility are immediately lost: and when responsibility ceases, slavery begins. It is the due restraint and not the moderation of rulers that constitutes a state of liberty; as the power to oppress, though never exercised, does a state of slavery.

The disposal of the whole of the western lands, at so low a rate even that now established by congress, as a *minimum*, is a measure of the policy of which, doubts may be entertained. . . . The western territory ought to be regarded as a national stock of wealth. It may be compared to bullion, or coin deposited in the vaults of a bank, which although it produces no present profit, secures the credit of the institution, and is ready to answer any emergency. This supposes the lands, like bullion, to remain always of the same value; but the lands must increase in value at the rate of compound interest, whenever population becomes considerable in those parts of the union. This we see is daily increasing with great rapidity; and the value of the lands can not fail to keep pace with it. The most fertile spots upon the globe are of no more value than those which are covered by the ocean, so long as they continue remote from population; as the most barren spots are rendered valuable by its progress, and approach. A reserve of one half, or some other considerable proportion of the lands remaining unsold, therefore, seems to be recommended by many prudential considerations.

Other considerable cessions have been made to the United States by other states in the union. The state of Connecticut, made a cession which appears to have been accepted by congress, September 14, 1786. The act of 6 Cong. c. 38, authorizes the president of the United States to release the soil of a tract lying west of the west line of Pennsylvania, and extending one hundred and twenty statue miles, westward, and from the completion of the forty-first, to the latitude of the forty-second degree and two

65. See Price's Observations on the American Revolution.

minutes, north, which was excepted by the state of Connecticut out of their cession, provided that state shall cede to the United States certain other lands, and relinquish her right of jurisdiction over the territory, the soil of which shall be thus released to that state. South-Carolina likewise appears to have made a cession of lands to the United States. The territory ceded by North-Carolina now constitutes the state of Tennessee. The acts of 5 Cong. c. 45, and 6 Cong. c. 50, authorize the acceptance of a cession of lands, or of the jurisdiction thereof, from the state of Georgia, on such terms as may seem reasonable to the commissioners appointed on the part of that state, and of the United States respectively. In the mean time the establishment of the Mississippi government is not in any respect to impair the right of the state of Georgia to the jurisdiction, or of the said state, or any person, to the soil of the territory thereof.

17. To give efficacy to these powers, congress is authorized to make all laws which shall be necessary and proper for carrying into execution the foregoing powers, and all other powers vested by the constitution in the government of the United States, or in any department, or officer thereof. C.U.S. Art. 1. Sec. 8.

After the satisfactory exposition of this article given in the Federalist,[66] that if the constitution had been silent on this head, there could be no doubt, that all the particular powers requisite, as the proper means of executing the general powers specified in the constitution, would have resulted to the federal government, by unavoidable implication; and that if there be any thing exceptionable in this particular clause, it must be sought for in the specific powers, upon which this general declaration is predicated: and after the explicit declaration contained in the twelfth article of the amendments to the constitution, that the powers not delegated to the United States by the constitution, nor prohibited by it to the states, are reserved to the states respectively, or to the people: we might have indulged a reasonable hope, that this clause would neither have continued to afford any ground of alarm, and apprehension, on the part

66. See the Federalist, No. 33, and 44.

of the people, or the individual states, nor any pretext for an assumption of any power not specified in the constitution, on the part of the federal government. But, notwithstanding this remarkable security against misconstruction, a design has been indicated to expound these phrases in the constitution, so as to destroy the effect of the particular enumeration of powers, by which it explains and limits them, which must have fallen under the observation of those who have attended to the course of public transactions.[67]

The plain import of this clause is, that congress shall have all the incidental or instrumental powers, necessary and proper for carrying into execution all the express powers; whether they be vested in the government of the United States, more collectively, or in the several departments, or officers thereof. It neither enlarges any power specifically granted, nor is it a grant of new powers to congress, but merely a declaration, for the removal of all uncertainty, that the means of carrying into execution those otherwise granted, are included in the grant. A single example may illustrate this matter. The executive has power to make treaties, and by the treaty with Algiers, a certain tribute is to be paid annually to that regency. But the executive have no power to levy a tax for the payment of this tribute; congress, therefore, are authorized by this clause, to pass a law for that purpose: without which the treaty, although it be a supreme law of the land, in its nature, and therefore binding upon congress, could not be executed with good faith. For the constitution expressly prohibits drawing any money from the treasury but in consequence of appropriations made by law.

Whenever, therefore, a question arises concerning the constitutional-

67. Witness, the act for establishing a bank; the act authorising the president to appoint officers to volunteer corps of militia; the act declaring that a paper not stamped agreeably thereto, shall not be admitted as evidence in a state court; the alien and sedition laws, &c. "not to multiply proofs on this subject, it may be sufficient to refer to the debates of the federal legislature, for several years, in which arguments have, on different occasions, been drawn with apparent effect from these phrases, in their indefinite meaning." See report of the committee of the general assembly of Virginia, on the alien and sedition laws, January 20, 1800.

ity of a particular power; the first question is, whether the power be expressed in the constitution? If it be, the question is decided. If it be not expressed, the next inquiry must be, whether it is properly an incident to an express power, and necessary to its execution. If it be, it may be exercised by congress. If it be not, congress cannot exercise it.... And this construction of the words "*necessary and proper*," is not only consonant with that which prevailed during the discussions and ratification of the constitution, but is absolutely necessary to maintain their consistency with the peculiar character of the government, as possessed of particular and defined powers, only; not of the general and indefinite powers vested in ordinary governments.

Under this construction of the clause in question, it is calculated to operate as a powerful and immediate check upon the proceedings of the federal legislature, itself, so long as the sanction of an oath, and the obligations of conscience, are regarded, among men. For, as every member is bound by oath to support the constitution, if he were to bring every measure that is proposed to the test here mentioned, and reject whatsoever could not stand the scrutiny, we should probably cease to hear any questions respecting the constitutionality of the acts of the federal government. To which we may add, that this interpretation of the clause is indispensably necessary to support that principle of the constitution, which regards the judicial exposition of that instrument, as the bulwark provided against undue extension of the legislative power. If it be understood that the powers implied in the specified powers, have an immediate and appropriate relation to them, as means, necessary and proper for carrying them into execution, questions on the constitutionality of laws passed for this purpose, will be a nature sufficiently precise and determinate, for judicial cognizance and control. If on the one hand congress are not limited in the choice of the means, by any such appropriate relation of them to the specified powers, but may use all such as they may deem capable of answering the end, without regard to the necessity, or propriety of them, all questions relating to means of this sort must be questions of mere policy, and expediency, and from which the judicial interposition and control are completely excluded.... If, for example, congress were to pass a law prohibiting any person from bearing arms, as a means of preventing insurrections, the judicial courts, under the construction of the words necessary and proper, here contended for, would be able to pronounce decidedly upon the constitutionality of these means. But if congress may use any means, which they choose to adopt, the provision in the constitution which secures to the people the right of bearing arms, is a mere nullity; and any man imprisoned for bearing arms under such an act, might be without relief; because in that case, no court could have any power to pronounce on the necessity or propriety of the means adopted by congress to carry any specified power into complete effect.

This finishes our view of the legislative powers granted to the federal government; great and extensive as they must appear, they are in general such as experience had evinced to be necessary, or as the principles of a federal government had recommended to experiment, at least. In many instances these powers have been guarded by wise provisions, and restraints; some of which have been already noticed; the remainder will soon pass under review. Experience has already evinced the benefit of these restraints; and had they been more numerous, and more effectual, there is little reason to doubt that it would have contributed largely to the peace and harmony of the union, both heretofore, and hereafter. All governments have a natural tendency towards an increase, and assumption of power; and the administration of the federal government, has too frequently demonstrated, that the people of America are not exempt from this vice in their constitution. We have seen that parchment chains are not sufficient to correct this unhappy propensity; they are, nevertheless, capable of producing the most salutary effects; for, when broken, they warn the people to change those perfidious agents, who dare to violate them.

The restraints imposed on the legislative powers of the federal government, are briefly comprised in the ninth section of the first article of the constitution, or in the amendments, proposed by the first congress, and since ratified in the mode prescribed by the constitution. Of these we shall take a brief survey, in the order in which they occur.

1. The migration, or importation of such persons, as any of the states now existing shall think proper to admit, shall not be prohibited by congress prior to the year 1808, but a tax or duty may be imposed on such importation, not exceeding ten dollars for each person. C.U.S. Art. 1. Sec. 9.

This article, at the time the constitution was framed, was deemed necessary to prevent an opposition, on that ground, to its adoption in those states which still permitted the importation of slaves from Africa, and other foreign parts. A more liberal policy has since prevailed, so far as to render it probable that congress will never have occasion to exert the right of prohibiting the importation of slaves, such importation being now prohibited by the laws of all the states in the union. But should any of them show an inclination to rescind the present prohibitions, congress, after the year 1808, will be able to interpose its authority to prevent it, and impose some partial restraint upon the farther extension of the miseries of mankind. How to remove the calamities of slavery from among us, is left to the wisdom of the state government; the federal government can only prevent the further importation of slaves after the period limited.

2. The privilege of the writ of *habeas corpus* shall not be suspended, unless when in cases of rebellion or invasion, the public safety may require it. C.U.S. Art. 1. Sec. 9.

The writ of *habeas corpus,* is the great and efficacious remedy provided for all cases of illegal confinement; and is directed to the person detaining another, commanding him to produce the body of the prisoner, with the day and cause of his caption and detention, to do, submit to, and receive whatsoever the judge or court awarding such writ shall consider in that behalf. In England this is a high prerogative writ, and issues out of the court of king's-bench, not only in term time, but during the vacation, by a *fiat* from the chief justice, or any other of the judges, and running into all parts of the king's dominions. In Virginia it may issue out of the high court of chancery, the general court, or the court of the district in which the person is confined, and may be awarded by any judge of either of those courts in vacation: and if any judge in vacation, upon view of the copy of the warrant of commitment or detainer, or upon affidavit made, that such copy was denied, shall refuse any writ of *habeas corpus,* required to be granted by law, such judge shall be liable to the action of the party aggrieved. And by the laws of the United States, all the courts of the United States, and either of the justices of the supreme court, as well as judges of the district courts, have power to grant writs of *habeas corpus* for the purpose of an inquiry into the cause of commitment.... Provided that writs of *habeas corpus* shall in no case extend to prisoners in gaol, unless they are in custody under, or by color of the authority of the United States, or are committed for trial before some court of the same, or are necessary to be brought into court to testify.

Here a question naturally occurs: if a person be illegally committed to prison in any state, under, or by color of the authority of the United States, can any judge, or color of the state in which he is confined, award a writ of *habeas corpus,* for the purpose of an inquiry into the cause of his commitment? To which, I answer, that if he be committed or detained for any crime, unless it be for treason or felony, plainly expressed in the warrant of commitment, and be neither convicted thereof, nor in execution by legal process, the writ (due requisites being observed) can not be refused him: for the act is imperative, as to awarding the writ. The court or judge, before whom the prisoner is brought, must judge from the return made to the writ, what course he ought to pursue: whether, to discharge him from his imprisonment, or bail him, or remand him again to the custody of the person from whom he may be brought.

In England the benefit of this important writ can only be suspended by authority of parliament. It has been done several times of late years, both in England and in Ireland, to the great oppression of the subject, as hath been said. In the United States, it can be suspended, only, by the authority of congress; but not whenever congress may think proper; for it cannot be suspended, unless in cases of actual rebellion, or invasion. A suspension under any other circumstances, whatever might be the pretext, would be unconstitutional, and consequently must be disregarded by those whose duty it is to grant the writ. The legislatures of the respective states are left, I presume, to judge of the causes which may induce a suspension within any particular state. This is the case, at least, in Virginia.

3. No bill of attainder, or *ex post facto,* shall be passed by congress, or by any state. C.U.S. Art. 1. Sec. 9. 10.

Bills of attainder are legislative acts passed for the special purpose of attainting particular individuals of treason, of felony, or to inflict pains and penalties beyond, or contrary to the common law. They are state-engines of oppression in the last resort, and of the most powerful and extensive operation, reaching to the absent and the dead, as well as to the present and the living. They supply the want of legal forms, legal evidence, and of every other barrier which the laws provide against tyranny and injustice in ordinary cases: being a legislative declaration of the guilt of the party, without trial, without a hearing, and often without the examination of witnesses, and subjecting his person to condign punishment, and his estate to confiscation and forfeiture. Instances of their application to these nefarious purposes occur in almost every page of the English history for every considerable period: and very few reigns have passed in which the power has not been exercised, though, to the honor of the nation, I believe, no instance of the kind has occurred for more than half a century.

In May, 1778, an act passed in Virginia, to attaint one Josiah Philips, unless he should render himself to justice, within a limited time: he was taken, after the time had expired, and was brought before the general court to receive sentence of execution pursuant to the directions of the act. But the court refused to pass the sentence, and he was put upon his trial, according to the ordinary course of law.... This is a decisive proof of the importance of the separation of the powers of government, and of the independence of the judiciary; a dependent judiciary might have executed the law, whilst they execrated the principles upon which it was founded.

If any thing yet more formidable, or more odious than a bill of attainder can be found in the catalogue of state-enginery, it is what the constitution prohibits in the same clause, by the name of *ex post facto* laws: whereby an action indifferent in itself, and not prohibited by any law at the time it is committed, is declared by the legislature to have been a crime, and punishment in consequence thereof, is inflicted on the person committing it. Happily, for the people of Virginia, I can not cite any case of an *ex post facto* law, (according to this definition, which I have borrowed from Judge Blackstone,) that has been made in this commonwealth, nor have I heard of any such, in any other of the United States, that I recollect.

4. To check any possible disposition in congress towards partiality in the imposition of burdens, it is further provided, that no capitation or other direct tax shall be laid, unless in proportion to the census, or enumeration, by the constitution directed to be taken. (C.U.S. Art. 1. Sec. 9.) And the fifth article of the constitution declares, that no amendment made prior to the year 1808, shall in any manner affect this, and the first clause of the ninth section, above noticed.

The acts of 3 Cong. c. 45, and 4 Cong. c. 37, laying duties upon carriages for the conveyance of persons, were thought to be infringements of this article, it being supposed, that such a tax was a direct tax, and ought to have been apportioned among the states. The question was tried in this state, in the case of the United States, against Hylton, and the court being divided in opinion, was carried to the supreme court of the United States, by consent. It was there argued by the proposer of it, (the first secretary of the treasury,) on behalf of the United States, and by the present chief justice of the United States, on behalf of the defendant. Each of those gentlemen was supposed to have defended his own private opinion. That of the secretary of the treasury prevailed, and the tax was afterwards submitted to, universally, in Virginia.

5. Upon similar principles of equity, and impartiality, the succeeding clause declares, that no tax or duty shall be laid on articles exported from any state. No preference shall be given by any regulation of commerce, or revenue, to the ports of one state, over those of another; nor shall vessels bound to, or from one state, be obliged to enter, clear, or pay duties, in another. . . . And the fourth article of the constitution, Sec. 3, further provides, that nothing in the constitution of the United States shall be so construed as to prejudice any claims of the United States, or of any par-

234	*View of the Constitution of the United States*

ticular state. The reasons of these several restrictions and explanations having been already noticed. I shall add nothing more to the subject here; they being mentioned in this place only for the sake of method.

6. No title of nobility shall be granted by the United States, or any state: and no person holding any office of profit or trust under the United States, shall, without consent of congress, accept of any present, emolument, office, or title of any kind whatever, from any king, prince, or foreign state. C.U.S. Art. 1. Sec. 9, 10.

The first of these prohibitions was indispensably necessary to preserve the several states in their democratic form, tone, and vigor. Distinctions between the citizens of the same state, are utterly incompatible with the principles of such governments. Their admission, therefore, can not be too cautiously guarded against: and their total exclusion seems to be the only mode by which this caution can operate effectually. We have already noticed, that the several acts passed for establishing an uniform rule of naturalization, require of every alien becoming a citizen, of the United States, an absolute renunciation, on oath, of any title of nobility, which he might have borne under any other prince or state. Without this wise provision, this clause of the constitution might have failed of some of those salutary effects which it was intended to produce. The second prohibition is not less important. Corruption is too subtle a poison to be approached, without injury. Nothing can be more dangerous to any state, than influence from without, because it must be invariably bottomed upon corruption within. Presents, pensions, titles and offices are alluring things. In the reign of Charles the second of England, that prince, and almost all his officers of state were either actual pensioners of the court of France, or supposed to be under its influence, directly, or indirectly, from that cause. The reign of that monarch has been, accordingly, proverbally disgraceful to his memory. The economy which ought to prevail in republican governments, with respect to salaries and other emoluments of office, might encourage the offer of presents from abroad, if the constitution and laws did not reprobate their acceptance. Congress, with great propriety, refused their assent to one of their ministers to a foreign court, accepting, what was called the usual presents, upon taking his leave: a precedent which we may reasonably hope will be remembered by all *future* ministers, and ensure a proper respect to this clause of the constitution, which on a former occasion is said to have been overlooked.

Thus far the restrictions contained in the constitution extend: "The conventions of a number of the states having, at the time of adopting the constitution, expressed a desire, in order to prevent misconstruction, or abuse of its powers, that further declaratory and restrict clauses should be added; and as extending the ground of public confidence in the government, will best ensure the beneficent ends of its institution."[68] The following articles were proposed by congress, as amendments to the constitution, which having been duly ratified by the several states, now form a part thereof.

7. Congress shall make no law respecting an establishment of religion, or prohibiting the free exercise thereof, or abridging the freedom of speech, or of the press, or the right of the people peaceable to assemble, and to petition the government for a redress of grievances.... Amendments to C.U.S. Art. 3.

On the first of these subjects, our state bill of rights contains, what, if prejudice were not incapable of perceiving truth, might be deemed an axiom, concerning the human mind. That "religion, or the duty we owe to our Creator, and the manner of discharging it, can be dictated only by reason and conviction, not by force or violence." In vain, therefore, may the civil magistrate interpose the authority of human laws, to prescribe that belief, or produce that conviction, which human reason rejects: in vain may the secular arm be extended, the rack stretched, and the flames kindled, to realize the tortures denounced against unbelievers by all the various sects of the various denominations of fanatics and enthusiasts throughout the globe. The martyr at the stake, glories in his tortures, and proves that human laws may punish, but cannot convince. The pretext of religion, and the pretenses of sanctity and humility, have been employed throughout the world, as the most direct means of gaining influence and power. Hence the numberless martyrdoms and massacres which have drenched the whole earth, with blood, from the first

---

68. Preamble to the amendments proposed by the 1 Cong. 1 Sess.

moment that civil and religious institutions were blended together. To separate them by mounds which can never be overleaped, is the only means by which our duty to God, the peace of mankind, and the genuine fruits of charity and fraternal love, can be preserved or properly discharged. This prohibition, therefore, may be regarded as the most powerful cement of the federal government, or rather, the violation of it will prove the most powerful engine of separation. Those who prize the union of the states will never think of touching this article with unhallowed hands. The ministry of the unsanctified sons of Aaron scarcely produced a flame more sudden, more violent, or more destructive, than such an attempt would inevitably excite. . . . I forbear to say more, in this place, upon this subject, having treated of it somewhat at large in a succeeding note.

The second part of this clause provides, against any law, abridging the freedom of speech, or of the press.

It being one of the great fundamental principles of the American governments, that the people are the sovereign, and those who administer the government their agents, and servants, not their kings and masters, it would have been a political solecism to have permitted the smallest restraint upon the right of the people to inquire into, censure, approve, punish or reward their agents according to their merit, or demerit. The constitution, therefore, secures to them the unlimited right to do this, either by speaking, writing, printing, or by any other mode of publishing, which they may think proper. This being the only mode by which the responsibility of the agents of the public can be secured, and practically enforced, the smallest infringement of the rights guaranteed by this article, must threaten the total subversion of the government. For a representative democracy ceases to exist the moment that the public functionaries are by any means absolved from their responsibility to their constituents; and this happens whenever the constituent can be restrained in any manner from speaking, writing, or publishing his opinions upon any public measure, or upon the conduct of those who may advise or execute it.

Our state bill of rights declares, that the freedom of the press is one of the great bulwarks of liberty, and can never be restrained but by despotic governments. The constitutions of most of the other states in the union contain articles to the same effect. When the constitution of the United States was adopted by the convention of Virginia, they inserted the following declaration in the instrument of ratification: "that among other essential rights, the liberty of conscience, and of the press, cannot be cancelled, abridged, restrained, or modified by any authority of the United States."

An ingenious foreigner seems to have been a good deal puzzled to discover the law which establishes the freedom of the press in England: after many vain researches, he concludes, (very rightly, as it relates to that government,) that the liberty of the press there, is grounded on its not being prohibited.[69] But with us, there is a visible solid foundation to be met with in the constitutional declarations which we have noticed. The English doctrine, therefore, that the liberty of the press consists only in this, that there shall be no previous restraint laid upon the publication of any-thing which any person may think proper, as was formerly the case in that country, is not applicable to the nature of our government, and still less to the express tenor of the constitution. That this necessary and invaluable liberty has been sometimes abused, and "carried to excess; that it has sometimes degenerated into licentiousness, is seen and lamented; but the remedy has not been discovered. Perhaps it is an evil inseparable from the good to which it is allied: perhaps it is a shoot which cannot be stripped from the stalk, without wounding vitally the plant from which it is torn. However desirable those measures might be which correct without enslaving the press, they have never yet been devised in America."[70]

It may be asked, is there no protection for any man in America from the wanton, malicious, and unfounded attacks of envenomed calumny? Is there no security for his good name? Is there no value put upon reputation? No reparation for an injury done to it?

To this we may answer with confidence, that the judicial courts of the

69. De Lolme on the English constitution.

70. Letter from the American envoys to the French minister of foreign affairs. This nervous passage bespeaks its author; a gentleman who now fills the highest judicial office under the federal government.

respective states are open to all persons alike, for the redress of injuries of this nature; there, no distinction is made between one individual and another; the farmer, and the man in authority, stand upon the same ground: both are equally entitled to redress for any false aspersion on their respective characters, nor is there any thing in our laws or constitution which abridges this right. But the genius of our government will not permit the federal legislature to interfere with the subject; and the federal courts are, I presume, equally restrained by the principles of the constitution, and the amendments which have since been adopted.

Such, I contend, is the true interpretation of the constitution of the United States: it has received a very different interpretation both in congress and in the federal courts. This will form a subject for a discussion on the freedom of the press, which the student will find more at large in another place.

The same article secures to the people the right of assembling peaceably; and of petitioning the government for the redress of grievances. The convention of Virginia proposed an article expressed in terms more consonant with the nature of our representative democracy, declaring, that the people have a right, peaceably to assemble together to consult for their common good, or to instruct their representatives: that every freeman has a right to petition, or apply to the legislature, for the redress of grievances. This is the language of a free people asserting their rights: the other savors of that style of condescension, in which favors are supposed to be granted. In England, no petition to the king, or either house of parliament for any alteration in church or state, shall be signed by above twenty persons, unless the matter thereof be approved by three justices of the peace, or a major part of the grand-jury in the county; nor be presented by more than ten persons. In America, there is no such restraint.

8. A well regulated militia being necessary to the security of a free state, the right of the people to keep, and bear arms, shall not be infringed. Amendments to C.U.S. Art. 4.

This may be considered as the true palladium of liberty.... The right of self defense is the first law of nature: in most governments it has been the study of rulers to confine this right within the narrowest limits possible. Wherever standing armies are kept up, and the right of the people to keep and bear arms is, under any color or pretext whatsoever, prohibited, liberty, if not already annihilated, is on the brink of destruction. In England, the people have been disarmed, generally, under the specious pretext of preserving the game: a never failing lure to bring over the landed aristocracy to support any measure, under that mask, though calculated for very different purposes. True it is, their bill of rights seems at first view to counteract this policy: but the right of bearing arms is confined to protestants, and the words suitable to their condition and degree, have been interpreted to authorize the prohibition of keeping a gun or other engine for the destruction of game, to any farmer, or inferior tradesman, or other person not qualified to kill game. So that not one man in five hundred can keep a gun in his house without being subject to a penalty.

9. No soldier shall in time of peace be quartered in any house without the consent of the owner; nor in time of war, but in a manner to be prescribed by law. Amendments to C.U.S. Art. 5.

Our state bill of rights, conforming to the experience of all nations, declares, that standing armies in time of peace, should be avoided as dangerous to liberty; this article of the constitution, seems by a kind of side wind, to countenance, or at least, not to prohibit them. The billeting of soldiers upon the citizens of a state, has been generally found burdensome to the people, and so far as this article may prevent that evil it may be deemed valuable; but it certainly adds nothing to the national security.

10. The right of the people to be secure in their persons, houses, papers, and effects, against unreasonable searches and seizures, shall not be violated; and no warrant shall issue, but upon probable cause supported by oath, or affirmation, and particularly describing the place to be searched, and the person or things to be seized. Amendments to C.U.S. Art. 6, and herewith agrees the tenth article of our state bill of rights.

The case of general warrants, under which term all warrants not comprehended within the description of the preceding article may be included, was warmly contested in England about thirty or thirty-five years ago, and after much alteration they were finally pronounced to be illegal by the common law. The constitutional sanction here given to the same doctrine, and the test which it affords for trying the legality of any warrant by which a man may be deprived of his liberty, or disturbed in the enjoyment of his property, cannot be too highly valued by a free people.

But, notwithstanding this constitutional sanction, and the security which it promises to all persons, an act passed during the second session of the fifth congress, entitled an act concerning aliens, which was supposed to violate this article of the constitution, in the most flagrant and unjustifiable degree: by authorizing the president of the United States to order all such aliens as he should judge dangerous to the peace and safety of the United States, or have reasonable grounds to suspect of any treasonable or secret machinations against the government thereof, to depart out of the territory of the United States within a limited time; and in case of disobedience, every alien so ordered was liable on conviction to be imprisoned for any term not exceeding three years. And any alien so ordered to depart, and remaining in the United States without a license from the president might be arrested, and sent out of them, by his order: and, in case of his voluntary return, might be imprisoned so long, as in the opinion of the president, the public safety might require. Alien friends, only, were the objects of this act, another act being passed at the same session, respecting alien enemies. . . . The general assembly of Virginia at their session in 1798, "protested against the palpable, and alarming infractions of the constitution in this act; which exercises a power no where delegated to the federal government; and which, by uniting legislative and judicial powers to those of executive, subverts the general principles of a free government, as well as the particular organization, and positive provisions of the federal constitution." Kentucky had before adopted a similar conduct.

Among the arguments used by the general assembly of Virginia in their strictures upon this act, the following seem to be more peculiarly apposite to the subject of this article.

In the administration of preventive justice, the following principles have been held sacred; that some probable ground of suspicion be exhibited before some judicial authority; that it be supported by oath or affirmation; that the party may avoid being thrown into confinement, by finding pledges or securities for his legal conduct, sufficient in the judgment of some judicial authority; that he may have the benefit of a writ of *habeas corpus,* and thus obtain his release, if wrongfully confined; and that he may at any time be discharged from his recognizance, or his confinement, and restored to his former liberty and rights, on the order of the proper judicial authority; if it shall see sufficient cause.

Let the student diligently compare these principles of the only preventive justice known to American jurisprudence, and he will probably find that they are all violated by the alien act. The ground of suspicion is to be judged of, not by any judicial authority, but by the executive magistrate, alone; no oath, or affirmation is required; if the suspicion be held reasonable by the president, (whatever be the grounds of it) he may order the suspected alien to depart, without the opportunity of avoiding the sentence by finding pledges for his future good conduct, as the president may limit the time of departure as he pleases, the benefit of the writ of *habeas corpus* may be suspended with respect to the party, although the constitution ordains, that it shall not be suspended, unless when the public safety may require it, in case of rebellion, or invasion, neither of which existed at the passage of that act: and the party being, under the sentence of the president, either removed from the United States, or punished by imprisonment, or disqualification ever to become a citizen on conviction of his not obeying the order of removal, or on returning without the leave of the president, he can not be discharged from the proceedings against him, and restored to the benefits of his former situation, although the highest judicial authority should see the most sufficient cause for it.

Among the reasons alleged by a committee of congress, in support of the constitutionality of the alien law, one was; "that the constitution was made for citizens, not for aliens, who of consequence have no rights under it, but remain in the country, and enjoy the benefit of the laws, not as matter of right, but merely as matter of favor and permission; which may be withdrawn whenever the government may judge their further continuance dangerous."[71]

To this it was answered; that, "although aliens are not parties to the constitution, it does not follow that the constitution has vested in Congress an absolute right over them; or that whilst they actually conform to it, they have no right to its protection. That if they had no rights under it, they might not only be banished, but even capitally punished, without a jury, or other incidents to a fair trial."[72] A doctrine so far from being sound, that a jury, one half of which shall be aliens, is allowed, it is believed, by the laws of every state, except in cases of treason. To which we may add that the word "*persons*" in this, and the subsequent articles of the amendments to the constitution, most clearly designate, that aliens, as *persons,* must be entitled to the benefits therein secured to all *persons* alike.... As we shall have occasion to mention the subject of this interesting controversy, again, in another place, I shall only add here, that the act was permitted to expire at the end of two years, without any attempt, I believe, to continue it.

11. No person shall be held to answer for a capital, or otherwise infamous crime, unless on a presentment, or indictment of a grand jury, except in cases arising in the land or naval forces, or in the militia in the time of war, or public danger; nor shall any person be subject for the same offense to be twice put in jeopardy of life or limb; nor be compelled in any criminal case, to be witness against himself, nor be deprived of life, liberty, or property, without due process of law; nor shall private property be taken for public use without just compensation. Amendments to C.U.S. Art. 7, and,

12. In all criminal prosecutions, the accused shall enjoy the right to a speedy and public trial, by an impartial jury of the state, and district, wherein the crime shall have been committed, which district shall have

71. Report of the committee of congress, on the petitions for repeal of the alien and sedition laws; February 25, 1799.

72. Report of the committee of the general assembly of Virginia, January 20, 1800.

been previously ascertained by law, and to be informed of the nature and cause of the accusation; to be confronted with witnesses against him; to have compulsory process for obtaining witnesses in his favor, and to have the assistance of counsel for his defense. Amendments to C.U.S. Art. 8.

13. Excessive bail shall not be required, nor excessive fines imposed, nor cruel, and unusual punishments inflicted. Amendments to C.U.S. Art. 10.

The subjects of these three articles are so immediately connected with each other, that I have chosen not to separate them. The first may be considered as a liberal exposition, and confirmation of the principles of that important chapter of Magna Carta, which declares, *"Nullus liber Homo aliquo modo destruatur nisi per legale judicium parium suorum,"* which words, *aliquo modo destruatur,* according to Sir Edward Coke, include a prohibition not only of killing and maiming, but also of torturing, and of every oppression by color of legal authority: and the words *liber Homo,* extend to every one of the king's subjects, "be he ecclesiastical or temporal, free or bond, man or woman, old or young, or be he outlawed, excommunicated, or any other, without exception".... for even a villein, as he tells us elsewhere, is comprehended under the term *liber Homo,* except against his lord.

The common law maxim, that no man is to be brought in jeopardy of his life more than once for the same offense, is here rendered a fundamental law of the government of the United States; as, is also, that other inestimable maxim of the common law, that no man shall be compelled in any criminal case to give evidence against himself; that he shall, moreover, be informed of the nature and cause of his accusation: that he shall be confronted with the witnesses against him; that he shall have compulsory process for obtaining witnesses in his favor;....a benefit long denied by the courts in England: and that he shall have the assistance of counsel for his defense;....not as a matter of grace, but of right; ....not for his partial defense, upon a point of law, but for his full defense, both on the law, and the evidence: and, that he shall, in no case, be deprived of life, liberty, or property, without due process of law. To all which, is added, the inestimable right of a trial by jury, of the state and district in which the crime shall have been committed. The importance of all which articles will more evidently appear, in the course of our examination of the various subjects to which they relate, in the first and fourth book of the Commentaries on the Laws of England. That part of the seventh article which declares that private property shall not be taken for public use, without just compensation, was probably intended to restrain the arbitrary and oppressive mode of obtaining supplies for the army, and other public uses, by impressment, as was too frequently practiced during the revolutionary war, without any compensation whatever. A law of the state of Virginia describes by whom, and in what cases, impresses may be made; and authorizes the commitment of the offender in case of any illegal impressment.

We have already noticed the act concerning aliens, as violating the sixth article of the amendments to the constitution. It was said, moreover, to violate the seventh and eighth. To this the congress answered, "that the provisions in the constitution relative to presentment and trial of offenses by juries, do not apply to the revocation of an asylum given to aliens. Those provisions solely respect crimes, and the alien may be removed without having committed any offense, merely from motives of policy, or security. The citizen, being a member of society, has a right to remain in the country, of which he cannot be disfranchised, except for offenses first ascertained, on presentment and trial by jury.... That the removal of aliens, though it may be inconvenient to them, cannot be considered as a punishment inflicted for an offense, but merely the removal, from motives of general safety, of an indulgence, which there is danger of their abusing, and which we are in no manner bound to grant or continue."[73]

To these arguments the general assembly of Virginia replied; that it can never be admitted that the removal of aliens authorized by the act, is to be considered, not as a punishment for an offense, but as a measure of precaution and prevention. If the banishment of an alien from a coun-

73. Report of the committee of congress, February 25, 1799.

try into which he has been invited, as the asylum most auspicious to his happiness; a country where he may have formed the most tender connections, where he may have vested his entire property, and acquired property of the real and permanent, as well as the moveable and temporary kind; where he enjoys under the laws, a greater share of the blessings of personal security, and personal liberty, than he can elsewhere hope for, and where he may have nearly completed his probationary title to citizenship; if, moreover, in the execution of the sentence against him, he is to be exposed, not only to the ordinary dangers of sea, but to the peculiar casualties incident to a crisis of war, and of unusual licentiousness on that element, and possibly to vindictive purposes which his emigration itself may have provoked; if a banishment of this sort be not a punishment, and among the severest of punishments, it will be difficult to imagine a doom, to which the name can be applied. And, if it be a punishment, it will remain to be shown, whether, according to the express provisions of these articles, it can be constitutionally inflicted, on mere suspicion, by the single will of the executive magistrate, on persons convicted of no personal offense against the laws of the land, nor involved in any offense against the law of nations, charged on the foreign state of which they were members."[74]

14. In suits at common law, where the value in controversy shall exceed twenty dollars, the right of trial by jury shall be preserved, and no fact tried by a jury shall be otherwise reexamined in any court of the United States than according to the rules of the common law. C.U.S. Art. 9. Amendments.

This article provides for the trial by jury in civil cases, as well as criminal, and supplies some omission in the constitution.

15. The enumeration in the constitution, of certain rights, shall not be construed to deny, or disparage others retained by the people. Amendments to C.U.S. Art. 11. and,

---

74. Report of the committee of the general assembly of Virginia, on the alien and sedition laws, January 20, 1800.

16. The powers not delegated to the United States by the constitution, nor prohibited by it to the states, are reserved to the states respectively, or to the people. C.U.S. Art. 12. Amendments.

All the powers of the federal government being either expressly enumerated, or necessary and proper to the execution of some enumerated power; and it being one of the rules of construction which sound reason has adopted; that, as exception strengthens the force of a law in cases not excepted, so enumeration weakens it, in cases not enumerated; it follows, as a regular consequence, that every power which concerns the right of the citizen, must be construed strictly, where it may operate to infringe or impair his liberty; and liberally, and for his benefit, where it may operate to his security and happiness, the avowed object of the constitution: and, in like manner, every power which has been carved out of the states, who, at the time of entering into the confederacy, were in full possession of all the rights of sovereignty, is in like manner to be construed strictly, wherever a different construction might derogate from the rights and powers, which by the latter of these articles, are expressly acknowledged to be reserved to them respectively.

The want of a bill of rights was among the objections most strongly urged against the constitution in its original form. The author of the Federalist undertakes to show, that a bill of rights was not only unnecessary, but would be dangerous. A bill of rights may be considered, not only as intended to give law, and assign limits to a government about to be established, but as giving information to the people. By reducing speculative truths to fundamental laws, every man of the meanest capacity and understanding may learn his own rights, and know when they are violated; a circumstance, of itself, sufficient, I conceive, to counterbalance every argument against one.

To comprehend the full scope and effect of the twelfth article, by which certain rights are said to be reserved to the states respectively, or to the people, it is to be recollected, that there are powers, exercised by most other governments, which in the United States are withheld by the people, both from the federal government and from the state governments: for instance, a tax on exports can be laid by no constitutional authority whatever, whether of the United States, or of any state; no bill of attainder, or *ex post facto* law can be passed by either; no title of nobility can be granted by either. Many other powers of government are neither delegated to the federal government, nor prohibited to the states, either by the federal or state constitutions. These belong to that indefinite class of powers which are supposed necessarily to devolve upon every government, in consequence of the very act of its establishment, where no restrictions are imposed on the exercise of them; such as the power of regulating the course in which property may be transmitted by deed, will, or inheritance; the manner in which debts may be recovered, or injuries redressed; the right of defining and punishing offenses against the society, other than such as fall under the express jurisdiction of the federal government; all which, and all others of a similar nature are reserved to, and may be exercised by the state governments. From those powers, which are in express terms granted to the United States, and though not prohibited to the states respectively, are not susceptible of a concurrent exercise of authority by them, the states, notwithstanding this article, will continue to be excluded; such is the power to regulate commerce, and to define and punish piracies and felonies committed upon the high seas; from which the states, respectively, are by necessary and unavoidable construction excluded from any share or participation. On the other hand, such of the powers granted by the constitution to the federal government, as will admit of a concurrent exercise of authority, both in the federal and the state governments; such for example, as the right of imposing taxes, duties, and excises (except duties upon imports or exports, or upon tonnage, which the states cannot do without consent of congress) may be exercised by the states respectively, concurrently with the federal government. And here it may not be improper to take a short review of the powers which are expressly prohibited to the individual states by the constitution; or can be exercised by them only with the consent of congress; they have been enumerated elsewhere, but seem to require a more particular notice in this place.

1. First, then; no state shall enter into any treaty, alliance, or confederation. C.U.S. Art. 1. Sec. 10.

A similar provision was contained in the articles of confederation, the terms of which are in reality more strong and definite than those of the constitution. The federal government being the organ through which the individual states communicate with foreign nations, and the interest of the whole confederacy being paramount to that of any member thereof; the power of making treaties and alliances with foreign nations, is with propriety vested exclusively in the federal government. Moreover, as congress is vested with the power of admitting new states into the union, it was necessary to prohibit any alliance or confederacy with such state, antecedent to its admission into the union; for such an alliance might contravene the principles of the constitution, and prevent or retard the proposed admission. And lastly, to preserve the union entire, and unbroken, no partial confederacy between any two or more states, can be entered into: for that would in fact dissolve the government of the United States, as now established.

2. Secondly; no state shall, without the consent of congress, enter into any agreement or compact with another state, or with any foreign power. C.U.S. Art. 1. Sec. 10.

Here we find a distinction between treaties, alliances, and confederations; and agreements or compacts. The former relate ordinarily to subjects of great national magnitude and importance, and are often perpetual, or made for a considerable period of time; the power of making these is altogether prohibited to the individual states: but agreements, or compacts, concerning transitory or local affairs, or such as cannot possibly affect any other interest but that of the parties, may still be entered into by the respective states, with the consent of congress. The compact between this state and Maryland, entered into in the year 1786, may serve as an example of this last class of public agreements.

3. No state shall grant letters of marque or reprisal.

As these measures ordinarily precede a declaration of war, the reasons for the total prohibition of the exercise of this power, by the states respectively, have been already mentioned: for otherwise the petulance and precipitation of any one state, whose citizens may have been injured by the subjects of a foreign nation, might plunge the union into a war.

4. No state shall, without consent of congress, keep troops, or ships of war, in time of peace; or engage in war, unless actually invaded, or in such imminent danger as will not admit of delay.

The prohibitions contained in this clause are not absolute, but are subject to the consent of congress, or imperious circumstances. The setting on foot an army or navy, in the time of profound peace, is often a just cause of jealousy between neighboring, and even remote nations. But there is not infrequently a period between the commencement of a quarrel between two nations, and a declaration of war, or commencement of actual hostility, when prudence makes it necessary to prepare for the issue of the dispute. During such a period, it might be necessary to call for the exertions of the several states, in aid of the federal strength. At this epoch, it might be the summit of indiscretion to check the ardor of the respective states, if disposed to raise an army or navy from its own resources. Congress therefore may permit it; and if the danger of an attack upon any particular state be so imminent, as not to admit of delay, or if it be actually invaded, it may adopt measures for its own defense, without waiting for the consent of congress. And when a war is actually begun, under the authority of the federal union, any state may, according to its resources and discretion, keep any number of troops or ships: for the prohibition ceases as soon as war begins.

5. No state shall coin money: emit bills of credit, make any thing but gold and silver coin a tender in payment of debts: or pass any law impairing the obligation of contracts.

The right of coining, and regulating the value of coin, being vested in the federal government, a participation in those rights could not be permitted to the respective states with any propriety. For the government must be responsible for the purity and weight of all coin issued under its authority: this could not be if the states were permitted to coin money according to the standard prescribed by the United States, as the officers of the mint would be under the directions of the state government. And if the several states were to issue coin of different standards, or denominations, the inconveniences to commerce would be infinite. They are therefore prohibited altogether from coining money.... The evils of paper money, the injury produced by it to public credit; the utter destruction of the fortunes of numberless individuals, by a rapid and unparalleled depreciation during the revolutionary war; the grievous hardships introduced, at the same period, by the tender laws, (an unhappy, but perhaps unavoidable expedient, to which both the federal, and state governments were constrained to have recourse, at the same time) by which a creditor was in some instances obliged to accept paper in a most depreciated state, for a just debt of an hundred times its real value, or incur the general odium of his fellow-citizens, probably gave rise to the prohibition against any state's emitting paper money, or making any thing but gold or silver a tender in payment of debts, or passing any law impairing the obligation of contracts. . . . But why was not the prohibition extended to the federal, as well as to the state governments? The federal government, during the revolutionary war, was not more exempt from just cause of censure upon these grounds, than the states respectively. Many of the laws passed by the states to support the credit of the continental money, by making it a tender in payment of debts, were passed on the recommendation of congress. The forty for one scheme originated there; why not prohibit some future congress from renewing the same breach of faith?

6. No state shall pass any bill of attainder, or *ex post facto* law; or grant any title of nobility.

These prohibitions being extended equally to the federal government, as to the states, have been already sufficiently noticed.

7. No state shall, without the consent of congress, lay any imposts or duties on imports or exports, except what may be absolutely necessary for executing its inspection laws; and the net produce of all duties and imposts, laid by any state on imports, or exports, shall be for the use of the treasury of the United States: and all such laws shall be subject to the revision and control of congress. Nor shall any state, without the consent of congress lay any duty of tonnage.

On the subject of these prohibitions, respectively, sufficient hath already been said, under the article which authorizes congress to regulate commerce.

Having thus taken a survey of the powers delegated to the congress of the United States, and of those prohibited thereto, by the constitution; as also, of those, which are either altogether prohibited to the states, individually, or can be exercised by them only, with the consent, and under the control of congress; and in the course of that survey, having pointed out according to the best of my abilities, those powers which are exclusively vested in the federal government; secondly, those powers, in which the federal, and state governments, may be presumed to possess concurrent jurisdiction, and authority: thirdly, those powers which are equally prohibited to the states, respectively, or can be exercised by them only, with the approbation and consent of the federal government; it follows that all other powers of government compatible with the nature and principle of democratic governments, and not prohibited by the bill of rights, or constitution of the respective states, remain with them, and may be exercised by them, respectively, in such manner as their several constitutions, and laws, may permit, or direct. And this right, is expressly recognized, as before-mentioned, by the twelfth article of the amendments to the federal constitution; declaring, that the powers not delegated to the United States by the constitution, not prohibited by it to the states, are reserved to the states respectively, or to the people. This numerous class of powers relates altogether to the civil institutions, or laws of the states; and the subject of them forms their several municipal codes, according to the constitutions and laws of each state, respectively.

Here let us again pause, and reflect, how admirably this division, and distribution of legislative power is adapted to preserve the liberty, and to promote the happiness of the people of the United States; by assigning to the federal government, objects which relate only to the common interests of the states, as composing one general confederacy, or nation; and reserving to each member of that confederacy, a power over whatever may affect, or promote its domestic peace, happiness, or prosperity: at the same time limiting, and restraining both, from the exercises, or assumption of powers, which experience has demonstrated, either in this, or in other countries, to be too dangerous to be entrusted with any man or body of men whatsoever. . . . Restraints upon the power of the legislature, says De Lolme, are more necessary than upon the executive; the former does in a moment, what the latter accomplishes only by successive steps. In England, all legislative power, without limitation, and without control, is concentrated in the two houses of parliament, with the king at their head; and their united power according to the maxims of that government, is omnipotent. In the United States, the great and essential rights of the people are secured against legislative as well as executive ambition.... They are secured, not by laws, only, which the legislature who makes them may repeal, and annul at its pleasure; but by constitutions, paramount to all laws: defining and limiting the powers of the legislature itself, and opposing barriers against encroachments, which it can not pass, without warning the people of their danger. Secondly, by that division, and distribution of power between the federal, and the state governments, by which each is in some degree made a check upon the excesses of the other. For although the states possess no constitutional negative upon the proceedings of the congress of the United States, yet it seems to be a just inference and conclusion, that as the powers of the federal government result from the compact to which the states are parties; and are limited by the plain sense of the instrument constituting that compact; they are no further valid, than as they are authorized by the grants enumerated therein: and, that in case of a deliberate, palpable, and dangerous exercise of other powers, not granted by that compact, the states, who are parties thereto, have the right, and are in duty bound, to interpose, for arresting the progress of the evil, and for maintaining within their respective limits, the authorities, rights, and liberties appertaining to them.[75] Thirdly, by the constitution of the legislative department itself, and the separation and division of powers, between the different branches, both of the congress, and of the state legislatures: in all which, an immediate dependence, either from the people, or the states, is happily, in a very great degree preserved. Fourthly, by the qualified negative which the constitution of the United States, gives

75. Resolutions of the general assembly of Virginia, December 21, 1798. Also the resolution of the general convention of Virginia, ratifying the constitution of the U. States.

to the president, upon all the proceedings of congress, except a question of adjournment. Fifthly, and lastly; by the separation of the judiciary from the legislative department; and the independence of the former, of the control, or influence of the latter, in any case where any individual may be aggrieved or oppressed, under color of an unconstitutional act of the legislature, or executive. In England, on the contrary, the greatest political object may be attained, by laws, apparently of little importance, or amounting only to a slight domestic regulation: the game-laws, as was before observed, have been converted into the means of disarming the body of the people: the statute *de donis conditionalibus* has been the rock, on which the existence and influence of a most powerful aristocracy, has been founded, and erected: the acts directing the mode of petitioning parliament, &c. and those for prohibiting riots: and for suppressing assemblies of free-masons, &c. are so many ways for preventing public meetings of the people to deliberate upon their public, or national concerns. The congress of the United States possesses no power to regulate, or interfere with the domestic concerns, or police of any state: it belongs not to them to establish any rules respecting the rights of property; nor will the constitution permit any prohibition of arms to the people; or of peaceable assemblies by them, for any purposes whatsoever, and in any number, whenever they may see occasion.

II. The second article of the federal constitution provides, that the executive power shall be vested in a president of the United States of America; that he shall be a natural born citizen, unless he was a citizen at the time of the adoption of the constitution, and in that case, that he shall have been fourteen years a resident in the United States; that he shall have attained the age of thirty-five years; that he shall continue in office four years; that he shall receive a stated compensation for his services, which shall neither be increased nor diminished during the period for which he is elected, and shall not receive within that period, any other emolument from the United States, or any of them; and that before he enters upon the execution of his office, he shall take an oath, "faithfully to execute the same, and to the best of his ability, preserve, protect, and defend the constitution of the United States."

The author of the Treatise on the English Constitution,[76] considers the unity of the executive among the advantages peculiar to that, as a free government. The advantages ordinarily attributed to that circumstance, are supposed to be a necessary and unavoidable unanimity; promptitude and dispatch, as a consequence of it: and, immediate and obvious, responsibility. If such are the real advantages of a single executive magistrate, we may contend that they are found in a much greater degree in the federal government, than in the English. In the latter it exists, only theoretically, in an individual; the practical exercise of it, being devolved upon ministers, councils, and boards. The king, according to the acknowledged principles of the constitution, not being responsible for any of his acts, the minister upon whom all responsibility devolves, to secure his indemnity acts by the advice of the privy council to whom every measure of importance is submitted, before it is carried into effect. His plans are often digested and canvassed in a still more secret conclave, consisting of the principal officers of state, and styled the cabinet-council, before they are communicated to the privy council: matters are frequently referred to the different boards, for their advice thereon, previously to their discussion, and final decision, in the council. Thus, in fact, the unity of the executive is merely ideal, existing only in the theory of the government; whatever is said of the unanimity, or dispatch arising from the unity of the executive power, is therefore without foundation. And with respect to responsibility, we have already observed that the nominal executive, is absolved from it by the constitution: all the responsibility that the government admits, is shared between the different ministers, privy council, and boards. The unity of the nominal executive, therefore, so far from ensuring responsibility, destroys it. If then the constitution of England be relied on as proving the superior advantages of unity in the executive department, it does not support any part of the position.

In the United States the unity of the executive authority is practically established, in almost every instance. For, the senate are constituted a

76. De Lolme.

council, rather for special, than for general purposes. It may reasonably be doubted, whether they have a right to advise the president, in any case, without being first consulted; and whether, when consulted, he is obliged to carry into effect any measure which they may advise: the constitution is perhaps defective in both these cases. To illustrate them, let it be supposed, that the senate, without being consulted should advise the sending an ambassador to a foreign court: is the president bound to nominate one to them for that purpose? Or, suppose an ambassador to have concluded a treaty, which the president disapproves, but, which the senate advise him to ratify; is he bound to do so? The constitution says, "*He shall have power,* by, and with, the advice and consent of the senate shall appoint ambassadors." These words appear rather to confer a discretionary authority, than to impose a mandate, or obligation. . . . But although the president may perhaps constitutionally decline the ratification of a treaty, or the appointment of an ambassador, notwithstanding the advice of the senate, yet he cannot adopt any measure, which they may advise him to reject, if the constitution requires their advice, or assent: so that, in general, whatever he does must have the sanction of the senate for its support: whatever he omits doing, is chargeable upon him, only, unless the measure shall have been submitted to the senate and rejected by them. The conduct of the first magistrate of a nation is as frequently liable to censure for his omissions, as for his acts. Whatever, therefore, is left undone, which the public safety may require to have been done, is chargeable upon the neglect of the president, exclusively: whatever may be done amiss is likewise chargeable upon him, in the first instance, as the author and propounder of the measure: although it should afterwards receive the approbation and consent of the senate. Responsibility, then, pursues him in every situation: whether active or passive; sleeping, or awake.

But although a king of England be not responsible, it is said that his ministers are; for they may be impeached: so may a president of the United States. . . . But I lay no stress upon this point, as a practical means of enforcing responsibility, for reasons that will be more fully explained hereafter. The true point of responsibility rests upon the shortness of the period for which a president of the United States is elected, and the power which the people possess, of rejecting him at a succeeding election: a power, the more formidable, and energetic, as it remains in their hands, is untrammelled by forms, and the exercise of it depends more upon opinion, than upon evidence. When brought before such a tribunal, in vain would a culpable president seek shelter under the flimsy veil, of advice of council; such a cobweb, like the net of Vulcan, would only expose him, more effectually.

On the ground of responsibility, then, an immense preference is due to the constitution of the United States: it is at least equal to that of Great-Britain on the ground of unanimity: for, as every executive measure must originate in the breast of the president, his plans will have all the benefit of uniformity, that can be expected to flow from the operations of any individual mind: let it be supposed that the senate reject one of his proposed measures; possessing a perfect acquaintance with the whole system of his own administration, he will naturally be led to adopt some other course, which shall neither retard, nor counteract any other part of his system. No British minister, whose measures are opposed in the cabinet, can do more; probably not so much: for a substitute may, perhaps, be obtruded upon him, by some other influential minister. But no such substitute can be obtruded upon a president of the United States; the power of the senate consisting rather in approving, or rejecting, than in advising or propounding, as already hinted.

The advantages of information, and dispatch, are probably equally in favor of the constitution of the American executive. The constitution of the United States has made ample provision for his aid in these respects, by assigning to him ministers to whom the conduct of each of the executive departments may be committed; from whom he may require all necessary information, as also their opinions in writing, upon any subject relating to the duties of their respective offices; and whom, he may, moreover, remove at pleasure. Here we find a single executive officer substituted for a numerous board, where responsibility is divided, until it is entirely lost, and where the chance of unanimity lessens in geometrical proportion to the number that compose it.

The perpetuity of the office, is another boasted advantage of the constitution of the supreme executive magistrate in Great Britain. "The king never dies.".... But Henry, Edward, or George may die, may be an infant in swaddling clothes, a superannuated dotard, or a raving maniac. Of what benefit is the immortality of the kingly office, in any of these instances? Can the puling infant, or the feeble hand of palsied age wield the scepter, or can it be entrusted to the raving Bedlamite? A president of the United States cannot be the first: it is highly improbable that he will ever be the second; the constitution has provided for the third case; and for all others, of a similar kind. For, in case of the removal of the president of the United States from office, or of his death, resignation, or inability to discharge the powers and duties of his office, the same shall devolve on the vice-president; and congress may by law provide for the case of removal, death, resignation, or inability, both of the president and vice-president, declaring what officer shall then act as president, and such officer shall act accordingly, until the disability be removed, or a president shall be elected. Such provision has been accordingly made by law, and the executive authority in such a case, would immediately devolve upon the president of the senate *pro tempore;* or if there be no president of the senate, upon the speaker of the house of representatives, for the time being. Nothing is wanting to the perpetuity of the office, but a provision for its continuance in case no president shall be elected at the period prescribed by the constitution. Such a case will probably not happen, until the people of the United States shall be weary of the present constitution and government, and adopt that method of putting a period to both. And it is, perhaps, among the recommendations of the constitution, that it thus furnishes the means of a peaceable dissolution of the government, if ever the crisis should arrive that may render such a measure eligible, or necessary. A crisis to be deprecated by every friend to his country.

To pursue the parallel between a king of England, and the president of the United States, a little further. A king of England is the fountain of honor, of office, and of privilege. Honors, as distinct from offices, are unknown in the United States; so likewise are privileges. At least there are none, which a president of the United States can constitutionally create, or bestow. It is not so with respect of offices; these he can not constitutionally create; they must first be established by law. But when established, he has the exclusive right of nomination to all offices, whose appointments are not otherwise provided for by the constitution, or by some act of congress, to which his assent may be necessary, or may have been previously given. The influence which this power gives him, personally, is one of those parts of the constitution, which assimilates the government, in its administration, infinitely more nearly to that of Great-Britain, than seems to consist with those republican principles, which ought to pervade every part of the federal constitution: at least so long as the union is composed of democratic states. On this subject we shall offer some further remarks hereafter.

The heir of a king of England may be born with all the vices of a Richard; with the tyrannical disposition, and cruelty of the eighth Henry; with the empty pride and folly of a James; with the cowardice and imbecility of a John; or with the stupid obstinacy, bigotry or other depravity of temper, of any of his successors; he must nevertheless succeed to the throne of his fathers; his person is sacred and inviolable as if he were an Alfred; and unless his misdeeds are so rank as to bring him to the block, or force him to an abdication, he continues the lord's anointed all his days. A president of the United States must have attained the middle age of life, before his is eligible to that office: if not a native, he must have been fourteen years a resident in the United States: his talents and character must consequently be known. The faculties of his mind must have attained their full vigor: the character must be formed, and formed of active, not of passive materials, to attract, and secure the attention, and approbation of a people dispersed through such a variety of element and situation, as the American people are. This activity of mind and of talent must have manifested itself on the side of virtue, before it can engage the favor of those who acknowledge no superiority of rights among individuals, and who are conscious that in promoting to office, they should choose a faithful agent, not a ruler, without responsibility. And should it happen, that they are after all deceived in their estimate of his character and worth, the lapse of four years enables them to correct their error, and dismiss him from their service. What nation governed by an hereditary monarch has an equal chance of happiness!

But, the tumult of popular elections, and the danger in elective monarchies, will be insisted on, as counterbalancing the advantage which we claim in behalf of the constitution of the executive magistrate in the United States. With regard to the latter, something will be said hereafter, when we examine the mode of electing a president of the United States. As to the former: if the sovereignty of the people of the United States, like that of the Roman and Grecian republics, resided in the inhabitants of a single city, or a small territory, the influence of men of popular talents would doubtless produce in certain conjunctures, similar events to those recorded in the annals of those republics. But nature herself seems to be enlisted on the side of the liberty and independence of the citizens of United America. Our cities are few; the population inconsiderable, compared with many of the capitals of ancient, or modern Europe: that population (from the unfavorable influence of climate for some years past) seems not likely to be extended very far beyond its present bounds, and probably will never bear any great proportion to the population of the country at large. This circumstance alone, would probably defeat any attempt to establish an undue influence in any part of the union. Agriculture is, and probably will for ages continue to be, the principal object of pursuit in the United States; and the period seems to be yet very far removed, when their population will be equal to the extent, and fertility of the soil. Europe has so far got the start of us in manufactures, that it is also probable, our population will not depend upon, nor derive any great increase from, them. Until it does, our towns will be principally confined to the sea coast, and, the interior of the United States will continue, as at present, the nurse of a hardy, independent yeomanry. A strong barrier between the United States and the countries which abound in the precious metals is devoutly to be wished by all, who can appreciate, properly, the blessings of liberty and peace. Whilst the ambition of America is limited to the cultivation of the arts of peace, and the science of free government; to the improvement, instead of the extension of her territory, and to the fortifying herself against enemies from within, as well as from without, by fostering, and encouraging the principles of genuine liberty; local influence can never be so formidable as to endanger the peace or happiness of the union, on any occasion. But, whenever our evil genius shall prompt us to aspire to the character of a military republic, and invite us to the field of glory: when rapacity, under the less odious name of ambition, shall lead us on to conquest; when a bold, though raw, militia shall be exchanged for a well trained, well disciplined and well appointed army; ready to take the field at the nod of an ambitious president, and to believe that the finger of heaven points to that course which his directs; then, may we regard the day of our happiness as past, or as hastening rapidly to its decline.

That provision in the constitution which requires that the president shall be a native-born citizen (unless he were a citizen of the United States when the constitution was adopted,) is a happy means of security against foreign influence, which, wherever it is capable of being exerted, is to be dreaded more than the plague. The admission of foreigners into our councils, consequently, cannot be too much guarded against; their total exclusion from a station to which foreign nations have been accustomed to, attach ideas of sovereign powers, sacredness of character, and hereditary right, is a measure of the most consummate policy and wisdom. It was by means of foreign connections that the stadtholder of Holland, whose powers at first were probably not equal to those of a president of the United States, became a sovereign hereditary prince before the late revolution in that country. Nor is it with levity that I remark, that the very title of our first magistrate, in some measure exempts us from the danger of those calamities by which European nations are almost perpetually visited. The title of king, prince, emperor, or czar, without the smallest addition to his powers, would have rendered him a member of the fraternity of crowned heads: their common cause has more than once threatened the desolation of Europe. To have added a member to this sacred family in America, would have invited and perpetuated among us all the evils of Pandora's Box.

The *personal* independence of the president is secured by that clause, which provides that he shall receive a compensation at stated periods, which shall not be diminished during his continuance in office. To guard against avarice, corruption, and venality, it is also provided, that it shall not be increased during the same period, nor shall be received within that period any other emolument from the United States, or either of them. His salary, as now fixed by law, seems to be fully adequate, though far below the income of many private persons in England, and even in America.

The *political* independence of the president of the United States, so far as it is necessary to the preservation, protection, and defense of the constitution, is secured, not only by the limitations and restrictions which the constitution impose upon the legislative powers of congress, but by a qualified negative on all their proceedings, as has been already mentioned elsewhere. This share in the proceedings of the federal legislature, which the constitution assigns to him, consists, like that of a king of England, in the power of rejecting, rather than resolving; a circumstance on which both judge Blackstone, and deLolme, lay considerable stress; and is one of the grounds upon which the latter founds his preference of that constitution to the republican system. In republics, he tells us, the laws usually originate with the executive; it is otherwise in all the American states. In England, the laws do, in fact, originate with the executive: a revenue bill is always proposed by the chancellor of the exchequer, or some member of that department; and it is understood to be the practice, that every other measure of considerable magnitude and importance is first discussed in the privy council, before it is brought into parliament; where it is generally introduced, and the bill prepared by some of the officers of the crown. The preference which de Lolme gives to the English constitution, therefore, is not altogether well founded. The negative of the president of the United States is not final, like that of the king of England, but suspensive. Neither is the expression of his assent absolutely necessary to the establishment of a law, for if he withholds his decision beyond the period of ten days (exclusive of Sundays) his assent shall be presumed. He may retard for a few days, but cannot prevent any beneficial measure, provided two-thirds of both houses concur in the

opinion of its expediency. Thus, the part assigned to him by the constitution is strictly preventative, and not creative; yet this preventive is so
modified as never to operate conclusively, but in those cases where it may
be presumed the congress have acted unadvisedly through haste or oversight: and we may safely conclude, that where the deliberate sense of two-
thirds of both houses of congress shall induce them to persist in any
measure to which the president shall have given his negative, it will neither militate with the constitution, nor with the interest of their constituents. There is one instance (besides a question of adjournment) in
which his assent appears not to be required; this is, when two-thirds of
both houses have concurred in proposing to the states any amendment
of the constitution: in this case, the concurrence of two-thirds of both
houses being required in the first instance, his assent is dispensed with,
as his dissent would be unavailing.

Let us now take a short view of the manner in which a president of
the United States is appointed.

Each state shall, within thirty-four days prior to the first Wednesday in
December, in every fourth year succeeding the last election, appoint a
number of electors equal to the whole number of representatives and
senators, to which such state may be entitled in congress, who shall meet
and give their votes on that day, at such place in each state as the legislature thereof may direct, for two persons, of whom one at least shall not
be an inhabitant of such state; three lists of the votes shall be made, one
of which shall be sent by an express, and another by post, to the president
of the senate; or, if there be no such officer at the seat of government, to
the secretary of state; and the third, to the judge of the district. The president of the senate shall, in the presence of both house of congress, open
the certificates on the second Wednesday in February next succeeding,
and the votes shall then be counted and the choice ascertained; the person having the greatest number of votes, if they be a majority of the
whole number of electors appointed, shall be president, and the person
having the next greatest number of votes shall be vice-president. If the
votes be equal for two persons having such majority, the house of representatives shall immediately choose by ballot one of them for president;

but in such cases they shall vote by states, each state having one vote; a quorum for this purpose shall consist of a member, or members from two-thirds of the states, and a majority of all the states be necessary to the choice. If no person have a majority of the electors, the house shall in like manner choose the president from the five highest on the list. The periods for which the president and vice-president are elected, shall always commence on the fourth day of March next succeeding such election. No senator or representative, or person holding an office of trust or profit under the United States, shall be an elector.

Such are the precautions which the constitution has provided for securing the tranquility of elections, the independence and integrity of the electors, and the wisdom of their choice; and such are the auxiliary regulations established by congress for the same purposes. Electors have been differently appointed in the different states. In some they have been appointed immediately by the legislature; in others they have been chosen by a general ticket throughout the state; in others, the state has been divided into districts, one elector being chosen by the freeholders of each district. This method was adopted in Virginia at first; but on a late occasion a general ticket was preferred. The reasons for this change seem to have been, that the whole strength of the state may be combined and united, instead of being divided, as on a former occasion.

The electors, we perceive, are to assemble on one and the same day, in all the different states, at as many different places, at a very considerable distance from each other, and on that day are simply to give their votes; no embarrassment can arise among them from the circumstance of an equality of votes, for different persons: they are to *vote only;* not to decide upon the result of their votes: they then disperse, and return to their respective habitations, and occupations, immediately. No pretext can be had for delay; no opportunity is furnished for intrigue, and cabal. The certificates of their votes are to be forwarded to different persons, and by different conveyances: they are to be publicly opened, and counted in the presence of the whole national legislature: there is no obligation of secrecy on the electors to conceal their votes; they are consequently known immediately, throughout the state, long before the opening the certificates at the seat of government: should any fraud be attempted, it must immediately be detected: whilst the constitution expressly incapacitates any man who may be presumed to labor under any undue bias, from serving as an elector, in the first instance, the salutary provisions which it contains, in other respects, seem to afford a sufficient guarantee against the arts of ambition, and the venality of corrupt minds. There is no room for the turbulence of a *Campus Martius,* or a *Polish Diet,* on the one hand, nor for the intrigues of the sacred college, or a Venetian senate, on the other; unless, when it unfortunately happens that two persons, having a majority of the whole number of electors, in their favor, have likewise an equal number of votes; or, where by any other means, the election may devolve upon the house of representatives. Then, indeed, intrigue and cabal may have their full scope: then, may the existence of the union be put in extreme hazard: then might a bold and desperate party, having the command of an armed force, and of all the resources of government, attempt to establish themselves permanently in power, without the future aid of forms, or the control of elections. Upon what principle, we may ask, is it that state influence is in this case permitted to operate in an inverse proportion to the ratio of population, and thus predominate over it. Upon what principle is it, that that ratio which gives to all the citizens of the United States an equal voice in the election of a president, in the first instance, shall give to the representative of the citizens of Delaware, in the second, a weight equal to nineteen representatives of the citizens of Virginia? Why then should the house of representatives vote by states on this great occasion? It is, perhaps, susceptible of proof, that if the arts of corruption should ever be practiced with success, in the election of a president, it will arise from this circumstance; the votes of a few individuals, in this instance, more than counterbalancing four times their number.[77] Had the senate been associated with the other house in the election, and each vote been sep-

77. It may be demonstrated, that twenty representatives, at the last election of a president and vice-president, might have carried the election against eighty-six: this supposes all the small states to have voted together.

arately counted, the mode of election might, at first view, appear less exceptionable: but their exclusion from any participation in the election of a president, is certainly founded upon the wisest policy: being associated with him in the exercise of his most important powers, and being chosen for a much longer period than the representatives, the presumption of undue influence, where the contest might be between a president in office, and any other person, would be altogether unavoidable.

Nothing in the constitution prohibits the re-election of a president as often as the approbation of his country may confer that distinction upon him. If his re-election were to depend entirely upon a majority of votes in the first instance, I should think the argument would be in favor of the principle. But what if a president of the United States should so far have lost the confidence of the people of the respective states, as not to have a majority of the votes of the state electors, in his favor? What, if he should so far have forfeited their esteem, as to be the lowest of five candidates, on the list, neither of whom should have such a majority, as to decide the election? Should we not, in such a case, with indignation behold him continued in office, by the votes of one fourth part of the house of representatives, against the other three? This might be sufficiently guarded against, by an amendment, providing that no president, for the time being, should ever be re-elected, unless he had not only the greatest number of votes in his favor, but a majority of the votes of all the electors appointed. As corruption can only be dreaded on the part of bad men, and is always to be dreaded from them, a president who may have lost the confidence of the citizens of the United States at large, would be the first person with whom the practice of corruption may be expected to commence.

The period of which a president is elected, as has been already noticed, is four years. By many it is thought too long: it seems long enough to give him an opportunity of bringing to a mature conclusion any measures which he may have undertaken for the good of the nation; and it has been thought short enough, for the people to displace him in sufficient time, where his conduct may not have merited approbation, on the one hand, or impeachment, on the other. Much evil, however, may be generated, and even matured, in the compass of four years.... Of removal from office by impeachment, no president will ever be in danger. But of this hereafter. I can see no inconvenience that would result from more frequent elections; there may be danger, if the constitution be not so amended as to provide for them.... The convention of this state proposed as an amendment to the constitution, That no person should be capable of being president of the United States for more than eight years, in any term of sixteen years. It might have been better to have selected the half of these periods, respectively.

The powers, or more properly, the duties, of the president of the United States, are various and extensive; though happily abridged of many others, which are considered as inseparable from the executive authority in monarchies: of these last, we have had frequent occasion to notice such as are transferred by the constitution to the congress of the United States; and of those which are assigned to the president,

1. The first is, That he shall be commander in chief of the army and navy of the United States, and of the militia of the several states, when called into the service of the United States. A power similar to that of the king of England, and of the stadtholder of Holland, before the late revolution; yet qualified, by some important restrictions, which I believe were not to be found in either of those governments. As, first; he cannot make rules for the regulation and government of the army and navy, himself, but they must be governed according to regulations established by congress. But notwithstanding this provision in the constitution, the act of 5 Cong. c. 74, authorized the president to make and establish such rules for training and disciplining the corps of volunteers, authorized to be raised by that act, as should be thought necessary to prepare them for actual service.... Secondly; the president of the United States hath not an unqualified right to appoint what officers he pleases; but such appointment (if there be no provision to the contrary made by law) must be made with the advice and consent of the senate: a restriction, perhaps of little importance, whilst the right of nomination, in all cases, and the right of filling up vacancies during the recess of the senate, remain uncontrollably in his power; to which may be added, the authority given

him by the act for raising a provisional army, (and perhaps some others) to appoint such officers as he may think proper in the recess of the senate; "the appointment of field officers to be submitted to the advice and consent of the senate, at their next subsequent meeting"; leaving the appointment of all officers of inferior rank to the discretion of the president.[78] The stadtholder of Holland derived his power and influence in great measure from a similar authority.... A third and infinitely more important check, than either of the former, so long as elections continue as frequent, as at present, is, that no appropriation for the support of an army can be made for a longer term than two years, the period for which congress is chosen. This puts it in the power of the people, by changing the representatives, to give an effectual check to the power of the executive at the end of that period.... In England, the power of raising armies, *ad libitum,* is vested in the king, though he is said to be dependent upon the parliament for their support; a supply bill, which is always limited to one year, passes accordingly, every session. Should it be refused, (a case which I believe has not happened for more than a century), a dissolution would pave the way, immediately, for a more complying parliament. Fourthly; the militia of the several states, though subject to his command when called into actual service, can only be called into service by the authority of congress, and must be governed according to law: the states, moreover, have the right appointing the officers, and training the militia, according to the discipline prescribed by congress, reserved to them by the constitution. But we have seen in what manner this very important clause has been evaded, by the acts of 5 Cong. c. 64, and 74, authorizing the president to accept companies of volunteers, and to appoint their officers, &c. A precedent, which if it be drawn into authority and practice in future, may be regarded as superceding every

---

78. L.U.S. 5 Cong. c. 64. The establishment of a large corps of officers, to be provisionally employed, might be compared to the establishment of the Legion of Honour, in France. The corps of volunteers, the officers of which were likewise to be appointed by the president, alone, may be regarded in the same light. Can it be doubted that such distinguished marks of presidential favour, must produce correspondent effects? Men ambitious of distinctions, are rarely ungrateful to their patrons in power.

part of the constitution, which reserves to the states any effectual authority over their militia.

2. The president has power to grant reprieves and pardons for offenses against the United States, except in cases of impeachment. C.U.S. Art. 2. Sec. 2.

The power of granting pardons, says judge Blackstone, is the most amiable prerogative of a king of England; and is one of the great advantages of monarchy, above any other form of government: in democracies, he adds, this power of pardon can never subsist. It is happy for the people of America that many speculative notions concerning the disadvantages and imperfections of democratic forms of government, have been found to be practically false. In all the democratic states of North America, the power of pardoning is regularly vested (as in the federal government of the United States) in the supreme executive magistrate; and this flower of monarchical prerogative has been found to flourish in a perfect republican soil, not less than in its native climate. The president of the United States is not, like a governor of Virginia, constrained to act by advice of a council, but the power of pardoning is left entirely to the dictates of his own bosom. The cases in which it has been exercised, manifest the propriety of the existence of such a power in every state, whatever be the form of its government. In cases of impeachment, as the prosecution is carried on by the representatives of the people, and the judgment can only extend to removal from, and disqualification to hold or enjoy any office under the United States, in future, the constitution has wisely provided, that the same person in whom the right of nomination to office is vested, shall not have the power to remove that disqualification, which the guilt of the offender has brought upon himself. In England, no pardon can be pleaded in bar of an impeachment; but the king may pardon after conviction upon an impeachment. He can not by an exercise of his prerogative avert the disgrace of a conviction; but he can avert its effects, and restore the offender to his credit.

3. The president hath power, by and with the advice and consent of the senate, to make treaties, provided two thirds of the senators present

concur; and the treaties so made, constitute a part of the supreme law of the land. C.U.S. Art. 2. Sec. 2. and Art. 6.

Treaties, as defined by Puffendorf, are certain agreements made by sovereigns, between one another, of great use both in war, and peace; of these, there are two kinds; the one such as reinforce the observance of what by the law of nature we were before obliged to; as the mutual exercise of civility, and humanity, or the prevention of injuries on either side; the second, such as add some new engagement to the duties of natural law; or at least determine what was before too general and indefinite in the same, to some thing particular, and precise.[79] Of those which add some new engagement to those duties which natural law imposes upon all nations, the most usual relate to, or in their operation may affect, the sovereignty of the state; the unity of its parts, its territory, or other property; its commerce with foreign nations, and *vice versa;* the mutual privileges and immunities of the citizens, or subjects of the contracting powers, or the mutual aid of the contracting nations, in case of an attack, or hostility, from any other quarter. To all these objects, if there be nothing in the fundamental laws of the state which contradicts it, the power of making treaties extends, and is vested in the conductors of states, according to the opinion of Vattel.

In our constitution, there is not restriction as to the subjects of treaties, unless perhaps the guarantee of a republican form of government, and of protection from invasion, contained in the fourth article, may be construed to impose such a restriction, in behalf of the several states, against the dismemberment of the federal republic. But whether this restriction may extend to prevent the alienation, by cession, of the western territory, not being a part of any state, may be somewhat more doubtful. The act of cession from Virginia militates, expressly, against such an alienation of that part of the western territory which was ceded by this state. Nevertheless, it is said to have been in contemplation soon after the establishment of the federal government, to cede the right of

79. Grotius.

pre-emption to the lands in that territory to the Indians, who were then supposed to be in treaty for the same with the crown of Great Britain. The president, who had not authorized any such article, and who is said to have disapproved of it, in submitting the treaty to the consideration of the senate, called their attention particularly to that part of it; in consequence of which it was rejected, though warmly supported in the senate, as has been said. If the power of making such a dismemberment be questionable at any rate, it is much more so, when it is recollected, that the constitution seems to have vested congress, collectively, and not any one or two branches of it only, with the power to dispose of that territory. The effect of this extraordinary treaty, if it had been ratified by the senate and the president, may easily be conceived. Great Britain, at that time not a little disposed to enmity towards the United States, would no doubt have insisted upon such an acquisition of territory, made under the faith of a treaty between the United States and the Indians; and thus the United States might either have been deprived of their territory by an unconstitutional treaty, or involved in a war for its preservation, by the proceedings of a body, whose authority does not extend to a final decision upon a question, whether war be necessary and expedient. This shows the collision which may possibly arise between the several branches of the congress, in consequence of this modification of the treaty-making power. For, being entrusted to a branch of the congress only, without the possibility of control or check by the other branch, so far as respects the conclusion and ratification of any treaty whatsoever, it may well happen, at some time or other, that the president and senate may overstep the limits of their just authority, and the house of representatives be so tenacious of their own constitutional rights, as not to yield to the obligations imposed upon them by a treaty, the terms of which they do not approve.

On the 24th of March, 1796, the house of representatives came to the following resolution: "That the president of the United States be requested to lay before the house a copy of the instructions to the minister of the United States, who negotiated the treaty with the king of Great

Britain, communicated by his message of the first of March, together with his correspondence and other documents relative to the said treaty; excepting such of said papers as any existing negotiation may render improper to be disclosed."

The president answered, "That the power of making treaties is exclusively vested in the president, by and with the advice and consent of the senate, provided two-thirds of the senators present concur; and that every treaty so made, and promulgated, henceforward becomes the law of the land." "That the necessity of caution and secrecy in foreign negotiations, was one cogent reason for vesting the power in that manner." "That to admit a right in the house of representatives to demand, and to have, as a matter of course, all the papers respecting a negotiation with a foreign power, would be to establish a dangerous precedent." "That it being perfectly clear to his understanding, that the assent of the house of representatives is not necessary to the validity of a treaty; as the treaty with Great Britain exhibits in itself all the objects requiring legislative provision, and on these the papers called for can throw no light; and as it is essential to the due administration of the government, that the boundaries fixed by the constitution between the different departments should be preserved. A just regard to the constitution, and to the duty of his office, under all the circumstances of the case, forbad a compliance with their request."

On the 6th of April following, the house of representatives came to the following resolution:

"Resolved, that it being declared by the second section of the second article of the constitution, that the president shall have power, by, and with the advice and consent of the senate, to make treaties, provided two thirds of the senators present concur, the house of representatives do not claim any agency in making treaties; but, that when a treaty stipulates regulations on any of the subjects submitted by the constitution to the power of congress, it must depend for its execution, as to such stipulations, on a law or laws to be passed by congress; and it is the constitutional right and duty of the house of representatives in all such cases, to deliberate on the expediency or inexpediency of carrying such treaty into effect, and to determine and act thereon, as in their judgment may be most conductive to the public good."

"Resolved, that it is not necessary to the propriety of any application from this house to the executive for information desired by them, and which may relate to any constitutional functions of the house, that the purposes for which such information may be wanted, or to which the same may be applied, should be stated in the application."

But the senate, in matters of treaty, are not only without control, they may be said also to be without even the least shadow of responsibility in the individuals who compose that body. In England, says judge Blackstone, lest this plenitude of authority should be abused to the detriment of the public, the constitution hath interposed a check by means of parliamentary impeachment, for the punishment of such members as from criminal motives advise or conclude any treaty, which shall afterwards be judged to derogate from the honor and interest of the nation. But where shall we find this responsibility in our constitution? Does it arise from the power of impeachment vested in the house of representatives by the constitution? It has been solemnly decided, that a senator is not a civil officer of the United States, and therefore not liable to impeachment.[80] Even were it otherwise, the power of impeachment would, in the case we are now speaking of, be nugatory, as will presently appear.... Does it consist then in the power of impeaching the ambassador, by whom it was concluded, or the president, by whom it has been ratified, both of whom are unquestionably impeachable, I presume? The ambassador is appointed by the president, with the advice and consent of the senate: it may be presumed that his instructions have been submitted to and approved by them, though a different practice is said to have been established. If the treaty be ratified, and the minister be impeached for concluding it, because it is derogatory to the honour, the interest, or per-

80. See the trial of William Blount, upon an impeachment, in which it was decided that a senator is not a civil officer within the meaning of the constitution of the United States, and therefore not liable to be impeached. January 7, and 10, 1799.

haps to the sovereignty and independence of the nation, who are to be his judges? The senate by whom it has been approved and ratified. If the president be impeached for giving improper instructions to the ambassador, and for ratifying the treaty concluded by him pursuant to his instructions, who are to be his judges? The senate, to whom the treaty has been submitted, by whom it has been approved, and by whose advice it has been ratified. The constitution requires, that a majority of two-thirds of the senate, at least, must advise the conclusion of a treaty, before it can be ratified by the president; it likewise requires that a majority of two-thirds at least must concur in the judgment in case of conviction. A quorum for the trial upon an impeachment, consequently cannot possibly be formed, without calling in some of those senators to be judges, who had either actually advised or dissented from the ratification of the treaty. Can such judges be deemed impartial? If they can, from which class shall they be chosen; from those who proposed the rejection of the treaty, or from those who advised its final ratification? Sophistry itself might be puzzled by the dilemma.

The Federalist attempts to vindicate this part of the constitution of the United States, with that zeal and ingenuity which runs through the work. "What other body, besides the senate," he asks, "would be likely to feel confidence enough in its own situation to preserve unawed, and uninfluenced the necessary impartiality between an individual, accused, and the representatives of the people, his accusers? Could the supreme court have been relied on, as answering this description? It is much to be doubted whether the members of that tribunal would at all times be endowed with so eminent a portion of fortitude, as would be called for in the execution of so difficult a task; and it is still more to be doubted, whether they would possess the degree of credit and authority, which might on certain occasions be indispensable towards reconciling the people to a decision that should happen to clash with an accusation brought forward by their immediate representatives." The author seems to have forgot, that senators may be discontinued from their seats, merely from the effect of popular disapprobation, but that the judges of the supreme court can not. He seems also to have forgot, that whenever the president of the United States is impeached, the constitution expressly requires that the chief justice of the supreme court shall preside, at the trial. Are all the confidence, all the firmness, and all the impartiality of that court supposed to be concentrated in the chief justice, and to reside in his breast, only? If that court could not be relied on for the trial of impeachments, much less would it seem worthy of reliance for the determination of any question between the United States, and any particular state: much less to decide upon the life and death of a person whose crimes might subject him to an impeachment, but whose influence might avert a conviction. Yet the courts of the United States are by the constitution regarded as the only proper tribunals, where a party convicted upon an impeachment, may receive that condign punishment, which the nature of his crimes may require: for it must not be forgotten, that a person convicted upon an impeachment, shall nevertheless be liable and subject to indictment, trial, judgment, and punishment, according to law.[81] And all this is those very courts, which the Federalist deems not sufficiently confident in their own situation to preserve unawed, and uninfluenced the necessary impartiality, to try him upon an impeachment. The question then might be retorted: can it be supposed that the senate, a part of whom must have been either *particeps criminis,* with the person impeached, by advising the measure for which he is to be tried, or must have joined the opposition to that measure, when proposed and debated in the senate, would be a more independent, or more unprejudiced tribunal, than a court composed of judges holding their offices during good behavior; and who could neither be presumed to have participated in the crime, nor to have prejudged the criminal? Wisely, then, was it proposed by the convention of this state, and some others, that some tribunal other than the senate should be provided for trying impeachments. In the state of Virginia, the trial of impeachments is to be in the general court of the commonwealth, except when a judge of that court may happen to be impeached, in which case the trial is to be

---

81. And as a conviction upon an impeachment, is no bar to a prosecution upon an indictment, so perhaps an acquittal may not be a bar.

in the court of appeals: the fact, as in other cases, is to be tried by a jury; to be summoned from the different counties of that senatorial district, in which the accused shall reside: and to prevent any undue influence from the sitting of the house of delegates, in whom the power of impeachment is vested, it is wisely provided, that no impeachment shall be tried during a session of the general assembly. A tribunal constituted upon similar principles for the trial of impeachments in the federal government, would probably produce some degree of responsibility, where there now seems to be none.

I have chosen to consider the power of trying impeachments, which the constitution vests in the senate, here, in order to place that of making treaties, which are to become a part of the supreme law of the land, and in which that body has a principle agency, in a stronger point of view. The union of these powers, in that body; and the total exemption of senators from an impeachment, seems to render this part of the federal constitution, the most defective and unsound, of any part of the fabric.

But, to return to the treaty-making power; it appears to be somewhat extraordinary, that that branch of the federal government, who are by the constitution required to concur, in a declaration of war, before any such declaration can be made, should be wholly precluded from voting at all, upon a question of peace.... They are judges of the causes of war; of the existence of those causes; of the resources, and ability of the states to prosecute and support a war; of the expediency of applying those resources to the obtaining redress, or satisfaction for the injury received; in short, of every possible circumstance that can induce the nation to incur the hazard, or expense of a war: and yet, if through timidity, venality, or corruption, the president, and two thirds of a majority of the senate can be prevailed upon to relinquish the prosecution of the war, and conclude a treaty, the house of representatives have not power to prevent, or retard the measure; although it should appear to them, that the object for which the war hath been undertaken, hath not been attained, and that it was neither relinquished from necessity, or inability to prosecute it, with effect.

These objections are not intended, to extend to the agency which the president and senate may have, in the formation of a treaty; nor to the principle that treaties with foreign nations should be regarded as a part of the supreme law of the land.... The honour and peace of the nation certainly require that its compacts should be duly observed, and carried into effect with perfect good faith. And though it may be the result of sound discretion to confide the formation of a treaty, in the first instance, to the president and senate, only; yet the safety of the nation seems to require that the final ratification of any compact, which is to form a part of the supreme law of the land, should, as well as other laws of the federal government, depend upon the concurrent approbation of every branch of the congress, before they acquire such a sanction as to become irrevocable, without the consent of a foreign nation; or without hazarding an imputation against the honor and faith of the nation, in the performance of its contracts.

It may not be improper here to add something on the subject of that part of the constitution, which declares that treaties made by the president and senate shall be a part of the supreme law of the land: acts of congress made pursuant to the powers delegated by the constitution are to be regarded in the same light. What then is the effect of a treaty made by the president and senate, some of the articles of which may contain stipulations on legislative objects, or such as are expressly vested in congress by the constitution, until congress shall make a law carrying them into effect? Is congress bound to carry such stipulations into effect, whether they approve or disapprove of them? Have they no negative, no discretion upon the subject? The answer seems to be, that it is in some respects, an inchoate act. It is the law of the land, and binding upon the nation in all its parts, except so far as relates to those stipulations. Its final fate, in case of refusal on the part of congress, to carry those stipulations into effect, would depend on the will of the other nation. If they were satisfied that the treaty should subsist, although some of the original conditions should not be fulfilled on our part, the whole, except those stipulations embracing legislative objects, might remain a treaty. But if the other nation chose not to be bound, they would be at liberty to say so, and the treaty would be defeated. And this construction seems to be consonant with that resolution, of the house of representatives,[82] wherein they declare, "That when a treaty stipulates regulations on any of the subjects submitted by the constitution to the power of congress, it must depend for its execution, as to such stipulations, on a law or laws to be passed by congress; and it is the constitutional right and duty of the house of representatives, in all such cases, to deliberate on the expediency, or inexpediency, of carrying such treaty into effect, and to determine and act thereon, as in their judgment, may be most conducive to the public good.". . . A contrary construction would render the power of the president and senate paramount to that of the whole congress, even upon those subjects upon which every branch of congress is, by the constitution, required to deliberate.[83] Let it be supposed, for example, that the president and senate should stipulate by treaty with any foreign nation, that in case of war between that nation and any other, the United States should immediately declare war against that nation: Can it be supposed that such a treaty would be so far the law of the land, as to take from the house of representatives their constitutional right to deliberate on the expediency or inexpediency of such a declaration of war, and to determine and act thereon, according to their own judgment?

4, and 5. The president shall nominate, and by and with the advice and consent of the senate, shall appoint ambassadors, other public ministers, and consuls: and he shall receive ambassadors, and other public ministers. C.U.S. Art. 2. Sec. 2., 3.

The intercourse with foreign nations requiring that ambassadors should be sent from one to another, the appointment of such ministers, is by our constitution vested in the same departments of government as the treaty making power; the exclusive right of nomination being vested in the president; the senate in this case, as in other cases of appointment

---

82. Resolution of the house of representatives, April 6, 1796.

83. Such a doctrine appears to have been strenuously advocated in congress, some years ago. See debates on the treaty making power: March and April 1796.

in which they have any concurrence, having simply the right of approving, or of rejecting, if they think proper; but they cannot propose any other person in the room of him whom they may reject; they may prevent the appointment of an agent in whom they have not a proper degree of confidence, but they cannot substitute a more fit one in his stead.

The president, alone, has authority to receive foreign ministers; a power of some importance, as it may sometimes involve in the exercise of it, questions of delicacy; especially in the recognition of authorities of a doubtful nature. A scruple is said to have been entertained by the president of the United States, as to the reception of the first ambassador from the French republic. But it did not prevent, or retard his reception, in that character.... These powers are respectively branches of the royal prerogative in England.

6. The president shall, moreover, nominate, and by and with the advice and consent of the senate, shall appoint judges of the supreme court, and all other officers of the United States, whose appointments are not otherwise provided for by the constitution, and which shall be established by law. But congress may, by law, vest the appointment of such inferior officers as they think proper, in the president alone, in the courts of law, or in the heads of departments. C.U.S. Art. 2. Sec. 2. And the president shall commission all the officers of the United States.... Ibid. Sec. 3.

Although the authority of the president of the United States does not extend, as has been already remarked, to the creation of offices, by his own authority, it is nevertheless astonishing to view the number to which he has been authorized in his discretion, to give existence. In the army, navy, and volunteer corps, only, this discretionary power, with which congress have from time to time most liberally vested him, must have amounted to the appointment of several thousand officers. If to these we add the civil officers whose appointments depend either upon the president, alone; or upon his nomination or influence in the senate; we shall find that the influence and patronage of that department are already as great, and probably greater than any friend to his country could wish to see them.[84] It is however, still more increased by the next clause.

7. The president shall have power to fill up all vacancies that may happen during the recess of the senate, by granting commissions, which expire at the end of their next session.

The act of 5 Cong. c. 153, authorized the president to make appointments to fill any vacancies in the army and navy which may have happened during that session of the senate. And this without any reservation of the right of the senate to approve, or reject, at a succeeding session. This was among the manifold acts of that period for increasing the power of the president, far beyond the limits assigned by the constitution; limits already sufficiently large for every beneficial purpose. The right of nomination to office in all cases where the senate are to be consulted upon the appointment, being the undoubted privilege of the president under the constitution, should he persist in the nomination of a person to office after the senate have rejected him, there is no constitutional control over him, by which he may be compelled to nominate any other person. The office then may be kept vacant through this disagreement between them. But if it should have happened that the office became vacant during the recess of the senate, and the vacancy were filled by a commission which should expire, not at the meeting of the senate, but at the end of their session, then, in case such a disagreement between the president and the senate, if the president should persist in his opinion, and make no other nomination, the person appointed by him during the recess of the senate would continue to hold his commission, until the end of their session: so that the vacancy would happen a second time during the recess of the senate, and the president consequently, would have the sole right of appointing a second time; and the person whom the senate have rejected, may be instantly replaced by a

84. See the speech of Mr. Gallatin on the foreign intercourse bill; by which it appears that the patronage of the executive amounted in March, 1798, to the enormous sum of two millions of dollars, annually. It is probably not less at this day, notwithstanding the immense changes that have been made.

new commission. And thus it is evidently in the power of the president to continue any person in office, whom he shall once have appointed in the recess of the senate, as long as he may think proper.[85] A circumstance which renders the power of nomination, and of filling up vacancies during the recess of the senate, too great, to require any further extension. Even the control of elections loses its force, in great measure, in such cases: the influence of a president, and the activity and zeal of his partisans increasing in proportion to the number of offices which he has power to fill, and to the measure of obligation which the persons preferred by his favor, may suppose they owe to him, for the distinction.

Perhaps these inconveniences might have been avoided, if the constitution had required more than one person to have been put in nomination by the president for those offices, where the concurrence of the senate is required to complete the appointment, or, that in case of disagreement between the president and senate, two thirds of the latter might appoint, without a previous nomination by the president, in case he should decline any further nomination, after the first had been rejected.

8. The president shall, from time to time, give to congress information of the state of the union, and recommend to their consideration such measures, as he may judge necessary and expedient. He may also on extraordinary occasions convene both houses, or either of them; and in case of disagreement between them with respect to the time of adjournment, he may adjourn them to such time as he shall think proper. C.U.S. Art. 2. Sec. 3.

As from the nature of the executive office it possesses more immediately the sources, and means of information than the other departments of government; and as it is indispensably necessary to wise deliberations and mature decisions, that they should be founded upon the correct knowledge of facts, and not upon presumptions, which are often false, and always unsatisfactory; the constitution has made it the duty of the supreme executive functionary, to lay before the federal legislature, a state

---

85. *Editor's note:* Tucker here anticipates what Andrew Jackson was to make a regular practice.

of such facts as may be necessary to assist their deliberations on the several subjects confided to them by the constitution. And as any inconveniences resulting from new laws, or for the want of adequate laws upon any subject, more immediately occur to those who are entrusted with the administration of the government, than to others, less immediately concerned therein; it is likewise provided, that the first magistrate of the union should recommend to the consideration of congress such measures as he shall judge necessary, and proper. But this power of recommending any subject to the consideration of congress, carries no obligation with it. It stands precisely on the same footing, as a message from the king of England to parliament; proposing a subject for deliberation, not pointing out the mode of doing the thing which it recommends. This is considered by De Lolme, as one of the favourable peculiarities of the English constitution, uniting the advantages of originating laws in select assemblies, with the freedom of the legislature, as vested in the representatives of the people. In France, under the present constitution, all laws originate with the executive department: than which, there cannot exist a stronger characteristic of a despotic government.

The power of the president to convene either or both houses of congress, was a provision indispensably necessary in a government organized as the federal government is by the constitution. Occasions may occur during the recess of congress, for taking the most vigorous and decisive measures to repel injury, or provide for the defense: congress, only, is competent to these objects: the president may therefore convene them for that purpose. Or it may happen that an important treaty hath been negotiated during the recess of the senate, and their advice thereupon be required, without delay, either, that the ratification may be exchanged in due time, or for some other important reason. On such extraordinary occasions as these, if there were not a power lodged in the president to convene the senate, or the congress, as the case might require, the affairs of the nation might be thrown into confusion and perplexity, or worse. The power of adjourning congress, in case of a disagreement between the two houses, as to the time of adjournment, was likewise necessary to prevent any inconvenience from that source, as, is too obvious to require any further remarks upon it.

9. Ninthly; the president, as was observed, elsewhere is *sub modo* a branch of the legislative department; since every bill, order, resolution, or vote, to which the concurrence of both houses of congress is necessary, must be presented to him for his approbation, before it can take effect. If he approve it, the measure is immediately final: if he disapprove, it must be sent back to congress for further consideration, as has been already shown. The importance which the executive department derives from this share in the legislative, hath been sufficiently discussed in its proper place, being here brought into view again, merely for the sake of method.

10. Lastly; it is the duty of the president to take care that the laws be faithfully executed; and, in the words of his oath, "to preserve, protect, and defend the constitution of the United States."

The obligation of oaths upon the consciences of ambitious men has always been very slight, as the general history of mankind but too clearly evinces. Among the Romans, indeed, they were held in great sanctity during the purer ages of the republic, but began to be disregarded as the nation approached to a state of debasement, that fitted them for slavery.[86] Among christian princes, they seem only to have been calculated for the worst, instead of the best purposes:[87] monarchs having long exercised, and seeming to claim, not less than the successors of St. Peter, a kind of dispensing power on this subject, in all cases affecting themselves. A due sense of religion must not only be wanting in such cases, but the moral character of the man must be wholly debased, and corrupted. Whilst these remain unsullied, in the United States, oaths may operate in support of the constitution they have adopted, but no longer. After that period an oath of office will serve merely to designate its duties, and not to secure the faithful performance of them; or, to restrain those who are disposed to violate them.

The right of issuing proclamations is one of the prerogatives of the

86. Montesquieu's Spirit of Laws. Grotius.
87. Vattel. Grotius.

crown of England. No such power being expressly given by the federal constitution, it was doubted, upon a particular occasion, whether the president possessed any such authority under it: Both houses of congress appear to have recognized the power as one that may be constitutionally exercised by him.[88] Independent of such authority, we might perhaps be justified, in concluding that the obligation upon the president to take care that the laws be faithfully executed, drew after it this power, as a necessary incident thereto. The commencement or determination of laws is frequently made to depend upon events, of which the executive may be presumed to receive and communicate the first authentic information: the notification of such facts seems therefore to be the peculiar province and duty of that department. If the nation be in a state of war with another nation, acts of hostility are justifiable, on the part of our citizens towards theirs; if a truce be concluded; such acts are no longer to be permitted. The fact that such a truce has been made, must be announced by the competent authority; and the law arising from the promulgation of this fact, according to the rules of war and peace, among civilized nations, is such, as to give to the proclamation the apparent effect of a new law to the people. But this is not really the case; it is the established law of nations which operates upon the fact disclosed by the proclamation, viz. That a truce has been concluded between the two nations, who were before at war. But if a proclamation should enjoin any thing to be done, which neither the law of nations, nor any previous act of the legislature, nor any treaty or compact should have made a duty, such injunction would not only be merely void, but an infringement of the constitution.[89] Proclamations are then only binding, when they reinforce

88. The occasion here alluded to, was the president's proclamation of neutrality in June, 1793. This was merely an admonition, to the people of the U. States, of the duty imposed on them by the law of nations, and an annunciation of the fact that we were at peace with all nations. Both houses of congress in the addresses to the president approved of the proclamation. 3 Cong. 1 Session.

89. The proclamation of the two former presidents recommending fasting and prayer, were of this nature; they were an assumption of power not warranted by the constitution, or rather prohibited, by the true spirit of the third article of the amendments. Some persons excused the act as amounting only to the advice of the president as an individual.

the observance of a duty, enjoined by law, but connected with some particular fact, which it may be the duty of the executive to make known.

The president of the United States may be removed from office on impeachment for, and conviction of treason, bribery, or other high crimes and misdemeanors: and the chief justice of the United States shall preside at his trial. C.U.S. Art. 2., Sec. 4. Art. 1., Sec. 3.

The exclusion of the vice-president in such cases, from his ordinary constitutional seat, as president of the senate, seems to have been both necessary and proper, not only in order to remove all suspicion of undue bias upon the mind of any member of the court; (since in case of conviction, the duties of the office of the president would devolve immediately upon the vice-president); but because it is presumable, that whenever a president may be actually impeached, he would be instantly incapacitated thereby from discharging the duties of his office, until a decision should take place; in which case also, the duties of the office of president, must devolve upon the vice-president. Machiavel ascribes the ruin of the republic of Florence, to the want of this mode of proceeding by impeachment against those who offend against the state. If the want of a proper tribunal for the trial of impeachments can endanger the liberties of the United States, some future Machiavel may, perhaps, trace their destruction to the same source.

In England, as we have more than once had occasion to remark, the law will not suppose the king capable of doing wrong. His person is sacred; he is above the reach of the laws, none having power to accuse, or to judge him. The people must be driven to a total violation, and subversion of the constitution, before he can be made responsible for the most flagrant act of tyranny, or abuse of authority. Our constitution, on the contrary, considers the president a man, and fallible; it contemplates the possibility of his being not only corrupt, but, in the highest degree criminal; even to the commission of treason, against the government which he is appointed to administer. How such a case may happen, will

---

Why then was it clothed with all the forms of authority, the seal of the United States, and the attestation of the secretary of state?

be the subject of future inquiry. Suffice it to say, the constitution supposes it, and has provided, however inadequately, for his punishment.

The administration of the federal government, from its first institution, has repeatedly given rise to doubts in my own breast, whether some important amendments are not necessary for the preservation of the liberty of the people of the United States, the necessary and proper independence of the several states, and the union of the confederacy. The limitations which the constitution has provided to the powers of the president, seem not to be sufficient to restrain this department within its proper bounds, or to preserve it from acquiring and exerting more than a due share of influence. To this cause it may be attributed, that in addition to the very extensive powers, influence, and patronage which the constitution gives to the president of the United States, congress have, from time to time, with a liberal hand, conferred others still more extensive; many of them altogether discretionary, and not infrequently questionable, as to their constitutionality. These circumstances but too well justify the remark, that if a single executive do not exhibit all the features of monarchy at first, like the infant Hercules, it requires only time to mature its strength, to evince the extent of its powers. *Crescit occulto velut arbor avo.*

Under the former confederation, the United States in congress assembled, had authority to appoint a committee to sit in the recess of congress, to be denominated "a committee of the states," and to consist of one delegate from each state: and to appoint one of their number to preside, provided that no person should be allowed to serve in the office of president more than one year, in any term of three years. This committee, or any nine of them, were authorized to execute, in the recess of congress, such of the powers of congress, as the United States in congress assembled, by the consent of nine states, might from time to time think expedient to vest them with; provided that no power be delegated to the said committee, for the exercise of which, by the articles of confederation, the voice of nine states, in the congress of the United States assembled, was requisite. An executive constituted somewhat upon this plan, composed of a member from each state, would, I conceive, have been more consistent with the principles of a federal union: it might have been so modified, as that a smaller number (consisting of one member from each quarter of the union,) might execute all the powers which are now vested in the president alone, whilst the whole should be consulted upon all points to which the advice and consent of the senate is now required by the constitution. The senate might then have been divested entirely of its executive powers, and confined to such as might properly be vested in a second branch of the legislature. Such an arrangement would have removed many of those objections which now apply to the union of legislative, executive, and judiciary powers, in that body. I well know that there are many objections to a numerous executive: but I conceive them to be fewer in a federal, than in a national government. One of the principal objections to the former congress, as an executive body, seems to have arisen from the plurality of members from the states, whose united voice was often necessary to give the state a vote. If the delegates from the same state were equally divided upon any question, the state had no vote. And as this not infrequently happened in the delegations from several states, upon the same question, the result was, that no determination could be had thereupon, for want of a sufficient number of states, voting either in the affirmative or negative. But where the representation from a state is confined to an individual, the former of these inconveniences could never happen, and the latter very rarely. How far experience, under the former articles of confederation, might have prompted or justified the preference given by the convention to a single executive, I cannot pretend to judge.

III. The constitution and powers of the judiciary department of the federal government have been equally the subject of applause and censure; of confidence and jealousy.[90] The unexceptionable mode of appointing the judges, and their constitutional independence of every other branch of the government merit an eulogium, which all would have concurred in bestowing on this part of the constitution of the

90. The papers in the Federalist, on the subject of the judiciary of the United States, are, in general, equal to any that will be found in that publication.

United States, had not the powers of that department been extended to objects which might hazard the tranquility of the union in attempting to secure it. No one doubted the necessity and propriety of a federal judiciary, where an ultimate decision might be had upon such questions as might arise under the law of nations, and eventually embroil the American nation with other sovereign powers: nor was it doubted that such a tribunal was necessary to decide such differences as might possibly arise between the several members of the confederacy, or between parties claiming lands under grants from different states. But the objects of the federal jurisdiction were originally far more numerous; extending to "all cases in law and equity arising under the constitution, the laws of the United States, and treaties made, or to be made, under the authority; to all cases affecting ambassadors, other public ministers and consuls; to all cases of admiralty and maritime jurisdiction; to controversies to which the United States shall be a party; and between two or more states; *between a state and citizens of another state;* between citizens of different states; between citizens of the same state claiming lands under grants of different states; and *between a state,* or the citizens thereof, and foreign states, *citizens or subjects.*" "These objects," a writer on the subject remarks, are so numerous, and the shades of distinction between civil causes are oftentimes so slight, that it is more than probable the state judicatories will be wholly superceded; for in contests about jurisdiction, the federal court, as the most powerful, will ever prevail."[91] This conclusion will not appear to be ill-founded, if we advert to the ingenious fictions which have been from time to time adopted in the courts of Great Britain, in order to countenance the claim of jurisdiction. But more solid objections seemed to arise from the want of a sufficient security from the liberty of the citizen in criminal prosecutions: the defect of an adequate provision for the trial by jury in civil cases; and the burdens and mischiefs which might arise from the re-examination of facts, upon an appeal. These objections, however, seem to be completely removed by the amendments proposed by the first congress, and since

91. Centinel.

ratified, and made a part of the constitution. Another important objection has been likewise in some degree obviated, by the act of 1 Cong. 1 Sess. c. 20. Sec. 11, which declares, that no district or circuit court shall have cognizance of any suit upon a promissory note, or other *chose* in action in favour of an assignee, except in cases of foreign bills of exchange, unless a suit might have been prosecuted in such court if no assignment had been made: it is, however, to be wished, that this provision had formed a part of the amendments to the constitution, which were proposed to the same session, since the objection, upon constitutional grounds, still remains: more especially, as a very serious attempt was made during the last session of the sixth congress to repeal this legislative provision. But the grand objection, that the states were made subject to the action of an individual, still remained for several years, notwithstanding the concurring dissent of several states at the time of accepting the constitution.[92] Nor was it till after several of the states had actually been sued in the federal courts, that the third congress proposed an amendment, which declares, "that the judicial power of the United States shall not be construed to extend to any suit in law or equity commenced or prosecuted against one of the United States, by the citizens of another state, or by the citizens or subjects of a foreign state." This amendment having been duly ratified now forms a part of the federal constitution. It is well calculated to secure the peace of the confederacy from the dangers which the former power might have produced, had any compulsory method been adopted for carrying into effect the judgment of a federal court against a state, at the suit of an individual. But whilst the propriety of the amendment is acknowledged, candor requires a further acknowledgment, that in order to render the judicial power completely efficacious, both in the federal and in the state governments, some mode ought to be provided, by which a pecuniary right, established by the judicial sentence of a court against a state, or against the government of the United States, may be enforced. It is believed, that instances might

92. The several conventions of Massachusetts, New Hampshire, Rhode-Island, New York, Virginia, and North Carolina, proposed amendments in this respect.

be adduced, where, although such rights have been judicially established, the claimants have not received any benefit from the judgment in their favour, because the legislature have neglected (perhaps wilfully) to provide a fund, or make the necessary appropriation required by the constitution, for the discharge of the debt. In this instance, the constitutions both of the federal and state governments seem to stand in need of reform.[93] For what avails it, that an impartial tribunal have decided, that a debt is due from the public to an individual, if those who hold the purse-strings of the government, may nevertheless refuse the payment of a just debt?

But whatever objection may be made to the extent of the judicial power of the federal government; in other respects, as it is now organized, and limited by the constitution itself, by the amendments before mentioned, and by the act referred to, it seems worthy of every encomium, that has ever been pronounced upon the judiciary of Great Britain, to which its constitution is in no respect inferior; being, indeed, in all respects assimilated to it, with the addition of a constitutional, instead of a legal independence, only. Whatever then has been said by Baron Montesquieu, De Lolme, or Judge Blackstone, or any other writer, on the security derived to the subject from the independence of the judiciary of Great Britain, will apply at least as forcibly to that of the United States. We may go still further. In England the judiciary may be overwhelmed by a combination between the executive and the legislature. In America (according to the true theory of our constitution,) it is rendered absolutely independent of, and superior to the attempts of both, to control, or crush it: First, by the tenure of office, which is during good behavior; these words (by a long train of decisions in England, even as far back as the reign of Edward the third) in all commissions and grants, public or private, importing an office, or estate, for the life of the grantee,

93. By the constitution of the United States, "no money can be drawn from the treasury, but in consequence of appropriations made by law." How shall an individual having a judgment against the United States, in his favour, recover his money, if the legislature chuse to keep him out of it? The case seems to be equally as bad in the state governments.

determinable only by his death, or breach of good behaviour. Secondly, by the independence of the judges, in respect to their salaries, which cannot be diminished. Thirdly, by the letter of the constitution which defines and limits the powers of the several coordinate branches of the government; and the spirit of it, which forbids any attempt on the part of either to subvert the constitutional independence of the others. Lastly, by that uncontrollable authority in all cases of litigation, criminal or civil, which, from the very nature of things is exclusively vested in this department, and extends to every supposable case which can affect the life, liberty, or property of the citizens of America under the authority of the federal constitution, and laws, except in the case of an impeachment.

The American constitutions appear to be the first in which this absolute independence of the judiciary has formed one of the fundamental principles of the government. Doctor Rutherforth considers the judiciary as a branch only, of the executive authority; and such, in strictness, perhaps, it is in other countries, its province being to advise the executive, rather than to act independently of it: thus when Titius demands a debt, or a parcel of land of Sempronius, the judgment of the court is, its advice to the executive, to whom the execution of the laws appertains, to levy the debt for the plaintiff, or put him in possession of the lands which he claims, or to dismiss his demand as unjust and ill founded. So also if Titius be accused of treason, murder, or other crime, and be thereof convicted, the judgment of the court, is its advice in what manner he shall be punished according to law; which advice is to be carried into effect by the executive officer. Or if he be acquitted, the judgment of the court is its advice that he be discharged from his confinement, and from further prosecution. In this sense it is, that the judges of the courts of law in England are reckoned among the number of the king's councils, they being his advisers in all cases where the subject matter is of a legal nature. But in the United States of America, the judicial power is a distinct, separate, independent, and *co-ordinate* branch of the government; expressly recognized as such in our state bill of rights, and constitution, and demonstrably so, likewise, by the federal constitution, from which the courts of the United States derive all their powers, in like manner as the legislative and executive departments derive theirs. The obligation which the constitution imposes upon the judiciary department to support the constitution of the United States, would be nugatory, if it were dependent upon either of the other branches of the government, or in any manner subject to their control, since such control might operate to the destruction, instead of the support, of the constitution. Nor can it escape observation, that to require such an oath on the part of the judges, on the one hand, and yet suppose them bound by acts of the legislature, which may violate the constitution which they have sworn to support, carries with it such a degree of impiety, as well as absurdity, as no man who pays any regard to the obligations of an oath can be supposed either to contend for, or to defend.

This absolute independence of the judiciary, both of the executive and the legislative departments, which I contend is to be found, both in the letter, and spirit of our constitutions, is not less necessary to the liberty and security of the citizen, and his property, in a republican government, than in a monarchy: if in the latter, the will of the prince may be considered as likely to influence the conduct of judges created occasionally, and holding their offices only during his pleasure, more especially in cases where a criminal prosecution may be carried on by his orders, and supported by his influence; in a republic, on the other hand, the violence and malignity of party spirit, as well in the legislature, as in the executive, requires not less the intervention of a calm, temperate, upright, and independent judiciary, to prevent that violence and malignity from exerting itself "to crush in dust and ashes" all opponents to its tyrannical administration, or ambitious projects. Such an independence can never be perfectly attained, but by a *constitutional tenure of office*, equally independent of the frowns and smiles of the other branches of the government. Judges ought not only to be incapable of holding any other office at the same time, but even of appointment to any but a judicial office. For the hope of favor is always more alluring, and generally more dangerous, than the fear of offending. In England, according to the principles of the common law, a judge cannot hold any other office; and according to the practice there for more than a century, no instance can,

I believe, be shown, where a judge has been appointed to any other than a judicial office, unless it be the honorary post of privy counsellor, to which no emolument is attached. And even this honourary distinction is seldom conferred but upon the chief justice of the king's bench, if I have been rightly informed.[94] To this cause, not less than to the tenure of their offices *during good behaviour,* may we ascribe that preeminent integrity, which amidst surrounding corruption, beams with genuine lustre from the English courts of judicature, as from the sun through surrounding clouds, and mists. To emulate both their wisdom and integrity is an ambition worthy of the greatest characters in any country.

If we consider the nature of the judicial authority, and the manner in which it operates, we shall discover that it cannot, of itself, oppress any individual; for the executive authority must lend its aid in every instance where oppression can ensue from its decisions: whilst on the contrary, its decisions in favour of the citizen are carried into instantaneous effect, by delivering him from the custody and restraint of the executive officer, the moment that an acquittal is pronounced. And herein consists one of the great excellencies of our constitution: that no individual can be

---

94. Much is it to be regretted that a similar conduct towards the judges of the courts of the United States, has not prevailed in the federal government. Already have we seen two chief justices of the United States, whose duties cannot, certainly, be performed in foreign parts, appointed envoys to distant nations, and still holding their offices in the supreme court of the federal government; offices altogether incompatible, yet held at the same time in manifest violation of every constitutional principle. For surely nothing is more incompatible with the nature of the federal government, than to suppose an office of such high trust and responsibility to have been intended as a *sine cure;* much less that it could have been intended as the means of extending executive influence, or of shielding the president against the effect of an impeachment. For what could more effectually strengthen the hands of an usurping president, than the power of sending into an honourable exile, the very officer whom the constitution expressly requires to preside at his trial, in case of his impeachment? To preserve the lustre of judicial purity, perfectly unsullied, it seems necessary, by an express amendment of the constitution, to disqualify the federal judges from appointment to any other than a judicial office; since such appointments have a natural tendency to excite hopes, and secure compliance, from the prospect or expectation of additional emolument, accumulated honours, or greater pre-eminence of station.

oppressed whilst this branch of the government remains independent, and uncorrupted; it being a necessary check upon the encroachments, or usurpations of power, by either of the other. Thus, if the legislature should pass a law dangerous to the liberties of the people, the judiciary are bound to pronounce, not only whether the party accused hath been guilty of any violation of it, but whether such a law be permitted by the constitution. If, for example, a law be passed by congress, prohibiting the free exercise of religion, according to the dictates, or persuasions of a man's own conscience; or abridging the freedom of speech, or of the press; or the right of the people to assemble peaceably, or to keep and bear arms; it would, in any of these cases, be the province of the judiciary to pronounce whether any such act were constitutional, or not; and if not, to acquit the accused from any penalty which might be annexed to the breach of such unconstitutional act. If an individual be persecuted by the executive authority, (as in any alien, the subject of a nation with whom the United States were at that time at peace, had been imprisoned by order of the president under the authority of the alien act, 5 Cong. c. 75) it is then the province of the judiciary to decide whether there be any law that authorizes the proceedings against him, and if there be none, to acquit him, not only of the present, but of all future prosecutions for the same cause: or if there be, then to examine its validity under the constitution, as before-mentioned. The power of pardon, which is vested in the executive, in its turn, constitutes a proper check upon the too great rigor, or abuse of power in the judiciary department. On this circumstance, however, no great stress ought to be laid; since in criminal prosecutions, the executive is in the eye of the law, always plaintiff; and where the prosecution is carried on by its direction, the purity of the judiciary is the only security for the rights of the citizen. The judiciary, therefore, is that department of the government to whom the protection of the rights of the individual is by the constitution especially confided, interposing its shield between him and the sword of usurped authority, the darts of oppression, and the shafts of faction and violence. Let us see in what manner this protection, is thus confided to the judiciary department by the constitution.

1. First, then; the judicial power of the United States extends to all cases in law and equity, arising under the constitution, the laws of the United States, and treaties made by their authority. 2. No person shall be deprived of life, liberty, or property, (and these are the objects of all rights) without due process of law; which is the peculiar province of the judiciary to furnish him with. 3. No person shall be held to answer for any crime, unless on presentment or indictment of a grand jury, except in cases arising in the land or naval forces, or in the militia, when in actual service, in time of war or public danger.... 4. In Criminal cases the accused shall have a speedy and public trial, by an impartial jury of the state and district, where the crime shall be committed. 5. He shall be informed of the nature and cause of his accusation. 6. He shall be confronted by the witnesses against him; and 7, Shall have compulsory process for obtaining witnesses in his favour.[95] 8. He shall not be compelled to be a witness against himself. 9. He shall not be subject, for the same offense, to be twice put in jeopardy of life or limb. 10. He shall have the aid of counsel for his defense. 11. His person, house, papers, and effects, shall be free from search or seizure, except upon warrants issued upon probable cause, supported by oath or affirmation, and particularly describing the place to be searched, and the person, or things to be seized. 12. Excessive bail shall not be required of him. 13. The benefit of the writ of *habeas corpus* shall not be denied him, unless in case of actual invasion, or rebellion, the public safety (of which congress are to judge, and suspend the benefit accordingly) may require the suspension of that privilege generally, and not in his particular case, only. 14. Excessive fines shall not be imposed, nor unusual punishments inflicted on him. 15. His private property shall not be taken for the public use without just com-

---

95. On the trial of Mr. Thomas Cooper, in the federal circuit court in Pennsylvania, for a libel against the president of the United States, under the sedition law, it is said, that Mr. Cooper applied to the court for a subpoena to summon the president as a witness in his behalf, and that the court refused to grant one. Upon what principle the application was refused, (notwithstanding this article) I have never been able to obtain satisfactory information. The case was certainly delicate, and might have been perplexing.

pensation. 16. He shall not be convicted upon any charge of treason, unless on the testimony of two witnesses, at least, to the same overt act, or on confession in open court. In all these respects, the constitution, by a positive injunction, prescribes the duty of the judiciary department; extending its powers, on the one hand, so far as to arrest the hand of oppression from any other quarter; and on the other prescribing limits to its authority, which if violated would be good cause of impeachment, and of removal from office. Thus if the privilege of the writ of *habeas corpus* should be suspended by congress, when there was neither an invasion, nor rebellion in the United States, it would be the duty of the judiciary, nevertheless, to grant the writ, because the act of suspension in that case, being contrary to the express terms of the constitution, would be void. On the other hand, if the benefit of the writ of *habeas corpus,* should be granted to any person, contrary to the provisions of an act for suspending it, during the time of an invasion or rebellion, this would be a good ground for impeaching a judge who should conduct himself in that manner. So, if a judge were to instruct a jury upon the trial of a person for treason, that he might be convicted upon the testimony of a single witness, if such instruction were advisedly, and corruptly given, (and not the mere effect of mistake and misapprehension) it would furnish a good ground for impeachment, and removal of such judge from his office. And any other gross misconduct of a judge in the execution of his office may be punished in like manner.

That absolute independence of the judiciary, for which we contend is not, then, incompatible with the strictest responsibility; (for a judge is no more exempt from it than any other servant of the people, according to the true principles of the constitution;) but such an independence of the other *co-ordinate* branches of the government as seems absolutely necessary to secure to them the free exercise of their constitutional functions, without the hope of pleasing, or the fear of offending. And, as from the natural feebleness of the judiciary it is in continual jeopardy of being overpowered, awed, or influenced by its coordinate branches, who have the custody of the purse and sword of the confederacy; and as nothing can contribute so much to its firmness and independence as permanency in office, this quality therefore may be justly regarded as an indispensable ingredient in its constitution; and in great measure as the citadel of the public justice and the public security.[96] Nor was it imagined that there was more than one opinion, upon this subject, in the United States, until a recent event proved the contrary.[97] It was supposed that there could not be a doubt that those tribunals in which justice is to be dispensed according to the constitution and laws of the confederacy; in which life, liberty and property are to be decided upon; in which questions might arise as to the constitutional powers of the executive, or the constitutional obligation of an act of the legislature; and in the decision of which the judges might find themselves constrained by duty, and by their oaths, to pronounce against the authority of either, should be stable and permanent; and not dependent upon the will of the executive or legislature, or both, for their existence. That without this degree of permanence, the tenure of office during good behavior, could not secure to that department the necessary firmness to meet unshaken every question, and to decide as justice and the constitution should dictate without regard to consequences. These considerations induced an opinion which it was presumed was general, if not universal, that the power vested in congress to erect from time to time, tribunals inferior to the supreme court, did not authorize them, at pleasure, to demolish them. Being built upon the rock of the constitution, their foundations were supposed to partake of its permanency, and to be equally incapable of being shaken by the other branches of the government. But a different construction of the constitution has lately prevailed; it has been determined that a power to ordain and establish from time to time, carries with it a discretionary power to discontinue, or demolish. That although the tenure of office be, *during good behaviour,* this does not prevent the separation of the office from the officer, by putting down the office; but only secures to the officer his station, upon the terms of good behaviour, so long as the

96. Federalist, No. 78.

97. See the act of 7 Cong. repealing the act of the preceding congress for the more convenient organization of the courts of the United States, and the debates thereon.

office itself remains.... Painful indeed is the remark that, this interpretation seems calculated to subvert one of the fundamental pillars of the free governments, and to have laid the foundation of one of the most dangerous political schisms that has ever happened in the United States of America.

In all cases affecting ambassadors, other public ministers and consuls, and those in which a state shall be a party, the supreme court of the United States shall have original jurisdiction. This, I presume, was intended to give the greater solemnity as well as dispatch to the decision of such important cases, by taking away all unnecessary delays, by appeal. But congress appears to have considered, that it was not necessary that the supreme court should have original jurisdiction, but that it might, in the discretion of congress, be invested with it in those cases. By the constitution, originally, the supreme court might have had appellate jurisdiction, both as to law and fact, in all cases. But the ninth article of amendments provides that no fact tried by a jury, shall be otherwise re-examined in any court of the United States, than according to the rules of the common law. A provision which has removed one of the most powerful objections made to this department.

The organization of the federal courts will form the subject of a future note; in which also will be attempted to give the students a view of the state courts.

It now only remains to examine some miscellaneous articles, which have either not yet been noticed, or have been but slightly mentioned.

1. No money shall be drawn from the treasury, but in consequence of appropriations made by law.

All the expenses of government being paid by the people, it is the right of the people, not only, not to be taxed without their own consent, or that of their representatives freely chosen, but also to be actually consulted upon the disposal of the money which they have brought into the treasury; it is therefore stipulated that no money shall be drawn from the treasury, but in consequence of appropriations, previously made by law: and, that the people may have an opportunity of judging not only of the propriety of such appropriations, but of seeing whether their money has been actually expended only, in pursuance of the same; it is further provided, that a regular statement and account of the receipts and expenditures of all public money shall be published from time to time. These provisions form a salutary check, not only upon the extravagance, and profusion, in which the executive department might otherwise indulge itself, and its adherents and dependents; but also against any misappropriation, which a rapacious, ambitious, or otherwise unfaithful executive might be disposed to make. In those governments where the people are taxed by the executive, no such check can be interposed. The prince levies whatever sums he thinks proper; disposes of them as he thinks proper; and would deem it sedition against him and his government, if any account were required of him, in what manner he had disposed of any part of them. Such is the difference between governments, where there is responsibility, and where there is none.

Yet even this excellent regulation has an inconvenience attending it, which was formerly hinted at. According to the theory of the American constitutions, the judiciary ought to be enabled to afford complete redress in all cases, where a man may have a just claim for compensation for any injury done him, or for any service which he may have rendered another, in expectation of a just recompence. According to the laws of Virginia, if a claim against the commonwealth be disallowed or abated by the auditor of public accounts, any person who may think himself aggrieved thereby may petition the high court of chancery, or the district court held at Richmond, according to the nature of his case, for redress; and such court shall proceed to do right thereon; and a like petition shall be allowed in all other cases to any person who is entitled to demand against the commonwealth any right in law or equity. But although redress is thus intended to be afforded in such cases, yet it seems to be held, that the treasurer cannot pay the money for which the claimant may have obtained a judgment, or decree, until the general assembly have passed a law making an appropriation, for that purpose, if no law authorizing such payment be previously passed. But whatever doubt there may be upon the subject, under the laws of the state, it seems to be altogether without a question, that no claim against the United

States (by whatever authority it may be established,) can be paid, but in consequence of a previous appropriation made by law; unless, perhaps, it might be considered as falling properly under the head of contingent charges against the government. An interpretation which may be somewhat strained, and which the executive department of the government, to which the management of the fund appropriated for contingent charges is committed, might be as little disposed to admit, as congress might be to pass a law making a specific appropriation.

Both the constitution and laws of the United States appear, then, to be defective upon this subject; inasmuch, as they neither provide in what manner a just claim against the United States, which may happen to be disallowed by the auditor and comptroller of the treasury, shall be judicially examined;[98] nor for the payment of any just claim which might be judicially established, without submitting it to the discretion of congress, whether they will make an appropriation for that purpose. As the congress are supposed, in all pecuniary cases, to have the same common interest with their constituents, they can hardly be considered in any other light than as parties, whenever a demand is made against the public. They cannot then be presumed to be altogether as impartial judges in such cases, as those who are sworn to do equal right to all persons, without distinction: and although the practice has been to petition them for any disputed claim against the United States, cases may arise where such a petition might be highly improper, and yet the nature of the case be such, as to entitle the party to obtain redress according to the dictates of

98. It hath been said on the floor of the house of representatives of the United States, "that it had been repeatedly decided, that the United States would not permit themselves to be brought into their own courts." The editor had supposed that that clause of the constitution, which declares that "the judicial power *shall* extend to *all cases*, in *law* and *equity*, arising under the constitution," &c. had prescribed a different rule of decision. Nor can he, even now, form a different opinion upon the subject; believing that there is as much reason that a *legal* or *equitable* claim *against* the United States, should receive a judicial discussion, and decision, as any similar claim which might be made on their *behalf*. And though he doubts, as to the mode in which a judicial enquiry into the justice of a pecuniary claim *against* them may be instituted, yet he cannot doubt that the constitution meant to afford the *right* to every citizen of the United States.

moral obligation. A judicial court is, according to the true spirit of the constitution, the proper place in which such a right should be inquired into, and from which redress might be finally obtained: and that, without impediment from any other department of the government. This might be effected by an amendment, declaring, that no money shall be drawn from the treasury but in consequence of appropriations made by law; or, of a judicial sentence of a court of United States.

2. Full faith and credit shall be given in each state to the public acts, records, and judicial proceedings of every other state. And congress may by general laws, prescribe the manner in which the same shall be proved, and the effect thereof. The act of 1 Cong. 2 Sess. c. 11, accordingly declares, that the acts of the legislature of the several states shall be authenticated by having the seal of their respective states affixed thereto; that the records and judicial proceedings of the courts of any state, shall be proved or admitted in any other court within the United States, by attestation of the clerk, and the seal of the court annexed, if there be a seal, together with a certificate of the judge, chief justice, or presiding magistrate, as the case may be, that such attestation is in due form. And records and judicial proceedings so authenticated, shall have such faith in every court within the United States, as they have by law or usage in the courts of the state, from whence they may be taken. The propriety and necessity of such a provision to be made between members of an extensive confederacy, are too obvious to escape observation. A similar provision was accordingly made by the former articles of confederation and perpetual union, Art. 4.

3. The citizens of each state shall be entitled to all the privileges and immunities of citizens of the several states.

This article, with some variation, formed a part of the confederation: we have in another place supposed, that the states retain the power of admitting aliens to become citizens of the states respectively, notwithstanding the several acts of congress establishing an uniform rule of naturalization. But such denizens, not being properly citizens, would not, I apprehend, be entitled to the benefit of this article in any other state. They would still be regarded as aliens in every state, but in that of which they may be denizens. Consequently, an alien before he is completely naturalized, may be capable of holding lands in one state, but not of holding them in any other.

4. A person charged in any state with treason, felony, or other crime, who shall flee from justice and be found in another state, shall, on demand of the executive authority of the state from which he fled, be delivered up to be removed to the state having jurisdiction of the crime.

This article likewise formed a part of the former confederation, and was necessary to cement and secure the harmony of the union. The act of 1784, c. 35. (V. L. Edi. 1794, c. 118.) provided for the mode of carrying it into execution; but a different provision is made by the act of 2 Cong. 51. ... Either mode may be adopted, I apprehend, according to the nature of the case. If the party accused be already in custody of the law, by virtue of process from the state courts, he may, on demand of the executive authority of the state from whence he fled, be sent thither in custody by order of the general court, or warrant of any two judges thereof in vacation: if he be not already in custody, the act of congress makes it the duty of the executive authority of the state to which he flies, upon a copy of an indictment found, or affidavit made before a magistrate of any state, charging him with any crime, to cause him to be arrested and secured, and notice to be given to the executive authority making the demand, or his agent, and the fugitive to be delivered up. But if no agent appear, within six months from the time of the arrest, the prisoner may be discharged.

5. No person held to service in one state, under the laws thereof, and escaping into another state, shall, in consequence of any law or regulation therein, be discharged from such service or labor, but shall be delivered up on claim of the party to whom such service is due.

This necessary provision had not a place in the former articles of confederation; in consequence of which numberless inconveniences were felt by the citizens of those states, where slavery prevails, from the escaping of their slaves into other states, where slavery was not tolerated by law, and where it was supposed no aid ought to be given to any other person claiming another as his slave. The act of 2 Cong. c. 51, prescribes the mode of proceeding in such cases; authorizing the master to seize his slave, and making it the duty of the district judge of the United States, and of the magistrates of the state to aid him therein; and imposing a penalty of five hundred dollars upon any person obstructing him.

6. The United States shall guarantee to every state in the union a republican form of government, and shall protect each of them against invasion; and on application of the legislature, or of the executive (when the legislature cannot be convened), against domestic violence. C.U.S. Art. 4. Sec. 4.

It is an observation of the enlightened Montesquieu, that mankind would have been at length obliged to submit to the government of a single person, if they had not contrived a kind of constitution, by which the internal advantages of a republic might be united with the external force of a monarchy; and this constitution is that of a confederacy of smaller states, to form one large one for their common defense. But these associations ought only to be formed, he tells us, between states whose form of government is not only similar, but also *republican.* The spirit of monarchy is war, and the enlargement of dominion; peace and moderation is the spirit of a republic. These two kinds of government cannot naturally subsist together in a confederate republic. Greece, he adds, was undone, as soon as the kings of Macedon obtained a seat among the Amphictions. If the United States wish to preserve themselves from a similar fate, they will consider the guarantee contained in this clause as a corner stone of their liberties.

The possibility of an undue partiality in the federal government in affording its protection to one part of the union in preference to another, which may be invaded at the same time, seems to be provided against, by that part of this clause which guarantees such protection to each of them. So that every state which may be invaded must be protected by the united force of the confederacy. It may not be amiss further to observe, that every pretext for intermeddling with the domestic concerns of any state, under color of protecting it against domestic violence is taken away, by that part of the provision which renders an application from the legislative, or executive authority of the state endangered, necessary to be made to the federal government, before its interference can be at all proper. On the other hand, this article secures an immense acquisition of strength; and additional force to the aid of any of the state governments, in case of an internal rebellion or insurrection against its authority.... The southern states being more peculiarly open to danger from this quarter, ought to be particularly tenacious of a constitution from which they may derive such assistance in the most critical periods.

7. All debts contracted, and engagements entered into, before the adoption of the constitution, are declared to be as valid against the United States under the same, as under the confederation. This declaration was probably inserted for the satisfaction, as well as the security of the public creditors, both foreign and domestic. The articles of confederation contained a similar stipulation in respect to the bills of credit emitted, monies borrowed, and debts contracted, by or under the authority of congress, before the ratification of the confederation. These declarations are merely acknowledgments of that which moral obligation imposed upon the United States as a duty. It might seem as if this act prohibited the making of any act of limitation in bar of such debts; but a different interpretation has been given to it by congress. L.U.S. 2 Cong. 2 Sess. c. 6.

8. The ratification of the conventions of nine states was declared to be sufficient for establishing the constitution between the states ratifying the same.

This article may now be regarded of little importance, the constitution having been ratified by all the members of the former confederacy. ... Had it been otherwise, after nine states had ratified the constitution, it might have been a question of some delicacy, in what relation those which failed to ratify, stood to the others which had. The adoption of the constitution and the establishing a new form of government by nine states only, would have been an undoubted breach of the articles of confederation, on their parts:[99] the remaining states might, at their election,

99. "The articles of this confederation shall be invioably observed by every state, and the union shall be perpetual; nor shall any alteration at any time hereafter be made in any of them; unless such alteration be agreed to in a congress of the United States, and be afterwards confirmed by the legislatures of every state." Art. 13.

have considered the confederacy as dissolved, or not. If they considered it as dissolved, they would have stood in the relation of other foreign states. If as still existing, they would have had a right to insist upon the performance of all mutual stipulations on the part of the other states, so long as they continued to perform their own, with good faith. The Federalist advances a different opinion: Happily for the United States it is now unnecessary to discuss the question any further.

9. The constitution, and the laws of the United States, made in pursuance of it; and all treaties made, and to be made, under the authority of the United States, shall be the supreme law of the land; and the judges in every state shall be bound thereby, any thing in the constitution or laws of any state to the contrary notwithstanding.

It may seem very extraordinary, that a people jealous of their liberty, and not insensible of the allurements of power, should have entrusted the federal government with such extensive authority as this article conveys: controlling not only the acts of their ordinary legislatures, but their very constitutions, also.

The most satisfactory answer seems to be, that the powers entrusted to the federal government being all positive, enumerated, defined, and limited to particular objects; and those objects such as relate more immediately to the intercourse with foreign nations, or the relation in respect to war or peace, in which we may stand with them; there can, in these respects, be little room for collision, or interference between the states, whose jurisdiction may be regarded as confided to their own domestic concerns, and the United States, who have no right to interfere, or exercise a power in any case not delegated to them, or absolutely necessary to the execution of some delegated power. That, as this control cannot possibly extend beyond those objects to which the federal government is competent, under the constitution, and under the declaration contained in the twelfth article, so neither ought the laws, or even the constitution of any state to impede the operation of the federal government in any case within the limits of its constitutional powers. That a law limited to such objects as may be authorized by the constitution, would, under the true construction of this clause, be the supreme law of the land; but a law not limited to those objects, or not made pursuant to the constitution, would not be the supreme law of the land, but an act of usurpation, and consequently void. A further answer seems also to be, that without this provision the constitution could not have taken effect in those states where the articles of confederation were sanctioned by the constitution; nor could it be supposed that the constitution of the United States would possess any stability so long as it was liable to be affected by any future change in the constitution of any of the states. Other reasons are assigned by the Federalist, for which I shall refer the student to that work.[100]

10. The senators and representatives in congress, and the members of the several state legislatures, and all executive and judicial officers of the United States, and of the several states, shall be bound by oath or affirmation to support the constitution.

That all those who are entrusted with the execution of the powers vested in the federal goverment, should, under the most solemn sanction, be bound to the due execution of the trusts reposed in them, could not be doubted. But the propriety of requiring a similar engagement from the members of the state legislatures, and the other public functionaries in the several states, was doubted. But it should be remembered, that the members and officers of the state governments will have an essential agency in giving effect to the federal government. The election of the senate depends upon the immediate agency of the state legislatures. In some of the states the electors for president and vice-president are chosen in the same manner. In all, the legislature must direct the mode in which they shall be appointed. The election of representatives must probably depend upon them also for aid; at least until congress shall pass a general law upon the subject. The judges of the state courts will not infrequently have to decide according to the constitution and laws of the United States. Decisions ought to be uniform, whether had in the federal courts, or the state courts. This uniformity can only be obtained by uniformity of obligation. The executive authority of the

100. Federalist, No. 33, No. 44.

states will also have an immediate agency in the appointment of senators, in case of vacancy during the recess of the legislature: in issuing writs of election to fill up vacancies in the house of representatives; in giving effect to the laws for calling the militia into the service of the United States; in officering the militia, and a variety of other occasions, all of which required that no adverse spirit, nor doubts of authority, or obligation, should be permitted to counteract, or retard the necessary operations of the federal government.

11. Lastly; the fifth article provides the mode by which future amendments to the constitution may be proposed, discussed, and carried into effect, without hazarding a dissolution of the confederacy, or suspending the operations of the existing government. And this may be effected in two different modes: the first on recommendation from congress, whenever two thirds of both houses shall concur in the expediency of any amendment. The second, which secures to the states an influence in case congress should neglect to recommend such amendments, provides, that congress shall, on application from the legislatures of two thirds of the states, call a convention for proposing amendments; which in either case shall be valid to all intents and purposes as part of the constitution, when ratified by the legislatures of three fourths of the several states, or by conventions in three fourths thereof, as the one or the other mode, of the ratification may be proposed by the congress. Both of these provisions appear excellent. Of the utility and practicability of the former, we have already had most satisfactory experience. The latter will probably never be resorted to, unless the federal government should betray symptoms of corruption, which may render it expedient for the states to exert themselves in order to the application of some radical and effectual remedy. Nor can we too much applaud a constitution, which thus provides a safe, and peaceable remedy for its own defects, as they may from time to time be discovered. A change of government in other countries is almost always attended with convulsions which threaten its entire dissolution; and with scenes of horror, which deter mankind from any attempt to correct abuses, or remove oppressions until they have become altogether

intolerable. In America we may reasonably hope, that neither of these evils need be apprehended; nor is there any reason to fear that this provision in the constitution will produce any degree of instability in the government; the mode both of originating and of ratifying amendments, in either mode which the constitution directs, must necessarily be attended with such obstacles, and delays, as must prove a sufficient bar against light, or frequent innovations. And as a further security against them, the same article further provides, that no amendment which may be made, prior to the year one thousand eight hundred and eight, shall, in any manner, affect those clauses of the ninth section of the first article, which relate to the migration or importation of such persons as the states may think proper to allow; and to the manner in which direct taxes shall be laid: and that no state, without its consent shall be deprived of its equal suffrage in the senate.

Among the amendments proposed by the several state conventions, some appear to have been proposed only for greater precaution, and security against misconstruction, or an undue extension of the powers vested in the federal government; whilst others seem to have been calculated to remedy some radical defects in the system.[101] The most important of those which have not yet received the approbation of both houses of congress may not improperly be brought into view in this place, although we have occasionally offered some remarks upon several of them in other parts of this essay.

1. That some tribunal other than the senate be provided for trying impeachments of senators.... This amendment seems to be the more necessary in consequence of the decision in William Blount's case, that a senator is not a civil officer, and therefore not impeachable. On this subject we have already spoken somewhat at large.

---

101. The following amendments were proposed by one or more of the following states; viz. Virginia, New-York, North-Carolina, Massachusetts, New Hampshire, Rhode-Island, or South-Carolina, in convention; or may be found in an address to the people of Maryland, or the proceedings at Harrisburg in Pennsylvania. The whole being collected in Carey's Museum, Vol. 3, 4, 7, and 8, to which I must refer the student.

2. That some reform be made, in the mode of choosing a president of the United States in those cases where the election may now devolve upon the house of representatives.

The necessity of such a reform, and the danger to which the federal union, may be exposed if it be not effected, have been brought into full view by the struggle between two parties almost equally balanced, at the election of a president of the United States in the year 1801. On this subject also, we have offered some remarks elsewhere. I shall only add, that sound policy would dictate that no president should be capable of being *re-elected*, that had not a majority of the whole number of votes of the state electors, in his favor; and that no preponderance ought to be given to the vote of one member of the house of representatives over that of another.

3. That all commercial treaties, and such whereby any cession of territory or of jurisdiction, or the right of fishing upon the coasts of the United States, or of the adjacent continent and islands, be made subject to the final ratification of congress, before they shall be deemed conclusive, on the part of the United States.

4. That the judiciary power of the United States be not construed to extend to any civil suit, where the cause of action was not originally cognizable in the federal courts; nor to any crime or misdemeanour whatsoever, which is not defined, and the punishment thereof prescribed, either in the constitution of the United States, or in some act of congress, made pursuant thereto; except the same be committed out of the jurisdiction of any particular state, and within the exclusive jurisdiction of the federal government.

The reasons for some further limitation of the judicial power of the United States have been repeatedly touched upon, already; some further reasons will be offered hereafter in the tract, upon the authority and obligation of the common law of England, in the United States. At the conclusion of the latter the student will find the sentiments of the general assembly of Virginia, upon that important subject, as connected with the extent of the judicial power of the United States; expressed in the most nervous language, that a just apprehension of the fatal consequences to be expected from the doctrine, that the common law of England has been adopted as the law of the federal government, could dictate.

5. That the articles which relate to direct taxes, and excises, might if possible be so modified as to remove the objections which have been made to them, by the several states.

6. That the exclusive power of legislation over the seat of government, &c. be limited to such regulations as respect the police and good government thereof.

7. That congress shall not alter, modify, or interfere in, the time, place, or manner, of holding elections for senators or representatives, except when the legislature of any state may neglect, or refuse, or be disabled by invasion or rebellion, to prescribe the same.

8. That no standing army, or regular forces, be kept up in time of peace, except for the necessary protection and defense of forts, dock yards, and arsenals, without consent of two thirds of both house of congress.

9. That congress shall not have power to grant monopolies, or to erect any companies with exclusive advantages of commerce.

10. That the president shall not command an army in person, without the consent, or desire of congress.

11. That congress shall not declare war, without the consent of two thirds of both houses.

12. That no law for the regulation of commerce, or navigation act, shall be made, unless with the consent of two-thirds of the members of both houses.

13. That the state legislatures may have power to recall, when they think it expedient, their senators, and to send others in their stead.

14. That the senators and representatives in congress shall be ineligible to any post or place under the United States during the term for which they were elected.... To which I will take the liberty of suggesting ... *"or for one year thereafter."*

The practical exercise of the federal government has evinced the indispensable necessity of an amendment upon this subject. It cannot be made too strict, or too rigorous.... The man who seeks a seat in congress, with the hopes by that means to retire upon a lucrative office, will be a venal sycophant towards those who have the power of fulfilling his wishes. We have seen that the most ready road to preferment in the federal government has been found to pass through the two house of congress; that offices have (almost invariably) been conferred on those, who have been the most distinguished supporters and promoters of the extension of the power and influence of the executive: that employments (lucrative in their nature) have been occasionally carved out for them, even during the time for which they have been elected.[102] He that can doubt that political corruption unavoidably springs from such a source, may, if he pleases, doubt that animal putrefaction is produced by the combined action of air, heat, and moisture. But neither the real philosopher, nor the enlightened politician, will feed a doubt upon either of these questions.

I have now finished the survey of the constitution of the United States, which I proposed making in this essay. Attached, from principle, and confirmed in that attachment from past experience, to a *federal* union of the American States, and to the principles of a democratic government, I have probably regarded with a jealous eye those parts of the constitution which seem to savor of monarchy, or aristocracy, or tend to a consolidated, instead of a federal, union of the states. I have been equally zealous in my endeavours to point out the excellencies of the constitution, as to expose its defects: a sincere attachment to the former will always lead an ingenuous mind to a candid investigation, and correction of the latter. Happily for us, and for our country, this correction has been found to be practicable without hazard, without tumult, and without the smallest interruption to the ordinary course of administering the government.

To shut our eyes against this inestimable advantage which we possess,

---

102. The mission of a senator, during a recess of congress, to visit the western posts, with a salary of eight dollars a day, and his expences paid, may serve as an instance of this practice.

beyond any other nation in the universe, would be an unpardonable act of ingratitude to that divine being, under whose providence we have accomplished the great work of our independence, and the establishment of free government, in every state, and an union of the whole upon such a solid foundation, as nothing but our own folly, or wickedness, can undermine. The man who first espies any defect, or decay in the fabric, should, therefore, be the first to point it out; that it may be amended, before the injury which it may have occasioned is too great to be repaired. Those who, perceiving the defect, deny that it exists, or wilfully obstruct the amendment, are the real enemies of the constitution: its real friends ought to pursue a different conduct. Governments of force may be preserved for a time by an obstinate perseverance in the same course, however pernicious: but a government of the people hath no foundation but the confidence of the people: if that be withdrawn, the government inevitably falls.

The very elaborate and masterly discussion of the constitution, in the Federalist, to which I have repeatedly referred the student in the course of this essay, would probably have saved me the labour of this attempt, if the defects of the constitution had been treated with equal candour, as the authors have manifested abilities in the developement of its eminent advantages. But, notwithstanding, those letters are not altogether free from objectionable parts, yet the far greater proportion of them contain so just a commentary upon the principles of republican government, and of a federal union of the states, that I cannot too warmly recommend the perusal of them to those who wish to make themselves perfectly acquainted with a subject so truly interesting to every American citizen, as the federal government of the United States.

WORKS USED BY TUCKER

Francis Bacon, *Advancement of Learning and Novum Organum.*
Matthew Carey, *American Museum* [magazine] (Philadelphia).
"Centinel" [Samuel Bryan], *On the Proposed Constitution for the United States of America. Letters of Centinel.*

Jean Louis De Lolme, *The Constitution of England*....

Hugo Grotius, *Concerning the Law of War and Peace.*

Sir James Mackintosh, *Vindiciae Gallicae: Defence of the French Revolution and Its English Admirers.*

Charles Louis de Secondat Montesquieu, *The Spirit of Laws.*

Thomas Paine, *The Rights of Man.*

Richard Price, *Observations on the Importance of the American Revolution, and the Means of Making It a Benefit to the World.*

Samuel, Baron von Pufendorf, *On the Law of Nature and of Nations.*

Thomas Rutherforth, *Institutes of Natural Law.*

Emerich de Vattel, *Law of Nations.*

❧ Of the Unwritten, or Common Law of England; And Its Introduction into, and Authority Within the United American States

The question of the role of the common law in federal jurisprudence was a major issue of the early American republic. Opposition to Federalist initiatives to establish such a role formed a large part of the Jeffersonian Republican attempts to restrain the imperial federal judiciary. As Tucker writes: "This question is of very great importance, not only as it regards the limits of the jurisdiction of the *federal courts;* but also, as it relates to the extent of the powers vested in the *federal government.* For, if it be true that the common law of England, has been adopted by the United States in their national, or federal capacity, the jurisdiction of the *federal courts* must be co-extensive with it; or, in other words, *unlimited....*" After a long struggle, lasting well into the nineteenth century, the doctrine against which Tucker contends was successfully grafted onto the federal system, largely through the untiring cleverness of Justice Joseph Story. The importance that Tucker ascribes to the question is indicated by his placing it in the first volume as Appendix E, immediately following *View of the Constitution of the United States.*

Having accompanied the commentator, to the fountain head, from whence he deduces the common law of England, it becomes us to trace its progress to our own shores. This, as it respects the commonwealth of Virginia, considered as an independant state, unconnected with any other, might have been regarded as an unnecessary trouble at this day; the convention, by which the constitution of the commonwealth was established, having expressly declared, "That the common law of England, and all statutes, or acts of parliament made in aid of the common law, prior to the fourth year, of James the first, which are of a general nature not local to that kingdom, together with the several acts of the colony then in force, so far as the same may consist with the several ordinances, declarations, and resolutions of the general convention, shall be considered as in full force, until the same shall be altered by the legislative power of the commonwealth." Ordinances of Convention May, 1776.

BUT SOME LATE INCIDENTS having given rise to an opinion, that the common law of England, is not only the law of the American States, respectively, according to the mode in which they may, severally have adopted it, but that it is likewise the law of the federal government, a much wider field for investigation is thereby opened; of the importance of which, the general assembly of Virginia, at their session in the winter of 1799, have thus expressed their sentiments, in behalf of themselves, and their constituents. "It is distressing to reflect, that it ever should have been made a question, whether the constitution of the United States on the whole face, of which, is seen so much labour to enumerate and define the several objects of federal power, could intend to introduce in the lump, in an indirect manner, and by a forced construction of a few phrases, the vast and multifarious jurisdiction involved in the common law; a law filling so many ample volumes; a law overspreading the entire field of legislation; a law that would sap the foundation of the constitution, as a system of limited, and specified powers."

My present purpose, therefore, is, in the compass of this note to enquire, how far the common law of England, is the law of the federal government of the United States? Should the enquiry seem long, to some of my readers, the importance of the subject I trust, will be deemed a sufficient apology for it.

A question has lately been agitated, whether the common, or, unwritten law of England, has been adopted in America, by the establishment of the constitution of the United States; or, in other words, how far the laws of England, both civil and criminal, make a part of the law of the American States, in their *united* and *national* capacity.

Judge Ellsworth is reported, on a late occasion, to have laid it down as a general rule, that the common law of England is the unwritten law of the United States, in their national or federal capacity.[1] Judge Washington, also, is said to have delivered a similar opinion, upon another occasion. The like opinion has been advanced on the floor of the federal house of representatives ... concurrent opinions from such respectable authority deserve to be candidly, and respectfully examined, where any doubt is entertained of their correctness; and where any such doubt is entertained, they ought to receive an early and full discussion; otherwise they will soon acquire the force of *precedents.* These are often more difficult to be shaken than the most cogent arguments, when drawn from reason alone.

This question is of very great importance, not only as it regards the limits of the jurisdiction of the *federal courts;* but also, as it relates to the extent of the powers vested in the *federal government.* For, if it be true that the common law of England, has been adopted by the United States in their national, or federal capacity, the jurisdiction of the *federal courts* must be co-extensive with it; or, in other words, *unlimited: so* also, must be the jurisdiction, and authority of the *other branches* of the federal government; that is to say, their powers respectively must be, likewise, *unlimited.* How far this may be the case, it is my present purpose to examine with candour.

In the prosecution of this subject it will be necessary to enquire,

1. Whether the several colonies of Great Britain, which now compose the United States of America, brought with them the laws of the mother-

---

1. Since this essay was transcribed for the press, I have seen an "account of the trial of Isaac Williams" in the federal district court, for the district of Connecticut: therein, the chief justice of the United States is reported to have delivered it as his opinion, that "the common law of this country remains the same, as it was before the revolution." This doctrine I apprehend, goes much farther than that which I have stated above. *Editor's note:* Tucker refers here to Chief Justice Oliver Ellsworth and Justice Bushrod Washington of the U.S. Supreme Court.

country, so far as they were applicable to the situation and circumstances of the colonies respectively, or not.

2. What part of those laws might be deemed applicable to the situation and circumstances of the colonies, respectively; and as such, adopted by them severally.

3. What part of those laws which might have been deemed applicable to their situations, respectively, as colonies, were abrogated and annulled by the revolution, or retained by the states; respectively, when they became independent and sovereign republics.

4. Lastly, how far that portion of the laws of England, which may have been retained by the states, respectively, has been engrafted upon, and made a part of, the constitution of the United States.

I. We are to enquire, whether the several colonies of Great Britain, which now compose the United States of America, brought with them the laws of the mother country, so far as they were applicable to the situation and circumstances of the colonies, respectively, or not.

Although very little doubt upon this part of our inquiry was, perhaps, ever entertained in America, yet the celebrated judge Blackstone in his commentaries on the laws of England, expressly denies that the common law of England, as such, had any allowance or authority in the British American colonies. "Plantations, or colonies in distant countries," as he observes, "are either such where the lands are claimed by the right of occupancy, only, by finding them desart and uncultivated, and peopling them from the mother country; or where, when already cultivated they have been either gained by conquest, or ceded by treaties. And both these rights are founded upon the law of nature, or at least upon that of nations. But there is a difference between the two species of colonies, with respect to the laws by which they are bound. For it hath been held, that if any uninhabited country be discovered, and planted by English subjects, all the English laws *then* in being, which are the birthright of every subject, are immediately there in force." . . . Afterwards he adds: "But in conquered or ceded countries, that have already laws of their own, the king may indeed alter and change those laws; but till he does actually change them, the ancient laws of the country remain, unless such as are against the laws of God, as in the case of an infidel country. Our American plantations are principally of this latter sort; being obtained in the last century, by right of conquest, and driving out the natives, or by treaties. And therefore the common law, as such, has no allowance or authority there."

As I apprehend the opinion here cited is not as correct as many others of the learned commentator, I shall venture to state some objections to it: observing by the way, that his conclusion is applicable only to the colony of New-York, which was originally settled by the Dutch, and afterwards conquered by the English, and ceded to the crown by the treaty of Breda in 1667; and perhaps, to the adjacent colony of Jersey, which was likewise ceded by the same treaty, and was also peopled at that time by the Dutch, the boundaries between the two colonies being not then established. But with respect to the other colonies; whether they were obtained by purchase from the Indian natives, as was certainly the case with Pennsylvania, and as it has been said, was the case with several others; or whether the territory was acquired by conquest; or by cession; in either case, as those persons by whom the colony was settled, were neither the people who were conquered, nor those who were ceded by treaty, to a different sovereignty; but the conquerors, themselves, or colonists, settling a vacant territory ceded by treaty, the conclusion here made by judge Blackstone will appear to be erroneous. For baron Puffendorf informs us, that sovereignty, by way of conquest, is acquired when a nation, having just reason to make war upon another people, reduces them by the superiority of their arms to the necessity of thenceforward submitting to the government of the *conquerors.* And with respect to countries ceded by treaty, Grotius tells us, it is not the people that are alienated, but the perpetual right of governing them as a people. Now the British emigrants by whom the colonies were settled were neither a conquered nor a ceded people, but free citizens of that state, by which, the conquest was made, or, to which, the territory was ceded; the Indians, the former people, having uniformly withdrawn themselves from the conquered, or ceded territory. What is here said by Mr. Blackstone, cannot, therefore, be applicable to any colony, which was settled by English emigrants, after the Indian natives had ceded, or withdrawn themselves from, the territory, however applicable it may be to New-York, where the Dutch settlers remained, after they were conquered, and after the perpetual right of governing them as a people, was ceded by the treaty of Breda before mentioned.

This distinction between the English emigrants, and the Indian natives, being once understood, we shall be able to apply to the former, what Grotius says upon this subject, viz. "When a people, by one consent, go to form colonies, it is the original of a new and independent people; for they are not sent out to be slaves, but to enjoy equal privileges and freedom." This sentiment he adopts from Thucydides, who, speaking of the second colony sent by the Corinthians to Epidamnus, says, they ordered public notice to be given, that such as were willing to go thither, should enjoy the same rights and privileges as those who staid at home; which corresponds precisely with the declaration contained in Queen Elizabeth's charter to Sir Walter Raleigh, bearing date March 25, 1584, whereby she promises and engages that for the purpose of "uniting in more perfect league and amity such lands and countries as the patentees should settle with the realms of England and Ireland, and for the better encouragement of those who would engage in the enterprize, the said countries so to be possessed and inhabited, should from thenceforth be in allegiance and protection of her, her heirs and successors; and further grants to the said Sir Walter Raleigh, his heirs and assigns, and to every other person or persons, to their and every of their heirs, that they and every of them that should thereafter be inhabiting in the said lands, countries, and territories, should and might have and enjoy all the privileges of free denizens, or persons native of England."[2] The like engagements and stipulations were contained in all the successive charters granted by King James, to the colony of Virginia; from whence it seems probable that the charters of all the other colonies contained the same. If this were the case, we may, without recurring to the authority of the writ-

2. Stith's History of Virginia.

ers on the law of nations, decide upon the ground of compact alone, that the English emigrants who came out to settle in America, did bring with them all the rights and privileges of free natives of England; and, consequently, did bring with them that portion of the laws of the mother country, which was necessary to the conservation and protection of those rights. A people about to establish themselves in a new country, remote from the parent state, would equally stand in need of some municipal laws, and want leisure, and experience to form a code adapted to their situation and circumstances. The municipal laws of the parent state being better known to them, than those of any other nation, a recurrence to them would naturally be had, for the decision of all questions of right and wrong, which should arise among them, until leisure and experience should enable them to make laws better adapted to their own peculiar situation. The laws of the parent state would from this circumstance acquire a tacit authority, and reception in all cases to which they were applicable. Of this applicability, the colonists themselves could be the only competent judges; the grant of a legislature of its own, to each colony, was a full recognition of this principle, on the part of the crown; and sanctioned the exercise of the right, thereby recognized, on all future occasions.

II. Let us now enquire, what part of the laws of the mother country might be deemed applicable to the situation of the colonies, respectively; and as such adopted by them severally.

I shall endeavour to consider this question, first, in a strictly legal point of view; secondly, in a more general, and political light; and lastly, I shall examine the conduct of the colonies, respectively, in the practical exercise of the right before spoken of; viz. of judging for themselves what parts of the laws of the mother country were applicable, or inapplicable, to their respective situations and circumstances.

1. It seems to be generally understood, that all the colonies were inhibited by the terms of their several charters, and provincial constitutions, from passing any act derogatory from the sovereignty and supremacy of the crown of England, as the head of the nation; and it was further pro-

vided by their charters, that all the laws which they should make should conform, as nearly as might be, to the laws and statutes of England, and not be repugnant thereto.

As, according to strict legal construction, all the laws and statutes of England in force at the time of their migration, might be considered as potentially existing in the colonies, so might they be regarded as actually existing there, whenever co-relative subjects occurred, upon which they could operate; except so far, and so far only, as their several charters might have permitted a departure from this general principle. The colonies under this construction, might be compared to corporations within the realm of England, many of which have power to make bye-laws, for the regulation of their own internal police; but in so doing, are bound to conform to the general laws of the realm, which are in all cases paramount to their own local institutions.

But this strict construction, however applicable to domestic corporations within the realm, where the administration of justice in a regular course was already established in courts of the most extensive jurisdiction; and where any defects in the existing laws of the realm, must be supposed to be subject to the immediate observation of the supreme legislature of the nation, by whom, if expedient, they could be immediately remedied; this construction, I say, must have been perfectly inapplicable to the circumstances of infant and remote colonies, surrounded by hostile savage nations, and equally destitute of support from the crown, as the supreme executive, for aid, or authority to repel their aggressions, and incursions; and of the means of application to the judicial courts of the realm for the redress of private injuries, or the punishment of such as were of a public nature: and not less destitute of the means of application to the national legislature for the remedy of such inconveniences of a public nature, as must continually have manifested themselves, under such circumstances. Some of the first charters, indeed, seem to have been intended to constitute a body politic, or trading company within the kingdom, rather than to establish foreign governments, beyond its limits; to which circumstance we may ascribe the omission of those more general and extensive powers contained in some subsequent charters.

These omissions the colonists themselves endeavoured to supply by voluntary consent and agreement among themselves, as was done in Massachusetts in the election of a representative body to assist in making law:[3] an innovation, which was not confined to that colony, but, which was acquiesced in, and even sanctioned by the crown, in its more recent charters, and provincial establishments. The highest act of sovereign authority likewise became necessary to be exercised upon criminals, in the privation of life, concerning which the first Massachusetts charter made no mention: but the government of that colony undertook to inflict capital punishments without recourse to the crown, for additional powers; without which, such a conduct was in strictness murder, in all concerned. In the same manner did they supply a defect of authority to erect judicatories for the probate of wills; to constitute courts of admiralty jurisdiction; to impose taxes; and to create towns, and other bodies corporate.[4] Although what is here said relates only to the colony of Massachusetts, there is reason to believe that a similar conduct was observed in the other New-England colonies, and perhaps in all those which were settled about the same time.

In examining this question, we must, therefore, abandon the ground of strict, legal, technical construction; since upon that ground the colonies must either have been swallowed in the vortex of anarchy, or have expired under the *peine forte et dure* of submission to rigid, and impracticable rules.

2. I shall, therefore, now proceed to consider this part of the question under the more liberal light of general policy.

We must here recollect, that the laws of England are divided into two distinct classes; the unwritten, and the written law: the former consisting of ancient, immemorial, general rules, maxims, and usages; the latter of written statutes, or acts of parliament, from time to time made in affirmance, or for the amendment, of the ancient unwritten law; or to rem-

---

3. According to Governor Hutchinson, all the colonies before the restoration of Charles the Second, except Maryland, settled a model of government for themselves. History of Massachusetts. A different policy was adopted after the restoration. Ibid.

4. Minot's History of Massachusetts.

edy some defect, mischief, or inconvenience therein; or finally, to repeal and annul it, altogether. Consequently, the common, or unwritten law must have been in a state of continual change, from the first institution of parliaments, in the thirteenth century, to the present time; a period of more than five hundred years; two centuries whereof have elapsed since the first migrations were made to America, under the authority of charters granted by the crown of England; though not quite half a century passed over, between the establishment of the colony of Georgia, and the declaration of independence.

The ancient, immemorial, unwritten law of England, may be divided into the *jus commune, common law,* or *folk-right,* of which the ancient English were so tenacious, and which they struggled so hard to maintain under the first princes of the Norman line: which subsequent princes so frequently promised to keep and restore, as the most popular act they could do, when pressed by foreign emergencies, or domestic discontents, and which depended solely upon custom; which carries this internal evidence of freedom along with it, that it was probably introduced by the voluntary consent of the *people.* And, secondly, the *jura coronae,* or prerogatives of the *crown,* as contradistinguished from the rights and privileges of the *people*: the foundation of which could only be discovered in many respects, to rest upon immemorial usurpations, exactions, and oppressions, generated by feudal tyranny, and enforced by irresistible military authority. From these two copious, and opposite springs are derived all those rules and maxims, which constitute the ground and foundation of the common law, *generally* so called. And it is in the admixture of these opposite characters and principles, that we discover, according as the scale of liberty, or prerogative has preponderated, a greater or less proportion of the one, or the other, in every subordinate rule and maxim, which, together, compose the whole body of the English common law.

The *jus commune,* or *folk-right,* above-mentioned, had for its object, the rights of persons; comprehending the rules, maxims, and usages adopted to ensure the legal and uninterrupted enjoyment of a man's life, his limbs, his body, his health, and his reputation; with the power of locomotion, or changing his situation, or moving to whatever place his own inclination may direct; and generally, of doing every thing that his own disposition might prompt, or suggest to him to do, that is not attended with injury to any other, or to the society at large, without imprisonment, molestation or restraint; and lastly, the free use, enjoyment, and disposal, of all his lawful acquisitions, without any control or diminution. These being the rights and privileges which were expressly guaranteed by the royal charters, there can be no reason to doubt that it was the intention of the colonists to adopt them, in all cases where they might be found applicable to their new condition. To judge of this applicability, time, and experience were both requisite; since it might happen that a rule which might have been highly beneficial and practicable in the mother country, might from local circumstances, or other considerations, be deemed inexpedient, or impracticable, in an infant colony. Thus we find that in Massachusetts they very soon disregarded that ancient rule of the common law, which constitutes the eldest son *sole* heir to his father, and divided the estate, whether personal, or real, according to circumstances, among all the branches of the family: A departure from the principles of the feudal law, of the propriety of which few Americans at this day entertain any doubt, yet certainly not authorised by the terms of their charter. Local circumstances, likewise, gave an early rise to a less justifiable departure from the principles of the common law in some of the colonies, in the establishment of slavery; a measure not to be reconciled either to the principles of the law of nature, nor even to the most arbitrary establishments in the English government at that period; absolute slavery, if it ever had existence in England, having been abolished long before. These instances shew that the colonists in judging of the applicability of the laws of the mother country to their own situations and circumstances, did not confine themselves to very strict, and narrow limits.

The *jura coronae*, or *lex prerogativa*, as denominated by Sir Matthew Hale, may be divided into two heads. First, those prerogatives which appertained strictly to the person of the prince; and secondly, such as regarded him in his political capacity, only; as the supreme head and ruler of the nation. Though all these which were not expressly given up by the crown in its charters, might, in strictness, be considered as potentially existing in every part of the nation, yet the exercise, or violation, of them, or a great part of them, being perfectly impracticable in remote colonies, such parts may well be considered as in abeyance, or perfectly dormant, there. All those prerogatives which were annexed to the person of the prince; as an individual, in whose case, that was law, which was not law in any case of a subject, must have been of this latter description; since the colonies could have nothing to do with them, in the internal administration of their affairs.... On the other hand those parts of the *jura coronae* which regard the prince, in his political capacity, only; that is, as the chief magistrate of the nation; the representative of his people; the administrator of the laws, and general conservator of the peace of his dominions, were applicable, or inapplicable, I apprehend, as circumstances might direct. Those laws, for example, which regard the king as supreme head of the national church, and punished non-conformity to its doctrines, and discipline, could not have been deemed applicable to the circumstances of a colony in which universal toleration in matters of religion was established by charter; and still less, perhaps, where the established, or prevailing religion of the colony differed from the church of England both in discipline, and in doctrine. Neither can we suppose the laws which regarded the king as supreme lord of the soil of his dominions, and those who held under him as military vassals, would be applicable to the condition of colonists who held their lands in free and common socage: yet the military tenures were not abolished in England, till near a century after the first charters granted to the colonies; and consequently that part of the common law which was founded upon the nature of these tenures remained in full force there, whilst it would have been perfectly absurd to suppose it could have been at all applicable to the colonies. Upon this ground we may infer that all the rules and maxims of the common law which sprung from that source, were equally inapplicable to the colonies; for *cessante ratione, cessat et ipsa lex.*

As to crimes and misdemeanors, no doubt the laws relating to such are *mala in se,* as murder, *mayhem,* and other offences which are universally admitted to be against the laws of God, and of nature, might have been deemed applicable to the situation of each colony; since the prevention and punishment of such offences are among the first objects of civil polity. But this was the case only with regard to such offences as might be strictly termed *mala in se;* and, as such, by the general consent of all civilized nations, admitted to be against the laws of God. Therefore the laws against heresy, witchcraft, sorcery, apostacy, and blasphemy, which, in some of the colonies, were regarded as among the most crying sins against God, and as such, punished with more severity than murder itself, could not have been deemed applicable, as was before observed, to those colonies, where universal toleration, in matters of religion, was established by charter. And as to that class of offences which are denominated *mala prohibita,* as not being contrary either to the laws of God, or to those of nature, but merely prohibited by the positive laws of society; the laws by which they were defined, restrained, or punished in the mother country, could not be deemed generally applicable to the colonies, because, in some of them there might be no co-relative subject for them to operate upon; as in the case of non-conformity to the worship of the church of England, before mentioned; which, although an offence in England which was punished with much severity, could not be deemed an offence in a colony, where universal toleration, or a different denomination of religion, was established; however it might continue to be deemed an offence in those colonies where the church of England was established as the religion of the colony. To this head we may likewise refer the whole class of offences against the prince, as an individual; whose personal prerogatives could be in no danger of violation in a colony, situated at the distance of a thousand leagues from his kingdom and residence. And many of those which were attached to the kingly office, must have been equally out of the reach of invasion, or attack, from so remote and feeble a quarter; and consequently could not have been deemed applicable to the situation and circumstances of colonies, of that description.

Nor must the motives and intentions of the colonists, in their respective migrations, be disregarded in an inquiry of this nature. Such of them, as allured by the hopes or prospects of immense riches, or a comfortable subsistence, at least, were induced by such motives, only, to leave their native country; to which, perhaps, they looked forward to return, may well be supposed to retain for its government and laws the same filial attachment as they felt for their *natale solum;* and would, consequently, conform as near as possible both in doctrine and in practice to all the institutions of the mother country. On the contrary, those who fled from what they accounted tyranny, both in church and state, and quitted their native country as a prison, in which they were exposed to all the terrors of persecution; preferring to it an asylum in the howling wilderness, where they might establish and enjoy freedom in a remote and unknown quarter of the globe, must have carried with them prejudices against the laws and government of the parent state, which would induce a general rejection of all such as were inimical to those principles, which prompted them to migrate. And as two strait lines, which diverge from each other at the same point, can never after meet, or become parallel, so the institutions of two countries, founded upon such discordant principles, could never after be assimilated to each other.

In addition to these sources of endless variety, and disagreement, between the civil institutions of the several colonies, there remain two others, equally copious, which have not yet been noticed, or but very slightly. The first, arising from the changes introduced by the English statute law, or acts of parliament made between the periods, when the several colonies were respectively settled; the whole amounting to somewhat more than one hundred and fifty years. Now it was held, that those English laws, only, which were in being, at the time of the settlement of each colony, respectively, were in force in such colony. Consequently the statutes made in England, between the period when Virginia was first settled, and that when Georgia was settled, amounting to one hundred and fifty-two years, and the consequent changes which those statutes made in the common law, had no effect or operation in Virginia; although, according to the principles which are generally agreed upon, those statutes, and the changes in the common law thereby produced, must have had an operation and authority in Georgia, so far as they were applicable to the situation and circumstances of that colony. Those who are acquainted with the prodigious changes made in the laws of England, during the period above-mentioned, will at once discover that there could be no common rule of law between those two colonies, unless that rule could be deduced, without alteration, from a period antecedent to the charter of Virginia. The same observation will hold as to all the other colonies, neither of which were bound by any English law that was not in being at the time of its own establishment.... The second source of variety and disagreement here referred to, and by far the most copious, had its rise in the power which the legislatures of the several colonies were perpetually engaged in exercising, viz. that of making laws adapted to the views, principles, situation, and circumstances of their respective inhabitants and countries. Being perfectly independent of each other, and without any other political relation or connection, except that of acknowledging the same common sovereign; and equally ignorant and regardless of the municipal institutions, or domestic policy of each other; each pursued that course which a regard to their own domestic concerns prompted them to take; until, like the radii of a circle, they arrived from the same common center to points diametrically opposite, or receding from each other in proportion to the length they were extended.

Nor must we forget, what was also before slightly mentioned, that a part of the present United States was first settled by a Dutch colony; and another part, by Swedes. The tract claimed by those two nations extended from the thirty-eighth to the forty-first degree of latitude, and was called the New Netherlands, comprehending the present states of New-York, New-Jersey, Pennsylvania, Delaware, and the Eastern Shore of Maryland: it was conquered by the English, and confirmed to the crown of England by the treaty of Breda in 1667. The Dutch inhabitants remained in their settlements in New-York, and a part of Jersey; the Swedes, if I mistake not, were removed from Delaware to New-York, where they likewise remained. According to judge Blackstone, the laws of England, as such, could have no allowance, or authority there; this being a conquered and ceded country, and not a colony originally planted by Englishmen: and according to his principles, also, the laws of Holland,

and of Sweden, were the municipal laws of those provinces, until the period of their conquest; and so continued until other laws were imposed upon them by the crown of England. When, and in what degree, a change was made in this manner; or whether any such change was ever formally made, can only be determined by recurrence to documents not within the reach of the author of these sheets.

From all these considerations it will appear, that in our inquiries how far the common law and statutes of England were adopted in the British colonies; or, in other words, what parts of those laws might be deemed applicable to their respective situations and circumstances, we must again abandon all hope of satisfaction from any *general theory,* and resort to their several charters, provincial establishments, legislative codes, and civil histories, for information. For although the colonial legislatures are understood to have been inhibited from passing any law derogatory from the sovereignty of the crown, or repugnant to the laws and statutes of England; which seems to have been the only common rule imposed upon them, yet the application of this rule in the several colonies will be found to have been as various as their respective soils, climates, and productions.

A research of this extensive nature is equally beyond the proposed limits of this essay, and the sources of information which its author possesses. Yet it may be neither unuseful, nor uninstructive, to turn our attention for a few moments towards such an inquiry; from whence we may possibly be made sensible how fruitless would be the labour of a further search after an uniform system of law in the British colonies.

The legislature of Virginia, the most ancient of the British colonies, was constituted by letters patent of March the 9th, 1607, in the fourth year of king James the first; the first charter granted by queen Elizabeth, to Sir Walter Raleigh, bore date March 25th, 1584, about three and twenty years before: it is not of much consequence from which of these periods we date the obligation of the laws of England. They seem to have been adopted by consent of the settlers, which might easily enough be done, whilst they were few, and living altogether. Of such adoption, however, we have no other proof, than their practice till the year 1661, when they were expressly adopted by an act of the assembly, which declares, "that they had endeavoured, in all things, as near as the capacity and constitution of the country would admit, to adhere to those excellent and often refined laws of England, to which they profess and acknowledge all reverence and obedience; and that the laws made by them are intended by them but as brief memorials of that which the capacity of the courts is utterly unable to collect out of its vast volumes, though sometimes perhaps, for the difference of condition, varying in small things." The several charters of queen Elizabeth and king James, stipulated that lands in Virginia should be held of the crown in free and common socage.

The first acts to be found in the colonial code of Virginia provide for building churches, appointing vestries, and laying out glebes in every parish. And by an act dated in 1642, it is provided, that for the preservation of purity and unity of doctrine, and discipline in the church, and the right administration of the sacraments, no minister should be admitted to officiate in Virginia, without producing to the governor a testimonial of his ordination from some bishop in England, and subscribing to be conformable to the orders and constitutions of the church of England, and the laws there established. All persons not having a lawful excuse, were obliged to attend their parish church every Sunday, under penalty of fifty pounds of tobacco; "but quakers and other recusants, who, out of non-conformity to the church, totally absented themselves, were made liable to such fines and punishments as by stat. 23, Eliza. were imposed upon them; being for every month's absence, twenty pounds sterling; and if they forbore a twelvemonth, then to give security for their good behaviour, besides payment of the before-mentioned fine. And all quakers, for assembling in unlawful assemblies, and conventicles were farther subject to a fine of two hundred pounds of tobacco, for each offence." The like penalty was extended two years after to any other separatist whatsoever, and the third offence, made the offender liable to banishment. Any person entertaining a quaker to teach, or preach, was subject to a fine of 5000 pounds of tobacco, and any justice of the peace, or other officer, neglecting the duties prescribed thereby for suppressing quakers, was subjected, likewise, to a penalty: and any master of a vessel bringing a quaker into the colony, was moreover liable to the penalty of 5000 pounds of tobacco.

Here then, we find not only the common law and statutes of England, so far as they were applicable to the situation of the colony, but also the hierarchy of the church of England, in its full vigour, established and adopted in Virginia.

But this general adoption of the laws of England was probably confined to the colony of Virginia, which, even to the period when the revolution commenced, was distinguished for its loyalty, beyond any other of the plantations. The New-England colonies owed their establishment to that spirit of independency, which afterwards shone forth there, in its full lustre, and received new accession from the aspiring character of those, who being discontented with the established church, and with regal government, sought for freedom amidst those savage desarts. But, even in Virginia, we find the distinction made, between acts of parliament antecedent to their settlement, and such as were subsequent thereto. Many of the latter were from time to time, either expressly declared to be in force in the colony, or, were introduced into the colonial code, in form of acts of the general assembly. The statute of 7 and 8 of William the third, which declares that "the solemn affirmation of quakers shall be accepted instead of an oath," for so much thereof as relates to such affirmation, was, by an act of assembly, passed in the year, 1705, declared to be in force in Virginia; the statute of 3 W. and M. c. 14. For relief of creditors against fraudulent devises was, in like manner declared to be in force in Virginia, by an act passed in the year 1726, and re-enacted in the year 1748. The statutes of limitations, 32 H. 8. c. 2. and 21 Ja. 1. c. 16. were enacted in the year 1710, with alterations in the former. The statutes of 21 Ja. 1. c. 27, to prevent the destroying of bastard children; and c. 24, concerning persons dying in execution, were likewise enacted about the same time. So was a part of the statute 16, and 17. Car. 2. c. 5, for preventing delays of execution by writ *of audita querela; as* also several clauses of the statute for preventing frauds and perjuries, 29 Car. 2. c. 3, whilst other parts of the same statute were either entirely omitted, or materially changed; as in the case of a will of lands: the statute requires 3 or 4 witnesses; the act of the Virginia assembly requires only two. Many other instances, if necessary, could be adduced to the like effect.

The Massachusetts colony may be considered as the parent of the other colonies of New-England; there being no importation of planters from England to any part of the continent northward of Maryland, except to Massachusetts, for more than fifty years after the colony began. The first settlement attempted in the year 1607, (the same in which the charter of James the first to Virginia bears date) soon failed.

The colony of New-Plymouth, which may be regarded as the most ancient establishment in New-England, owed its existence to that bigotry and persecution which prevailed at that time among christians of every sect and denomination. The adventurers procured a patent from the Virginia company in 1620, and, eight years after, a charter was obtained from the crown: the settlement having been previously effected. This charter, according to governor Hutchinson, was intended to constitute a corporation in England, like that of the East India company; but on the proposal of several gentlemen of figure and estate, who were dissatisfied with the arbitrary proceedings both in *church* and *state,* and pleased themselves with the prospect of the enjoyment of *liberty* in *both,* in America, it was resolved the succeeding year, by the general consent of the company, that the government and patent should be settled in New-England. In 1630, they established rules for proceeding in all civil actions, and instituted subordinate powers for punishing offenders. In civil actions, equity, according to the circumstances of the case, seems to have been their rule of determining; the judges had recourse to no authority but common reason and understanding.[5] In 1634, they began to think about a body of laws suited to the circumstances of the colony, civil and religious; and in the year 1648, (the same in which the regal government was subverted in England) the whole collected together, were ratified by the general court, and then first printed. The principal characters in Massachusetts during this period were the intimate friends of the lead-

5. Hutchinson.

ing members of parliament, Pym, Hampden, &c. and whilst Cromwell was at the head of affairs, he shewed them all the indulgence they desired; from 1640 to 1660, they approached very near to an independent commonwealth.

In the system of laws and government which they established they departed from their charter, and instead of making the laws of England the ground work of their code, they preferred the laws of Moses.[6] In that branch of law more especially, which is distinguished by the name of crown law, they professed to have no regard to the rules of the common law of England. It seems to have been the general opinion that acts of parliament had no other force than what they derived from acts made by the general court to establish, or confirm them. High treason was not mentioned, conspiracy to invade their own commonwealth, or any treacherous perfidious attempt to alter and subvert fundamentally the frame of their polity and government, was made capital. Murder, sodomy, witchcraft, arson, and rape of a child under ten years of age, were the only crimes made capital in the colony, which were capital in England. They made no distinction between murder and manslaughter, and the statutes which allowed, or denied the benefit of clergy were disregarded. The worship of any other God besides the Lord God, was capital. Governor Hutchinson doubts whether a Roman catholic for the adoration of the host, might not have come within that law. Blasphemy, man-stealing, adultery with a married woman, wilful perjury in certain cases, cursing, or smiting a parent by a child above the age of sixteen years, except in one or two particular cases, were all capital offences. A stubborn and rebellious son, according to Deuteronomy c. 21. upon conviction was also to suffer death. There were several trials under this law. Rape was left to the court to punish with death or other grievous punishment at discretion. Several offences were capital upon a second conviction; as the returning of a Romish priest, or a quaker, after banishment upon the first conviction: The denial of either of the books of the old and new testament, to be the written and infallible word of God, was either banish-

6. Ibid.

ment, or death, for the second offence, at the discretion of the court. Burglary and theft in a house, or field, on the Lord's day, were capital upon a third conviction: larceny, or theft was punishable by fine or whipping, and restitution of treble the value; fornication, by enjoining marriage, by fine, or corporal punishment. Common fowlers, tobacco-takers, and idlers, the constables were required to present to the next magistrate; and the select men of every town were required to oversee the families: to distribute the children into classes, and to take care that they were employed in spinning and other labour according to their age and condition. Contempt of authority was punished with great severity, by fine, imprisonment, or corporal punishment. Lesser offences were punished at the discretion of the court. Such are the outlines of their penal code: it would be mispending time to attempt to shew the numerous departures therein, from the principles both of the common, and statute law of England.

Nor were many of the civil regulations less dissimilar. Marriages from the first settlement of the colony were celebrated by magistrates, and not by clergymen. At the revolution they were solemnized by the clergy. A man who struck his wife, or a woman her husband, was liable to a penalty of ten pounds, or corporal punishment. In testamentary causes they at first so far allowed the civil law, as to consider real estates, as mere *bona*, and did not confine themselves to any rules of distribution in England. They considered the family and estate in all their circumstances, as was before mentioned, and sometimes assigned a greater portion to one branch than another; and sometimes they settled all upon the widow; executors or administrators were not held, as at the common law, to prefer a debt due by judgement, or bond, to a simple contract debt; fee-simple estates descended to every child; but estates tail to the eldest son, or other heir at common law. Traitors and felons might dispose of their estates, real and personal, by will, after sentence; and if they died intestate, distribution was made as in other cases. No free inhabitant of any town could sell his lands therein, but to some other free inhabitant of the same town; unless the town gave consent, or refused to give what others offered without fraud; which was agreeable to the law of Moses, which forbad the alienation of lands from one tribe to another. The clergy were at all times exempted from taxes, on their persons, or estates, under their own improvement. Nor was their ecclesiastical polity at less variance with the laws and statutes of England, which regard the king as the supreme head of the church, and make it penal not to conform to the doctrine and discipline of that church. Upon their removal they supposed their relation both to the civil and ecclesiastical government, except so far as a special reserve was made by their charter, was at an *end;* and that they had a right to form such new model of both, as best pleased them. Accordingly they established an ecclesiastical polity of their own, totally differing from the mother country, it being one of the principles upon which their platform, or church-government was formed, "that there is no jurisdiction to which particular churches are, or ought to be subject, by way of authoritative censure, nor any other church power, extrinsical to such churches, which they ought to depend upon any other sort of men for the exercise of." In general the ordination of ministers was by imposition of the hands of their brethren in the ministry; but some churches called for the aid of no ministers of other churches, but ordained their ministers by the imposition of the hands of some of their own brethern. They laid aside the fasts and feasts, as well as the doctrine and discipline of the church of England; yet they appointed days of fasting and thanksgiving occasionally, and any person absenting himself from public worship on those days, was liable to a fine: and non-conformity was attended with the deprivation of more civil privileges than in England. This intolerant spirit occasioned complaints to be preferred against the colony, after the restoration, not only by episcopalians, but by baptists, quakers, and other sectarists; which, together with other reasons, produced the abrogation of their charter, by a decree of the high court of chancery in England, in the year 1684. A new charter was obtained in 1691, upwards of sixty years after the date of the former, and seventy years from the first settlement of the colony of New-Plymouth, and near half a century from the period when a system of laws the most discordant to those of the mother country had been established. In the mean time the laws of England had undergone many very material alterations, and the system of government had twice been wholly changed. The new charter contained nothing of an ecclesiastical constitution. Liberty of conscience was allowed to all except papists. On the publication of the new charter, there was room to question what was the law in civil and criminal matters, and how far the *common law* and what *statutes* took place. The general court soon after passed an act declaring that all the laws of the colony of Massachusetts, and the colony of New-Plymouth, not being repugnant to the laws of England, nor inconsistent with the charter, should be in force in the respective colonies to the 10th of November, 1692, except where other provision should be made by act of assembly. Instead of committing to a few select and able men, the duty of preparing, and digesting a complete code, or system of laws, upon a preconcerted plan, the whole of which each person should have kept in view: which after being submitted to, and approved by the general assembly, might have been sent to England, to be finally ratified there, by the crown; it was proposed that the members of the general court should, during the recess, consider of such laws as were necessary to be established. This improvident step according to governor Hutchinson, produced consequences by which the people of the province were ever after sufferers; "the construction of many laws," he tells us, "has been doubtful and varying, it being impossible to reconcile the several parts to any general principle of law whatever." Many of the subsequent acts of assembly were passed from time to time, one after another, as they happened to be brought in; and when sent to England for allowance, some were disapproved; others, which depended upon, or had some connexion with those which were disapproved, were allowed. The legislature consisting of many of the same persons who had composed the same body under the old charter, the same spirit prevailed in most of the laws which were passed, as in the former code: many of them were consequently disallowed; others were approved, among which is enumerated an act for punishing criminal offences, in many parts mitigating the penalties at common law; as also an act for the settlement of intestates' estates, which continued in force until the period when Hutchinson wrote his history; and is, not improbably, the law of the land at this day.

By this act such estates were to be divided among all the children, giving to the eldest son a double portion; and where there were no children, the whole was to go to the next of kin to the intestate. This act was variously interpreted, the courts, where there were no children, at first adjudging that the estate should go to the heir at common law; but later judgments have assigned it to the half blood, to the father, and also to the mother. Notwithstanding which general entails were adjudged not to be partible.

A body of people receding from the established government and religion of a country can not, as was before remarked, be supposed to have carried with them any great affection for its laws. To this cause we must attribute that immediate departure from the conditions of their first charter, which prohibited the making any laws repugnant to those of England. A strict compliance with this condition would require the aid of learned counsel, whose professional pursuits might enable them to point out the conformity required by the charter. Of such counsel the general court are said to have acknowledged the want. Under such circumstances, had there been every disposition to adhere strictly to the terms of their charter, it would have been impossible. A single instance will shew what extensive consequences flowed from these causes. By the charter of Massachusetts, (which agrees perfectly with the charters of the other colonies, in this respect,) it was stipulated that the colonists should hold their lands in free and common socage, as of the manor of East-Greenwich in the county of Kent. In Massachusetts this was interpreted to include all the properties and customs of gavel-kind; one of which is, that lands are partible among all the sons; and another, that they are not subject to forfeiture for treason or felony, according to the maxim, the father to the bough, the son to the plough. This interpretation gave a correspondent stamp to their laws, before noticed. In Virginia that part of the charter was interpreted to establish the common law rule of descents, in favour of the eldest son, or next collateral kinsman of the whole blood, in exclusion of all others in equal degree; and the law of forfeiture, in cases of treason or felony, was adopted in its fullest latitude. Two ships sailing from the equator to the opposite poles would scarcely pursue more different courses, or arrive at more opposite points. If such different interpretations could be made where the text was so short, familiar, and explicit, what irreconcileable variances might we not expect in the construction of the numerous, and often discordant dogmas, contained in the vast volumes of common law reports, and statutory provisions?

The colonies of Connecticut and New-Hampshire, which, according to governor Hutchinson, grew out of Massachusetts, severally adopted institutions, both civil and religious, which bore a great conformity to those of Massachusetts. Perhaps the spirit of civil independence run higher in Connecticut, even than in Massachusetts; and that of religious intolerance towards all who differed from them in doctrine, or in discipline, was certainly equal in both.[7] Toleration was preached against as a sin in rulers, which would bring down the judgments of heaven upon the land. This spirit of intolerance in Massachusetts produced the settlement of Rhode-Island, where religious freedom seems first to have erected her standard, under the protection of the charter granted by Charles the second, in the fourteenth year of his reign, A.D. 1662, which declared, that no person within that colony, at any time thereafter, should be any wise molested, punished, disquieted, or called in question for any differences of opinion in matters of religion, who do not actually disturb the civil peace of the colony. Universal toleration was not long after established in Pennsylvania, and there flourished more than in any other country. Popery, the abomination of the religious bigots of New England, seems to have been rather favoured, than discouraged in Maryland. In no other colony, except Rhode-Island and Pennsylvania was it tolerated. It is not improbable that in every colony the prevailing sentiments and laws respecting religion, had a corresponding effect upon their civil institutions. Of this Peters mentions a remarkable instance in Connecticut, not many years before the American revolution. A negro was brought to trial before the superior court at Hertford for castrating his master's son: the court could find no law to punish him. The lawyers

7. Belknap's History of N.H.; Peters's History of Conn.

quoted the English statute against maiming; the court were of opinion that statute did not reach the colony, because it had not been passed in the general assembly.[8] At length, however, the court had recourse to the vote of the first settlers at New-Haven, viz. that the bible should be their law, till they could make others more suitable to their circumstances. The court were of opinion that vote was in full force, as it had not been revoked; and thereupon tried the negro by the Jewish law, "eye for eye, tooth for tooth"; and he suffered accordingly. Mr. Swift, in his system of the laws of Connecticut, tells us, that the English common law had never been considered as more obligatory there, than the Roman laws had been in England. That there is no general rule to ascertain what part of it is binding; that the running the line of distinction is a subject of embarrassment to the courts; and that it has no other foundation there, than the voluntary reception of it by the general (implied) consent of the people, (in particular cases, I presume.) That the first settlers there instead of considering it to be the basis of their jurisprudence, and in all cases binding, have only considered it as auxilary to their statutes.... That a consequence of this doctrine has been, the introduction of many new rules and principles, which have greatly improved the legal system of that state; from whence he adduces a second branch of what he stiles the common law of the state, founded upon the adjudications of the courts, in all cases of defect of the common law not supplied by statute.[9] In Virginia, it would be a violation of the constitution for the *courts* to undertake to supply all defects of the common law not already supplied by statute. That is the exclusive province of the *legislature.*

From this specimen, my readers will readily perceive that it would require the talents of an Alfred to harmonize and digest into one system such opposite, discordant, and conflicting municipal institutions, as composed the codes of the several colonies at the period of the revolution; united with the coercive arm of the Norman tyrant to enforce obe-

8. Castration was mayhem at the common law, and by that law might have been punished as felony. It would seem that the court neither considered the common law nor the statute of Mayhem, as in force in Connecticut.

9. Swift's System of the Laws of Connecticut.

dience to it, when digested. In vain then should we attempt, by any *general theory*, to establish an uniform authority and obligation in the common law of England, over the American colonies, at any period between the first migrations to this country, and that epoch, which annihilated the sovereignty of the crown of England over them. I shall, therefore, proceed to consider,

3. Thirdly; what part of the laws of England were abrogated by the revolution, or retained by the several states, when they became sovereign, and independent republics.

And here we may premise, that by the rejection of the sovereignty of the crown of England, not only all the laws of that country by which the dependence of the colonies was secured, but the whole *lex prerogativa* (or *Jura Coronae* before mentioned) so far as respected the person of the sovereign and his prerogatives as an individual, was utterly abolished: and, that so far as respected the kingly office, and government, it was either modified, abridged, or annulled, according to the several constitutions and laws of the states, respectively: consequently, that every rule of the common law, and every statute of England, founded on the nature of regal government, in derogation of the natural and unalienable rights of mankind; or, inconsistent with the nature and principles of democratic governments, were absolutely abrogated, repealed, and annulled, by the establishment of such a form of government in the states, respectively. This is a natural and necessary consequence of the revolution, and the correspondent changes in the nature of the governments, unless we could suppose that the laws of England, like those of the Almighty Ruler of the universe, carry with them an intrinsic moral obligation upon all mankind. A supposition too gross and absurd to require refutation.

In like manner, all other parts of the common law and statutes of England, which, from their inapplicability, had not been brought into use and practice during the existence of the colonial governments, must, from the period of their dissolution, be regarded not only as obsolete, but as incapable of revival, except by constitutional, or legislative authority. For they no longer possessed even a potential existence, (as being the laws of the British nation, and as such, extending, in theoretical strictness, to the remotest part of the empire,) because the connexion, upon which this theoretical conclusion might have been founded, was entirely at an end: and having never obtained any authority from usage, and custom, they were destitute of every foundation upon which any supposed obligation could be built.... This is a regular consequence of that undisputed right which every free state possesses, of being governed by its own laws.... And as all laws are either written; or acquire their force and obligation by long usage and custom, which imply a tacit consent; it follows, that where these evidences are wanting, there can be no obligation in any supposed law.

Another regular consequence of the revolution was this: when the American states declared themselves independent of the crown of Great-Britain, each state from that moment became sovereign, and independent, not only of Great-Britain, but of all other powers, whatsoever. Each had its own separate constitution and laws, which could not, in any manner, be affected or controlled by the laws, or constitutions of any other. From that moment there was no common law amongst them but the general law of nations, to which all civilized nations conform. And as no law could thereafter be imposed upon the people of any state, but by the legislature thereof, so no law could be obligatory in one state, merely because it was obligatory in another. And how much soever their municipal institutions might agree, one with another, yet as it was in the power of their legislatures, respectively, to alter the whole, or any part of them, whenever they should think proper, therefore, such coincidence by no means established a common rule amongst them; because, as was before observed, the establishment of a law within the jurisdiction of one state, gave it no authority within the jurisdiction of any other. From hence it follows, that the adoption of the common law, or statutes of England, in one state, or in several, or even in all, although it might produce a general conformity in their municipal codes, yet as such adoption was the separate act of each state, it could not operate so as to give to those laws a sanction superior to any other laws of the states, respectively; inasmuch as each state would still have retained the power of changing, or rejecting them, whenever it should think proper: and much less, could the adoption of them under various modifications, limitations, and restrictions, (as was actually the case,) create such a superior sanction, as thereafter to render them *paramount,* not only to the legislative authority, but even to the *constitutions,* of the respective states.

These things being premised, we shall now proceed to enquire what was actually done by the several states, in regard to the subject, here spoken of.

The constitution of Massachusetts,[10] declares, that, "the people of that commonwealth have the sole and exclusive right of governing themselves as a free, sovereign, and independent state; and do, and forever thereafter shall, exercise and enjoy every power, jurisdiction, and right, which is not, or may not thereafter, be by them expressly delegated to the United States of America, in congress assembled.". . . This is merely a declaration of the law of nations: and as such, applies equally to every other state in the union, as to the commonwealth of Massachusetts. And though, perhaps, it will be objected, that by the confederation formed between the states, they were, respectively abridged of a very large portion of that sovereignty, which some other nations exercise; yet this objection admits of several answers, viz. First, The articles of confederation, were not agreed upon, nor ratified, till several years after the states became independent.[11] Secondly, when agreed upon, and ratified, they contained an express declaration, in conformity to the law of nations,[12] "that each state retains its sovereignty, freedom and independence, and every power, jurisdiction, and right, which is not thereby expressly delegated to the United States in congress assembled.". . . Thirdly, that no power is therein delegated to congress, whereby that body was authorised to introduce, or to establish the common law, or statutes of England, or of any other country or nation, in the United States, as the general law of the land, therein.

The constitution of Massachusetts further declares, that, "all the laws

10. Established, March, 1780.
11. They were not finally agreed upon and ratified till the first day of March 1781.
12. Vattel.

which had been theretofore adopted, used and approved, in the province, colony, or state of Massachusetts-bay, and usually practised on, in the courts of law, shall still remain and be in full force, until altered, or repealed by the legislature; such parts only excepted, as are repugnant to the rights, and liberties contained in that constitution." Among those rights we find the following declaration, that, "all power residing originally, in the people, and being derived from them, the several magistrates and officers of government, vested with authority whether legislative, executive, or judicial, are their substitutes, and agents, and are, at all times, accountable to them." Again.... That government is instituted for the common good; for the protection, safety, prosperity, and happiness of the people and not for the profit, honour, or private interest of any one man, family, or class of men."... And again; that, "the people have a right to require of their law-givers and magistrates an exact, and constant observance of the fundamental principles, of the constitution, in the formation and execution of all laws." And further; that, "the *liberty* of the *press,* is essential to the security of freedom, in a state; and ought not, therefore, to be restrained in that commonwealth."

These constitutional declarations (among many others of a similar nature, contained, not only in the constitution of Massachusetts, but in those of the far greater part of the states in the union) establish, beyond the reach of doubt, I apprehend, the several points premised, under this head. And here we may remark, in the way, that by these constitutional declarations all the colonial laws, (of whose validity, as being repugnant to the common law, and statutes of England, great doubts had been entertained during the colonial government), were, thenceforth, unquestionably established, how repugnant, soever, they might have been to the common law, or statutes of England, or the conditions of their charter. The adoption of the laws of England, we see was confined to such as had been theretofore adopted, used, and approved, *within* the colony, and usually practised on, in the courts of law; with an exception as to such parts as were repugnant to the rights and liberties contained in the constitution. It was therefore essential to the force and obligation of any rule of the common law, that it had been before that time actually adopted, used, or approved, *in* the colony: and further, that it should not be repugnant to the rights and liberties contained in the constitution. Otherwise, although it might be found in every law treatise from Bracton, and Glanville, to Coke, Hale, Hawkins, and Blackstone; or in every reporter from the year-books to the days of Lord Mansfield, it would have no more force in Massachusetts, than an edict of the emperor of China.

But let us now proceed to inquire what other states have done upon this subject.

The constitution of New-York, ordains, and declares, that *such parts* of the common law of England, and of the statute law of England and Great Britain, and of the acts of the legislature of the colony of New-York, as together did form the law of the said colony on the 19th day of April, 1775, shall be, and continue the law of the land, subject to such alterations and provisions, as the legislature of the state shall, from time to time make, concerning the same. That all such parts thereof as may be construed to establish any particular denomination of christians, or concerns the allegiance, theretofore yielded to, and the supremacy, sovereignty, government, or *prerogatives,* claimed or exercised by the king of England or his predecessors, over the colony or its inhabitants, or are repugnant to that constitution, are thereby abrogated, and rejected.

The constitution of New-Jersey, declares, that, the common law of England, as well as so much of the statute law, as had been theretofore practised in that colony, shall still remain in force, until they shall be altered by a future law of the legislature; such parts only excepted, as are repugnant to the rights and privileges contained in that charter.

The constitution of Delaware, declares, nearly in the same words, that the common law of England, as well as so much of the statute law, as had theretofore been adopted in practice in that state, shall remain in force; unless they shall be altered by a future act of the legislature; such parts only excepted, as are repugnant to the rights and privileges contained in that constitution.

The constitution of Maryland declares, that the inhabitants thereof are entitled to the common law of England, and the trial by jury according to the course of that law, and to the benefit of such English statutes as existed, at the time of their *first emigration,* and which by experience have been found applicable to their local and other circumstances, and of such others as have since been made in England, or Great-Britain, and have been since introduced, used, and practised by the courts, &c. except such as may be altered by acts of convention, or that declaration of rights, subject to the revision, amendment, or repeal, of the legislature of that state.

The convention of Virginia, declared, that the common law of England, and all statutes or acts of parliament made in aid of the common law, prior to the fourth year of James the first, which are of a general nature, not local to that kingdom, together with the several acts of the colony then in force, so far as the same may consist with the several ordinances, declarations, and resolutions of the general convention, shall be considered as in full force, until the same shall be altered by the legislative power of the commonwealth. This has since been done, and at this day, no statute of England, or Great-Britain, as such, has any authority in Virginia, except in one or two special cases, particularly saved by the act of repealing them; and the common law, both in criminal and civil cases, has undergone a most extensive change.

The constitution of South-Carolina, established March 19, 1778, declares, that the resolutions of the late Congresses of that state, and all laws then in force there, and not thereby repealed, shall so continue until altered, or repealed, by the legislature of the state, unless where they are temporary.

The constitutions of the other states, so far as I have had an opportunity of consulting them, are silent on the subject of the adoption of the common law, or statutes of England. But I apprehend, that what I have here selected is sufficient to shew, that in every state, where they have been adopted, they have the force of laws, only, *sub graviori lege;* like the civil and canon laws, in England: being modified, limited, restrained, repealed, or annulled, by the provisions contained in their several constitutions, bills of rights, legislative codes, and judicial usages, and practice; and in all cases subject to the *future* amendment, repeal, and control, of the legislatures of the several states, respectively. These modifications, restrictions, and limitations, being different in the different states, according to the difference of their several constitutions and laws, and the different terms of adoption, it would be altogether a hopeless attempt, to endeavour to extract from such discordant materials, an uniform system of national jurisprudence, were there any grounds in the American constitutions to warrant such an undertaking. Hitherto, I apprehend, we have met with nothing of the kind. It only remains to inquire,

4. How far that portion of the common law and statutes of England, which has been retained by the several states, respectively, has been engrafted upon, or made a part of the constitution of the United States.

It will be remembered, that the object of the several states in the adoption of that instrument, was not the establishment of a general consolidated government, which should swallow up the state sovereignties, and annihilate their several jurisdictions, and powers, as *states;* but a federal government, with powers limited to certain determinate objects; viz. their intercourse and concerns with foreign nations; and with each other, as separate and independent states; and, as members of the same confederacy: leaving the administration of their internal, and domestic concerns, to the absolute and uncontrolable jurisdiction of the states, respectively; except in one or two particular instances, specified, and enumerated in the constitution. And because this principle was supposed not to have been expressed with sufficient precision, and certainty, an amendatory article was proposed, adopted, and ratified; whereby it is expressly declared, that, "the powers not delegated to the United States by the constitution, nor prohibited by it to the states, are reserved to the states respectively, or to the people." This article is, indeed, nothing more than an express recognition of the law of nations; for Vattel informs us, "that several sovereign, and independent states may unite themselves together by a perpetual confederacy, without each in particular ceasing to be a perfect state. They will form together a federal republic: the deliberations in common will offer no violence to the sovereignty of each member, though they may in certain respects put some constraint on the exercise of it, in virtue of voluntary engagements." And with respect to the construction and interpretation of that article, the great Bacon gives us the following rule: "As exception strengthens the force of a law in cases not excepted; so enumeration weakens it, in cases not enumerated."[13] Now, the powers prohibited by the constitution to the states, respectively, are all exceptions to powers, which they before enjoyed; the powers granted to congress, are all enumerations of new powers thereby created: the prohibition on the states, operating, therefore, as an exception, strengthens their claim to all powers not excepted: on the other hand, the grant of powers to the federal government operating only by way of enumeration, weakens its claim in all cases not enumerated.

These things being premised, I shall take a short survey of the constitution of the United States, with a view to discover, whether that instrument contains any grant of general jurisdiction in common law cases, to the federal government; or prohibits the states from the exercise of such general jurisdiction: except only, in some few cases, particularly enumerated. For without such grant the federal government cannot exercise such a jurisdiction; and without such prohibition, the states, respectively, cannot be abridged of it.

1. The powers delegated to congress, are not all legislative: Many of them have been usually supposed to belong to the executive department; such are,

The power of declaring war; granting letters of marque and reprisal; raising and supporting armies, and navies; and borrowing money; none of which contain, or can be presumed to imply, any grant of general jurisdiction in common law cases. The legislative powers of congress, are also determinate, and enumerated, being,

1. To lay and collect taxes, duties, imposts, and excises, to pay the debts, and provide for the common defence, and welfare of the United States.

2. To regulate commerce with foreign nations, and among the several states, and the Indian tribes: leaving the regulation of the internal commerce of each state, to the states, respectively.

13. Bacon, of the advancement of learning.

3. To establish an uniform rule of naturalization: this being a branch of common law jurisdiction, particularly *enumerated*, leaves all others not *enumerated*, with the states, respectively.

4. To establish uniform laws on the subject of bankruptcies. This was no part of the common law of England, the name, as well as the wickedness of bankrupts, according to sir Edward Coke, being fetched from foreign nations. The grant of special authority, upon this branch of commercial polity, and of the English statute law, shews it was not intended to vest congress with the power of legislating upon all subjects of that nature; all others *not enumerated*, remaining with the states, respectively.

5. To coin money, regulate the value thereof, and of foreign coin, and fix the standard of weights and measures. These are, respectively, branches of the royal prerogative in England, and being specially *enumerated*, shew that it was not intended to trust the exercise of other branches of that prerogative to the federal government; all others *not enumerated*, (and consistent with the nature and constitution of democratic republics) being reserved to the states, respectively.

6. To provide for the punishment of counterfeiting the securities, and current coin of the United States. Forgery, is an offence at common law; but this clause gives no power to congress over the subject of forgery, generally; but over that branch, only, which relates to counterfeiting the securities of the United States. Counterfeiting the current coin was also treason, by the common law. But congress have not power to declare it to be treason in the United States: the special power hereby granted, shews that it was not intended to vest congress with the power of punishing offences of this nature, generally, but such only as are *enumerated: all others not enumerated* being reserved to the jurisdiction of the states, respectively.

7. To establish post-offices, and post-roads; and,

8. To promote the progress of science and useful arts, by securing to the authors and inventors, for a limited time, the exclusive right to their writings and discoveries. These determinate objects of legislation, upon subjects of general polity, may be referred to the same class as the subject

of bankruptcy; and being particularly *enumerated* leave all others *not enumerated,* to the jurisdiction of the states, respectively.

9. To constitute tribunals inferior to the supreme court: another branch of the royal prerogative in England, to which we may refer what was said on the subject of coining money.

10. To *define* and *punish* piracies, and felonies, committed on the *high seas;* and against the law of nations: The power of *defining* and punishing all felonies and offences *committed upon land,* in all cases *not enumerated,* being reserved to the states, respectively.

11. To make rules for the government and regulation of the land and naval forces: that is of the *military* and *maritime* states, employed in the service of the union; the government of the *civil* state, in all cases *not enumerated,* being reserved to the states, respectively.

12. To provide for calling forth the militia, to execute the laws of the union, suppress insurrections, and repel invasions; and to provide for organizing, arming, and disciplining them; and for governing such parts of them, as may be employed in the service of the United States. The right of appointing officers of the militia, and of training, and calling them forth, and of governing them in all other cases, *not enumerated,* being reserved to the states, respectively.

13. To declare the punishment of treason, under certain restrictions. The definition of treason, being contained in the constitution itself.

14. To exercise exclusive legislation in all cases whatsoever, over such district *not exceeding ten miles square,* as may by cession of particular states, and the acceptance of congress, become the seat of government of the United States; and to exercise like authority over all places purchased by consent of the legislature in which the same shall be, for the erection of forts, magazines, arsenals, dock-yards, and other needful buildings. The *exclusive power of* legislating in all cases whatsoever, except *within the precincts* of the seat of government, *not exceeding ten miles square;* and except *within the precincts* of such forts, magazines, arsenals, dock-yards, and other such needful buildings, as may be erected by congress with the consent of the state, in which the same shall be, being reserved to the states, respectively.

Such are the *enumerated powers,* of congress; to give efficacy to them, as also to the powers expressly granted to the other departments of the federal government, there is an express declaration, of what was perhaps before implied, viz.

15. That congress shall have power to make all laws which shall be *necessary* and *proper* for carrying into execution the foregoing powers, and all other vested by the constitution in the government of the United States, or in any department or officer thereof.

This clause, I apprehend, cannot be construed to enlarge any power before specifically granted; nor to grant any new power, not before specifically enumerated; or granted in some other part of the constitution. On the contrary it seems calculated to restrain the federal government from the exercise of any power, not *necessarily* an *appendage* to, and *consequence* of some power particularly *enumerated.* Acts of congress to be binding, must be made pursuant to the constitution; otherwise they are *not laws,* but a mere *nullity;* or what is worse, *acts of usurpation.*[14] The people are not only not bound by them, but the several departments and officers of the governments, both federal, and state, are *bound by oath to oppose them;* for, being bound by oath to support the constitution, they must violate that oath, whenever they give their sanction, by obedience, or otherwise, to any unconstitutional act of any department of the government.

If the reader can discover in any of the powers before enumerated, that which contains a grant of general jurisdiction in common law cases to the federal government, our enquiry is at an end. And he will render an incomparable act of service to his country, by laying his finger upon that clause, and pointing it out to his fellow-citizens, that they may no longer puzzle themselves, or their agents, about a question of such importance.... But, if he can not do this, and is not yet convinced that no such grant is contained in the constitution, I must request him patiently to attend me, whilst we hunt for it in some other part of that instrument.

14. See the Federalist, No. 33. and No. 44.

2. Then; we are to seek for this grant in that article which relates to the powers and duties of the executive department.

The president, by that article, is declared to be commander in chief of the army and navy of the United States, and of the militia of the several states, when called into the actual service of the United States: he may require the opinion, in writing, of the principal officer of each of the executive departments, upon any subject relating to the duties of their respective offices, and hath power to grant reprieves and pardons for offences against the United States, except in cases of impeachment. He may with advice and consent of the senate, make treaties; and may nominate, and with consent of the senate, appoint ambassadors, other public ministers and consuls, judges of the supreme court, and all other officers whose appointments are not otherwise provided for; he may fill up all vacancies that may happen during the recess of the senate, by temporary commissions; it is his duty to give congress information of the state of the union, and he may recommend to their consideration such measures as he may judge necessary and expedient; he may on extraordinary occasions convene both houses, or either of them; and in case of disagreement between them with respect to the time of adjournment, may adjourn them; he hath a qualified negative upon all the other acts, and proceedings; he is to receive ambassadors and other public ministers; he is to take care that the laws be faithfully executed; and to commission all officers of the United States.

The most dextrous political empyric would, I apprehend, be puzzled to extract from the preceding enumeration any thing, which could bear the most distant resemblance to a grant of general jurisdiction in common law cases: we, are driven then, in the last resort to seek for it.

3. In that article, which relates to the constitution and powers of the judiciary department. It is therein declared,

That the judicial power shall extend to all cases in law and equity, arising under the constitution; the laws of the United States; and treaties made, or which shall be made, under their authority; to all cases affecting ambassadors, other public ministers, and consuls; to all cases of admiralty; to controversies to which the United States shall be a party; to controversies between two, or more states; between citizens of different states; between citizens of the same state, claiming lands under grants from different states; and between a state and foreign states.

Such is the power of the judiciary department, as now limited by the thirteenth article of the amendments to the constitution of the United States. I shall endeavour to analize the whole.

1. The judicial power of the federal government extends to all cases in law and equity arising under the constitution. Now, the powers granted to the federal government, or prohibited to the states, being all enumerated, the cases arising under the *constitution*, can only be such as arise out of some *enumerated* power delegated to the federal government, or prohibited to those of the several states. These general words include what is comprehended in the next clause, viz. Cases arising under the laws of the United States. But as contra-distinguished from that clause, it comprehends some cases afterwards enumerated, e. g. Controversies between two or more states; between a state and foreign states; between citizens of the same state claiming lands under grants of different states; all which may arise under the *constitution*, and not under any law of the U. States. Many other cases might be enumerated, which would fall strictly under this clause, and no other. As, if a citizen of one state should be denied the privileges of a citizen in another; so, if a person held to service or labour in one state, should escape into another and obtain protection there, as a free man; so, if a state should coin money, and declare the same to be a legal tender in payment of debt, the validity of such a tender, if made, would fall within the meaning of this clause. So also, if a state should, without consent of congress, lay any duty upon goods imported, the question as to the validity of such an act, if disputed, would come within the meaning of this clause, and not of any other.... In all these cases equitable circumstances may arise, the cognizance of which, as well as such as were strictly legal, would belong to the federal judiciary, in virtue of this clause.

2. The judicial power of the United States extends to all cases arising under the laws of the United States; .... now as the subjects upon which congress have the power to legislate, are all specially enumerated, so the

judicial authority, under this clause, is limited to the same subjects as congress have power to legislate upon. Thus congress being authorised to pass uniform laws of naturalization, the question whether a person is an alien, or not, falls under this head, provided the party were an alien born. So, also, if a person be accused of counterfeiting the public securities of the United States, this question would be cognizable in the federal courts, under this clause; but if he were accused of any other forgery: of this offence the state courts, and not the federal courts, possess jurisdiction.

3. The power of the federal judiciary extends to cases arising under treaties; as well those already made, as to such as might be made after the adoption of the constitution.... Of the former kind were the questions concerning the validity of payments made into the state treasuries by British debtors, during the war; of the latter sort, may be such questions as may hereafter arise under the treaty of 1794, enabling British subjects, though aliens, to hold and inherit lands, within the U. States.... In neither of the preceding clauses can we find any thing like a grant of general jurisdiction in common law cases.

4. To all cases affecting ambassadors, other public ministers, and consuls; these cases, although provided for in some countries by statute, where that is not the case, belong to the law of nations, and not to the common law.

5. To all cases of admiralty and maritime jurisdiction; these were never held to be within the jurisdiction of the common law.

6. To *controversies* to which the United States shall be a party. The word *cases* used in the preceding clauses of this article comprehends, generally, I apprehend all cases, whether civil or criminal, which are capable of falling under these heads, respectively, instances of which it might be unnecessary here to repeat: I shall however add to what I have before said, that it comprehends such *criminal* cases as may arise within the precincts of the seat of government, not exceeding ten miles square; or within the precincts of forts, dockyards, magazines, and arsenals, purchased with the consent of the state in which they may be; and finally, treason against the U. States; piracies and felonies committed upon the

high seas; and offences against the law of nations; and against the revenue laws of the U. S.

The word controversies, as here used, must be understood merely as relating to such as are of a *civil* nature. It is probably unknown in any other sense, as I do not recollect ever to have heard the expression, *criminal controversy*. As here applied, it seems particularly appropriated to such disputes as might arise between the U. States, and any one or more states, respecting territorial, or fiscal, matters. . . . Or between the U. States and their debtors, contractors, and agents. This construction is confirmed by the application of the word in the ensuing clauses, where it evidently refers to disputes of a *civil* nature only, such for example, as may arise between two or more states; or between citizens of different states; or between a state, and the citizens of another state; none of which can possibly be supposed to relate to such as are of a criminal nature, unless we could suppose it was meant to deprive the states of the power of punishing murder or theft, if committed by a foreigner, or the citizen of another state.

7. The judicial power extends likewise to controversies between two or more states; and between a state, and foreign states. These must be proceeded in, and determined according to the law of nations, and not according to the common law.

8. To controversies between citizens of different states; and between citizens of any state and the subjects or citizens of foreign states. . . . In these cases, the municipal law of the place where the cause of controversy arises, whether that be one of the United States, or Great Britain, France, Spain, Holland, Hamburg, or any other country; or the general law of merchants; or, the general law of nations according to the nature and circumstances of the case, must be the rule of decision, in whatever court the suit may be brought. Thus if a bond be given in Philadelphia, the rate of interest must be settled according to the laws of Pennsylvania. If a bill of exchange be drawn in Virginia, the rate of damages must be settled by the law of that state. If in England, Hamburg, or Cadiz, the custom of merchants in those places, respectively, must govern. If a ran-

som bill be drawn at sea, the law of nations in that case must be consulted. If the controversy relate to lands, the law of the state where the lands lie must be referred to; unless the lands be claimed under grants from different states; in which case the territorial rights of each state must be inquired into. The same must be done, in the last case which remains to be noticed; viz:

9. Controversies between citizens of the same state claiming lands under grants of different states. None of the cases enumerated in this, and the preceding paragraph can be construed to give general jurisdiction in cases at common law, or such as ordinarily arise between citizens of the same state; under which description, civil suits, in general, (with the exception of the case here supposed) are comprehended; or such as may arise between a state, and its own citizens, or subjects; under which head crimes and misdemeanors are comprehended. This being the only enumerated case, in which the federal courts can take cognizance of any civil controversy between citizens of the same state, it can not extend to such common law cases, as may arise between them; all such cases being reserved to the jurisdiction of the states, respectively. And on the other hand, as it does not extend to *any case* that may arise between a state and its own citizens or subjects; nor to any case between a state, and foreign citizens or subjects, or the citizens of any other state[15]... so every such case, whether civil or criminal, and whether it arise under the law of nations, the common law, or law of the state, belongs exclusively, to the jurisdiction of the states, respectively. And this, as well from the reason of the thing, as from the express declarations contained in the twelfth and thirteenth articles of the amendments to the constitution.

Having thus minutely examined *all* the *enumerated powers*, which are vested in the federal government, or any of its departments, and not finding any grant of general jurisdiction in cases at common law, we are warranted, under the twelfth article of amendments, in concluding, that *no such jurisdiction* has been *granted;* and consequently, that it remains with the *states, respectively, in all cases not enumerated;* so far, as their sev-

15. *Editor's note:* Eleventh Amendment.

eral constitutions and legislative acts, may admit the authority and obligation of the common law, or statutes of England, in each state, respectively.

But it has, I believe, been said, that if this general jurisdiction in common law cases has not been granted to the federal government in express terms, yet it is given by *implication*. This admits of several answers:

1. The twelfth article of the amendments[16] was proposed, adopted and ratified, for the express purpose of rebutting, this doctrine of grant by *implication:* since it expressly declares, that the *powers not delegated* to the United States, by the constitution, *nor prohibited* by it to the states, are *reserved* to the states respectively, or to the people. And this I hold to be a full answer to the conceit.... But,

2dly. If this were not the case, it would be absurdity in the extreme, to suppose a grant, by *implication,* of general power to the federal government to revive, and enforce such parts of the common law, or statutes of England, as the *states* by their respective constitutions had severally condemned in express terms; and rejected, repealed, and annulled as dangerous, absurd, or incompatible with that system of government which they had, respectively, established.

3dly. This is probably the first instance in which it has been supposed that sovereign and independent states can be abridged of their rights, as sovereign states, by *implication,* only.... For, no free nation can be bound by any law but its own will; and where that will is manifested by any written document, as a convention, league, treaty, compact, or agreement, the nation is bound, only according as that will is expressed *in* the instrument by which it binds itself. And as every nation is bound to preserve itself, or, in other words, its independence; so no interpretation whereby its destruction, or that of the state, which is the same thing, may be hazarded, can be admitted in any case where it has not, in the *most express terms,* given its consent to such an interpretation.[17] Now if this

16. *Editor's note:* Here as elsewhere, Tucker means the Tenth Amendment by "the twelfth article of the amendments."

17. See Vattel, Book the first.

construction were once established, that the federal government possesses general jurisdiction over all cases at common law, what else could be the consequence, but, at one stroke, to annihilate the states altogether; and to repeal and annul their several constitutions, bills of rights, legislative codes, and political institutions in all cases whatsoever. For, what room, or occasion, could there be for a constitution, if the common law of England, be *paramount* thereto; or for a state legislature, if their acts are not laws, but mere nullities; or for courts, if their decisions, founded upon the constitutions and laws of the states, are for that reason null and void?

4thly. If it were admitted, that the federal government, by implication, possesses general jurisdiction over all cases at common law; this construction could not be carried into practice, without annihilating the states, and repealing, and annulling, their several constitutions, bills of rights, and legislative codes: as a few instances will demonstrate.

The constitution of Virginia declares, and the constitutions of the other states agree therewith, that the legislative, executive, and judiciary departments shall be separate and distinct: the common law unites all three in one and the same person.

The constitution of Maryland declares there shall be no forfeiture of any part of the estate of any person for any crime, except murder, or treason against the state; the laws of Virginia have abolished forfeitures in all cases: The doctrine of forfeiture, in case of conviction, or attainder for any crime, is one of the pillars of criminal jurisprudence, by the common law.

The constitution of Pennsylvania declares, that the penal laws as theretofore used in that state, shall be reformed, and punishment made less sanguinary, and more proportionate to crimes. If the common law be revived, this article is a mere nullity. South-Carolina has an article in it's constitution to the same effect.

The same constitution declares, that the printing presses shall be free to every person who undertakes to examine the proceedings of the legislature, or any part of the government. It is contended by some persons in power, that the common law does not permit this freedom to any person.

The constitution of Georgia declares, that no grand-jury shall consist of fewer than eighteen persons; the common law deems sixteen a sufficient number.

The same constitution will not allow of a special verdict in any case: The practice of the common law courts in England for five hundred years past, has been to the contrary.

The constitution of North Carolina, declares, that every foreigner who comes to settle in that state, having first taken an oath of allegiance to the same, may purchase, or by other just means acquire, hold, and transfer land, or other real estate; and after one year's residence shall be deemed a free citizen. The constitution of Pennsylvania, has an article to the same effect.... The foreigner is not naturalized immediately upon taking the oath of allegiance; he continues an alien for a year; and if he departs before its expiration, remains an alien: yet he may acquire, hold, and transfer lands: by the common law, an alien can not hold lands.

The constitution of Georgia, prohibits entails; and declares that the real estate of a person dying intestate shall be divided equally among his children: that the widow shall have a child's part, or her dower, at her option. And if there be no children the estate shall be divided among the next of kin. The common law admits of entails; and absolutely rejects the other provisions of this article.

The constitutions and laws of all the states of the union, (except Massachusetts, where there have been judicial decisions to the contrary), admit slavery. The common, as understood for many centuries past in England, absolutely rejects slavery.... Should a question arise upon that subject in Maryland, Virginia, North Carolina, South Carolina or Georgia, it might be of serious consequence, if the common law were pronounced to be paramount to the laws of the states.

Lastly, The constitutions and laws of all the states, in which the common law and statutes of England have been expressly adopted, in a certain degree, declare that those laws are not to be construed so as to

impair any of the rights and privileges contained in their respective constitutions and laws; and further subject them to be repealed, altered, or
annulled, by acts of their respective legislatures: the construction contended for, would render the common law *paramount* to those constitutional declarations, and to all legislative acts. These cases might be
multiplied without end; I shall only add one more, which may serve to
illustrate the consequences likely to flow from this doctrine, were it possible it should be established.

The constitution of Pennsylvania, declare, that all men have a natural
inherent right to emigrate from one state to another that will receive
them, whenever they think, that thereby, they may promote their own
happiness. Virginia, made a law to the same effect, in the year, 1783, which
still continues to be a part of her code. The English jurists deny to the
subjects of the crown of Great Britain the right of expatriation, a doctrine which they contend is derived from the common law. In those
states which have adopted the common law under certain limitations,
but have made no declaration in their constitution, nor any legislative
act upon the subject, the right of expatriation may still be questionable.
But ought it to be questioned in Pennsylvania, or Virginia, (both which
states have, in the most solemn and explicit manner repealed the law,)
because it is still questionable in Connecticut, where the law was, perhaps, not repealed, because the right had never before been questioned.
What a snare is it for the feet of the citizens of the United States, if obsolete maxims of this kind, may be revived at the discretion of a judge, and
enforced with severe penalties, notwithstanding they may have been
expressly repealed and annulled in the most solemn manner by the
authority of the states, respectively! What principle can be established,
more inimical to the independence of sovereign states, or more destructive to the liberty, security, and happiness of the citizen, than, that the
unwritten law of a foreign country, differing from them in the fundamental principles of government, is paramount to their own written
laws, and even to those *constitutions*, which the *people* had sealed with
their blood, and declared to be *forever inviolable!* Such, however, is the
necessary, and inevitable consequence, of this constructive grant of juris-

diction in all cases at *common law,* to the courts of the United States, or to any department of the federal government.

But, were it possible that the consequence above mentioned would not follow, which, however, seems to be altogether inevitable, another consequence, scarcely less mischevous, must follow from the rule contended for; if, in reducing it to practice in the *federal courts,* it should be admitted, that the common law might be repealed in certain states, in virtue of their constitutions or legislative acts, but remain in full vigour in others. Thus, if it be admitted in the federal courts that a native citizen of Pennsylvania, or Virginia, may expatriate himself, because the constitution of the former, and the law of the latter, expressly permit him to do so; but that a native citizen of Connecticut, cannot expatriate himself, because the common law has not been repealed in that state; here the same action must, by the same judge, be decided to be lawful in one part of the United States, and unlawful in another. Consequently, a native citizen of Connecticut, may be punished, as a citizen of the United States, for doing that, which a native of Pennsylvania, or Virginia, may do with impunity. On the other hand, if the right of expatriation be denied, in the case of a native of Pennsylvania, or Virginia, would not such a denial amount to a declaration, that the common law of England is *paramount* to the law of the one, and the constitution of the other? This dilemma proves, that it could not be the intention of the several states to grant a power so unbounded in its operation, and so destructive to those principles which they deemed inseparable from their constitutions, and therefore sacred, and inviolable.

But perhaps it will be contended, that the power of establishing an uniform rule of naturalization, includes in it the power to prohibit the right of expatriation. This admits of more than one answer.

1. If it be true; (which is by no means admitted) congress alone have power to prohibit the exercise of that right; which, not having yet done, the right, until they do so, remains as before the adoption of the federal constitution.

2. The power of establishing an uniform rule of naturalization, relates to aliens; that of prohibiting expatriation to citizens: the first, to rights to

be acquired; the second, to rights to be abandoned. The first relates to such persons as thereafter submit themselves to our jurisdiction; the second, to such as thenceforward renounce their connexion with us, forever.... The former to political, the latter to natural, right.

5th. But to return to our subject; there are certain passages in the constitution, and the amendments thereto, not yet noticed, which perhaps may be relied on to establish this doctrine of a grant of general jurisdiction to the federal courts or government, in cases at common law, by *implication:* These are,

1. The privilege of the writ of *habeas corpus* shall not be suspended, unless when in cases of rebellion or invasion, the public safety may require it.

2. The trial of all crimes, except in cases of impeachment, shall be by jury.

3. In suits at common law, the right of trial by jury, shall, (in general) be preserved: and no fact tried by a jury, shall be otherwise re-examined in any court of the United States, than according to the rules of the common law.

In all these passages, we may be told, the common law is evidently referred to as the *law* of the *land.* This is not the case; it is referred to as a known law: and might in strictness have been referred to as the law of the several states, so far as their constitutions and legislative codes, respectively, have admitted or adopted it. Will any man who knows any thing of the laws of England, affirm, that the civil, or Roman imperial law, is the general law of the land in England, because many of its maxims, and its course of proceedings, are generally admitted and established in the high court of chancery, which is the highest court of civil jurisdiction, except the parliament, in the kingdom? Or that the canon, or Roman ecclesiastical law, is the general law of the land, because marriages are solemnized according to its rites; or because simony, which is an ecclesiastical offence, is also made an offence by statute?

But it will be asked, what is meant by suits at common law, the cognizance of which, from this article, appears to belong to the federal courts. The answer is easy; in many of the states, the courts are distinguished by the epithets of common law courts, and courts of equity. In the former, the rules and mode of proceeding in the English courts of common law jurisdiction, have under different modifications been adopted; the latter pursue the course of the civil law. Suits cognizable in these courts, respectively, are consequently denominated, suits at common law, and suits in equity, comprehending under these terms *all* civil suits, except such as are of a maritime nature. . . . The trial by jury being the usual mode of trial in all the states, except in the courts of equity, it was thought expedient to preserve the same mode of trial in the federal courts, as in the state courts. The article gives not *a new* jurisdiction, not before expressly granted, in the third article of the constitution; it merely prescribes a mode of trial.

We may fairly infer from all that has been said that the common law of England stands precisely upon the same footing in the federal government, and courts of the United States, *as such,* as the civil and ecclesiastical laws stand upon in England: That is to say, it's maxims and rules of proceeding are to be adhered to, whenever the written law is silent, in cases of a similar, or analogous nature, the cognizance whereof is by the constitution vested in the federal courts; it may govern and direct the course of proceeding, in such cases, but cannot give jurisdiction in *any case,* where jurisdiction is not expressly given by the constitution. The same may be said of the *civil law;* the rules of proceeding in which, whenever the written law is silent, are to be observed in cases of equity, and of admiralty, and maritime jurisdiction. In short, as the matters cognizable in the federal courts, belong, (as we have before shewn, in reviewing the powers of the judiciary department) partly to the law of nations, partly to the common law of England; partly to the civil law; partly to the maritime law, comprehending the laws of Oleron and Rhodes; and partly to the general law and custom of merchants; and partly to the municipal laws of any foreign nation, or of any state in the union, where the cause of action may happen to arise, or where the suit may be instituted; so, the law of nations, the common law of England, the civil law, the law maritime, the law merchant, or the *lex loci,* or law of the foreign nation, or state, in which the cause of action may arise, or shall be decided, must in their turn be resorted to as the rule of decision, according to the nature and circumstances of each case, respectively. So that each of these laws may be regarded, so far as they apply to such cases, respectively, as the law of the land. But to infer from hence, that the common law of England is the general law of the United States, is to the full as absurd as to suppose that the laws of Russia, or Germany, are the general law of the land, because in a controversy respecting a contract made in either of those empires, it might be necessary to refer to the laws of either of them, to decide the question between the litigant parties. Nor can I find any more reason for admitting the penal code of England to be in force in the United States, (except so far as the states, respectively, may have adopted it, within their several jurisdictions) than for admitting that of the Roman empire, or of Russia, Spain, or any other nation, whatever.

One or two instances, in addition to those already mentioned, may set this matter in a clearer light. If a suit be brought in a federal court upon a bond executed in England, the bond must be actually sealed, because the common law of England requires that every bond, deed, or covenant, should be executed in that manner; and if it be not, it is not a bond, but merely a simple contract; but if the bond be executed in Virginia, where a scroll by way of seal, is by law declared to be as effectual as if the instrument were actually sealed, there the law of the state shall prevail, and turn that contract into a specialty, by which the lands of the obligor may be bound, which in England would only bind his goods and chattles, after his decease. So if a bill of exchange be drawn in Virginia, an action of debt may be maintained thereupon, in that state; but if it be drawn in any other state, or country, the action I apprehend, must be brought, even in that state upon the custom of merchants. Thus, the *lex loci* may operate not only so as to determine the nature of the contract, but of the remedy. And with respect to the mode of proceeding, in order to a remedy, wherever the constitution and laws of the United States are silent, there, I apprehend, the law of the state, where the suit is brought, ought to be observed as a guide: thus if a suit be brought upon a bond the plaintiff may demand bail, in Virginia, as of course, and an endorsement to that effect will be sufficient to compel the sheriff, who executes the writ, to take bail at his peril. But in England, the plaintiff in that case, must make an affidavit of the sum actually due upon the bond, otherwise the sheriff is not obliged to take bail. So in the same case, if the sheriff neglects to take bail where he ought to do it, the plaintiff may proceed, in Virginia, against the defendant and sheriff, at the same time, and shall have judgment for his debt against both at once, unless special bail be put in; whereas in England, he must bring a special action on the case, against the sheriff, for neglect of his duty, instead of having the remedy which the laws of Virginia furnish him with. So also, if a bond be executed in London, and a suit be brought thereupon, in the state of Virginia, the defendant cannot plead *non est factum*, as is the usual course of pleading in England, unless he verifies his plea by affidavit; without which it cannot be received; and the same course of proceeding, I apprehend, is to be observed in the federal, as in the state courts.

From the whole of the preceding examination, we may deduce the following conclusions:

First. . . . That the common law of England, and every statute of that kingdom, made for the security of the life, liberty, or property of the subject, before the settlement of the British colonies, respectively, so far as the same were applicable to the nature of their situation and circumstances, respectively, were brought over to America, by the first settlers of the colonies, respectively; and remained in full force therein, until repealed, altered, or amended by the legislative authority of the colonies, respectively; or by the constitutional acts of the same, when they became sovereign and independent states.

Secondly. . . . That neither the common law of England, nor the statutes of that kingdom, were, at any period antecedent to the revolution, the general and uniform law of the land in the British colonies, now constituting the United States.

Thirdly. . . . That as the adoption or rejection of the common law and statutes of England, or any part thereof, in one colony, could not have any operation or effect in another colony, possessing a constitutional legislature of its own; so neither could the adoption or rejection thereof by the constitutional, or legislative act of one sovereign and independent state, have any operation or effect in another sovereign independent state; because every such state hath an exclusive right to be governed by its own laws only.

Fourthly. . . . Therefore the authority and obligation of the common law and statutes of England; as such in the American states, must depend solely upon the constitutional or legislative authority of each state, respectively; as contained in their several bills of rights, constitutions, and legislative declarations . . . . which, being different in different states, and wholly independent of each other, cannot establish any uniform law, or rule of obligation in all the states.

Fifthly. . . . That neither the articles of confederation and perpetual union, nor, the present constitution of the United States, ever did, or *do,* authorize the federal government, or any department thereof, to declare the common law or statutes of England, or of any other nation, to be the law of the land in the United States, generally, as one nation; nor to legislate upon, or exercise jurisdiction in, any case of municipal law, not delegated to the United States by the constitution.

POSTSCRIPT

Since the publication of the preceding tract, I have met with the case of the United States against Worral, which I had not before seen.

The defendant was charged with an attempt to bribe Tench Coxe, commissioner of the revenue; it was admitted that the offence did not come within the act of 1 Congress, 2 Session, c. 9, §. 21. and a question was asked of the attorney for the U. States, by Judge Chase, whether he meant to support his indictment solely at common law? If you do, said he, I have no difficulty upon the subject. The indictment cannot be maintained in this court, viz. The circuit court of the U. States, for the district of Pennsylvania.

The attorney for the United States, answering in the affirmative; Chase, justice, stopped the counsel for the defendant, and delivered an opinion to the following effect.

CHASE, *Justice.* "This is an indictment for an offence highly injurious

to morals, and deserving the severest punishment; but as it is an indictment at common law, I dismiss, at once, every thing that has been said
about the constitution and laws of the United States.

"In this country, every man sustains a two-fold political capacity; one
in relation to the state, and another in relation to the United States: for
the constitution of the union is the source of all the jurisdiction of the
national government; so that the departments of the government can
never assume any power that is not expressly granted by that instrument,
nor exercise a power in any other manner than is there prescribed.
Besides the particular cases, which the eighth section of the first article
designates, there is a power granted to congress to create, define, and
punish crimes and offences, whenever they shall deem it necessary and
proper by law to do so, for effectuating the objects of the government;
and although bribery is not among the crimes and offences specially
mentioned, it is certainly included in this general provision. The question, however, does not arise about the power: whether the courts of the
United States can punish a man for any act, before it is declared by a law
of the United States, to be criminal? Now, it appears to my mind, to be as
essential, that congress should define the offences to be tried and apportion the punishment to be inflicted, as that they should erect courts to try
the criminal, or to pronounce a sentence on conviction.

"It is attempted, however, to supply the silence of the constitution,
and statutes, of the union, by resorting to the common law, for a definition and punishment of the offence which has been committed: but, in
my opinion, the United States, as a federal government, have no common law. If indeed the U. States, can be supposed for a moment, to have
a common law, it must, I presume, be that of England; and yet it is
impossible to trace, when, or how, the system was adopted, or introduced. With respect to the individual states, the difficulty does not occur.
When the American colonies were first settled by our ancestors, it was
held, as well by the settlers, as by the judges and lawyers of England, that
they brought hither as a birthright and inheritance, so much of the common law, as was applicable to their situation, and change of circumstances. But each colony judged for itself, what parts of the common law

were applicable to its new condition; and in various modes, by legislative acts, by judicial decisions, or by constant usage, adopted some parts, and rejected others. Hence, he who shall travel through the different states, will soon discover, that the whole of the common law of England, has been no where introduced; that some states have rejected what others have adopted; and that there is, in short, a great and essential diversity, in the subjects to which the common law is applied, as well as in the extent of the application. The common law, therefore, of one state, is not the common law of another; but the common law of England, is the law of each state, so far as each state has adopted it; and it results from that position, connected with the judicial act, that the common law will always apply to suits between citizen and citizen, whether they are instituted in a federal, or state court.

"But the question recurs, when and how, have the courts of the United States acquired a common law jurisdiction in criminal cases? The United States must possess the common law themselves, before they can communicate it to their judicial agents: now the United States did not bring it with them from England; the constitution does not create it; and no act of congress has assumed it. Besides, what is the common law, to which we are referred? Is it the common law entire, as it exists in England; or modified as it exists in some of the states; and of the various modifications, which are we to select; the system of Georgia, or New-Hampshire, Pennsylvania or Connecticut?

"Upon the whole, it may be a defect in our political institutions, it may be an inconvenience in the administration of justice, that the common law authority, relating to crimes and punishments, has not been conferred upon the government of the United States, which is a government in other respects also of a limited jurisdiction: but judges cannot remedy political imperfections, nor supply any legislative omission. I will not say whether the offence is at this time cognizable in a state court. But certainly congress might have provided, by law, for the present case, as they have provided for other cases of a similar nature; and yet if congress had even declared and defined the offence, without prescribing a punishment, I should still have thought it improper to exercise a discretion upon that part of the subject."

PETERS, *Justice*.[18] "Whenever a government has been established, I have always supposed, that a power to preserve itself, was a necessary, and an inseparable concomitant. But the existence of the federal government would be precarious, it could no longer be called an independent government, if, for the punishment of offences of this nature, tending to obstruct and pervert the administration of its affairs, an appeal must be made to the state tribunals, or the offenders must escape with absolute impunity.

"The power to punish misdemeanors, is originally and strictly a common law power; of which, I think, the United States are constitutionally possessed. It might have been exercised by congress in form of a legislative act; but it may, also, in my opinion, be enforced in a course of judicial proceeding. Whenever an offence aims at the subversion of any federal institution, or at the corruption of its public officers, it is an offence against the well-being of the United States; from its very nature, it is cognizable under their authority; and, consequently, it is within the jurisdiction of this court, by the 11th section of the judicial act."

Here then are two opposite opinions on this great question. On the trial of Isaac Williams, in the district court of Connecticut, February 27, 1797, for accepting a commission under the French Republic, and under the authority thereof committing acts of hostility against Great-Britain, the defendant alledged, and offered to prove that he had expatriated himself from the United States, and become a French citizen before the commencement of the war between France and England. This produced a question as to the right of expatriation; when Judge Ellsworth, then chief justice of the United States, is said to have delivered an opinion nearly to the following effect.

---

18. *Editor's note:* At this time, U.S. Supreme Court justices sat with U.S. District Court judges (in this case Richard Peters) to form the circuit court of appeals. Judge Chase was Justice Samuel Chase of the U.S. Supreme Court.

"The common law of this country remains the same as it was before the revolution. The present question is to be decided by two great principles; one is, that all the members of a civil community are bound to each other by compact; the other is, that one of the parties to this compact cannot dissolve it by his own act. The compact between our community and its members is, that the community shall protect its members, and on the part of the members, that they will at all times be obedient to the laws of the community, and faithful in its defence. It necessarily results that the member cannot dissolve this compact, without the consent or default of the community. There has been no consent.... no default. Express consent is not claimed; but it is argued that the consent of the community is implied, by its policy.... its conditions.... and its acts. In countries so crouded with inhabitants, that the means of subsistence are difficult to be obtained, it is reason and policy to permit emigration; but our policy is different; for our country is but scarcely settled, and we have no inhabitants to spare.

"Consent has been argued from the condition of the country, because we were in a state of peace. But though we were in peace, the war had commenced in Europe. We wished to have nothing to do with the war; but the war would have something to do with us. It has been extremely difficult for us to keep out of this war; the progress of it has threatened to involve us. It has been necessary for our government to be vigilant in restraining our own citizens from those acts which would involve us in hostilities. The most visionary writers on this subject do not contend for the principle in the unlimited extent, that a citizen may, at any, and at all times, renounce his own, and join himself to a foreign country.

"Consent has been argued from the acts of our government permitting the naturalization of foreigners. When a foreigner presents himself here, we do not inquire what his relation is to his own country; we have not the means of knowing, and the inquiry would be indelicate; we leave him to judge of that. If he embarrasses himself by contracting contradictory obligations, the fault and folly are his own; but this implies no consent of the government that our own citizens should also expatriate themselves.... It is, therefore, my opinion, that these facts which the prisoner offers to prove, in his defence, are totally irrelevant," &c. The prisoner was accordingly found guilty, fined and imprisoned. See the account of his trial, National Magazine, No. 3, p. 254. I presume not to answer for the correctness of it.

As the learned judge in this opinion, refers to no express prohibitory law, except the common law, (by which I presume was meant the common law of England) we must understand his opinion, as founded upon the doctrine that the common law of England is the common law of the United States, in their federal, and national capacity and character. How far reason is on the side of that opinion, the student may form some judgement from what has been said in the foregoing essay.

And here it will be proper to subjoin an instruction from the general assembly of Virginia, to the senators from this state, in congress, January 11, 1800.

"The general assembly of Virginia would consider themselves unfaithful to the trust reposed in them, were they to remain silent, whilst a doctrine has been publicly advanced, novel in its principle, and tremendous in its consequences: That the common law of England is in force under the government of the United States. It is not at this time proposed to expose at large the monstrous pretentions resulting from the adoption of this principle. It ought never, however, to be forgotten, and can never be too often repeated, that it opens a new tribunal for the trial of crimes never contemplated by the federal compact. It opens a new code of sanguinary criminal law, both obsolete and unknown, and either wholly rejected or essentially modified in almost all its parts by state institutions. It arrests, or supercedes, state jurisdictions, and innovates upon state laws. It subjects the citizens to punishment, according to the judiciary will, when he is left in ignorance of what this law enjoins as a duty, or prohibits as a crime. It assumes a range of jurisdiction for the federal courts, which defies limitation or definition. In short it is believed, that the advocates for the principle would, themselves, be lost in an attempt, to apply it to the existing institutions of federal and state courts, by separating with precision their judiciary rights, and thus preventing the constant and mischievous interference of rival jurisdictions.

"Deeply impressed with these opinions, the general assembly of Virginia, instruct the senators, and request the representatives from this state, in congress, to use their best efforts. . . .

"To oppose the passing of any law, founded on, or recognizing the principle lately advanced, 'that the common law of England, is in force under the government of the United States;' excepting from such opposition, such particular parts of the common law, as may have a sanction from the constitution, so far as they are necessarily comprehended in the technical phrases which express the powers delegated to the government; . . . . and excepting, also, such other parts thereof as may be adopted by congress as necessary and proper for carrying into execution the powers expressly delegated."

WORKS USED BY TUCKER

Francis Bacon, *Advancement of Learning and Novum Organum.*
Jeremy Belknap, *History of New Hampshire.*
Thomas Hutchinson, *The History of the Colony and Province of Massachusetts Bay.*
George Minot, *Continuation of the History of Massachusetts Bay.*
Samuel Andrew Peters, *A General History of Connecticut.*
William Stith, *The History of the First Discovery and Settlement of Virginia.*
Zephaniah Swift, *A System of the Laws of the State of Connecticut.*
Emerich de Vattel, *Law of Nations.*

❧ Of the Right of Conscience; And of the Freedom of Speech and of the Press

Here Tucker sets forth the basis of personal rights and individual liberty, that is, freedom from government oppression in matters of opinion, in the United States. This was one of the things that distinguished the governments of the people in the New World from those of unlimited authority in the Old World. The immediate context is the Sedition Act, an attempt of the Federalist majority in Congress to punish criticism of the government as long as they controlled it. Tucker's response is that the federal government is not the judge of its own powers and may be restrained by the people of the states. This is the doctrine that Virginia and Kentucky had asserted in 1798–99 and South Carolina was to assert in 1832–33.

THE RIGHT of personal security in the United States comprehends, likewise, the uninterrupted enjoyment of a person's conscience in all matters respecting religion; and of his opinions in all matters of a civil nature.

The right of personal opinion is one of those absolute rights which man hath received from the immediate gift of his Creator, but which the policy of all governments, from the first institution of society to the foundation of the American republics, hath endeavoured to restrain, in some mode or other. The mind being created free by the author of our nature, in vain have the arts of man endeavoured to shackle it: it may indeed be imprisoned a while by ignorance, or restrained from a due exertion of its powers by tyranny and oppression; but let the rays of science, or the dawn of freedom, penetrate the dungeon, its faculties are instantly rarified and burst their prison. This right of personal opinion, comprehends first, liberty of conscience in all matters relative to religion; and, secondly, liberty of speech and of discussion in all speculative matters, whether religious, philosophical, or political.

1. Liberty of conscience in matters of religion consists in the absolute and unrestrained exercise of our religious opinions, and duties, in that mode which our own reason and conviction dictate, without the control or intervention of any human power or authority whatsoever. This liberty though made a part of our constitution, and interwoven in the nature of man by his Creator, so far as the arts of fraud and terrors of violence have been capable of abridging it, hath been the subject of coercion by human laws in all ages and in all countries as far as the annals of mankind extend. The infallibility of the rulers of nations, in matters of religion, hath been a doctrine practically enforced from the earliest periods of history to the present moment among jews, pagans, mahometans, and christians, alike. The altars of Moloch and of Jehovah have been equally stained with the blood of victims, whose conscience did not receive conviction from the polluted doctrines of blood thirsty priests and tyrants. Even in countries where the crucifix, the rack, and the flames have ceased to be the engines of proselitism, civil incapacities have been invariably attached to a dissent from the national religion: the ceasing to persecute by more violent means, has in such nations obtained the name of toleration. In liberty of conscience says the elegant Dr. Price, I include much more than toleration. Jesus Christ has established a perfect equality among his followers. His command is, that they shall assume no jurisdiction over one another, and acknowledge no master besides himself. It is, therefore, presumption in any of them to claim a right to any superiority or pre-eminence over their brethren. Such a claim is implied, whenever any of them pretend to tolerate the rest. Not only all christians, but all men of all religions, ought to be considered by a state as equally entitled to its protection, as far as they demean themselves honestly and peaceably. Toleration can take place only where there is a civil establishment of a particular mode of religion; that is, where a predominant sect enjoys exclusive advantages, and makes the encourage-

ment of it's own mode of faith and worship a part of the constitution of the state; but at the same time thinks fit to suffer the exercise of other modes of faith and worship. Thanks be to God, the new American states are at present strangers to such establishments. In this respect, as well as many others, they have shewn in framing their constitutions, a degree of wisdom and liberality which is above all praise.

Civil establishments of formularies of faith and worship, are inconsistent with the rights of private judgment. They engender strife.... they turn religion into a trade.... they shore up error.... they produce hypocrisy and prevarication.... they lay an undue bias on the human mind in its inquiries, and obstruct the progress of truth.... genuine religion is a concern that lies entirely between God and our own souls. It is incapable of receiving any aid from human laws. It is contaminated as soon as worldly motives and sanctions mix their influence with it. Statesmen should countenance it only by exhibiting, in their own example, a conscientious regard to it in those forms which are most agreeable to their own judgments, and by encouraging their fellow citizens in doing the same. They cannot, as public men, give it any other assistance. All, besides, that has been called a public leading in religion, has done it an essential injury, and produced some of the worst consequences.

The church establishment in England is one of the mildest sort. But even there what a snare has it been to integrity? And what a check to free inquiry? What dispositions favourable to despotism has it fostered? What a turn to pride and narrowness and domination has it given the clerical character? What struggles has it produced in its members to accommodate their opinions to the subscriptions and tests which it imposes? What a perversion of learning has it occasioned to defend obsolete creeds and absurdities? What a burthen is it on the consciences of some of its best clergy, who, in consequence of being bound down to a system they do not approve, and having no support except that which they derive from conforming to it, find themselves under the hard necessity of either prevaricating or starving? No one doubts but that the English clergy in general could with more truth declare that they do not, than that they do give their unfeigned assent to all and every thing contained in the thirty-nine articles, and the book of common prayer: and, yet, with a solemn declaration to this purpose, are they obliged to enter upon an office which above all offices requires those who exercise it to be examples of simplicity and sincerity.... Who can help execrating the cause of such an evil?

But what I wish most to urge is the tendency of religious establishments to impede the improvement of the world. They are boundaries prescribed by human folly to human investigation; and enclosures, which intercept the light, and confine the exertions of reason. Let any one imagine to himself what effects similar establishments would have in philosophy, navigation, metaphisics, medicine, or mathematics. Something like this, took place in logic and philosophy, while the *ipse dixit* of Aristotle, and the nonsense of the schools, maintained, an authority like that of the creeds of churchmen; and the effect was a longer continuance of the world in the ignorance and barbarity of the dark ages. But civil establishments of religion are more pernicious. So apt are mankind to misrepresent the character of the Deity, and to connect his favour with particular modes of faith, that it must be expected that a religion so settled will be what it has hitherto been....a gloomy and cruel superstition, bearing the name of religion.

It has been long a subject of dispute, which is worse in its effects on society, such a religion or speculative atheism. For my own part, I could almost give the preference to the latter.... Atheism is so repugnant to every principle of common sense, that it is not possible it should ever gain much ground, or become very prevalent. On the contrary, there is a particular proneness in the human mind to superstition, and nothing is more likely to become prevalent.... Atheism leaves us to the full influence of most of our natural feelings and social principles; and these are so strong in their operation, that, in general, they are a sufficient guard to the order of society. But superstition counteracts these principles, by holding forth men to one another as objects of divine hatred; and by putting them on harrassing, silenceing, imprisoning and burning one another, in order to do God service.... Atheism is a sanctuary for vice, by taking away the motives to virtue arising from the will of God, and the fear of future judgment. But superstition is more a sanctuary for vice, by teaching men ways of pleasing God, without moral virtue; and by leading them even to compound for wickedness, by ritual services, by bodily penances and mortifications; by adoring shrines, going pilgrimages, saying many prayers, receiving absolution from the priests, exterminating heretics, &c. . . . Atheism destroys the sacredness and obligation of an oath. But is there not also a religion (so called) which does this, by teaching, that there is a power which can dispense with the obligation of oaths; that *pious* frauds are right, and that faith is not to be kept with heretics.

It is indeed only a rational and liberal religion; a religion founded on just notions of the Deity, as a Being who regards equally every sincere worshipper, and by whom all are alike favoured as far as they act up to the light they enjoy: a religion which consists in the imitation of the moral perfections of an Almighty but Benevolent Governor of Nature, who directs for the best, all events, in confidence in the care of his providence, in resignation to his will, and in the faithful discharge of every duty of piety and morality from a regard to his authority, and the apprehension of a future righteous retribution. It is only this religion (the inspiring principle of every thing fair and worthy, and joyful, and which, in truth is nothing but the love of God to man, and virtue warming the heart and directing the conduct). It is only this kind of religion that can bless the world, or be an advantage to society. This is the religion that every enlightened friend to mankind will be zealous to support. But it is a religion that the powers of the world know little of, and which will always be best promoted by being left free and open.[1] The following passage from the same author, deserves too much attention to be pretermitted: "Let no such monster be known there, [in the United States] as human authority in matters of religion. Let every honest and peaceable man, whatever is his faith, be protected there; and find an effectual defence against the attacks of bigotry and intolerance. In the United States may religion flourish! They cannot be very great and happy if it

---

1. Price's observations on the American revolution.

does not. But let it be a better religion than most of those which have been hitherto professed in the world. Let it be a religion which enforces moral obligations; not a religion which relaxes and evades them.... A tolerant and catholic religion; not a rage for proselytism.... A religion of peace and charity; not a religion that persecutes curses and damns. In a word, let it be the genuine gospel of peace, lifting above the world, warming the heart with the love of God and his creatures, and sustaining the fortitude of good men, by the assured hope of a future deliverance from death, and an infinite reward in the everlasting kingdom of our Lord and Saviour."

This inestimable and imprescriptible right is guaranteed to the citizens of the United States, as such, by the constitution of the United States, which declares, that no religious test shall ever be required as a qualification to any office or public trust under the United States; and by that amendment to the constitution of the United States, which prohibits congress from making any law respecting the establishment of religion, or prohibiting the free exercise thereof; and to the citizens of Virginia by the bill of rights, which declares, "that religion, or the duty which we owe to our Creator, and the manner of discharging it, can be directed only by reason and conviction, not by force or violence, and therefore all men are equally entitled to the free exercise of religion, according to the dictates of conscience: and that it is the mutual duty of all to practice christian forbearance, love, and charity, towards each other." And further, by the act for establishing religious freedom, by which it is also declared, "that no man shall be compelled to frequent or support any religious worship, place, or ministry, whatsoever, nor shall be enforced, restrained, molested or burthened in his body or goods, nor shall otherwise suffer on account of his religious opinions or belief; but that all men shall be free to profess, and by argument maintain their opinions in matters of religion, and that the same shall in no wise diminish, enlarge, or affect their civil capacities."

2. Liberty of speech and of discussion in all speculative matters, consists in the absolute and uncontrollable right of speaking, writing, and publishing, our opinions concerning any subject, whether religious, philosophical, or political; and of inquiring into and, examining the

nature of truth, whether moral or metaphysical; the expediency or inexpediency of all public measures, with their tendency and probable effect; the conduct of public men, and generally every other subject, without restraint, except as to the injury of any other individual, in his person, property, or good name. Thought and speech are equally the immediate gifts of the Creator, the one being intended as the vehicle of the other: they ought, therefore, to have been wholly exempt from the coersion of human laws in all speculative and doctrinal points whatsoever: liberty of speech in political matters, has been equally proscribed in almost all the governments of the world, as liberty of conscience in those of religion. A complete tyranny over the human mind could never have been exercised whilst the organ by which our sentiments are conveyed to others, was free: when the introduction of letters among men afforded a new mode of disclosing, and that of the press, a more expeditious method of diffusing their sentiments, writing and printing also became subjects of legal coersion; even the expression of sentiments by pictures and hieroglyphics attracted the attention of the Argus-government, so far as to render such expressions punishable by law. The common place arguments in support of these restraints are, that they tend to preserve peace and good order in government; that there are some doctrines both in religion and politics, so sacred, and others of so bad a tendency, that no public discussion of them ought to be suffered. To these the elegant writer before referred to, gives this answer: "were this a right opinion, all the persecution that has ever been practised, would be justified. For if it is a part of the duty of civil magistrates, to prevent the discussion of such doctrines, they must, in doing this, act on their own judgments of the nature and tendency of doctrines; and consequently, they must have a right to prevent the discussion of all doctrines which they think to be too sacred for discussion, or too dangerous in their tendency; and this right they must exercise in the only way in which civil power is capable of exercising it, by inflicting penalties on all who oppose sacred doctrines, or who maintain pernicious opinions."[2]

In England during the existence of the court of star chamber, and after

2. Ibid.

its abolition, from the time of the long parliament to the year 1694, the liberty of the press, and the right of vending books, was restrained to very narrow limits, by various ordinances and acts of parliament; all books printed were previously licensed by some of the great offices of state, or the two universities, and all foreign books were exposed to a similar scrutiny before they were vended. No shopkeeper could buy a book to sell again, or sell any book, unless he were a licensed bookseller. By these and other restrictions the communication of knowledge was utterly subjected to the control of those, whose interest led them rather to promote ignorance than the knowledge of truth. In 1694, the parliament refused to continue these prohibitions any longer, and thereby, according to De Lolme, established the freedom of the press in England. But although this negative establishment may satisfy the subjects of England, the people of America have not thought proper to suffer the freedom of speech, and of the press to rest upon such an uncertain foundation, as the will and pleasure of the government. Accordingly, when it was discovered that the constitution of the United States had not provided any barrier against the possible encroachments of the government thereby to be established, great complaints were made of the omission, and most of the states instructed their representatives to obtain an amendment in that respect; and so sensible was the first congress of the general prevalence of this sentiment throughout America, that in their first session they proposed an amendment since adopted by all the states and made a part of the constitution, "that congress shall make no law abridging the freedom of speech, or of the press." And our state bill of rights declares, "that the freedom of the press is one of the great bulwarks of liberty, and cannot be restrained, but by despotic governments." And so tenacious of this right, was the convention of Virginia, by which the constitution of the United States was ratified, that they further declared, as an article of the bill of rights then agreed to, "that the people have a right to the freedom of speech, and of writing and publishing their sentiments; that the freedom of the press is one of the greatest bulwarks of liberty, and ought not to be violated." Nay, so reasonably jealous were they of the possibility of this declaration being disregarded, as not

forming a part of the constitution, at that time, that the following declaration is inserted in, and forms a part of, the instrument of ratification, viz. "That the powers granted under the constitution, being derived
from the people of the United States, may be resumed by them, whensoever the same shall be perverted to their injury or oppression; and that,
every power not granted thereby, remains with them, and at their will:
that, therefore no right; of any denomination, can be cancelled, abridged,
restrained, or modified by the congress, by the senate, or house of representatives, acting in any capacity; by the president, or any department,
or officer of the United States, except in those instances where power is
given by the constitution for those purposes: that among other essential
rights, the liberty of conscience, and of the press, cannot be cancelled,
abridged, restrained, or modified, by any authority of the United States."

As this latter declaration forms a part of the instrument by which the
constitution of the United States became obligatory upon the state, and
citizens of Virginia; and as the act of ratification has been accepted in
that form; no principle is more clear, than that the state of Virginia is no
otherwise bound thereby, than according to the very tenor of the instrument, by which she has bound herself. For as no free state can be bound
to another, or to a number of others, but, by its own voluntary consent
and act, so not only the evidence of that consent, but the nature and
terms of it, can be ascertained only by recurrence to the very instrument,
by which it was first given. And as the foregoing declaration not only
constitutes a part of that instrument, but contains a preliminary protest
against any extension of the enumerated powers thereby granted to the
federal government, it could scarcely have been imagined, that any violation of a principle so strenuously asserted, and made, as it were, the
sole ground of the pragmatic sanction, would ever have been attempted
by the federal government.

But however reasonable such an expectation might have been, a very
few years evinced a determination on the part of those who then ruled
the public councils of the United States, to set at nought all such
restraints. An act accordingly was passed by the congress, on the fourteenth of July 1798, whereby it was enacted, that "if any person shall

write, print, utter or publish any false and malicious writing against the government of the United States, or either house of congress, or the president, with intent to defame them, or either of them, or to bring them or either of them into contempt, or disrepute; or to excite against them or either of them, the hatred of the good people of the United States, then such person, being thereof convicted before any court of the United States having jurisdiction thereof shall be punished by a fine not exceeding two thousand dollars, and by imprisonment not exceeding two years." The act was limited in its duration to the third day of March, 1801, the very day on which the period for which the then president was elected, was to expire; and, previous to which the event of the next presidential election must be known.

The consequences of this act, as might have been fourseen, were a general astonishment, and dissatisfaction, among all those who considered the government of the United States, as a limited system of government; in its nature altogether federal, and essentially different from all others which might lay claim to unlimited powers; or even to national, instead of federal authority. The constitutionality of the act was accordingly very generally denied, or questioned, by them. They alleged, that it is to the freedom of the press, and of speech, that the American nation is indebted for its liberty, its happiness, its enlightened state, nay more, for its existence. That in these states the people are the only sovereign: that the government established by themselves, is for their benefit; that those who administer the government, whether it be that of the state, or of the federal union, are the agents and servants of the people, not their rulers or tyrants. . . . That these agents must be, and are, from the nature and principles of our governments, responsible to the people, for their conduct. That to enforce this responsibility, it is indispensibly necessary that the people should inquire into the conduct of their agents; that in this inquiry, they must, or ought to scrutinize their motives, sift their intentions, and penetrate their designs; and that it was therefore, an unimpeachable right in them to censure as well as to applaud; to condemn or to acquit; and to reject, or to employ them again, as the most severe scrutiny might advise. That as no man can be forced into the service of the people against his own will and consent; so if any man employed by them in any office, should find the tenure of it too severe, because responsibility is inseparably annexed to it, he might retire: if he can not bear scrutiny, he might resign: if his motives, or designs, will not bear sifting; or if censure be too galling to his feelings, he might avoid it in the shades of domestic privacy. That if flattery be the only music to his ear, or the only balm to his heart; if he sickened when it is withheld, or turned pale when denied him; or if power, like the dagger of Macbeth, should invite his willing imagination to grasp it, the indignation of the people ought immediately to mark him, and hurl him from their councils, and their confidence forever. That if this absolute freedom of inquiry may be, in any manner, abridged, or impaired by those who administer the government, the nature of it will be instantly changed from a federal union of representative democracies, in which the people of the several states are the sovereign, and the administrators of the government their agents, to a consolidated oligarchy, aristocracy, or monarchy, according to the prevailing caprice of the constituted authorities, or of those who may usurp them. That where absolute freedom of discussion is prohibited, or restrained, responsibility vanishes. That any attempt to prohibit, or restrain that freedom, may well be construed to proceed from conscious guilt. That the people of America have always manifested a most jealous sensibility, on the subject of this inestimable right, and have ever regarded it as a fundamental principle in their government, and carefully engrafted in the constitution. That this sentiment was generated in the American mind, by an abhorrence of the maxims and principles of that government which they had shaken off, and a detestation of the abominable persecutions, and extrajudicial dogmas, of the still odious court of star-chamber; whose tyrannical proceedings and persecutions, among other motives of the like nature, prompted and impelled our ancestors to fly from the pestilential government of their native country, to seek an assylum here; where they might enjoy, and their posterity establish, and transmit to all future generations, freedom, unshackled, unlimited, undefined. That in our time we have vindicated, fought for, and established that freedom by our arms, and made it the solid, and immovable basis and foundation both of the state, and federal government. That nothing could more clearly evince the inestimable value that the American people have set upon the liberty of the press, than their uniting it in the same sentence, and even in the same member of a sentence, with the rights of conscience, and the freedom of speech. And since congress are equally prohibited from making any law abridging the freedom of speech, or of the press, they boldly challenged their adversaries to point out the constitutional distinction, between those two modes of discussion, or inquiry. If the unrestrained freedom of the press, said they, be not guaranteed, by the constitution, neither is that of speech. If on the contrary the unrestrained freedom of speech is guaranteed, so also, is that of the press. If then the genius of our federal constitution has vested the people of the United States, not only with a censorial power, but even with the sovereignty itself; if magistrates are, indeed, their agents: if they are responsible for their acts of agency; if the people may not only censure whom they disapprove, but reject whom they may find unworthy; if approbation or censure, election or rejection, ought to be the result of inquiry, scrutiny, and mature deliberation; why, said they, is the exercise of this censorial power, this sovereign right, this necessary inquiry, and scrutiny to be confined to the freedom of speech? Is it because this mode of discussion better answers the purposes of the censorial power? Surely not. The best speech can not be heard, by any great number of persons. The best speech may be misunderstood, misrepresented, and imperfectly remembered by those who are present. To all the rest of mankind, it is, as if it had never been. The best speech must also be short for the investigation of any subject of an intricate nature, or even a plain one, if it be of more than ordinary length. The best speech then must be altogether inadequate to the due exercise of the censorial power, by the people. The only adequate supplementary aid for these defects, is the absolute freedom of the press. A freedom unlimited as the human mind; viewing all things, penetrating the recesses of the human heart, unfolding the motives of human actions, and estimating all things by one invaluable standard, truth; applauding those who deserve well; censuring the undeserving; and condemning the unworthy, according to the measure of their demerits.

In vindication of the act, the promoters and supporters of it, said,[3] that a law to punish false, scandalous, and malicious writings against the government, with intent to stir up sedition, is a law necessary for carrying into effect the power vested by the constitution in the government of the United States, and consequently such a law as congress may pass. To which it was answered, that even were the premises true, it would not authorize congress to pass an act to punish writings calculated to bring congress, or the president into contempt or disrepute. Inasmuch as such contempt or disrepute may be entertained for them, or either of them, without incurring the guilt of sedition, against the government, and without the most remote design of opposing, or resisting any law, or any act of the president done in pursuance of any law: one or the other of which would seem necessary to constitute the offence, which this argument defends the right of congress to punish, or prevent.

It was further urged in vindication of the act, that the liberty of the press consists not in a licence for every man to publish what he pleases, without being liable to punishment for any abuse of that licence; but in a permission to publish without previous restraint; and, therefore, that a law to restrain the licentiousness of the press, cannot be considered as an abridgment of its liberty.

To which it was answered that this exposition of the liberty of the press, was only to be found in the theoretical writings of the commentators on the *English* government, where the liberty of the press rests upon no other ground, than that there is now no law which imposes any actual previous restraint upon the press, as was formerly the case: which is very different from the footing upon which it stands in the United States, where it is made a fundamental article of the constitutions, both of the federal and state governments, that no such restraint shall be imposed by the authority of either. . . . That if the sense of the state governments be wanting on the occasion, nothing can be more explicit than the meaning and intention of the state of Virginia, at the moment of adopting the constitution of the United States; by which it will clearly appear that it

---

3. See the report of a committee of congress, respecting the alien and sedition laws, Feb. 25, 1799.

never was the intention of that state (and probably of no other in the union) to permit congress to distinguish between the liberty and licentiousness of the press; or, in any manner to "cancel, abridge, restrain, or modify" that inestimable right.

Thirdly it was alleged, that the act could not be unconstitutional because it made nothing penal, which was not penal before, being merely declaratory of the common law, viz. of England.

To this it was, among other arguments, answered. That the United States as a federal government have no common law. That although the common law of England, is, under different modifications, admitted to be the common law of the states respectively, yet the whole of the common law of England has been no where introduced: that there is a great and essential difference, in this respect, in the several states, not only in the subjects to which it is applied, but in the extent of its application. That the common law of one state, therefore, is not the common law of another. That the constitution of the United States has neither created it, nor conferred it upon the federal government. And, therefore, that government has no power or authority to assume the right of punishing any action, merely because it is punishable in England, or may be punishable in any, or all the states, by the common law.

The essential difference between the British government and the American constitutions was moreover insisted on, as placing this subject in the clearest light. In the former, the danger of encroachments on the rights of the people, was understood to be confined to the executive magistrate. The representatives of the people in the legislature are not only exempt themselves, from distrust, but are considered as sufficient guardians of the rights of their constituents against the danger from the executive. Hence it is a principle, that the parliament is unlimited in its power, or, in their own language, is omnipotent. Hence too, all the ramparts for protecting the rights of the people, such as their *magna charta*, their bill of rights, &c. are not reared against the parliament, but against the royal prerogative. They are mere legislative precautions against executive usurpations. Under such a government as that, an exemption of the press from previous restraints, by licencers from the king, is all the freedom that can be secured to it, there: but, that in the United States the case is altogether different. The people, not the government, possess the absolute sovereignty. The legislature, no less than the executive, is under limitations of power. Encroachments are regarded as possible from the one, as well as from the other. Hence in the United States, the great and essential rights of the people, are secured against legislative, as well as against executive ambition. They are secured, not by laws paramount to prerogative; but by constitutions paramount to laws. This security of the freedom of the press requires, that it should be exempt, not only from previous restraint by the executive, as in Great-Britain; but from legislative restraint also; and this exemption, to be effectual, must be an exemption, not only from the previous inspection of licencers, but from the subsequent penalty of laws. . . . A further difference between the two governments was also insisted on. In Great-Britain, it is a maxim, that the king, an hereditary, not a responsible magistrate, can do no wrong; and that the legislature, which in two thirds of its composition, is also hereditary, not responsible, can do what it pleases. In the United States, the executive magistrates are not held to be infallible, nor the legislatures to be omnipotent; and both being elective, are both responsible. That the latter may well be supposed to require a greater degree of freedom of animadversion than might be tolerated by the genius of the former. That even in England, notwithstanding the general doctrine of the common law, the ministry, who are responsible to impeachment, are at all times animadverted on, by the press, with peculiar freedom. That the practice in America must be entitled to much more respect: being in most instances founded upon the express declarations contained in the respective constitutions, or bill of rights of the confederated states.⁴ That even in those states where no such guarantee

4. See the Virginia bill of rights, Art. 12. Massachusetts, Art. 16. Pennsylvania, Art. 12. Delaware, Art. 23. Maryland, Art. 38. North-Carolina, Art. 15. South-Carolina, Art. 43. Georgia, Art. 61. The constitution of Pennsylvania, Art. 35, declares, "That the printing presses shall be free to every person who undertakes to examine the proceedings of the legislature or any part of the government." And the bill of rights of Vermont, Art. 15, is to the same effect.

could be found, the press had always exerted a freedom in canvassing the merits, and measures of public men of every description, not confined to the limits of the common law. That on this footing the press has stood even in those states, at least, from the period of the revolution.

The advocates and supporters of the act alleged, fourthly; That had the constitution intended to prohibit congress from legislating at all, on the subject of the press, it would have used the same expressions as in that part of the clause, which relates to religion, and religious tests; whereas, said they, there is a manifest difference; it being evident that the constitution intended to prohibit congress from legislating at all, on the subject of religious establishments, and the prohibition is made in the most express terms. Had the same intention prevailed respecting the press, the same expression would have been used, viz. "Congress shall make no law respecting the press." They are not, however, prohibited, added they, from legislating at all, on the subject, but merely from abridging the liberty of the press. It is evident, therefore, said they, that congress may legislate respecting the press: may pass laws for its regulation, and to punish those who pervert it into an engine of mischief, provided those laws do not abridge its liberty. A law to impose previous restraints upon the press, and not one to inflict punishment on wicked and malicious publications, would be a law to abridge the liberty of the press.

To this it was answered, that laws to regulate, must, according to the true interpretation of that word, impose rules, or regulations, not before imposed; that to impose rules is to restrain; that to restrain must necessarily imply an abridgment of some former existing rights, or power: consequently, when the constitution prohibits congress from making any law abridging the freedom of speech, or of the press, it forbids them to make any law respecting either of these subjects. That this conclusion was an inevitable consequence of the injunction contained in the amendment, unless it could be shown, that the existing restraints upon the freedom of the press in the United States, were such as to require a remedy, by a law regulating (but not abridging) the manner in which it might be exercised with greater freedom and security. A supposition, which it was believed no person would maintain. That the necessary consequence of these things is, that the amendment was meant as a positive denial to congress, of any power whatever, on the subject.

As an evidence on this subject, which must be deemed absolutely conclusive, it was observed, That the proposition of amendments made by congress, is introduced in the following terms. "The conventions of a number of states, having, at the time of their adopting the constitution, expressed a desire, in order to prevent misconstruction, or abuse of its powers, that further declaratory and restrictive clauses should be added; and, as extending the ground of public confidence in the government, will best ensure the beneficent ends of its institution": which affords the most satisfactory and authentic proof, that the several amendments proposed, were to be considered as either declaratory, or restrictive; and whether the one or the other, as corresponding with the desire expressed by a number of states, and as extending the ground of public confidence in the government. That under any other construction of the amendment relating to the press, than that it declared the press to be wholly exempt from the power of congress.... the amendment could neither be said to correspond with the desire expressed by a number of the states, nor be calculated to extend the ground of public confidence in the government. Nay more; that the construction employed to justify the "Sedition Act," would exhibit a phœnomenon without a parrallel in the political world. It would exhibit a number of respectable states, as denying first that any power over the press was delegated by the constitution; as proposing next, that an amendment to it should explicitly declare, that no such power was delegated; and finally as concurring in an amendment actually recognizing, or delegating such a power.

But, the part of the constitution which seems to have been most recurred to, and even relied on, in defence of the act of congress, is the last clause of the eighth section of the first article, empowering congress "to make all laws which shall be necessary and proper for carrying into execution the foregoing powers, and all other powers vested by the constitution in the government of the United States, or in any department or officer thereof."[5]

To this it was answered, that the plain import of that clause is, that congress shall have all the incidental, or instrumental powers, necessary and proper for carrying into execution all the express powers; whether they be vested in the government of the United States, more collectively, or in the several departments, or officers thereof. That it is not a grant of new powers to congress, but merely a declaration, for the removal of all uncertainty, that the means of carrying into execution, those otherwise granted, are included in the grant. Whenever, therefore, a question arises concerning the constitutionality of a particular power, the first question is, whether the power be expressed in the constitution. If it be, the question is decided. If it be not expressed, the next inquiry must be, whether it is properly incidental to an express power, and necessary to its execution. If it be, it may be exercised by congress. If it be not, congress cannot exercise it.... That, if the sedition law be brought to this kind of test, it is not even pretended by the framers of that act, that the power over the press, which is exercised thereby, can be found among the powers expressly vested in congress. That if it be asked, whether there is any express power, for executing which, that act is a necessary and a proper power: the answer is, that the express power which has been selected, as least remote from that exercised by the act, is the power of "suppressing insurrections"; which is said to imply a power to prevent insurrections, by punishing whatever may lead, or tend to them. But it surely cannot, with the least plausibility, be said, that a regulation of the press, and the punishment of libels, are exercises of a power to suppress insurrections. That if it be asked, whether the federal government has no power to prevent, as well as punish, resistance to the laws; the proper answer is, that they have the power, which the constitution deemed most proper in their

5. See the report of a committee of congress, Feb. 25, 1799; and the answer of the senate and house of representatives of Massachusetts, (Feb. 9th and 13th, 1799), to the communications from the state of Virginia, on the subject of the alien and sedition laws.

hands for the purpose. That congress has power, before it happens, to pass laws for punishing such resistance; and the executive and judiciary have a power to enforce those laws, whenever it does actually happen. That it must be recollected by many, and could be shewn to the satisfaction of all, that this construction of the terms "necessary and proper," is precisely the construction which prevailed during the discussions and ratifications of the constitution: and that it is a construction absolutely necessary to maintain their consistency with the peculiar character of the government, as possessed of particular and defined powers only; not of the general and indefinite powers vested in ordinary governments. That if this construction be rejected, it must be wholly immaterial, whether unlimited powers be exercised under the name of unlimited powers, or be exercised under the name of unlimited means of carrying into execution limited powers.

To those who asked, if the federal government be destitute of every authority for restraining the licentiousness of the press, and for shielding itself against the libellous attacks which may be made on those who administer it; the reply given was, that the constitution alone can answer the question: that no such power being expressly given; and such a power not being both necessary and proper to carry into execution any express power; but, above all, such a power being expressly forbidden by a declaratory amendment to the constitution, the answer must be, that the government is destitute of all such authority.[6]

This very imperfect sketch may be sufficient to afford the student some idea of the magnitude and importance of a question, which agitated every part of the United States, almost to a degree of convulsion: the controversy not being confined to the closets of speculative politicians, or to the ordinary channels of discussion through the medium of

6. In the preceding sketch of the arguments used to demonstrate the unconstitutionality of the act of congress, I have extracted a few of those contained in the report of the committee of the house of delegates of Virginia, agreed to by the house, Jan. 11, 1800, and afterwards concurred in by the senate. This most valuable document is very long, and is incapable of being abridged, without manifest injury.

the press; but engrossing the attention, and calling forth the talents and exertions of the legislatures of several of the states in the union, on the one hand, and of the federal government, and all its branches, legislative, executive, and judiciary, on the other. For no sooner had the act passed, than prosecutions were commenced against individuals in several of the states: they were conducted, in some cases, with a rigour, which seemed to betray a determination to convert into a scourge that, which it had been pretended was meant only to serve as a shield.

The state of Kentucky was the first which took the act under consideration, and by a resolution passed with two dissenting voices only, declared the act of congress not law, but altogether void, and of no force. The state of Virginia, though posterior to her younger sister in point of time, was not behind her in energy. The general assembly at their first session after the passage of the act, did "explicitly and peremptorily declare, that it views the powers of the federal government, as resulting from the compact, to which the states are parties; as limited by the plain sense and intention of the instrument constituting that compact; as no further valid than they are authorized by the grants contained in that compact; and that in case of a deliberate, palpable, and dangerous exercise of other powers, not granted by the said compact, the states who are parties thereto have the right, and are in duty bound, to interpose for arresting the progress of the evil, and for maintaining within their respective limits the authorities, rights, and liberties appertaining to them.".... "That a spirit hath, in sundry instances, been manifested by the federal government, to enlarge its powers, by forced constructions of the constitutional charter which defines them; and to expound certain general phrases (copied from the very limited grant of powers in the former articles of confederation, and therefore less liable to be misconstrued) so as to destroy the meaning and effect of the particular enumeration, which necessarily explains and limits the general phrases; so as to consolidate the states, by degrees, into one sovereignty." That the "general assembly doth, particularly protest against the palpable and alarming infractions of the constitution, in the two cases of the alien and sedition acts, passed at the last session of congress; the first of which exercises a power no where delegated to the federal government; and the other exercises, in like manner, a power not delegated by the constitution; but, on the contrary, expressly and positively forbidden by one of the amendments thereto; a power which, more than any other, ought to produce universal alarm; because it is levelled against that right of freely examining public characters and measures, and of free communication among the people thereon, which has ever been justly deemed the only effectual guardian of every other right.

"That this state having by its convention, which ratified the federal constitution, expressly declared, that among other essential rights, 'the liberty of conscience, and of the press cannot be cancelled, abridged, restrained, or modified, by any authority of the United States,' and from its extreme anxiety to guard these rights from every possible attack of sophistry, or ambition, having, with other states, recommended an amendment for that purpose, which amendment was, in due time, annexed to the constitution; it would mark a reproachful inconsistency and criminal degeneracy, if an indifference were now shewn, to the most palpable violation of the rights, thus declared and secured; and to the establishment of a precedent, which may be fatal to the other.

"That feeling the most sincere affection for their sister states; the truest anxiety for establishing and perpetuating the union; and the most scrupulous fidelity to the constitution which is the pledge of mutual friendship; and solemnly appealing 'to the like dispositions of the other states, in confidence that they will concur with this commonwealth in declaring, (as it does hereby declare,) that the acts aforesaid are unconstitutional; and that the necessary and proper measures will be taken by each, for co-operating with this state, in maintaining the authorities, rights and liberties, reserved to the states respectively, or to the people.'"[7]

Answers were received from the legislatures of seven states, disap-

---

7. *Editor's note:* The reports quoted here by Tucker were, of course, written by James Madison.

proving of the resolutions of Virginia and Kentucky, which had also been transmitted with a similar proposition. The general assembly of Massachusetts, alone, condescended to reason with her sister states; the others scarcely paid them the common respect that is held to be due from individuals, to each other. The assembly of Virginia at their next session, entered into a critical review and examination of their former resolutions, and supported them by a train of arguments, and of powerful, convincing, and unsophistic reasoning, to which, probably, the equal cannot be produced in any public document, in any country. They concluded this examination and review (which occupied more than eighty pages) with resolving, "That having carefully and respectfully attended to the proceedings of a number of the states, in answer to their former resolutions, and having accurately and fully re-examined and re-considered the latter, they found it to be their indispensible duty to adhere to the same, as founded in truth, as consonant with the constitution, and as conducive to its preservation; and more especially to be their duty, to renew, as they do hereby renew their protest against the alien and sedition acts, as palpable and alarming infractions of the constitution."

Mean time, petitions had been presented to congress for the repeal of those obnoxious acts: on the 25th of February 1799, congress agreed to the report of a committee advising them, that it would be inexpedient to repeal them. A majority of four members, only, prevailed on this occasion. During the session which succeeded, strenuous exertions were made for the continuance of the act commonly called the sedition act, (the other concerning aliens, having expired): After a severe struggle, the attempt failed, and the act was permitted to expire, at the same moment that put a period to the political importance of those, for whose benefit, alone, it seems to have been intended.

We may now, I trust, say with our former envoys to the republic of France: "The genius of the constitution can not be overruled by those who administer the government. Among those principles deemed sacred in America; among those sacred rights, considered as forming the bulwark of their liberty, which the government should contemplate with awful reverence, and approach only with the most cautious circumspection, there is none of which the importance is more deeply impressed on the public mind, than the liberty of the press."[8]

It may be asked, perhaps: is there no remedy in the United States for injuries done to the good fame and reputation of a man; injuries, which to a man of sensibility, and of conscious integrity, are the most grievous that can be inflicted; injuries, which when offered through the medium of the press, may be diffused throughout the globe, and transmitted to latest posterity; may render him odious, and detestable in the eyes of the world, his country, his neighbours, his friends, and even his own family; may seclude him from society as a monster of depravity, and iniquity; and even may deprive him of sustenance, by destroying all confidence in him, and discouraging that commerce, or intercourse with him, which may be necessary to obtain the means?

Heaven forbid, that in a country which boasts of rational freedom, and of affording perfect security to the citizen for the complete enjoyment of all his rights, the most valuable of all should be exposed without remedy, or redress, to the vile arts of detraction and slander! Every individual, certainly, has a right to speak, or publish, his sentiments on the measures of government: to do this without restraint, control, or fear of punishment for so doing, is that which constitutes the genuine freedom of the press. The danger justly apprehended by those states which insisted that the federal government should possess no power, directly or indirectly, over the subject, was, that those who were entrusted with the administration might be forward in considering every thing as a crime against the government, which might operate to their own personal disadvantage; it was therefore made a fundamental article of the federal compact, that no such power should be exercised, or claimed by the federal government; leaving it to the state governments to exercise such jurisdiction and control over the subject, as their several constitutions and laws permit. In contending therefore for the absolute freedom of the press, and its total exemption from all restraint, control, or jurisdiction

---

8. See the letters from Messrs Marshall, Pinckney, and Gerry, to Mons. Talleyrand, minister of foreign affairs in France, 1798.

of the federal government, the writer of these sheets most explicitly dis-
avows the most distant approbation of its licentiousness. A free press,
conducted with ability, firmness, decorum, and impartiality, may be regarded as the chaste nurse of genuine liberty; but a press stained with
falsehood, imposture, detraction, and personal slander, resembles a contaminated prostitute, whose touch is pollution, and whose offspring
bears the foul marks of the parent's ignominy.

Whoever makes use of the press as the vehicle of his sentiments on
any subject, ought to do it in such language as to shew he has a deference
for the sentiments of others; that while he asserts the right of expressing
and vindicating his own judgment, he acknowledges the obligation to
submit to the judgment of those whose authority he cannot legally, or
constitutionally dispute. In his statement of facts he is bound to adhere
strictly to the truth; for any deviation from the truth is both an imposition upon the public, and an injury to the individual whom it may
respect. In his restrictures on the conduct of men, in public stations, he
is bound to do justice to their characters, and not to criminate them
without substantial reason. The right of character is a sacred and invaluable right, and is not forfeited by accepting a public employment. Whoever knowingly departs from any of these maxims is guilty of a crime
against the community, as well as against the person injured; and though
both the letter and the spirit of our federal constitution wisely prohibit
the congress of the United States from making any law, by which the freedom of speech, or of the press, may be exposed to restraint or persecution under the authority of the federal government, yet for injuries done
the reputation of any person, as *an individual,* the state-courts are always
open, and may afford ample, and competent redress, as the records of
the courts of this commonwealth abundantly testify.

WORK USED BY TUCKER

Richard Price, *Observations on the Importance of the American Revolution, and
the Means of Making It a Benefit to the World.*

⟨⟨ Of the Cognizance of Crimes and Misdemeanours

> In this brief treatise on jurisdiction in a federal system, Tucker
> draws together the legal applications of some of his major
> themes: the limitation of the federal government, including its
> courts, to its specific delegated powers; and the inapplicability
> of the common law to such a system. This is Appendix A in the
> fifth volume of Tucker's *Blackstone.*

THE COMPLICATED system of government in the United States, imposes upon us the necessity of a frequent recurrence to fundamental
principles, in order to ascertain to what department of it any particular
subject appertains. In no respect is this recurrence more necessary, than
in the examination of the nature of crimes and misdemeanours; the cognizance of which, by the *federal* courts, will depend altogether upon the
nature and tenor of that instrument, upon which the jurisdiction is
founded: in the exposition of which, we have been repeatedly obliged to
recur to the nature of the compact, for a due exposition of the text. If
for example, the constitution of the United States had been intended for
the establishment of a consolidated national government, instead of a
federal republic, the same strict interpretation, which is at present necessary, in order to preserve to the states, respectively, whatever rights they
had no design to part with, might perhaps, in many instances have been
dispensed with.

It has been well observed by one of the judges of the supreme court of
the United States, that "in this country every man sustains a twofold
political capacity: one in relation to the *state,* and another in relation to
the *United States.* In relation to the state, he is subject to various municipal regulations, founded upon the state constitution and policy, which
do *not* affect him in his relation to the *United States:* For the constitution

of the union is the source of all the jurisdiction of the national government; so that the departments of *that* government, can never assume any power, that is not expressly granted by that instrument, nor exercise a power, in any other manner than is there prescribed."[1] This is, indeed, a short, clear, and comprehensive exposition of the principles of a limited government, founded upon compact between sovereign and independent states.

For it cannot, I presume, be denied, or even doubted, that the constitution of the United States, is the instrument by which the federal government was *created;* its powers defined; their extent limited; the duties of the public functionaries prescribed; and the principles according to which the government is to be administered, delineated;

That the federal government of the United States, is that *portion,* only, of the sovereign power, which, in the opinion of the people of the several states, could be more advantageously administered in common, than by the states respectively;

That the several states at the time of adopting that constitution, being free, sovereign, and independent states, and possessing all the rights, powers, and jurisdictions, incident to civil government, according to their several constitutions; and having expressly stipulated, that the powers not delegated to the United States by the constitution, nor prohibited by it, to the states, are reserved to the states respectively, or to the people; every power which has been carved out of the sovereignty of the states, respectively, must be construed strictly, wherever it may derogate from any power which they possessed antecedently;

And, on the other hand, that all the powers granted to the *federal* government, are either expressly enumerated, and positive; or must be both necessary, and proper to the execution of some enumerated power, which is expressly granted.

If these be the genuine principles of the federal constitution, as, I apprehend they are, then it seems impossible to refuse our full assent to

---

1. *Editor's note:* Here and later on, Tucker quotes from the decision of Justice Samuel Chase in the case of *U.S. vs. Worral.*

the learned judge's observations on the subject. Adopting them therefore as our guide, let us proceed in our enquiry.

A crime or misdemeanour, as defined by judge Blackstone, "is an act committed, or omitted in violation of a PUBLIC LAW, either forbidding, or commanding it": from whence it follows, that the cognizance and punishment of all crimes and misdemeanours, belongs exclusively to that body politic, or state to which the right to enact such a public law belongs.

The cognizance of all crimes and misdemeanours committed within the body of any state, therefore, belongs exclusively to the jurisdiction of that state; unless it hath by compact or treaty surrendered its jurisdiction in any particular cases to some other power. And in like manner the cognizance of all crimes and misdemeanours committed on the high seas (where all nations have a common jurisdiction) by citizens of the same state against each other; or, by common pirates, or robbers, against the citizens of any state, belongs to that particular state to whose citizens the injury is offered. And consequently the American states respectively, as soon as they became sovereign, and independent states, were entitled to exclusive jurisdiction in the case of all crimes and misdemeanours, whatsoever, committed within the body of such states, respectively, or upon the high seas, in every case where any other state or nation might claim jurisdiction under similar circumstances.

By the articles of confederation concluded between the states some years after; each state, expressly, "retained its sovereignty, freedom, and independence, and every power, *jurisdiction*, and right, which was not, by that confederation, expressly delegated to the United States in Congress assembled." The ninth article ceded to congress, the sole and exclusive right of making *rules* for the government, and regulation of the land and naval forces of the United States; and of appointing courts for the trial of *piracies* and *felonies committed on the high seas:* so that the states *retained* the exclusive cognizance of all *civil* crimes and misdemeanours, whatsoever, except in the cases therein mentioned. And this exclusive jurisdiction they continued to retain until the adoption of the present constitution.

By the third article of that instrument it is declared, "that the judicial power of the United States, shall extend to all cases arising under the constitution, the laws of the United States, and treaties made, or which shall be made under their authority." The same article defines the offence of treason against the United States, but leaves to Congress the power to declare the punishment, thereof, under certain limitations. Treason against the *United States,* is, therefore, one of those crimes, to which the jurisdiction of the federal courts extends.

The eighth section of the first article, among other things, declares, that congress shall have power to *provide* for the *punishment* of counterfeiting the securities and current coin of the United States; to define and punish piracies, and felonies committed on the high seas, and offences against the law of nations; to exercise exclusive jurisdiction within certain specified limits; and to make all laws, which shall be *necessary* and *proper* for carrying into execution the foregoing powers, and all other powers vested by the constitution in the government of the United States, or in any department or officer thereof.

To apply then, the observations of the learned judge; since neither Congress, nor any other department of the *federal* government, can ever assume any power that is not expressly granted by the constitution, nor exercise it, in any other manner, than is there prescribed, it appears to be essential that congress should define all offences against the United States, except treason; and prescribe the punishment to be inflicted for that and every other offence against the United States, before the federal courts can proceed to try a criminal or to pronounce sentence upon him in case of conviction.

If this be doubted, let us suppose that any person had committed treason against the United States, before the passage of the act of Congress, declaring the punishment of that offence; could the federal courts, or any other, have proceeded to judgment against him for the same, or, if they could, what judgment could they have pronounced? Let us suppose again that congress having defined the offence of piracy, had omitted to declare the punishment; could the federal courts have supplied this omission by pronouncing such a sentence as they might suppose the crime deserved? Again, let us suppose that congress may have omitted altogether to define or to declare the punishment of any other offence committed upon the high seas; will it be contended that the federal courts could in any such case punish the offender, however atrocious his offence regarded in a moral light may appear? In none of these cases (as I apprehend) could the federal courts proceed to punish the delinquent, although in every one of them, the offence may be clearly acknowleged to arise under the constitution of the United States.

If in cases arising upon the high seas, (in all which the federal courts, under the federal constitution and laws, possess a jurisdiction, altogether exclusive of the state courts) it be necessary that an offence be first defined, and the punishment thereof declared by congress; how much more necessary is it, that offences committed within the body of any state should, in the same manner, be first defined, and the punishment thereof declared by a law of the United States, before the courts of the United States can undertake to inquire into or punish it? For the presumption is, that every offence, committed within the body of any state, is an offence against that state only; and, that the state courts have the sole and exclusive cognizance and punishment thereof, unless it be shewn, that the federal constitution, or some act of congress made in pursuance of it, have altogether divested the state courts of jurisdiction over the subject. For although we may readily admit, that besides the particular case of treason and those which the eighth section of the first article designates, there is a power granted to congress to *create* and to define and punish offences, whenever it may be *necessary* and *proper* to do so, in order to carry into execution, the specific powers granted to the federal government, still it appears indispensably necessary, that congress should first *create*, (that is, define and declare the punishment of,) every such offence, before it can have existence as such, against the United States.

It has been attempted, however, to supply the silence of the constitution and statutes of the union, by resorting to the common law for the definition and punishment of offences in such cases. To which, the same judge has given the following clear and emphatical answer. "In my opinion, the *United States* as a *federal government have no common law:* and consequently, no indictment can be maintained in their courts for offences merely at the common law. If indeed the United States can be supposed for a moment to have a common law, it must, I presume, be that of England; and *yet it is impossible to trace, when, or how, the system was adopted, or introduced.* With respect to the individual states, the difficulty does not occur. When the American colonies were first settled by our ancestors, it was held, as well by the settlers as by the judges and lawyers of England, that they brought hither, as a birth right and inheritence, so much of the common law as was applicable to their local situation, and change of circumstances. But each colony judged for itself, what parts of the common law were applicable to its new condition; and in various modes, by legislative acts, by judicial decisions, or by constant usage, adopted some parts and rejected others. Hence, he who shall travel through the different states will soon discover, that the *whole* of the *common law* has been *no where* introduced; that some states have rejected what others have adopted; and that there is, in short, a *great* and *essential diversity* in the *subjects* to which the *common law* is applied, as well as in the *extent* of its application. The common law, therefore, of one state, is not the common law of another; but the common law of England is the law of each state, *so far as each state has adopted it;* and the results from that position connected with the judicial act, that the common law will always apply to suits between citizen and citizen.

"But the question recurs, when and how, *the courts of the United States* acquired a *common law jurisdiction in* CRIMINAL *cases?* The United States must possess the law themselves, before they can communicate it to their judicial agents: now the *United States* did not bring it with them from England; *the constitution does not create it;* and no act of congress has *assumed it.* Besides, what is the common law to which we are referred? Is it the common law *entire,* as it exists in England; or *modified,* as it exists in some of the states; and, of the various modifications, which are we to select, the system of Georgia or New-Hampshire, of Pennsylvania or Connecticut?

"Upon the whole," he concludes, "it *may* be a defect in our political institutions, it may be an inconvenience in the administration of justice, that the common law authority relating to crimes and punishments, has not been conferred upon the government of the *United States,* which is a government, in other respects also, of a limitted jurisdiction: *but judges cannot remedy political imperfections, or, supply any legislative omission."*

Unfortunately, perhaps, for the United States, this opinion did not prevail, the court being divided in their judgments.... We are, therefore, not only without a precedent: but, what is infinitely more important, a principle, which might have been deemed clear, and well ascertained, is now, in some degree, rendered doubtful. Nevertheless, until a contrary division shall have subverted the apparently solid foundation of that which I have cited, I shall venture to recommend it to the student, as containing the most clear, correct, and convincing, illustration of the principles of the federal constitution.

From what has been said, we may venture to draw the following conclusions.

1. That the cognizance of every crime and misdemeanor, whatsoever, committed within the body of any state, belongs to the courts of that state, in which the offence is committed, *exclusively;* unless it can be shewn that a power over the subject hath been *expressly* granted to the United States, by the federal constitution.

2. That the federal courts possess no jurisdiction, whatsoever, over any crime or misdemeanor, which is an offence by the *common law, only,* and not declared to be such, by the constitution, or some statute of the United States.

3. That although a certain class of offences, may, by the constitution of the United States, be declared to be within the jurisdiction of the federal courts, yet those courts cannot proceed to take cognizance thereof, unless they be first defined, by the constitution; or by statute; nor to punish them, unless the punishment be likewise *prescribed* by a *statute* of the *United States.*

On the State of Slavery in Virginia

Tucker's plan for the gradual elimination of slavery in Virginia was first published as a pamphlet in 1796: *A Dissertation on Slavery: With a Proposal for the Gradual Abolition of It, in the State of Virginia* (Philadelphia: Matthew Carey). He incorporated the essay whole as an appendix to his edition of *Blackstone's Commentaries* a few years later.

Like many of the great Southerners of the early republic, Tucker considered Negro slavery an undesirable element of the American body politic, and hoped for its eventual elimination, though, like Jefferson, and later Lincoln, he felt that emancipation would best be followed by removal of the freed people from American society.

Tucker is writing in the light of very recent events—the horrendous uprising and massacre of whites in Santo Domingo—of which Americans were very aware. And he was writing before the appearance of an aggressive, evangelistic Northern abolition movement, so that the question was still open to discussion by Virginia gentlemen.

Perhaps the most important things about Tucker's essay for later times are the following: it shows the potential in the South for constructively addressing the most difficult issue in American society before the time when it became necessary to defend against outside control; and, it demonstrates that Tucker's state rights understanding of the Constitution is not merely a rationalization in defense of slavery, a misunderstanding that is a mainstay of conventional accounts of American history.

IN THE preceding Enquiry[1] into the absolute rights of the citizens of united America, we must not be understood as if those rights were equally and universally the privilege of all the inhabitants of the United States, or even of all those, who may challenge this land of freedom as their native country. Among the blessings which the Almighty hath showered down on these states, there is a large portion of the bitterest draught that ever flowed from the cup of affliction. Whilst America hath been the land of promise to Europeans, and their descendants, it hath been the vale of death to millions of the wretched sons of Africa. The genial light of liberty, which hath here shone with unrivalled lustre on the former, hath yielded no comfort to the latter, but to them hath proved a pillar of darkness, whilst it hath conducted the former to the most enviable state of human existence. Whilst we were offering up vows at the shrine of Liberty, and sacrificing hecatombs upon her altars; whilst we swore irreconcilable hostility to her enemies, and hurled defiance in their faces; whilst we adjured the God of Hosts to witness our resolution to live free, or die, and imprecated curses on their heads who refused to unite with us in establishing the empire of freedom; we were imposing upon our fellow men, who differ in complexion from us, a *slavery*, ten thousand times more cruel than the utmost extremity of those grievances and oppressions, of which we complained. Such are the inconsistencies of human nature; such the blindness of those who pluck not the beam out of their own eyes, whilst they can espy a moat, in the eyes of their brother; such that partial system of morality which confines rights and injuries, to particular complexions; such the effect of that self-love which justifies, or condemns, not according to principle, but to the agent. Had we turned our eyes inwardly when we supplicated the Father of Mercies to aid the injured and oppressed; when we invoked the Author of Righteousness to attest the purity of our motives, and the Justice of our cause;[2] and

1. The subject of a preceding Lecture, with which the present was immediately connected, was, An Enquiry into the Rights of Persons, as Citizens of the United States of America.

2. The American standard, at the commencement of those hostilities which terminated in the revolution, had these words upon it—AN APPEAL TO HEAVEN!

implored the God of battles to aid our exertions in its defence, should we not have stood more self convicted than the contrite publican! Should we not have left our gift upon the altar, that we might be first reconciled to our brethren whom we held in bondage? Should we not have loosed their chains, and broken their fetters? Or if the difficulties and dangers of such an experiment prohibited the attempt during the convulsions of a revolution, is it not our duty to embrace the first moment of constitutional health and vigor, to effectuate so desirable an object, and to remove from us a stigma, with which our enemies will never fail to upbraid us, nor our consciences to reproach us? To form a just estimate of this obligation, to demonstrate the incompatibility of a state of slavery with the principles of our government, and of that revolution upon which it is founded, and to elucidate the practicability of its total, though gradual, abolition, it will be proper to consider the nature of slavery, its properties, attendants, and consequences in general; its rise, progress, and present state not only in this commonwealth, but in such of our sister states as have either perfected, or commenced the great work of its extirpation; with the means they have adopted to effect it, and those which the circumstances and situation of our country may render it most expedient for us to pursue, for the attainment of the same noble and important end.[3]

According to Justinian, the first general divisions of persons, in respect to their rights, is into freemen and slaves. It is equally the glory and the happiness of that country from which the citizens of the United States derive their origin, that the traces of slavery, such as at present exists in several of the United States, are there utterly extinguished. It is not my design to enter into a minute enquiry whether it ever had existence there, nor to compare the situation of villeins, during the existence of pure villenage, with that of modern domestic slaves. The records of those times, at least such as have reached this quarter of the globe, are too few

3. The Author here takes the liberty of making his acknowledgments to the reverend Jeremiah Belknap, D. D. of Boston, and to Zephaniah Swift, Esq. representative in congress from Connecticut, for their obliging communications; he hath occasionally made use of them in several parts of this Lecture, where he may have omitted referring to them.

to throw a satisfactory light on the subject. Suffice it that our ancestors migrating hither brought not with them any prototype of that slavery which hath been established among us. The first introduction of it into Virginia was by the arrival of a Dutch ship from the coast of Africa having *twenty* negroes on board, who were sold here in the year 1620. In the year 1638 we find them in Massachusetts. They were introduced into Connecticut soon after the settlement of that colony; that is to say, about the same period. Thus early had our forefathers sown the seeds of an evil, which, like a leprosy, hath descended upon their posterity with accumulated rancour, visiting the sins of the fathers upon succeeding generations.—The climate of the northern states less favourable to the constitution of the natives of Africa than the southern, proved alike unfavourable to their propagation, and to the increase of their numbers by importants. As the southern colonies advanced in population, not only importations increased there, but Nature herself, under a climate more congenial to the African constitution, assisted in multiplying the blacks in those parts, no less than in diminishing their numbers in the more rigorous climates to the north; this influence of climate, more over, contributed extremely to increase or diminish the value of the slave to the purchasers, in the different colonies. White labourers, whose constitutions were better adapted to the severe winters of the New England colonies, were there found to be preferable to the negroes,[4] who, accustomed to the influence of an ardent sun, became almost torpid in those countries, not less adapted to give vigour to their laborious exercises, than unfavorable to the multiplication of their species; in those colonies where the winters were not only milder, and of shorter duration, but succeeded by an intense summer heat, as invigorating to the African, as debilitating to the European constitution, the negroes were not barely more capable of performing labour than the Europeans or their descendants, but the multiplication of the species was at least equal; and, where they met with humane treatment, perhaps greater than among the whites. The purchaser therefore calculated not upon the value of the

4. Dr. Belknap. Zephan. Swift.

labour of his slave only, but, if a female, he regarded her as "the fruitful mother of an hundred more": and many of these unfortunate people have there been in this state, whose descendants even in the compass of two or three generations have gone near to realize the calculation.—The great increase of slavery in the southern, in proportion to the northern states in the union, is therefore not attributable, *solely,* to the effect of sentiment, but to natural causes; as well as those considerations of profit, which have, perhaps, an equal influence over the conduct of mankind in general, in whatever country, or under whatever climate their destiny hath placed them. What else but considerations of this nature could have influenced the merchants of the freest nation, at that time in the world, to embark in so nefarious a traffic, as that of the human race, attended, as the African slave trade has been, with the most atrocious aggravations of cruelty, perfidy, and intrigues, the objects of which have been the perpetual fomentation of predatory and intestine wars? What, but similar considerations, could prevail on the government of the same country, even in these days, to patronize a commerce so diametrically opposite to the generally received maxims of that government. It is to the operation of these considerations in the parent country, not less than to their influence in the colonies, that the rise, increase, and continuance of slavery in those British colonies which now constitute united America, are to be attributed, as I shall endeavour to shew in the course of the present enquiry. It is now time to enquire into the nature of slavery, in general, and take a view of its consequences, and attendants in this commonwealth, in particular.

Slavery, says a well informed writer on the subject,[5] has been attended with circumstances so various in different countries, as to render it difficult to give a general definition of it. Justinian calls it a constitution of the law of nations, by which one man is made subject to another, contrary to nature. Grotius describes it to be an obligation to serve another for life, in consideration of diet, and other common necessaries. Dr. Rutherforth,

5. Hargrave's case of negroe Somerset.

rejecting this definition, informs us, that perfect slavery is an obligation to be directed by another in all one's actions. § Baron Montesquieu defines it to be the establishment of a right, which gives one man such a power over another, as renders him absolute master over his life and fortune. These definitions appear not to embrace the subject fully, since they respect the condition of the slave, in regard to his *master* only, and not in regard to the *state*, as well as the *master*. The author last mentioned observes, that the constitution of a state may be free, and the subject not so. The subject free, and not the constitution of the state. Pursuing this idea, instead of attempting a general definition of slavery; I shall, by considering it under a threefold aspect, endeavour to give a just idea of its nature.

I. When a nation is, from any external cause, deprived of the right of being governed by its own laws, only, such a nation may be considered as in a state of *political slavery*. Such is the state of conquered countries, and generally, of colonies, and other dependent governments. Such was the state of united America before the revolution. In this case, the personal rights of the subject may be so far secured by wholesome laws, as that the individual may be esteemed free, whilst the state is subject to a higher power: this subjection of one nation or people, to the will of another, constitutes the first species of slavery, which, in order to distinguish it from the other two, I have called political; inasmuch as it exists only in respect to the governments, and not to the individuals of the two countries. Of this, it is not our business to speak, at present.

II. Civil liberty being no other than natural liberty, so far restrained by human laws, and no farther, as is necessary and expedient for the general advantage of the public, whenever that liberty is, by the laws of the state, further restrained than is necessary and expedient for the general advantage, a state of *civil slavery* commences immediately: this may affect the whole society, and every description of persons in it, and yet the constitution of the state be perfectly free. And this happens whenever the laws of a state respect the form, or energy of the government, more than the happiness of the citizen; as in Venice, where the most oppressive species of civil slavery exists, extending to every individual in the state, from the poorest gondolier to the members of the senate, and the doge himself.

This species of slavery also exists whenever there is an inequality of rights, or privileges, between the subjects or citizens of the same state, except such as necessarily result from the exercise of a public officer; for the pre-eminence of one class of men must be founded and erected upon the depression of another; and the measure of exaltation in the former, is that of the slavery of the latter. In all governments, however consti-tuted, or by what description soever denominated, wherever the distinc-tion of rank prevails, or is admitted by the constitution, this species of slavery exists. It existed in every nation, and in every government in Europe before the French revolution. It existed in the American colonies before they became independent states; and notwithstanding the maxims of equality which have been adopted in their several constitutions, it exists in most, if not all, of them, at this day, in the persons of our free negroes and mulattoes; whose civil incapacities are almost as numerous as the civil rights of our free citizens. A brief enumeration of them, may not be improper before we proceed to the third head.

Free negroes and mulattoes are, by our constitution, excluded from the right of suffrage,[6] and by consequence, I apprehend, from office too: they were formerly incapable of serving in the militia, except as drum-mers or pioneers, but now I presume they are enrolled in the lists of those that bear arms, though formerly punishable for presuming to appear at a muster-field. During the revolution war many of them were enlisted as soldiers in the regular army. Even slaves were not rejected from military service at that period, and such as served faithfully dur-ing the period of their enlistment, were emancipated by an act passed after the conclusion of the war. An act of justice to which they were enti-

6. The Constitution of Virginia, art 7. declares, that the right of suffrage shall remain as then exercised, the act of 1723, c. 4 (edit. 1733,) sect. 23, declared, that no negroe, mulat-toe, or Indian, shall have any vote at the election of burgesses, or any other election what-soever.—This act, it is presumed, was in force at the adoption of the constitution.—The act of 1785, also expressly excludes them from the right of suffrage.

tled upon every principle. All but house-keepers, and persons residing upon the frontiers are prohibited from keeping or carrying any gun, powder, shot, club, or other weapon offensive or defensive: Resistance to a white person, in any case, was, formerly, and now, in any case, except a wanton assault on the negroe or mulattoe, is punishable by whipping. No negroe or mulattoe can be a witness in any prosecution, or civil suit in which a white person is a party. Free negroes, together with slaves, were formerly denied the benefits of clergy in cases where it was allowed to white persons; but they are now upon an equal footing as to the allowance of clergy, though not as to the consequence of that allowance, inasmuch as the court may superadd other corporal punishments to the burning in the hand usually inflicted upon white persons, in the like cases. Emancipated negroes may be sold to pay the debts of their former master contracted before their emancipation; and they may be hired out to satisfy their taxes where no sufficient distress can be had. Their children are to be bound out apprentices by the overseer of the poor. Free negroes have all the advantages in capital cases, which white men are entitled to, except a trial by a jury of their own complexion: and a slave sueing for his freedom shall have the same privilege. Free negroes residing, or employed to labour in any town must be registered; the same thing is required of such as go at large in any county. The penalty in both cases is a fine upon the person employing, or harbouring them, and imprisonment of the negroe. The migration of free negroes or mulattoes to this state is also prohibited; and those who do migrate hither may be sent back to the place from whence they came. Any person, not being a negroe, having one-fourth or more negroe blood in him is deemed a mulattoe. The law makes no other distinction between negroes and mulattoes, whether slaves or freemen. These incapacities and disabilities are evidently the fruit of the third species of slavery, of which it remains to speak; or, rather, they are scions from the same common stock: which is,

III. That condition in which one man is subject to be directed by another in all his actions; and this constitutes a state of *domestic slavery;* to which state all the incapacities and disabilities of civil slavery are incident, with the weight of other numerous calamities superadded thereto. And here it may be proper to make a short enquiry into the origin and foundation of domestic slavery in other countries, previous to its fatal introduction into this.

Slaves, says Justinian, are either born such, or become so. They are born slaves when they are children of bond women; and they become slaves, either by the laws of nations, that is, by captivity; for it is the practice of our generals to sell their captives, being accustomed to preserve, and not to destroy them: or by the civil law, which happens when a free person, above the age of twenty, suffers himself to be sold for the sake of sharing the price given for him. The author of the Commentaries on the Laws of England thus combats the reasonableness of all these grounds:[7] "The conqueror," says he, "according to the civilians, had a right to the life of his captives; and having spared that, has a right to deal with him as he pleases. But it is an untrue position, when taken generally, that by the law of nature or nations, a man may kill his enemy: he has a right to kill him only in particular cases; in cases of absolute necessity for self-defence; and it is plain that this absolute necessity did not subsist, since the victor did not actually kill him, but made him prisoner. War itself, is justifiable only on principles of self-preservation; and therefore it gives no other right over prisoners but merely to disable them from doing harm to us, by confining their persons: much less can it give a right to kill, torture, abuse, plunder, or even to enslave an enemy, when the war is over. Since therefore the right of *making* slaves by captivity, depends on a supposed right of slaughter, that foundation failing, the consequence drawn from it must fail likewise. But, secondly, it is said slavery may begin *jure civili;* when one man sells himself to another. This, if only meant of contracts to serve, or work for another, is very just: but when applied to strict slavery, in the sense of the laws of old Rome or modern Barbary, is also impossible. Every sale implies a price, a *quid pro quo,* an equivalent given to the seller, in lieu of what he transfers to the buyer; but what equivalent can be given for life and liberty, both of which, in absolute

7. Blackstone.

slavery, are held to be in the master's disposal? His property, also, the very price he seems to receive, devolves, *ipso facto* to his master, the instant he becomes a slave. In this case, therefore, the buyer gives nothing, and the seller receives nothing: of what validity, then, can a sale be, which destroys the very principles upon which all sales are founded? Lastly we are told, that besides these two ways by which slaves are acquired, they may also be hereditary; '*servi nascuntur;*' the children of acquired slaves are, '*jure naturæ,*' by a negative kind of birthright, slaves also.—But *this, being built on the two former rights,* must *fall* together with them. If neither captivity, nor the sale of one's self, can by the law of nature and reason reduce the parent to slavery, *much less* can they reduce the offspring." Thus, by the most clear, manly, and convincing reasoning, does this excellent author refute every claim upon which the practice of slavery is founded, or by which it has been supposed to be justified, at least, in modern times.[8] But were we even to admit, that a captive taken in a *just war,* might by his conqueror be reduced to a state of slavery, this could not justify the claim of Europeans to reduce the natives of Africa to that state: it is a melancholy, though well-known fact, that in order to furnish supplies of these unhappy people for the purposes of the slave trade, the Europeans have constantly, by the most insidious (I had almost said infernal) arts, fomented a kind of perpetual warfare among the ignorant and miserable people of Africa; and instances have not been wanting, where, by the most shameful breach of faith, they have trepanned and made slaves of the *sellers* as well as the *sold.*[9] That such horrid practices have been sanctioned by a civilized nation; that a nation ardent in the cause of liberty, and enjoying its blessings in the fullest extent, can continue to vindicate a right established upon such a foundation; that a people who have declared, "That *all men* are by nature *equally*[10] *free* and *independent,*" and have made this declaration the first article in the foundation of their government, should, in defiance of so

8. These arguments are, in fact, borrowed from the Spirit of Laws.

9. The Law of Retribution by Granville Sharpe, Esq.; Historical Account of South Carolina and Georgia. Anonymous. London—printed in 1779.

10. Bill of Rights [of Virginia].

sacred a truth, recognized by themselves in so solemn a manner, and on so important an occasion, tolerate a practice incompatible therewith, is such an evidence of the weakness and inconsistency of human nature, as every man who hath a spark of patriotic fire in his bosom must wish to see removed from his own country. If ever there was a cause, if ever an occasion, in which all hearts should be united, every nerve strained, and every power exerted, surely the restoration of human nature to its inalienable right is such: Whatever obstacles, therefore, may hitherto have retarded the attempt, he that can appreciate the honour and happiness of his country, will think it time that we should attempt to surmount them.

But how loudly soever reason, justice, and (may I not add) religion, condemn the practice of slavery, it is acknowledged to have been very ancient, and almost universal. The Greeks, the Romans, and the ancient Germans also practiced it, as well as the more ancient Jews and Egyptians. By the Germans it was transmitted to the various kingdoms which arose in Europe out of the ruins of the Roman empire. In England, it subsisted for some ages under the name of *villeinage*. In Asia, it seems to have been general, and in Africa, universal, and so remains to this day. In Europe, it hath long since declined; its first declension there, is said to have been in Spain, so early as the eighth century; and it is alleged to have been general about the middle of the fourteenth, and was near expiring in the sixteenth, when the discovery of the American continent, and the eastern and western coasts of Africa gave rise to the introduction of a new species of slavery. It took its origin from the Portugese, who, in order to supply the Spaniards with persons able to sustain the fatigue of cultivating their new possessions in America, particularly the islands, opened a trade between Africa and America for the sale of negroes, about the year 1508. The expedient of having slaves for labour was not long peculiar to the Spaniards, being afterwards adopted by other European colonies: and though some attempts have been made to stop its progress in most of the United States, and several of them have the fairest prospects of success in attempting the extirpation of it, yet in others, it hath taken such deep root, as to require the most strenuous exertions to eradicate it.

The first introduction of negroes into Virginia happened, as we have already mentioned, in the year 1620; from that period to the year 1662, there is no compilation of our laws, in print, now to be met with. In the revision made in that year, we find an act declaring that no Englishman, trader, or other, who shall bring in any Indians as servants and assign them over to any other, shall sell them for *slaves,* nor for any other time than English of like age should serve by act of assembly. The succeeding session, all children born in this country were declared to be bond, or free, according to the condition of the mother. In 1667 it was declared, "That the conferring of baptism doth not alter the condition of the person baptized, as to his bondage or freedom." This was done, "that divers masters freed from this doubt may more carefully endeavour the propagating of Christianity, by permitting their slaves to be baptized." It would have been happy for this unfortunate race of men, if the same tender regard for their bodies had always manifested itself in our laws, as is shown for their souls in this act. But this was not the case; for two years after, we meet with an act, declaring, "That if any slave resist his master, or others, by his master's orders correcting him, and by the extremity of the correction should chance to die, such death should not be accounted felony: but the master or other person appointed by his master to punish him, be acquit from molestation: *since it could not be presumed that prepensive malice* which alone makes *murder, felony,* should induce any man to destroy his own estate."[11] This cruel and tyrannical act, was, at three different periods re-enacted, with very little alteration; and was not finally repealed till the year 1788—above a century after it had first disgraced our code. In 1668, we meet with the first traces of emancipation, in an act which subjects negroe women set free to the tax on titheables. Two years after, an act passed prohibiting *Indians* or negroes, manumitted, or otherwise set free, though baptized, from purchasing

---

11. Among the Israelites, according to the Mosaical law, "If a man smote his servant, or his maid, with a rod, and he died under his hand, he should surely be punished—notwithstanding if he continue a day or two, he should not be punished": for, saith the text, he is *his money.* Our legislators appear to have adopted the reason of the latter clause, without the humanity of the former part of the law. Exod., c. 21.

Christian servants. From this act it is evident that *Indians* had *before* that time been made slaves, as well as negroes, though we have no traces of the original act by which they were reduced to that condition. An act of the same session recites that disputes had arisen whether Indians taken in war by any other nation, and by that nation sold to the English, are servants for *life,* or for a term of years; and declaring that all *servants,* not being Christians, imported into this country by *shipping,* shall be *slaves* for their life-time; but that what shall come by land, shall serve, if boys and girls, until thirty years of age; if men and women, twelve years, and no longer. On a rupture with the Indians in the year 1679, it was, for the *better encouragement of soldiers,* declared that what *Indian* prisoners should be *taken in war* should be free purchase to the soldier *taking* them. Three years after, it was declared that all *servants* brought into this country, by sea or land, not being Christians, whether negroes, Moors, mulattoes or Indians, except Turks and Moors in amity with Great Britain, and all Indians which should thereafter be sold by neighbouring Indians, or any others trafficking with us, as slaves, should be slaves to all intents and purposes. This act was re-enacted in the year 1705, and afterwards in 1753, nearly in the same terms. In 1705 an act was made, authorizing a free and open trade for all persons, at all times, and at all places, with all Indians whatsoever. On the authority of this act, the general court, in April term 1787, decided that no Indians brought into Virginia since the passing thereof, nor their descendants, can be slaves in this commonwealth. In October 1778 the general assembly passed the first act which occurs in our code for prohibiting the importation of slaves; thereby declaring that no slave should thereafter be brought into this commonwealth, by land or by water; and that every slave imported contrary thereto, should upon such importation be free: with an exception as to such as might belong to persons migrating from the other states, or be claimed by descent, devise, or marriage, or be at that time the actual property of any citizen of this commonwealth, residing in any other of the United States, or belonging to travellers making a transient stay, and carrying their slaves away with them.—In 1785 this act unfortunately underwent some alteration, by declaring that slaves thereafter brought into this commonwealth, and kept therein one whole *year together,* or so long at different times as shall *amount to a year,* shall be free. By this means the difficulty of proving the right to freedom will not be a little augmented: for the fact of the first importation, where the right to freedom immediately ensued, might have been always proved without difficulty; but where a slave is subject to removal from place to place, and his right to freedom is postponed for so long a time as a whole year, or perhaps several years, the provisions in favour of liberty may be too easily evaded. The same act declares that no persons shall thenceforth be slaves in this commonwealth, except such as were so on the first day of that session (Oct. 17th, 1785), and the descendants of the females of them. This act was re-enacted in the revival made in 1792. In 1793, an additional act passed, authorizing and requiring any justice of the peace having notice of the importation of any slaves, directly or indirectly, from any part of Africa or the West Indies, to cause such slave to be immediately apprehended and transported out of the commonwealth. Such is the rise, progress, and present foundation of slavery in Virginia, so far as I have been able to trace it. The present number of slaves in Virginia, is immense, as appears by the census taken in 1791, amounting to no less than 292,427 souls: nearly two-fifths of the whole population of the commonwealth.[12] We may console ourselves with the hope that this proportion will not increase,—the further importation of slaves being prohibited, whilst the free migrations of white people hither is encouraged. But this hope affords no other relief from the evil of slavery, than a diminution of those apprehensions which are naturally excited by the detention of so large a number of oppressed individuals among us, and

---

12. *Editor's note:* Here Tucker included a note giving a detailed recapitulation of the distribution of slaves in Virginia. "Although it be true that the number of slaves in the *whole* state bears the proportion of 292,427, to 747,610, the whole number of souls in the state, that is, nearly as *two* to *five;* yet this proportion is by no means *uniform* throughout the state.... It is obvious from this statement that almost all the dangers and inconveniences which may be apprehended from a state of slavery on the one hand, or an attempt to abolish it, on the other, will be confined to the people eastward of the blue ridge of mountains."

the possibility that they may one day be roused to an attempt to shake off their chains.

Whatever inclination the first inhabitants of Virginia might have to encourage slavery, a disposition to check its progress and increase, manifested itself in the legislature even before the close of the last century. So long ago as the year 1669 we find the title of an act, laying an imposition upon *servants,* and *slaves,* imported into this country; which was either continued, revised, or increased, by a variety of temporary acts, passed between that period and the revolution in 1776.—One of these acts passed in 1723, by a marginal note, appears to have been repealed by proclamation, Oct. 24, 1724. In 1732 a duty of five per cent, was laid on slaves imported, to be paid by the buyers; a measure calculated to render it as little obnoxious as possible to the *English* merchants trading to Africa, and not improbably suggested by them, to the privy council in England. The preamble to this act is in these remarkable words, "We, your majesty's most dutiful and loyal subjects, &c. taking into our serious consideration the exigencies of your government here, and that the duty laid upon liquors will not be sufficient to defray the necessary expenses thereof, do humbly represent to your majesty, that *no other* duty can be laid upon our import or export, without oppressing your subjects, than a duty upon *slaves imported,* to be paid by the buyers, *agreeable to your majesty's instructions* to your lieutenant governor." This act was only for the short period of four years, but seems to have been continued from time to time till the year 1751, when the duty expired, but was revived the next year. In the year 1740, an additional duty of five per cent. was imposed for four years, for the purpose of an expedition against the Spaniards, &c. to be likewise paid by the buyers: and in 1742 the whole duty was continued till July 1, 1747.—The act of 1752, by which these duties were revived and continued, (as well as several former acts), takes notice that the duty had been found *no ways burdensome to the traders* in slaves. In 1754, an additional duty of five per cent. was imposed for the term of three years, by an act for encouraging and protecting the settlers on the Mississippi; this duty, like all the former, was to be paid by the buyers. In 1759, a duty of 20 per cent. was imposed upon all slaves imported into Virginia from Maryland, North Carolina, or other places in America, to continue for seven years. In 1769, the same duty was further continued. In the same session, the duty of five per cent. was continued for three years, and an additional duty of ten per cent. to be likewise paid by the buyers, was imposed for seven years; and a further duty of five per cent. was, by a separate act of the same session, imposed for the better support of the contingent charges of government, to be paid by the buyers. In 1772, all these duties were further continued for the term of five years from the expiration of the acts then in force: the assembly at the same time petitioned the throne, *to remove all those restraints which inhibited* his majesty's governors assenting to such *laws as might check so very pernicious a commerce,* as that of slavery.[13]

In the course of this enquiry it is easy to trace the desire of the legis-

---

13. The folowing extract from a petition to the throne, presented from the house of burgesses of Virginia, April 1, 1772, will shew the sense of the people of Virginia on the subject of slavery at that period.

"The many instances of your majesty's benevolent intentions and most gracious disposition to promote the prosperity and happiness of your subjects in the colonies, encourages us to look up to the throne, and implore your majesty's paternal assistance in averting a calamity of a most alarming nature.

"The importation of slaves into the colonies from the coast of Africa hath long been considered as a trade of great inhumanity, and under its *present encouragement,* we have too much reason to fear *will endanger the very existence* of your majesty's American dominions.

"We are sensible that some of your majesty's subjects of *Great Britain* may reap emoluments from this sort of traffic, but when we consider that it greatly retards the settlement of the colonies with *more useful* inhabitants, and may, in time, have the most destructive influence, we presume to hope that the *interest of a few* will be disregarded when placed in competition with the security and happiness of such numbers of your majesty's dutiful and loyal subjects.

"Deeply impressed with these sentiments, we most humbly beseech your majesty to *remove all those restraints* on your majesty's governors of this colony, *which inhibit their assenting to such laws as might check so very pernicious a commerce.*" Journals of the House of Burgesses, page 131.

This petition produced no effect, as appears from the first clause of our CONSTITUTION, where among other acts of misrule, "the inhuman use of the royal negative" in refusing us permission to exclude slaves from among us by law, is enumerated, among the reasons for *separating from Great Britain.*

lature to put a stop to the further importation of slaves; and had not this desire been uniformly opposed on the part of the crown, it is highly probable that event would have taken effect at a much earlier period than it did. A duty of five per cent. to be paid by the buyers, at first, with difficulty obtained the royal assent. Requisitions from the crown for aids, on particular occasions, afforded a pretext from time to time for increasing the duty from five, to ten, and finally to twenty per cent. with which the *buyer* was uniformly made chargeable. The wishes of the people of this colony, were not sufficient to counterbalance the interest of the English merchants, trading to Africa, and it is probable, that however disposed to put a stop to so infamous a traffic by law, we should never have been able to effect it, so long as we might have continued dependent on the British government: an object sufficient of itself to justify a revolution. That the legislature of Virginia were *sincerely* disposed to put a stop to it, cannot be doubted; for even during the tumult and confusion of the revolution, we have seen that they availed themselves of the earliest opportunity, to crush for ever so pernicious and infamous a commerce, by an act passed in October 1778, the penalties of which, though apparently lessened by the act of 1792, are still equal to the value of the slave; being two hundred dollars upon the importer, and one hundred dollars upon every person buying or selling an imported slave.

A system uniformly persisted in for nearly a whole century, and finally carried into effect, so soon as the legislature was unrestrained by "the inhuman exercise of the royal negative," evinces the sincerity of that disposition which the legislature had shewn during so long a period, to put a check to the growing evil. From the time that the duty was raised above five per cent. it is probable that the importation of slaves into this colony decreased. The demand for them in the more southern colonies probably contributed also to lessen the numbers imported into this: for some years immediately preceding the revolution, the importation of slaves into Virginia might almost be considered as at an end; and probably would have been entirely so, if the ingenuity of the merchant had not found out the means of evading the heavy duty, by pretended sales at which the slaves were bought in by some friend, at a quarter of their real value.

Tedious and unentertaining as this detail may appear to all others, a citizen of Virginia will feel some satisfaction at reading so clear a vindication of his country, from the opprobrium, but too lavishly bestowed upon her, of fostering slavery in her bosom, whilst she boasts a sacred regard to the liberty of her citizens, and of mankind in general. The acrimony of such censures must abate, at least in the breasts of the candid, upon an impartial review of the subject here brought before them; and if, in addition to what we have already advanced, they consider the difficulties attendant on any plan for the abolition of slavery, in a country where so large a proportion of the inhabitants are slaves; and where a still larger proportion of the cultivators of the earth are of that description of men, they will probably feel emotions of sympathy and compassion, both for the slave and for his master, succeed to those hasty prejudices, which even the best dispositions are not exempt from contracting, upon subjects where there is a deficiency of information.

We are next to consider the condition of slaves in Virginia, or the legal consequences attendant on a state of slavery in this commonwealth; and here it is not my intention to notice those laws, which consider slaves, merely as *property,* and have from time to time been enacted to regulate the disposition of them, *as such;* for these will be more properly considered elsewhere: my intention at present is therefore to take a view of such laws, only, as regard slaves, as a distinct class of *persons,* whose rights, if indeed they possess any, are reduced to a much narrower compass, than those, of which we have been speaking before.

Civil rights, we may remember, are reducible to three primary heads; the right of personal security; the right of personal liberty; and the right of private property. In a state of slavery, the two last are wholly abolished, the person of the slave being at the absolute disposal of his master; and property, what he is incapable, in that state, either of acquiring, or holding, in his own use. Hence it will appear how perfectly irreconcilable a state of slavery is to the principles of a democracy, which form the *basis* and *foundation* of our government. For our bill of rights declares, "that all men are by nature *equally free* and independent, and have certain rights of which they cannot deprive or divest their posterity, namely, the enjoyment of life and *liberty,* with the means of *acquiring* and *possessing property.*" This is indeed no more than a recognition of the first principles of the law of nature, which teaches us this equality, and enjoins every man, whatever advantages he may possess over another, as to the various qualities or endowments of body or mind, to practice the precepts of the law of nature to those who are in these respects his *inferiors,* no less than it enjoins his *inferiors* to practice them towards *him.* Since he has no more right to insult *them,* than they have to injure him. Nor does the *bare unkindness of nature* or of fortune condemn a man to a *worse* condition than others, as to the enjoyment of common privileges.[14] It would be hard to reconcile reducing the negroes to a state of slavery to these principles, unless we first degrade them below the rank of human beings, not only politically, but also physically and morally. The Roman lawyers look upon those only properly as *persons* who are *free,*—putting *slaves* into the rank of *goods* and *chattels;* and the policy of our legislature, as well as the practice of slave-holders in America in general, seems conformable to that idea: but surely it is time we should admit the evidence of moral truth, and learn to regard them as our fellow men, and equals, except in those particulars where accident, or perhaps nature, may have given us some advantage; a recompense for which they perhaps enjoy in other respects.

Slavery, says Hargrave, always imports an obligation of perpetual service, which only the consent of the master can dissolve: it also generally gives to the master an arbitrary power of administering every sort of correction, however inhuman, not immediately affecting life or limb, and even these in some countries, as formerly in Rome, and, at this day among the Asiatics and Africans, are left exposed to the arbitrary will of a master, or protected only by fines or other slight punishments. The property of the slave also is absolutely the property of his master, the

14. Puffendorf.

slave himself being the subject of property, and as such saleable, or transmissible at the will of his master.—A slavery, so malignant as that
described, does not leave to its wretched victims the least vestige of any
civil right, and even divests them of all their natural rights. It does not,
however, appear, that the rigours of slavery in this country were ever as
great, as those above described: yet it must be confessed, that, at times,
they have fallen very little short of them.

The first severe law respecting slaves, now to be met with in our code,
is that of 1669, already mentioned, which declared that the death of a
slave *resisting* his master, or other person correcting him by his order,
happening by extremity of the correction, should not be accounted felony.
The alterations which this law underwent in three successive acts, were
by no means calculated effectually to mitigate its severity; it seems rather
to have been augmented by the act of 1723, which declared that a person
indicted for the murder of a slave, and found guilty of *manslaughter,*
should not incur any punishment for the same.[15]

All these acts were at length repealed in 1788. So that homicide of a
slave stands now upon the same footing, as in the case of any other person. In 1672 it was declared lawful for any person pursuing any runaway
negroe, mulattoe, Indian slave, or *servant for life,* by virtue of an *hue and
cry,* to kill them in case of resistance, without being questioned for the
same. A few years afterwards this act was extended to persons *employed
to apprehend* runaways. In 1705, these acts underwent some small alteration; two justices being authorized by proclamation to *outlaw* runaways,
who might thereafter be *killed* and destroyed by any person whatsoever,
by *such ways and means* as he may think fit, without accusation or
impeachment of any crime for so doing: And if any such slave were
apprehended, he might be punished at the discretion of the county
court, either *by dismembering,* or in any other manner *not touching life.*

---

15. In December term, 1788, one John Huston was tried in the general court for the
murder of a slave; the jury found him guilty of manslaughter, and the court, upon a
motion in arrest of judgment, discharged him without any punishment. The general
assembly being then sitting, some of the members of the court mentioned the case to
some leading characters in the legislature, and the act was at the same session repealed.

The inhuman rigour of this act was afterwards extended to the venial offence of going abroad by night, if the slave was *notoriously* guilty of it.—Such are the cruelties to which a state of slavery gives birth; such the horrors to which the human mind is capable of being reconciled, by its adoption. The dawn of humanity at length appeared in the year 1769, when the power of dismembering, even under the authority of a county court, was restricted to the single offence of *attempting* to ravish a white woman, in which case perhaps the punishment is perhaps not more than commensurate to the crime. In 1772 some restraints were laid upon the practice of outlawing slaves, requiring that it should appear to the *satisfaction* of the justices that the slaves were outlying, and *doing mischief*. These loose expressions of the act, left too much in the discretion of men, not much addicted to weighing their import.—In 1792, every thing relative to the outlawry of slaves was *expunged* from our code, and I trust will never again find a place in it. By the act of 1680, a negroe, a mulattoe, or Indian, bond or *free*, presuming to lift his hand in opposition to any Christian, should receive thirty lashes on his bare back for every offence. The same act prohibited slaves from carrying any club, staff, gun, sword, or other weapon, offensive or defensive. This was afterwards extended to all negroes, mulattoes and Indians whatsoever, with a few exceptions in favour of housekeepers, residents on a frontier plantation, and such as were enlisted in the militia. Slaves, by these and other acts, are prohibited from going abroad without leave in writing from their masters, and if they do, may be whipped: any person suffering a slave to remain on his plantation for four hours together, or dealing with him without leave in writing from his master, is subject to a fine. A runaway slave may be apprehended and committed to jail, and if not claimed within three months (being first advertised) he shall be hired out, having an iron collar first put about his neck: and if not claimed within a year, shall be sold. These provisions were in general re-enacted in 1792, but the punishment to be inflicted on a negroe or mulattoe, for lifting his hand against a white person, is restricted to those cases, where the former is not wantonly assaulted. In this act the word Indian appears to have been designedly omitted: the small number of these people, or their descendants remaining among us, concurring with a more liberal way of thinking, probably gave occasion to this circumstance. The act of 1748, c. 31, made it felony, without benefit of clergy, for a slave to prepare, exhibit, or administer any medicine whatever, without the order or consent of the master; but *allowed clergy* if it appeared that the medicine was not administered with an *ill intent;* the act of 1792, with more justice, directs that in such case he shall be acquitted. To consult, advise, or conspire, to rebel, or to plot, or conspire the death of any person whatsoever, is still felony, without benefit of clergy, in a slave. Riots, routs, unlawful assemblies, trespasses and seditious speeches by slaves, are punishable with stripes, at the discretion of a justice of the peace.—The master of a slave permitting him to go at large and trade as a freeman, is subject to a fine; and if he suffers the slave to hire himself out, the latter may be sold, and twenty-five per cent. of the price be applied to the use of the county.—Negroes and mulattoes, whether slaves or not, are incapable of being witnesses, but against, or between negroes and mulattoes; they are not permitted to intermarry with any white person; yet no punishment is annexed to the offence in the slave; nor is the marriage void; but the white person contracting the marriage, and the clergyman by whom it is celebrated are liable to fine and imprisonment; and this is probably the only instance in which our laws will be found more favorable to a negroe than a white person. These provisions though introduced into our code at different periods, were all re-enacted in 1792.

From this melancholy review, it will appear that not only the right of property, and the right of personal liberty, but even the right of personal security, has been, at times, either wholly annihilated, or reduced to a shadow: and even in these days the protection of the latter seems to be confined to very few cases. Many actions, indifferent in themselves, being permitted by the law of nature to all mankind, and by the laws of society to all free persons, are either rendered highly criminal in a slave, or subject him to some kind of punishment or restraint. Nor is it in this respect only, that his condition is rendered thus deplorable by law. The measure of punishment for the same offence, is often, and the manner of trial and conviction is always, different in the case of a slave, and a free-man.

If the latter be accused of any crime, he is entitled to an examination before the court of the county where the offence is alleged to have been committed; whose decision, if in his favor, is held to be a legal and final acquittal, but it is not final if against him; for after this, both a grand jury, and a petit jury of the county, must successively pronounce him guilty; the former by the concurrent voices of twelve at least, of their body, and the latter, by their unanimous verdict upon oath. He may take exception to the proceedings against him, by a motion in arrest of judgment; and in this case, or if there be a special verdict, the same unanimity between his judges, as between his jurors, is necessary to his condemnation. Lastly, though the punishment which the law pronounces for his offence amount to death itself, he shall in many cases have the benefit of clergy, unless he has before received it. But in the case of a slave, the mode was formerly, and still remains essentially different. How early this distinction was adopted I have not been able to discover. The title of an act occurs, which passed in the year 1705 for the *speedy* and *easy* prosecution of slaves committing capital crimes. In 1723 the governor was authorized, whenever any slave was committed for any capital offence, to issue a special commission of oyer and terminer, to *such persons as he should think fit,* the number being left to his discretion, who should thereupon proceed to the trial of such slave, taking for evidence the confession of the defendant, the oath of one or more credible witnesses, or such testimony of negroes, mulattoes, or Indians, bond or free, with pregnant circumstances, as to them should seem convincing, without the solemnity of a jury. No exception, formerly, could be taken to the proceedings, on the trial of a slave, but that proviso is omitted in the act of 1792, and the justices moreover seem bound to allow him counsel for his defence, whose fee shall be paid by his master. In case of conviction, execution of the sentence was probably very speedily performed, since the act of 1748, provides that, thereafter, it should not be performed in less than ten days, except in case of insurrection or rebellion; and further, that if the court be divided in opinion the accused should be acquitted. In 1764, an act passed, authorizing general, instead of special, commissioners of oyer and terminer, constituting all the justices of any county, judges for the trial of slaves, committing capital offences, within their respective counties; any four of whom, one being of the quorum, should constitute a court for that purpose. In 1772 one step further was made in favour of humanity, by an act declaring that no slave should thereafter be condemned to die unless four of the court should concur in opinion of his guilt. The act of 1786, c. 58, confirmed by that of 1792, constitutes the justices of every county and corporation justices of oyer and terminer for the trial of slaves; requires *five* justices, at least, to constitute a court, and *unanimity* in the court for his condemnation; allows him counsel for his defence, to be paid by his owner, and, I apprehend, admits him to object to the proceedings against him; and finally enlarges the time of execution to *thirty* days, instead of ten (except in cases of conspiracy, insurrection, or rebellion), and extends the benefit of clergy to him in all cases, where any other person should have the benefit thereof, except in the cases before mentioned.

To an attentive observer these gradual, and almost imperceptible amendments in our jurisprudence respecting slaves, will be found, upon the whole, of infinite importance to that unhappy race. The mode of trial in criminal cases, especially, is rendered infinitely more beneficial to them than formerly, though perhaps still liable to exception for want of the aid of a jury: the solemnity of an oath administered the moment the trial commences, may be considered as operating more forcibly on the mind, than a general oath of office, taken, perhaps, twenty years before. Unanimity may also be more readily expected to take place among *five* men, than among *twelve*. These objections to the want of a jury are not without weight: on the other hand it may be observed, that if the number of triers be not equal to a full jury, they may yet be considered as more select; a circumstance of infinitely greater importance to the slave. The unanimity requisite in the court in order to conviction, is a more happy acquisition to the accused, than may at first appear; the opinions of the court must be delivered openly, immediately, and seriatim, beginning with the youngest judge. A single voice in favour of the accused, is an acquittal; for unanimity is not necessary, as with a jury, to acquit, as well as to condemn: there is less danger in this mode of trial, where the suffrages are to be openly delivered, that a few will be brought over to the opinion of the majority as may too often happen among jurors, whose deliberations are in *private*, and whose impatience of confinement may go further than real conviction, to produce the requisite unanimity. That this happens not unfrequently in civil cases, there is too much reason to believe; that it may also happen in criminal cases, especially where the party accused is not one of their equals, might not unreasonably, be apprehended. In New-York, before the revolution, a slave accused of a capital crime, should have been tried by a jury if his master required it. This is, perhaps, still the law of that state. Such a provision might not be amiss in this; but considering the ordinary run of juries in the county-courts, I should presume the privilege would be rarely insisted upon.

Slaves, we have seen are now entitled to the benefit of clergy in all cases where it is allowed to any other offenders, except in cases of consulting, advising, or conspiring to rebel, or make insurrection; or plotting or conspiring to murder any person; or preparing, exhibiting, or administering medicine with an *ill* intent. The same lenity was not extended to them formerly. The act of 1748, c. 31, denied it to a slave in case of manslaughter; or the felonious breaking and entering *any* house, in the night time: or breaking and entering *any* house in the day time, and taking therefrom goods to the value of twenty shillings. The act of 1764, c. 9, extended the benefit of clergy to a slave convicted of the manslaughter of a slave; and the act of 1772, c. 9, extended it further, to a slave convicted of house-breaking in the night time, unless such breaking be burglary; in the latter case, other offenders would be equally deprived of it. But wherever the benefit of clergy is allowed to a slave, the court, besides burning him in the hand (the usual punishment inflicted on free persons) may inflict such further corporal punishment as they may think fit; this also seems to be the law in the case of free negroes and mulattoes. By the act of 1723, c. 4, it was enacted that when *any negroe* or *mulattoe* shall be found, upon due proof made, or *pregnant circumstances*, to have given false testimony, every such offender shall, *without further trial*, have his ears successively nailed to the pillory for the space of an hour, and then cut off, and moreover receive thirty-nine lashes on his bare back, or such other punishment as the court shall think proper, not extending to life or limb. This act, with the exception of the words *pregnant circumstances,* was re-enacted in 1792. The punishment of perjury, in a *white* person, is only a fine and imprisonment. A slave convicted of hog stealing, shall, for the first offence, receive thirty-nine lashes: any other person twenty five: but the latter is also subject to a fine of thirty dollars, besides paying eight dollars to the owner of the hog. The punishment for the second and third offence, of this kind, is the same in the case of a free person, as of a slave; namely, by the pillory and loss of ears, for the second offence; the third is declared felony, to which clergy is, however, allowed. The preceding are the only positive distinctions which now remain between the punishment of a slave, and a white person, in those cases, where the latter is liable to a determinate corporal punishment. But we must not forget, that many actions, which are either not punishable at all when perpetrated by a white person, or at most, by fine and imprisonment, only, are liable to severe corporal punishment, when done by a slave; nay, even to death itself, in some cases. To go abroad without a written permission; to keep or carry a gun, or other weapon; to utter any seditious speech; to be present at any unlawful assembly of slaves; to lift the hand in opposition to a white person, unless wantonly assaulted, are all offences punishable by whipping. To attempt the chastity of a white woman, forcibly, is punishable by dismemberment: such an attempt would be a high misdemeanor, in a white free man, but the punishment would be far short of that of a slave. To administer medicine without the order or consent of the master, unless it *appear not to have been done with an ill intent;* to *consult,* advise, or conspire, to rebel or make insurrection; or to *conspire* or *plot* to *murder* any person, we have seen, are all capital offences, from which the benefit of clergy is utterly excluded. But a *bare intention* to commit a felony, is not punishable in the case of a free white man; and even the attempt, if not attended with an actual breach of the peace, or prevented by such circumstances, only, as do not tend to lessen the guilt of the offender, is at most a misdemeanor by the common law: and in statutable offences in general, to consult advise, and even to procure any person to commit a felony, does not constitute the crime of felony in the adviser or procurer, unless the felony be actually perpetrated.

From this view of our jurisprudence respecting slaves, we are unavoidably led to remark, how frequently the laws of nature have been set aside in favour of institutions, the pure result of prejudice, usurpation, and tyranny. We have found actions, innocent or indifferent, punishable with a rigour scarcely due to any, but the most atrocious offences against civil society; justice distributed by an unequal measure to the master and the slave; and even the hand of mercy arrested, where mercy might have been extended to the wretched culprit, had his complexion been the same with that of his judges: for, the short period of ten days, between his condemnation and execution, was often insufficient to obtain a pardon for a slave, convicted in a remote part of the country, whilst a free man, condemned at the seat of government, and tried before the governor himself, in whom the power of pardoning was vested, had a respite of thirty days to implore the clemency of the executive authority.—It may be urged, and I believe with truth, that these rigours do not proceed from a sanguinary temper in the people of Virginia, but from those political considerations indispensably necessary, where slavery prevails to any great extent: I am moreover happy to observe that our police respecting this unhappy class of people, is not only less rigorous than formerly, but perhaps milder than in any other country where there are so many slaves, or so large a proportion of them, in respect to the free inhabitants: it is also, I trust, unjust to censure the present generation for the existence of slavery in Virginia: for I think it unquestionably true, that a very large proportion of our fellow-citizens lament that as a misfortune, which is imputed to them as a reproach; it being evident from what has been already shown upon the subject, that, *antecedent to the revolution,* no exertion to abolish, or even check the progress of slavery in Virginia, could have received the smallest countenance from the crown, without whose assent the united wishes and exertions of every individual here, would have been wholly fruitless and ineffectual: it is, perhaps, also demonstrable, that at no period since the revolution, could the abolition of slavery in this state have been safely undertaken until the foundations of our newly established governments had been found capable of supporting the fabric itself, under any shock, which so arduous an attempt might have produced. But these obstacles being now happily removed, considerations of policy, as well as justice and humanity, must evince the necessity of eradicating the evil, before it becomes impossible to do it, without tearing up the roots of civil society with it.

Having in the preceding part of this enquiry shewn the origin and foundation of slavery, or the manner in which men have become slaves, as also who are liable to be retained in slavery, in Virginia, at present, with the legal consequences attendant upon their condition; it only remains to consider the mode by which slaves have been or may be emancipated; and the legal consequences thereof, in this state.—Manumission, among the Israelites, if the bondman were an Hebrew, was enjoined after six years' service, by the Mosaical law, unless the servant chose to continue with his master, in which case the master carried him before the judges, and took an awl, and thrust it through his ear into the door,[16] and from thenceforth he became a servant for ever: but if he sent him away free, he was bound to furnish him liberally out of his flock, and out of his floor, and out of his wine-press.[17] Among the Romans, in the time of the commonwealth, liberty could be conferred only three ways. By testament, by the *census,* and by the *vindicta,* or lictor's rod. A man was said to be free by the census, "*liber censu,*" when his name was inserted in the censor's roll, with the approbation of his master. When he was freed by the vindicta, the master placing his hand upon the head of the slave, said in the presence of the praetor, it is my desire that this man may be free, "*hunc hominem liberem esse volo*"; to which the praetor replied, I pronounce him free after the manner of the Romans, "*dico cum liberum esse more quiritum.*"—Then the lictor, receiving the *vindicta,* struck the new freed man several blows with it, upon the head, face, and back, after which his name was registered in the roll of freed-men, and his head being close shaved, a cap was given him as a token of liberty.

16. Exod., c. 21.
17. Deut., c. 15.

Under the imperial constitutions liberty might have been conferred by several other methods, as in the face of the church, in the presence of friends, or by letter, or by testament.—But it was not in the power of every master to manumit at will; for if it were done with an intent to defraud creditors, the act was void: that is, if the master were insolvent at the time of manumission, or became insolvent by manumission, and intentionally manumitted his slave for the purpose of defrauding his creditors. A minor, under the age of twenty years, could not manumit his slave but for a just cause assigned, which must have been approved by a council, consisting of the praetor, five senators, and five knights.—In England, the mode of enfranchising villeins is said to have been thus prescribed by a law of William the Conqueror. "If any person is willing to enfranchise his *slave,* let him with his right hand, deliver the slave to the sheriff in a full county, proclaim him exempt from the bond of servitude by manumission, shew him open gates and ways, and deliver him *free arms,* to wit, a lance and a sword; thereupon he is a free man."—But after that period, freedom was more generally conferred by deed, of which Mr. Harris, in his notes upon Justinian, has furnished a precedent.

In what manner manumission was performed in this country during the first century after the introduction of slavery does not appear: the act of 1668, before mentioned, shews it to have been practised before that period. In 1723 an act was passed, prohibiting the manumission of slaves, upon any pretence whatsoever, except for meritorious services, to be adjudged, and allowed by the governor and council. This clause was re-enacted in 1748, and continued to be the law, until after the revolution was accomplished. The number of manumissions under such restrictions must necessarily have been very few. In May 1782 an act passed authorizing, generally, the manumission of slaves, but requiring such as might be set free, not being of sound mind or body, or being above the age of forty-five years, or males under twenty-one, or females under eighteen, to be supported by the person liberating them, or out of his estate. The act of manumission may be performed either by will, or by deed under the hand and seal of the party, acknowledged by him, or proved by two witnesses in the court of the county where he resides.

There is reason to believe that great numbers have been emancipated since the passing of this act. By the census of 1791 it appears that the number of free negroes, mulattoes and Indians in Virginia, was then 12,866. It would be a large allowance, to suppose that there were 1800 free negroes and mulattoes in Virginia when the act took effect; so that upwards of ten thousand must have been indebted to it for their freedom.[18] The number of Indians and their descendants in Virginia at present, is too small to require particular notice. The progress of emancipation in Virginia, is at this time continual but not rapid; a second census will enable us to form a better judgment of it than at present. The act passed in 1792 accords in some degree with the Justinian code, by providing that slaves emancipated may be taken in execution to satisfy any debt contracted by the person emancipating them, before such emancipation is made.[19]

18. There are *more* free negroes and mulattoes in Virginia alone, than are to be found in the four New England states, and Vermont in addition to them. The progress of emancipation in this state is therefore much greater than our *Eastern* brethren may at first suppose. There are only 1087 free negroes and mulattoes in the States of New-York, New-Jersey and Pennsylvania, *more* than in Virginia. Those who take a subject in the gross, have little idea of the result of an exact scrutiny. Out of 20,348 inhabitants on the Eastern Shore of Virginia 1185 were free negroes and mulattoes when the census was taken. The number is since much augmented.

19. The act of 1795. c. 11 enacts, that any person held in slavery may make complaint to a magistrate, or to the court of the district county or corporation wherein he resides, and not elsewhere. The magistrate, if the complaint be made to him, shall issue his warrant to summon the owner before him, and compel him to give bond and security to suffer the complainant to appear at the next court, to petition the court to be admitted to sue *in formâ pauperis.* If the owner refuse, the magistrate shall order the complainant into the custody of the officer serving the warrant, at the expence of the master, who shall keep him until the sitting of the court, and then produce him before it. Upon petition to the court, if the court be satisfied as to the material facts, they shall assign the complainant council, who shall state the facts with his opinion thereon to the court; and unless from the circumstances so stated, and the opinion thereon given, the court shall *see manifest reason to deny their interference,* they shall order the clerk to issue process against the owner, and the complainant shall remain in the custody of the sheriff until the owner shall give bond and security to have him forthcoming to answer the judgment of the court. And by the general law in case of pauper's suits, the complainants shall have writs of subpoena gratis; and by the practice of the courts, he is permitted to attend the

Among the Romans, the *libertini,* or freedmen, were formerly distinguished by a threefold division. They sometimes obtained what was called the greater liberty, thereby becoming *Roman citizens.* To this privilege, those who were enfranchised by testament, by the census, or by the vindicta, appear to have been alone admitted: sometimes they obtained the lesser liberty only, and became *Latins;* whose condition is thus described by Justinian. "They never enjoyed the right of succession [to estates].—For although they led the lives of free men, yet with their last breath they lost both their lives and liberties; for their possessions, like the goods of slaves, were detained by the manumitter." Sometimes they obtained only the inferior liberty, being called *dedititii:* such were slaves who had been condemned as criminals, and afterwards obtained manumission through the indulgence of their masters: their conditions was equalled with that of conquered revolters, whom the Romans called, in reproach, *dedititii, quia se suaque omnia dediderunt:* but all these distinctions were abolished by Justinian, by whom all freed men in general were made citizens of Rome, without regard to the form of manumission.—In England, the presenting the villein with *free arms,* seems to have been the symbol of his restoration to all the rights which a feudatory was entitled to. With us, we have seen that emancipation does not confer the rights of citizenship on the person emancipated; on the contrary, both he and his posterity, of the same complexion with himself, must always labour under many civil incapacities. If he is absolved from personal restraint or corporal punishment, by a master, yet the laws restrain his actions in many instances, where there is none upon a free white man. If he can maintain a suit, he cannot be a witness, a juror or a judge in any controversy between one of his own complexion and a white person. If he can acquire property in lands, he cannot exercise the right of suffrage, which such a property would confer on his former master; much less can he assist in making those laws by which he is bound. Yet, even under these disabilities, his present condition bears an enviable

---

taking the depositions of witnesses, and go and come freely to and from court, for the prosecution of his suit.

pre-eminence over his former state. Possessing the liberty of locomotion, which was formerly denied him, it is in his choice to submit to
that civil inferiority, inseparably attached to his condition in this country, or seek some more favorable climate, where all distinctions between
men are either totally abolished, or less regarded than in this.

The extirpation of slavery from the United States is a task equally
arduous and momentous. To restore the blessings of liberty to near a
million of oppressed individuals, who have groaned under the yoke of
bondage, and to their descendants, is an object, which those who trust in
Providence, will be convinced would not be unaided by the divine
Author of our being, should we invoke his blessing upon our endeavours. Yet human prudence forbids that we should precipitately engage
in a work of such hazard as a general and simultaneous emancipation.
The mind of man must in some measure be formed for his future condition. The early impressions of obedience and submission, which slaves
have received among us, and the no less habitual arrogance and assumption of superiority, among the whites, contribute, equally, to unfit the
former for *freedom,* and the latter for *equality.*[20] To expel them all at once,

20. Mr. Jefferson most forcibly paints the unhappy influence on the manners of the
people produced by the existence of slavery among us. The whole commerce between
master and slave, says he, is a perpetual exercise of the most boisterous passions, the most
unremitting despotism on the one part, and degrading submissions on the other. Our
children see this, and learn to imitate it; for man is an imitative animal. This quality is the
germ of education in him. From his cradle to his grave he is learning what he sees others do. If a parent had no other motive either in his own philanthropy or his self love for
restraining the intemperance of passion toward his slave, it should always be a sufficient
one that his child is present. But generally it is not sufficient. The parent storms, the child
looks on, catches the lineaments of wrath, puts on the same airs in the circle of smaller
slaves, gives a loose to his worst of passions; and thus nursed, educated, and daily exercised in tyranny, cannot but be stamped by it with odious peculiarities. The man must be
a prodigy who can retain his manners and morals undepraved by such circumstances.
And with what execration would the statesman be loaded, who permitting one half the
citizens thus to trample on the rights of the other, transforms them into despots, and
these into enemies, destroys the morals of the one part, and the amor patriae of the other.
For if a slave can have a country in this world, it must be any other in preference to that
in which he is born to live and labour for another: in which he must lock up the faculties of his nature, contribute as far as depends on his individual endeavors to the evan-

from the United States, would in fact be to devote them only to a lingering death by famine, by disease, and other accumulated miseries: "We have in history but one picture of a similar enterprise, and there we see it was necessary not only to open the sea by a miracle, for them to pass, but more necessary to close it again to prevent their return."[21] To retain them among us, would be nothing more than to throw so many of the human race upon the earth without the means of subsistence: they would soon become idle, profligate, and miserable. Unfit for their new condition, and unwilling to return to their former laborious course, they would become the caterpillars of the earth, and the tigers of the human race. The recent history of the French West Indies exhibits a melancholy picture of the probable consequences of a general, and momentary emancipation in any of the states, where slavery has made considerable progress. In Massachusetts the abolition of it was effected by a single stroke; a clause in their constitution: but the whites at that time, were as sixty-five to one, in proportion to the blacks. The whole number of free persons in the United States, south of Delaware state, are 1,233,829, and

---

ishment of the human race, or entail his own miserable condition on the endless generations proceeding from him. With the morals of the people, their industry also, is destroyed. For in a warm climate, no man will labour for himself who can make another labour for him. This is so true, that of the proprietors of slaves a very small proportion indeed are ever seen to labour. And can the liberties of a nation be ever thought secure when we have removed their only firm basis, a conviction in the minds of the people, that these liberties are of the gift of God? That they are not to be violated but with his wrath? Indeed I tremble for my country when I reflect that God is just: that his justice cannot sleep for ever: that considering numbers, nature, and natural means only, a revolution of the wheel of fortune, an exchange of situation is among possible events: that it may become probable by supernatural interference! The Almighty has no attribute which can take side with us in such a contest.—But it is impossible to be temperate and to pursue this subject through the various considerations of policy, of morals, of history, natural and civil. We must be contented to hope they will force their way into every one's mind. I think a change already perceptible, since the origin of the present revolution. The spirit of the master is abating, that of the slave rising from the dust; his condition mollifying; the way I hope preparing, under the auspices of Heaven, for a total emancipation, and that this is disposed in the order of events, to be with the consent of their masters, rather than by their extirpation. Notes on Virginia, 298.

21. Letter from Jas. Sullivan, Esq. to Dr. Belknap.

there are 648,439 slaves; the proportion being less than two to one. Of the cultivators of the earth in the same district, it is probable that there are four slaves for one free white man.—To discharge the former from their present condition, would be attended with an immediate general famine, in those parts of the United States, from which not all the productions of the other states, could deliver them; similar evils might reasonably be apprehended from the adoption of the measure by any one of the southern states; for in all of them the proportion of slaves is too great, not to be attended with calamitous effects, if they were immediately set free.[22] These are serious, I had almost said unsurmountable obstacles, to a general, simultaneous emancipation.—There are other considerations not to be disregarded. A great part of the *property* of individuals consists in *slaves*. The laws have sanctioned this species of property. Can the laws take away the property of an individual without his own consent, or without a *just compensation:* Will those who do not hold slaves agree to be taxed to make this compensation? Creditors also, who have trusted their debtors upon the faith of this visible property will be defrauded. If justice demands the emancipation of the slave, she also, *under these circumstances,* seems to plead for the owner and for his creditor. The claims of nature, it will be said are stronger than those which arise from social institutions, only. I admit it, but nature also dictates to us to provide for our *own* safety, and authorizes all *necessary* measures for that purpose. And we have shewn that our own security, nay, our very existence, might be endangered by the hasty adoption of any measure for the *immediate* relief of the *whole* of this unhappy race. Must we then quit the subject, in despair of the success of any project for the amendment of their, as well as our own condition? I think not.—Strenuously as

---

22. What is here advanced is not to be understood as implying an opinion that the labour of slaves is more productive than that of freemen.—The author of the Treatise on the Wealth of Nations, informs us, "That it appears from the experiences of all ages and nations, that the work done by freemen comes cheaper in the end than that done by slaves. That it is found to do so, even in Boston, New-York and Philadelphia, where the wages of common labour are very high." Admitting this conclusion, it would not remove the objection that emancipated slaves would not willingly labour.

436 On the State of Slavery in Virginia

I feel my mind opposed to a simultaneous emancipation, for the reasons already mentioned, the abolition of slavery in the United States, and especially in that state, to which I am attached by every tie that nature and society form, is *now* my *first,* and will probably be my last, expiring wish. But here let me avoid the imputation of inconsistency, by observing, that the abolition of slavery may be effected without the *emancipation* of a single slave; without depriving any man of the *property* which he *possesses,* and without defrauding a creditor who has trusted him on the faith of that property. The experiment in that mode has already been begun in some of our sister states. Pennsylvania, under the auspices of the immortal Franklin,[23] begun the work of gradual abolition of slavery in the year 1780, by enlisting nature herself, on the side of humanity. Connecticut followed the example four years after. New-York very lately made an essay which miscarried, by a very inconsiderable majority. Mr. Jefferson informs us that the committee of revisors, of which he was a member, had prepared a bill for the emancipation of all slaves born after passing that act. This is conformable to the Pennsylvanian and Connecticut laws.—Why the measure was not brought forward in the general assembly I have never heard. Possibly because objections were foreseen to that part of the bill which relates to the disposal of the blacks, after they had attained a certain age.[24] It certainly seems liable to many, both as to the policy and the practicability of it. To establish such a

23. Dr. Franklin, it is said, drew the bill for the gradual abolition of slavery in Pennsylvania.

24. The object of the amendment proposed to be offered to the legislature, was to emancipate all slaves born after a certain period; and further directing that they should continue with their parents to a certain age, then be brought up at the public expence, to tillage, arts, or sciences, according to their geniuses, till the females should be eighteen, and the males twenty-one years of age, when they should be colonized to such a place as the circumstances of the time should render most proper; sending them out with arms, implements of household and of the handicraft arts, seeds, pairs of the useful domestic animals, &c. to declare them a free and independent people, and extend to them our alliance and protection, till they shall have acquired strength; and to send vessels at the same time to other parts of the world for an equal number of white inhabitants; to induce whom to migrate hither, proper encouragements should be proposed. Notes on Virginia, 251.

colony in the territory of the United States, would probably lay the foundation of intestine wars, which would terminate only in their extirpation, or final expulsion. To attempt it in any other quarter of the globe would be attended with the utmost cruelty to the colonists, themselves, and the destruction of their whole race. If the plan were at this moment in operation, it would require the annual exportation of 12,000 persons. This requisite number must, for a series of years be considerably increased, in order to keep pace with the increasing population of those people. In twenty years it would amount to upwards of twenty thousand persons; which is half the number which are now supposed to be annually exported from Africa.—Where would a fund to support this expence be found? Five times the present revenue of the state would barely defray the charge of their passage. Where provisions for their support after their arrival? Where those necessaries which must preserve them from perishing?—Where a territory sufficient to support them?—Or where could they be received as friends and not as invaders? To colonize them in the United States might seem less difficult. If the territory to be assigned them were beyond the settlements of the whites, would they not be put upon a forlorn hope against the Indians? Would not the expence of transporting them thither, and supporting them, at least for the first and second year, be also far beyond the revenues and abilities of the state? The expence attending a small army in that country hath been found enormous. To transport as many colonists, annually, as we have shewn were necessary to eradicate the evil, would probably require five times as much money as the support of such an army. But the expence would not stop there: they must be assisted and supported at least for another year after their arrival in their new settlements. Suppose them arrived. Illiterate and ignorant as they are, is it probable that they would be capable of instituting such a government, in their new colony, as would be necessary for their own internal happiness, or to secure them from destruction from without? European emigrants, from whatever country they arrive, have been accustomed to the restraints of laws, and to respect for government. These people, accustomed to be ruled with a rod of iron, will not easily submit to milder restraints. They would become hordes of vagabonds, robbers and murderers. Without the aids of an enlightened policy, morality, or religion, what else could be expected from their still savage state, and debased condition?—"But why not retain and *incorporate the blacks into the state?*" This question has been well answered by Mr. Jefferson,[25] and who is there so free from prejudices among us, as candidly to declare that he has none against such a measure? The recent

25. It will probably be asked, why not retain the blacks among us and *incorporate them into the state?* Deep-rooted prejudices entertained by the whites; ten thousand recollections by the blacks, of the injuries they have sustained; new provocations; the *real distinctions* which *nature* has made; and many other circumstances will divide us into parties and produce convulsions, which will probably never end but in the extermination of one or the other race. To these objections which are political may be added others which are physical and moral. The first difference which strikes us is that of colour.—&c. The circumstance of superior beauty is thought worthy attention in the propagation of our horses, dogs, and other domestic animals; why not in that of man? &c. In general their existence appears to participate more of sensation than reflection. Comparing them by their faculties of memory, reason, and imagination, it appears to me that in memory they are equal to the whites; in reason much inferior; that in imagination they are dull, tasteless and anomalous. &c. The improvement of the blacks in body and mind, in the first instance of their mixture with the whites, has been observed by every one, and proves that their inferiority is not the effect merely of their condition of life. We know that among the Romans, about the Augustan age, especially, the condition of their slaves was much more deplorable, than that of the blacks on the continent of America. Yet among the Romans, their slaves were often their rarest artists. They excelled too, in science, insomuch as to be usually employed as tutors to their master's children. Epictetus, Terence, and Phaedrus were slaves. But they were of the race of whites. It is not their condition then, but nature, which has produced the distinction. The opinion that they are inferior in the faculties of reason and imagination, must be hazarded with great diffidence. To justify a general conclusion requires many observations. &c.—I advance it therefore as a suspicion only, that the blacks, whether originally a distinct race, or made distinct by time and circumstances, are inferior to the whites both in the endowments of body and mind. &c. This unfortunate difference of colour, and perhaps of faculty, is a powerful obstacle to the emancipation of these people. Among the Romans, emancipation required but one effort. The slave, when made free, might mix with, without staining, the blood of his master. But with us, a second is necessary, unknown to history.—See the passage at length, Notes on Virginia.

"In the present case, it is not only the slave who is beneath his master, it is the Negroe who is beneath the white man. No act of enfranchisement, can efface this unfortunate distinction." Chastellux's Travels in America.

scenes transacted in the French colonies in the West Indies are enough to make one shudder with the apprehension of realizing similar calamities in this country. Such probably would be the event of an attempt to smother those prejudices which have been cherished for a period of almost two centuries. Those who secretly favour, whilst they affect to regret, domestic slavery, contend that in abolishing it, we must also abolish that scion from it which I have denominated *civil* slavery. That there must be no distinction of rights; that the descendants of Africans, as men, have an equal claim to all civil rights, as the descendants of Europeans; and upon being delivered from the yoke of bondage have a right to be admitted to all the privileges of a citizen.—But have not men when they enter into a state of society, a right to admit, or exclude any description of persons, as they think proper? If it be true, as Mr. Jefferson seems to suppose, that the Africans are really an inferior race of mankind,[26] will not sound policy advise their exclusion from a society in which they have not yet been admitted to participate in civil rights; and even to guard against such admission, at any future period, since it may eventually depreciate the whole national character? And if prejudices have taken such deep root in our minds, as to render it impossible to eradicate this opinion, ought not so general an error, if it be one, to be respected? Shall we not relieve the necessities of the naked diseased beggar, unless we will invite him to a seat at our table; nor afford him shelter from the inclemencies of the night air, unless we admit him also to share our bed? To deny that we ought to abolish slavery, without incorporating the negroes into the state, and admitting them to a full participation of all our civil and social rights, appears to me to rest upon a similar foundation. The experiment so far as it has been already made among us, proves that the emancipated blacks are not ambitious of civil rights. To prevent the generation of such an ambition, appears to comport with sound pol-

26. The celebrated David Hume, in his Essay on National Character, advances the same opinion; Doctor [James] Beattie, in his Essay on Truth, controverts it with many powerful arguments. Early prejudices, had we more satisfactory information than we can possibly possess on the subject at present, would render an inhabitant of a country where negroe slavery prevails, an improper umpire between them.

icy; for if it should ever rear its head, its partizans, as well as its opponents, will be enlisted by nature herself, and always ranged in formidable array against each other. We must therefore endeavor to find some middle course, between the tyrannical and iniquitous policy which holds so many human creatures in a state of grievous bondage, and that which would turn loose a numerous, starving, and enraged banditti, upon the innocent descendants of their former oppressors. *Nature, time,* and *sound policy* must co-operate with each other to produce such a change: if either be neglected, the work will be incomplete, dangerous, and not improbably destructive.

The plan therefore which I would presume to propose for the consideration of my countrymen is such as the number of slaves, the difference of their nature, and habits, and the state of agriculture, among us, might render it *expedient,* rather than *desirable* to adopt: and would partake partly of that proposed by Mr. Jefferson, and adopted in other states; and partly of such cautionary restrictions, as a due regard to situation and circumstances, and even to *general* prejudices, might recommend to those, who engage in so arduous, and perhaps unprecedented an undertaking.

1. Let every female born after the adoption of the plan be free, and transmit freedom to all her descendants, both male and female.

2. As a compensation to those persons, in whose families such females, or their descendants may be born, for the expence and trouble of their maintenance during infancy, let them serve such persons until the age of twenty-eight years; let them then receive twenty dollars in money, two suits of clothes, suited to the season, a hat, a pair of shoes, and two blankets. If these things be not voluntarily done, let the county courts enforce the performance, upon complaint.

3. Let all negroe children be registered with the clerk of the county or corporation court, where born, within one month after their birth: let the person in whose family they are born take a copy of the register, and deliver it to the mother, or if she die to the child, before it is of the age of twenty-one years. Let any negroe claiming to be free, and above the age

of puberty, be considered as of the age of twenty-eight years, if he or she be not registered as required.

4. Let all such negroe servants be put on the same footing as white servants and apprentices now are, in respect to food, raiment, correction, and the assignment of their service from one to another.

5. Let the children of negroes and mulattoes, born in the families of their parents, be bound to service by the overseers of the poor, until they shall attain the age of twenty-one years.—Let all above that age, who are not housekeepers, nor have voluntarily bound themselves to service for a year before the first day of February annually, be then bound for the remainder of the year by the overseers of the poor. Let the overseers of the poor receive fifteen per cent. of their wages, from the person hiring them, as a compensation for their trouble, and ten per cent. per annum out of the wages of such as they may bind apprentices.

6. If at the age of twenty-seven years, the master of a negroe or mulattoe servant be unwilling to pay his freedom dues, above mentioned, at the expiration of the succeeding year, let him bring him into the county court, clad and furnished with necessaries as before directed, and pay into court five dollars, for the use of the servant, and thereupon let the court direct him to be hired by the overseers of the poor for the succeeding year, in the manner before directed.

7. Let no negroe or mulattoe be capable of taking, holding, or exercising, any public office, freehold, franchise or privilege, or any estate in lands or tenements, other than a lease not exceeding twenty-one years.— Nor of keeping, or bearing arms, unless authorized so to do by some act of the general assembly, whose duration shall be limited to three years. Nor of contracting matrimony with any other than a negroe or mulattoe; nor be an attorney; nor be a juror; nor a witness in any court of judicature, except against, or between negroes and mulattoes. Nor be an executor or administrator; nor capable of making any will or testament; nor maintain any real action; nor be a trustee of lands or tenements himself, nor any other person to be a trustee to him or to his use.

8. Let all persons born after the passing of the act, be considered as

entitled to the same mode of trial in criminal cases, as free negroes and mulattoes are now entitled to.

The restrictions in this place may appear to favour strongly of prejudice: whoever proposes any plan for the abolition of slavery, will find that he must either encounter, or accommodate himself to prejudice.— I have preferred the latter; not that I pretend to be wholly exempt from it, but that I might avoid as many obstacles as possible to the completion of so desirable a work as the abolition of slavery. Though I am opposed to the banishment of the negroes, I wish not to encourage their future residence among us. By denying them the most valuable privileges which civil government affords, I wished to render it their inclination and their interest to seek those privileges in some other climate. There is an immense unsettled territory on this continent[27] more congenial to their natural constitutions than ours, where they may perhaps be received upon more favorable terms than we can permit them to remain with us. Emigrating in small numbers, they will be able to effect settlements more easily than in large numbers; and without the expence or danger of numerous colonies. By releasing them from the yoke of bondage, and enabling them to seek happiness wherever they can hope to find it, we surely confer a benefit, which no one can sufficiently appreciate, who has not tasted of the bitter curse of compulsory servitude. By excluding them from offices, the seeds of ambition would be buried too deep, ever to germinate: by disarming them, we may calm our apprehensions of their resentments arising from past sufferings; by incapacitating them from holding lands, we should add one inducement more to emigration and effectually remove the foundation of ambition, and party-struggles. Their personal rights, and their property, though lim-

---

27. The immense territory of Louisiana, which extends as far south as the lat. 25° and the two Floridas, would probably afford a ready asylum for such as might choose to become Spanish subjects. How far their political rights might be enlarged in these countries, is, however questionable: but the climate is undoubtedly more favourable to the African constitution than ours, and from this cause, it is not improbable that emigrations from these states would in time be very considerable.

ited, would, whilst they remain among us, be under the protection of the laws; and their condition not at all inferior to that of the *labouring* poor in most other countries. Under such an arrangement we might reasonably hope, that time would either remove from us a race of men, whom we wish not to incorporate with us, or obliterate those prejudices, which now form an obstacle to such incorporation.

But it is not from the want of liberality to the emancipated race of blacks that I apprehend the most serious objections to the plan I have ventured to suggest.—Those slave holders (whose numbers I trust are few) who have been in the habit of considering their fellow creatures as no more than cattle, and the rest of the brute creation, will exclaim that they are to be deprived of their *property,* without compensation. Men who will shut their ears against this moral truth, that all men are by nature *free,* and *equal,* will not even be convinced that they do not possess a *property* in an *unborn* child: they will not distinguish between allowing to *unborn* generations the absolute and unalienable rights of human nature, and taking away that which they *now possess;* they will shut their ears against truth, should you tell them, the loss of the mother's labour for nine months, and the maintenance of a child for a dozen or fourteen years, is amply compensated by the services of that child for as many years more, as he has been an expence to them. But if the voice of reason, justice and humanity be not stifled by sordid avarice, or unfeeling tyranny, it would be easy to convince even those who have entertained such eroneous notions, that the right of one man over another is neither founded in nature, nor in sound policy. That it cannot extend to those *not in being;* that no man can in reality be *deprived* of what he doth not possess: that fourteen years labour by a young person in the prime of life, is an ample compensation for a few months of labour lost by the mother, and for the maintenance of a child in that coarse homely manner that negroes are brought up: And lastly, that a state of slavery is not only perfectly incompatible with the principles of government, but with the safety and security of their masters. History evinces this. At this moment we have the most awful demonstrations of it. Shall we then neglect a duty, which every consideration, moral, religious, political, or *selfish*, recommends. Those who wish to postpone the measure, do not reflect that every day renders the task more arduous to be performed. We have now 300,000 slaves among us. Thirty years hence we shall have double the number. In sixty years we shall have 1,200,000. And in less than another century from this day, even that enormous number will be doubled. Milo acquired strength enough to carry an ox, by beginning with the ox when he was yet a calf. If we complain that the calf is too heavy for our shoulders, what will not the ox be?

To such as apprehend danger to our agricultural interest, and the depriving the families of those whose principal reliance is upon their slaves, of support, it will be proper to submit a view of the gradual operation, and effects of this plan. They will no doubt be surprized to hear, that whenever it is adopted, the number of slaves will not be diminished for forty years after it takes place; that it will even increase for thirty years; that at the distance of sixty years, there will be one-third of the number at its first commencement: that it will require *above a century* to complete it; and that the number of blacks *under twenty-eight*, and consequently bound to service, in the families they are born in, will always be at least as great, as the present number of slaves. These circumstances I trust will remove many objections, and that they are truly stated will appear upon enquiry. It will further appear, that females only will arrive at the age of emancipation within the first forty-five years; all the males during that period, continuing either in slavery, or bound to service till the age of twenty-eight years. The earth cannot want cultivators, whilst our population increases as at present, and three-fourths of those employed therein are held to service, and the remainder compellable to labour. For we must not lose sight of this important consideration, that these people must be *bound* to labour; if they do not *voluntarily* engage therein. Their faculties are at present only calculated for that object; if they be not employed therein they will become drones of the worst description. In absolving them from the yoke of slavery, we must not forget the interests of the society. Those interests require the exertions of every individual in some mode or other; and those who have not wherewith to support themselves honestly without corporal labour, whatever be their complexion, ought to be compelled to labour. This is the case in England where domestic slavery has long been unknown. It must also be the case in every well ordered society; and where the numbers of persons without property increase, there the coertion of the laws becomes more immediately requisite. The proposed plan would necessarily have this effect, and therefore ought to be accompanied with such a regulation. Though the rigours of our police in respect to this unhappy race ought to be softened, yet, its regularity, and punctual administration should be increased, rather than relaxed. If we doubt the propriety of such measures, what must we think of the situation of our country, when instead of 300,000, we shall have more than *two millions* of SLAVES among us. This *must happen within a* CENTURY, if we do not set about the abolition of slavery. Will not our posterity curse the days of their nativity with all the anguish of Job? Will they not execrate the memory of those ancestors, who, having it in their power to avert evil, have, like their first parents, entailed a curse upon all future generations? We know that the rigour of the law respecting slaves unavoidably must increase with their numbers: What a blood-stained code must that be which is calculated for the restraint of *millions* held in bondage! Such must our unhappy country exhibit within a century, unless we are both wise and just enough to avert from posterity the calamity and reproach, which are otherwise unavoidable.

I am not vain enough to presume the plan I have suggested entirely free from objection; nor that in offering my own ideas on the subject, I have been more fortunate than others: but from the communication of sentiment between those who lament the evil, it is possible that an effectual remedy may at length be discovered. Whenever that happens the golden age of our country will begin. Till then,

———*Non hospes ab hospite tutus,*
Non Herus a Famulis: fratrum quoque gratia rara.

WORKS USED BY TUCKER

Francis Hargrave, *An Argument in the Case of James Sommersett, a Negro, Where-in It Is Attempted to Demonstrate the Present Unlawfulness of Domestic Slavery in England.*
François Jean, Marquis de Chastellux, *Travels in North America.*
Thomas Jefferson, *Notes on Virginia.*
Charles Louis de Secondat Montesquieu, *The Spirit of Laws.*
Samuel, Baron von Pufendorf, *On the Law of Nature and of Nations.*
Granville Sharp, *A Tract on the Law of Nature and Principles of Action in Man.*

Index

Abolitionism, in North, xvi, 402
Abraham, 167n
Achaia, 78
Adams, John: and British constitution, xiv, 68n; and federal government's powers, xii; monarchical aspirations of, 146n; political style of, xiii; and restraint of democracy, 21
Admiralty jurisdiction, 117, 131, 287, 350, 352, 361
Africa: governments of, 58; slave trade of, 406, 415, 416, 417n; and slavery, 403, 405, 411, 412, 420
Agreements, state governments prohibited from, 248
Agriculture: and emancipation, 444–45; United States as agrarian society, 44, 64, 259; and wealth, 65
Alexander of Macedon, 43
Alfred the Great, 30
Alien Act: and amendments, 244–45; and federal government's powers, 227n; and Federalists, xiv; and judiciary, xiv, 293; North's support for, xiii; and president, 240, 241; support of, 241–42; and Virginia, xiv, 240–41, 244–45, 388n, 389n, 390–92; and writ of *habeas corpus*, 241
Aliens, 199, 200, 240, 300–301, 359

Ambassadors: and Congress, 210; and executive department, 131, 255; and federal courts, 287; and federal government, 47; impeachment of, 272; and judiciary, 131, 350, 352; presidential appointment of, 277–78, 350; and Supreme Court of the United States, 116–17, 297
Amendments: and Alien Act, 244–45; and Congress, 121, 235–47, 306; as correctional device, 310, 311; and due process of law, 148–49; and federal courts, 287–88, 288n, 289; federal government's powers limited by, xi, 387; and federal versus national government, 99–100; and ratification of Constitution, xii; requirements of, 121, 306–7; and sovereignty of people of United States, 6, 31–32; and state legislatures, 95, 121, 132, 306; and state sovereignty, 104–5; states' proposals of, 288n, 307–9, 307n; and taxation, 178–79; and trial by jury, 297; Tucker's numbering of, xxi, 77n, 93n; Virginia's proposals for, xxi, 115–18, 288n, 307n. *See also* specific amendments and freedoms
American Indians: and apportionment, 138; and British settlement in America, 318; commerce with,

447

representation, 155–56, 171–72; and slavery, 411, 420; of state governments, 142; of states' suffrage in Senate, 307; and taxation, 180, 189

Ex post facto laws, 135, 232–33, 247, 250

Excise taxes: and Congress, 175, 180, 184, 346; and manufacturing, 182, 184–85; and proportional taxes, 177; and state legislatures, 132, 247

Executive department: and ambassadors, 131, 255; and constitutional oath, 305–6; and duration of Congress, 173; and judges, 131, 292n; and judiciary powers, xv, 290, 296; and mixed governments, 66–67; and pardons, 293; powers of, 98, 131, 149, 253–86, 350; and president, 47–48, 253; and responsibility, 255–56; and Senate, 146, 174, 254–55, 286; and separation of powers, 47, 112, 137; suspension of, 86–87; and taxation, 298; unity of, 254–55. *See also* President; State executive departments

Expatriation, 358–60, 367–69

Export taxes: prohibition of, 246–47, 250; state exports, 175, 233–34; and state legislatures, 132, 184n

Factions, 37, 42, 62

Federal courts: and amendments, 287–88, 288n, 289; and common law, 359, 360–61; and Congress, 211, 348, 398–99; and criminal justice, 395; and freedom of the press, 238;

and judiciary, 131, 208–10; jurisdiction of, xv–xvi, 136, 287, 313, 315, 369, 401; and law of nations, 287, 361; organization of, 297; and states' rights, xv; and treason, 398; and treaties, 287; uniform decisions of, 305; and writ of *habeas corpus*, 231

Federal district, and Congress, 116, 130–31, 217–19, 348

Federal government: amendments as limitation on power of, xi, 387; binding of, to state governments, 94, 120–23; and civil power division, 45; and commerce, 47, 108, 127, 134, 247; and common law, 314, 315, 346, 349, 354–63, 384, 399–400; and common rule, 102–3; and Constitution of the United States, 34, 120–21, 123–33, 396; dissolution of, 87; federal versus national character of, 97–100, 127, 286, 310, 395; Federalist Papers and, xii; and foreign affairs, 127, 134, 136, 248; intra-American conflict on powers of, xiii; and judiciary's powers, xv, 103; jurisdiction of, 81, 82, 99, 126–29, 247, 251–52, 396; and Northern political faction, xii; organization of, 123–33; partiality in protection, 302; powers of, xii, 129–31, 134–35, 135n, 175, 226–29, 227n, 247, 313, 315, 346, 354, 371; recovery of judgments against, 289, 289n, 298–99, 299n; role of, after Civil War, vii, xi; and sovereignty of people of

This book is set in Minion, a contemporary digital type
designed by Robert Slimbach and issued by Adobe Systems
in 1989. A neohumanist face, Minion has no single source but
is inspired by the classic typefaces of the late Renaissance.
Slimbach called his typeface Minion after a word that in early
printing denoted a typeface size of about seven points.

Printed on paper that is acid-free and meets the requirements
of the American National Standard for Permanence of Paper
for Printed Library Materials, z39.48-1992. ∞

Book design by Sandra Strother Hudson,
Athens, Georgia
Composition by Brad Walrod, High Text Graphics,
Brooklyn, New York
Printed and bound by Sheridan Books, Inc.,
Chelsea, Michigan